MAN
takes control

CULTURAL DEVELOPMENT AND AMERICAN AID

Charles J. Erasmus

UNIVERSITY OF MINNESOTA PRESS, MINNEAPOLIS

To Julian Steward

Acknowledgments

M Y DEEP gratitude goes out to every person who helped make this book possible:

I owe a very special debt to George Foster for first arousing my interest in the problems of foreign aid and applied anthropology in 1951 while he was my boss in the Smithsonian Institution. No one has influenced the direction of my professional interests so much as he.

My sincere thanks go to Drs. Gómez de la Torre, Wilson Salazar, and Julio Falcony, of the Servicio Cooperativo Interamericano de Salud Pública in Ecuador, for their assistance back in 1952 in arranging for and administering the tests on folk beliefs discussed in Chapter III. All three doctors helped me in the identification of folk ailments, the medical evaluation of my interview material, and the wording of my test questions.

For the help they gave me while analyzing technical aid programs under their supervision in Ecuador, Colombia, Chile, and Haiti from 1951 to 1954, I am grateful to those able administrators, Preston Blanks, John Cady, Albion Patterson, and Vance Rodgers.

I am indebted to both the University of Illinois and to the Ford Foundation for their financial support of the field work on which my Mexican case study is based. This book was written while I was a member of the Culture Change Project at the University of Illinois, the first two parts in 1957 before leaving for Mexico and the third part upon my return in the spring of 1959. I am deeply grateful to Julian H. Steward, director of the University of Illinois Culture Change Project, for allowing me the freedom to do my own work in my own way while under the financial and administrative auspices of his project from 1956 to 1959.

My sincere thanks go also to Doña Rosa de Gutierrez, dedicated and respected schoolteacher in Mesquital de Tesia for over twenty years, for her assistance during 1958 in collecting the data on Mesquital discussed in the Mexican case study.

I am very grateful to Eric Wolf for reading the manuscript and offering valuable suggestions. I am also extremely indebted to Edward Spicer not only for his detailed and painstaking critique of the manuscript and for a helpful visit to me in Sonora while the case study was in progress but for twelve years of friendship that have been a great source of stimulation and encouragement to me. It was at his suggestion that I first went to Sonora in 1948. Neither Dr. Wolf nor Dr. Spicer is responsible for any errors of fact or judgment in this work.

I also wish to thank all the students in my graduate seminar at Yale, who served as an experimental audience in reading and criticizing the manuscript: Robin Brooks, Robert Dentan, David Eyde, Patrick Gallagher, Edgar Gregersen, Denise O'Brien, Paul Ray, Anne Renouf, Joan Rubin, and Bruce Trigger.

Finally, for assistance well beyond the call of duty, warm thanks go to my editor, Miss Marcia Strout.

Table of Contents

141, 309

INTRODUCTION

I

A Man from the Past

For several months in 1948, I studied the life of Mayo Indian peasants in an isolated village on the coast of southern Sonora in northwestern Mexico. When I left, I decided to take one of the villagers back to the United States so that I might observe his reactions to modern urban life. Juan was an intelligent young man of about thirty who had become a close friend during my stay in his village. Since in many ways life in Las Bocas was more like that of the sixteenth century than that of the twentieth, I was in a sense transporting him from the past into the present. Had I foreseen all the consequences of my action, I doubt that I would have brought him to the United States, for when I saw him again several months after his return to his village he was despondent and unhappy. His experience had engendered a host of new wants which he felt he had little hope of ever satisfying in his own "world of the past."

Most of the world is made up of Juans — people of the "past" who daily see more of industrial society and its material products. We are all familiar with the magazine photograph which shows a modern factory or hotel alongside primitive huts and oxcarts. The picture often bears such a caption as "Mexico — Land of Contrasts" or "India — Past and Present." In these underdeveloped areas we find the "dual societies" [1] in which past and future are juxtaposed to a greater degree than

3

they were at any time during the development of Western civilization. In these dual societies, where contrasts in living standards are greater than ever before, wants are often created much faster than the people of the "past" can hope to satisfy them by their own efforts.

This book is directly concerned with the people of the "past" — the undercapitalized populations — and their relation to industrialized society. Juan's story provides a microcosmic view of the situation — of the clash of "past" and "present" in the preindustrial, underdeveloped areas of the world, where people still follow a way of life closer to mankind's tribal and peasant past than to his industrial present. Juan's wants increased much faster than his expectations of satisfying them, but subsequent events have given him some hope of expanding his expectations as well. Let us review his story.

Before I met him, Juan had never been more than forty miles from his home. Included within that forty mile radius, however, are the Mayo River towns of Huatabampo and Navojoa, small commercial centers that cater to the needs of the rich farming area bordering the river. Here, of course, is where a strict analogy with the past breaks down: Juan had already seen automobiles and radios and trains, for example. But his meetings with these had been brief and fleeting; they had played no important part in his life before 1948.

Las Bocas, his native village, is primitive in most respects. The houses are constructed either of sun-baked adobes or of mud and wattle, the latter a framework of posts and pliable branches plastered over with mud. The villagers' material possessions are few; many do not have so much as a change of clothing, and others have only one extra set for wear at social and ceremonial occasions. Because of the insufficient rainfall and the lack of water for irrigation, farming provides only a small part of the village food supply. Those who own cattle allow them to forage in the thorn forest surrounding the village and sell the meat and cheese in the river towns. Villagers without cattle work at various crafts or in industries. Some extract fiber from the leaf of the maguey plant that grows wild in the thorn forest, spin it into cord, and weave it into feed and market bags. Some manufacture lime, which is used for softening corn before grinding it to make tortillas. Others gather firewood in the thorn forest. The towns along the Mayo River provide a ready market for all of these products.

Although the village has an old adobe school building, no teacher has been willing to live for long on a meager government salary in such an isolated place. In 1948, Las Bocas had not had a teacher for several years, the last one having improved her economic position by becoming a prostitute in Huatabampo. It is not surprising, therefore, that even those who can understand and speak Spanish in addition to their native Indian tongue are unable to read or write. The villagers' knowledge of the world is correspondingly limited. Though most of them are dependent on regional markets for the sale of local products and the purchase of their staple foods and are thus full participants in a money economy, their wants are few. In many of the details of their daily life, Las Bocans differ from the villagers of other preindustrial areas; but in their outlook on the larger world and their understanding of that world and of themselves, they are as much like their preliterate contemporaries as they are like their preliterate past. Nominally the villagers are Mayo Indians, but they are no longer "pure" Indians either genetically or culturally. Their culture is a blend of early colonial Spanish and native American Indian customs, with the Spanish component definitely outweighing the Indian.

The villagers are peasants rather than tribal Indians and as such are much like rural people everywhere in the world except in the most industrialized nations. Las Bocans are peasants because they are no longer socially self-contained and economically self-sufficient. They recognize the authority and jurisdiction of Mexican federal and local government, to which the ceremonial vestiges of their native social organization have long been subsidiary. Their practice of purchasing most of their food staples with money earned by the sale of local products makes them highly dependent on the outside world. Yet, despite these two important ways in which the structure of Las Bocas is integrated with that of the Mexican nation, it is still in many ways a closed structure. Las Bocans have seen the material evidences of the higher standard of living enjoyed by prosperous Mexican families along the river, but because they lack opportunities and even expectations, they do not emulate the expanding consumption patterns of middle-class Mexicans.

Such was the social and cultural environment Juan left when I took him to California in 1948. He found the United States a paradise of unbelievable wealth and comfort. To him all gringos were rich, and using *his* standard of living as a comparison, who could disagree? The variety and quantity of our food was one of the things that impressed him most.

5

He was amazed to learn that we enjoyed the luxury of eating meat every day, for like so many peasants faced with a storage problem in warm climates, Las Bocans seldom butcher their own livestock. Pigs and cows are sold on the hoof in the river towns where the market for fresh meat is large enough to absorb the meat before it spoils.

Our dairy products and pastries were also a great treat for Juan. He became especially fond of blueberry pie à la mode and, on my visit to Las Bocas several months after his return, he told me sadly how much he wished I could have brought him just one dish of his favorite dessert. He was amused and at the same time annoyed when he discovered canned food for dogs and cats among the wonders of our supermarkets. His people could not afford to buy canned food at all — and we could give it to our pets.

A feature of our daily life that seemed particularly luxurious to Juan in contrast to his own desert environment was the abundance of water. Water was piped everywhere, even into our homes. Women did not have to walk to a well several times a day to fetch it in a bucket or jar balanced on their heads. We even irrigated patches of worthless grass in front of our houses. If only there were water like this for the fields of Las Bocas, what crops it would be possible to grow! And to Juan even a very modest middle-class house seemed a thing of extraordinary beauty and comfort with its spacious rooms, its heating system, its carpeted floors, its stoves that cooked without fire, its machines to wash clothes, its soft beds, and its storage spaces full of food and clothing.

In three short weeks Juan had vastly increased his wants as he acquired a taste for a great number of new products. But he had learned nothing from the experience that could help him increase his expectations of satisfying those new felt needs. This was the tragedy of my experiment; when I returned to Las Bocas the following summer I found Juan a changed man. He was no longer my happy-go-lucky companion of the year before. He had become irritable and morose and had taken to drinking heavily. "I have lost my patience," he said.

By *paciencia* or "patience" he meant inner contentment and outward calmness of manner, a condition which had been violently upset by his new wants. One incident in particular illustrates the change of which even Juan himself was aware. Before his trip he had never seriously objected to the occasional raids made by the village children on his small orchard of fruit trees. It was a standing joke in Las Bocas that if one did not eat his fruit green he would eat none at all. Juan had not attempted to defend his harvest by chasing away the children. He simply picked his fruit green. Once when I pointed out the value of oranges in the market at Huatabampo he smiled and said, "Yes, I could make more money by guarding my fruit, but those poor children! They must live too, and they are hungry." Generosity is a great virtue in a closed society. But on more than one occasion during my visit in the summer of 1949, I saw Juan shout angrily at the children in his orchard. "Our farm should not be a highway for every child in the village," he told his father. "I shall put up a fence!" In Juan the easygoing, live-for-today philosophy of the society which awards prestige for conspicuous giving was being replaced by the spirit of the acquisitive society in which prestige is awarded the man whose conspicuous consumption is individualistic.

To Juan the hopeless realization that he would never be a part of that great world of new things to which he had been briefly introduced was a source of considerable frustration, for he could see no opportunities in his own environment to raise his standard of living. He had no special training, and he had no capital. Even worse, he was afraid. So long had he lived the humble life that he felt insecure with the townspeople he would have to deal with in order to improve his lot.

One hot summer day six years after my brief second visit in 1949, I rode once more down the dusty desert trail leading through the thorn forest to Las Bocas, wondering if I would find my friend alive and well and whether he had regained his *paciencia*. I was relieved to find that Juan's initial despondency had disappeared, but despite his readjustment to his old way of life, his experience had left a permanent mark, evident not only in the fence around his orchard, but also in the fact that he was still restlessly searching for a way to satisfy his new wants.

Juan made his living primarily by farming a few acres of land flood-irrigated with sheet runoff from heavy rains. From two shallow wells he also hand-irrigated his orchard and a small vegetable garden. Not long after I had last seen him in 1949, he got the idea of irrigating a larger area with well water by means of a gasoline-powered pump. By working several months as a ranch hand on a nearby farm, he had saved up enough money to buy a secondhand pump from a Mexican in Navojoa. But the venture failed, for when the pump stopped running Juan did not know how to repair it. Discouraged at the prospect of depend-

7

ing on the Mexican mechanics in the river towns, imagining himself having to make frequent trips into town carrying the pump by horse-drawn cart to have it repaired, he began to feel that he had been taken advantage of by the Mexican who had sold it to him. He was further disheartened by the fact that the fuel cost more than he had expected.

It was Juan's brother and father who told me about the pump incident, because Juan was ashamed of his failure and reticent about it. Instead, he was eager to talk about his plans for the future — he was now working on a new scheme to improve his lot. It was said that when the irrigation system of the Fuerte River was finished, the northernmost canal would terminate just south of Las Bocas on the coast. Surveyors had already staked out its course. The land south of this canal, including a part of the indigenous reserve which any resident still had the right to clear, would some day be rich, irrigated farm land. Seeing his opportunity, Juan was busy clearing land in that part of the reserve which would fall within the projected zone of irrigation. In anticipation of the highly profitable cultivation that would some day be possible, he was extending the size of his fields each year. His hopes for a future with a wider range of satisfactions had been raised, and because his expectations had been increased, he could afford to be patient once again.

Few underprivileged inhabitants of preindustrial areas receive an introduction to our high living standards as abrupt and dramatic as a vacation in California. In this sense Juan's case was unusual. But in many places people *are* experiencing rapid increases in wants, often with few visible means of increasing their expectations. Such an increase in felt needs without any compensatory increase in expectations may cause frustrations leading to messianic or utopian movements. The so-called cargo cults that have grown up on many of the Melanesian islands of the South Pacific are an example of the first.[2] The cargo cults are led by prophets who predict that the spirits of the dead will return to the islands in ships and planes bringing a great abundance of goods. In expectation, some native groups have built wharves into the sea for ships to dock and others have cleared airfields in the jungles. Here the natives acquired wants for the goods of Western civilization faster than they could find means of satisfying them. This situation was particularly severe in cases where the withdrawal of foreign troops after the Pacific war resulted in a sudden reduction in the supply of the outside goods the natives had become accustomed to.

In cases like the cargo cults the gap between felt needs and real expectations is so great and the comprehension of the people so poor that it can be bridged only by delusion. When such a gap between wants and expectations occurs among sophisticated peoples at the national level, the result may be "utopian" expropriations of foreign and domestic capital. Since cargo cults present no threat to the United States' security, we read about them with a mixture of curiosity and amusement. The spreading Communist cult has been a constant source of worry to us, however, because of its potential threat to our peace and security. Motivated largely by fear, the United States since World War II has spent billions of dollars in foreign aid, which has helped the rest of the world increase its expectations.

Fear has not been the only reason for our aid, though. There has been a growing understanding of world conditions in this country, and an increasing ability on the part of the public to identify themselves with peoples in other lands and to tolerate other points of view. The same motive of self-preservation which led earlier generations into isolationism and even war has been channeled by the rising level of knowledge into activities of a new order.

Orientation and Objectives

Although this book is concerned with preindustrial peoples of "underdeveloped" areas and their relation to industrialized society, its purpose is not simply to present and discuss examples of technical or financial aid. Basically it is concerned with the much broader and older question of what makes men act the way they do: I am curious about what causes behavior and how it develops. Because of my experience as an anthropological observer of technical aid programs in Latin America, I am examining these larger questions by looking at problems of directing culture change. The United States is doing something altogether new in human history by helping people on an international scale, and I am interested in the significance of this phenomenon for a general theory of cultural development. Implicit in international aid programs, moreover, is the assumption that man can cognitively direct changes in cultural behavior. This assumption introduces questions about the very nature of cultural causality, for it implies that man is a cognitive causal agent of culture.

One of the objectives of this book, then, is to formulate a simple scheme of cultural causality, congenial to an applied interest in culture change. A second objective is to advance — on the basis of the causal scheme — a general theory of culture development to assist us in understanding some of the problems of development in dual society and our role in helping to deal with those problems. In line with these objectives the book is in three parts. The first (Chapters II to V) deals with cultural causality, the second (Chapters VI to VIII) with cultural development, and the third (Chapters IX to XII) with a case study of economic development and culture change.

The first part — the next four chapters — deals largely with cases of directed change that illustrate the causal theory of culture I have adopted. By "culture" I shall mean all behavior learned by men as members of social groups, including social behavior. More will be said about the nature of culture in Chapter VI.

In this section I shall oppose the concept of cultural determinism, which makes *man* in the abstract sense of *the individual* a pawn of cultural forces. "The individual," this concept says, cannot prevent a war, cannot invent a new idea or technique unless his "culture" is "ready" for it, and cannot change the general "patterns" of his "culture." In this unequal contest between abstractions, "the individual" is bound to lose. I wish to make it very clear at the outset that the abstraction "man" as used in the title of this book and throughout the text means "men in interaction" — not "the individual."

I do not object to cultural determinism because I believe in free will, but because it explains so little. If people do thus and so simply because of their cultural heritage, the past becomes *sufficient* explanation of the present. The sufficiency of culture to cause itself is unsatisfying to me both as an explanation and as a guide to action.

Cultural determinism as a causal theory is not in itself objectionable. But because causal explanations can lead to anthropomorphic thinking, they have fallen into ill repute among physical scientists, and social scientists have tended to copy their more prestigeful colleagues in this regard; causal explanations, however, can be useful heuristic devices. Important as it is to recognize the difference between correlation and causal interpretation, this does not remove the usefulness of causal interpretation for daily living.

On the basis of laboratory experiments and controlled observations, various correlations have been found, for example, between tobacco smoking and lung cancer. Many people have given up smoking as a consequence. They have drawn a causal inference from these correlations and used it as a basis for action. The tobacco interests reiterate the scientific view that a correlation is not a cause, but men do not have to wait for all scientific investigations to end before deriving a causal inference for action. Nor must all men take the same action on the same evidence.

When people make a causal interpretation of either casual or laboratory evidence and this interpretation significantly changes their behavior, cultural change takes place. This process cannot be regarded simply as anthropomor*phic*, for it is legitimately anthropomor*phous*. It is perfectly true that such a view emphasizes the cognitive and creative side of human intelligence, and, admittedly, when one concentrates on the relatively static and primitive peoples, culture hardly seems to justify such an emphasis. The small, isolated "folk" society as conjured up in its ideal and unadulterated state does indeed seem like some Durkheimian social organism composed of non-cognitive cells. But my interest here is not in primordial, pristine societies nor even primitive peoples as such, but in the dynamic and changing world of today.

In this changing world of cultural behavior I view man's motivational and cognitive attributes as the active agents of causality, and his environmental conditions (both physical and cultural) as passive — passive in the sense that they determine culture only as a consequence of man's actions. The pins in a pinball machine determine the path of the ball only when the ball has been set in motion. Limitative causes of culture determine human behavior as man is set in motion by his basic motivations and as he employs his cognitive abilities to innovate alternative behaviors or "controls" to deal with his limitations. Limitative causes of culture are biological, physical, or even cultural. As situational factors affecting the probability of the occurrence or disappearance of any given cultural behavior, they are passive and random and do not involve purposive or planned action. Motivation is the stimulus to action, but cognition introduces a creative element without which action would not take symbolic and cultural form. These two causal components are psychological attributes of the human agents of culture, who produce cultural behavior through interaction with limitative causes. All cultural growth and change stems from the individual human beings who make up the basic units of the cultural phenomenon,

11

whereas limitative causes include the ecological, social, and technological factors which affect the probability of the occurrence or disappearance of given forms of cultural behavior at a particular time
and place.

Although all three components of the structure of culture are necessary causes of any given cultural behavior, none by itself is a sufficient
cause. If this fact is kept in mind, there need be no fear that a motivation component will repeat the excesses of the early twentieth-century
instinct psychologists, who used an infinite number of innate drives to
account for most of human behavior. I shall use only three basic motivations here: (1) the desire for self-preservation or survival, (2) the desire
for sexual gratification, and (3) the desire for prestige, social status, or
achievement. These motivations exist in all cultures, but the ways of
satisfying them may differ greatly from one group to another. Some
people hunt their food in order to survive, others farm, and still others
produce manufactures or services rather than food. In some societies
the person who is accorded the greatest prestige is the one who gives
most to his fellows. In others a person acquires distinction through the
conspicuous ownership of goods which he himself consumes.

To me, the most plausible explanations of the prestige motivation
are those advanced by Richard T. LaPiere and David C. McClelland.[3]
The two explanations are similar and complement each other well. Both
men assign what is called here a "prestige" motivation to learning situations universally provided by certain biological limitations. LaPiere
calls the motivation "status need," and McClelland calls it a concern
with "achievement." Both ascribe the motivation to the process of
socialization (or what some might call "enculturation") and both to
pan-cultural limitative factors in human maturation. McClelland emphasizes the fact that in all societies people must "learn to do things
for themselves — e.g., learn to walk, talk, eat by themselves, fish, hunt,
read, or whatever," a condition which in time arouses "motivating an-
ticipations of success or failure." LaPiere stresses the fact that the
period of human maturation is very long and creates in each person
"a growing psychological dependency" on others, which in "its later
manifestations," LaPiere designates as "regard for status." Both men
point out that the intensity of the motivation can vary with the person
as well as with the culture.

Thus, desire for prestige is neither purely biological nor purely cultural. Because of the long maturation period of social dependency during which the human child is subject to many tests of achievement, persons in all human societies become victims to some degree of invidious comparison and the concern for status. Although the intensity of this socially mediated awareness of the self varies among societies as well as among persons within the same society, the prestige motivation which it engenders is pan-social.

What I label here a "survival" motivation some might prefer to call a "security" or "deficiency" motive. It includes the avoidance of hunger, thirst, pain, cold, and other bodily discomforts. Again there are biological reasons for these avoidances, but the abstraction I call "survival motivation" is not simply innate; it derives in part from the human being's early conditioning. The important thing again is its pan-social nature. Desire for sexual gratification is clear enough, and such widespread institutions as marriage and the family attest to its universality.

Throughout this work I shall use the terms "felt needs" and "wants" synonymously, but they should not be confused with basic motivation. Motivations for survival, sex, and prestige are pan-social, but at the level of wants or felt needs they differentiate and take varied forms among distinctive social groups. Motivation and cognition are inseparable within each person, but cognition, interacting with the limitative causes inherent in every situation, is responsible for the variety of felt needs that results. Basic motivations are not directly observable apart from the forms of felt needs which they take in particular cultural settings; they are indirectly observable as common denominators in cross-cultural comparisons.

In Part I, I shall give more attention to cognition and limitation than to motivation. In Part II, I shall view prestige motivation as the stimulus to cultural development, and cultural relativism will become my primary target. In the process of cultural development through specialization, prestige motivation takes different forms, and to characterize these forms I shall lean heavily on Thorstein Veblen's concepts of conspicuous consumption and invidious comparison. The former I divide into two correlative concepts — conspicuous giving and conspicuous ownership — and to them I add a third, conspicuous production. Invidious comparison I shall subdivide into invidious sanction, invidious emulation, and invidious promotion, each of which accompanies one of the three forms of prestige-seeking.

13

While prestige motivation provides the stimulus for development, man's cognitive and symbolizing faculty provides the necessary creative ingredient. Through the process of specialization the cognitive faculty leads to increasing knowledge and control of the environment. As this takes place, different forms of prestige motivation predominate. We shall see why conspicuous giving is the most characteristic form in the "closed" or primitive society whereas with the opening of society through specialization, conspicuous ownership and conspicuous production become more prominent.

Part III is a case study of economic development and culture change in the dual society of northwestern Mexico. The dual or underdeveloped society is to some extent both "closed" and "open." A very large part of the population in a dual society is illiterate, uneducated, and impoverished; this segment is often a peasantry made up of subsistence farmers and day laborers with few specialized skills. The "open" part usually lives in cities and is more likely to be literate, specialized in work skills, and engaged in commerce and industry.

The illiterate part of a dual society has little voice in the management of national affairs and maintains a relatively weak sanctioning position in the total society. As a consequence, it is usually subordinated to the "open" part, either by means of totalitarian controls or by means of graft. The dual society we shall analyze is graft-ridden, and therefore particularly interesting for our purposes because it thus is typical of most free underdeveloped nations in which the desire to possess a great variety of new goods is rapidly taking precedence over older patterns of sharing and redistribution. These are the societies where we are most likely to have the opportunity to give aid. Here affluence is the privilege of a few, and most people, as their opportunities increase, make invidious comparisons leading to emulation through conspicuous ownership. We shall see how a strong middle class with its own "Protestant" ethic is arising in Roman Catholic Sonora.

In the conclusions I shall discuss the implications of my findings for our own free society, a society of affluence in a world of want. Are we justified in trying to help the rest of the world increase its expectations? If so, what kinds of help should be given priority and how can the social scientist be of service in rendering this aid? These are some of the questions with which the final chapter is concerned.

PART I. CULTURAL CAUSALITY

II

Motivation and Cognition

T HE "needs" a social planner feels or perceives for his subjects may be quite different from those felt by the subjects themselves. Unless otherwise stated, "wants" and "felt needs" are used synonymously in this work to refer to needs felt by the public rather than the expert or the social planner. How motivation and cognition produce wants or felt needs will be illustrated in this chapter by examples of technical assistance. Special attention is given to the process of "frequency interpretation" and to the way it operates among preliterate or uneducated peoples, who learn chiefly through casual rather than technical observation. The first study compares two soil conservation programs — one in Chile and one among the Papago of Arizona.

Two Soil Conservation Programs

Early in 1952, soil conservationist Grover Kincaid arrived in Chile as a new member of the United States government's Point Four agricultural program in that country. His specialty was certainly one of highest priority on the list of Chilean needs, at least in the opinion of experts. William Vogt, in his book *Road to Survival*, had recently expressed great alarm over the extent of erosion in Chile, accusing her people of committing national suicide.[1] But soil conservation is usually very difficult to introduce among the rural populations of underdeveloped areas. One might assume that Kincaid's biggest job would have been to promote or sell his technical know-how to Chilean farmers, but he did not regard his job in that light.

As chief of one of the five soil conservation work groups in the United States to receive the Superior Service Award in 1951, Kincaid had a simple explanation for his success as a soil conservation expert. "I never give farmers the idea they're doing me a big favor to let me help them. I wait for them to come to me, but the job I do for them leaves no doubt as to who's received the favor." He said he had no intention of ever working with farmers who did not freely solicit his aid. This may seem a rather uncooperative attitude in a man with a foreign aid assignment, but Kincaid proved very successful, not in spite of his attitude but because of it.

Most of Chile's population, its farm land, and its manmade erosion are concentrated in the central part of the country. To the north lie arid deserts and to the south virgin forests and natural pastures. Within the central zone we can roughly demarcate three major subareas on the basis of the different technical and socioeconomic problems each would present as the object of a soil conservation program. Of the three, the mountainous coastal area has been the most severely damaged by erosion. There the farming of steep hillside slopes not suited to cultivation has led to conditions which in many cases could be remedied only by pasture development and reforestation. Such drastic measures would mean that much of the farm land would have to be taken out of production, thereby causing a serious socioeconomic problem; for while the coastal range has some of the least desirable farm land in the entire central zone, it is crowded with small farmers, many of whom produce little more than enough to provide a bare subsistence. Before any significant conservation measures could be effected here, many families would have to be relocated.

The central valley north of the Bío-Bío River, a region of large landholdings, also suffers from considerable erosion and soil exhaustion, although the situation is not so bad as it is in the coastal range. Farm management is largely in the Spanish colonial tradition: haciendas are operated by foremen while their absentee owners spend most of their time in the city. Instead of increasing production and the efficiency of their farm management, the owners are content to maintain a traditional and somewhat conspicuous standard of living by relying on an abundance of cheap labor. In this area, where size and production of farm units are great enough to make soil conservation measures feasible, the main problem is apathy.

In the agricultural provinces south of the Bío-Bío River the problem of soil conservation is least severe. Much of this land has been brought under the plow only recently. This region, as compared to the others, is characterized by medium-sized farms, a greater abundance of farm machinery, and a larger number of resident landowners. It is much more progressive than the other two because of the greater number of first-, second-, and third-generation European immigrants, mainly of German and English stock, who are actively interested in improving their farming practices.

In the last area, near the town of Temuco, lived a moderately prosperous farmer of English ancestry who, shortly before Kincaid's arrival, had read Vogt's *Road to Survival* and had become very much concerned about soil erosion. Actually, his farm was among those least eroded in the area, but the book made the dangers of erosion very real to him. Because of his great desire to learn new agricultural practices, he kept close watch on the United States technical assistance program. As soon as he heard of Kincaid's arrival, he eagerly requested help. And thus, even before Kincaid had a chance to fully appraise the situation, his conditions had been met. By the end of his first year in Chile, the soil conservation program begun on the Englishman's farm had stimulated enough requests for help in the vicinity of Temuco to keep the initial staff of Chilean trainees busy for three more years.

Kincaid was an expert in planning and laying terraces, a soil conservation measure particularly suited to the rolling hill country south of the Bío-Bío River. Terracing checks erosion by breaking the profile of a sloping hillside into a series of low steps, each constructed with a gradient so gentle that it drains off excess rainwater without carrying off the topsoil. Contour terraces along the sloping wheatfields could slow the run-off after heavy downpours and prevent the gullies that were deepening each year on most farms. On some farms fence posts at the foot of hillside plots had been half buried by the sliding soil in just the few years since the land was first cleared.

The percentage of slope and the channel capacity of terraces are usually figured on the basis of soil analyses and maximum rainfall statistics, neither of which was available in this part of the world. Therefore Kincaid built his first terraces experimentally, with slightly different slopes and channel capacities, diligently checking them after rain and modifying them accordingly. As a result, not a single terrace failed when the area was subjected to a downpour of flood proportions. The erosion caused by the storm on neighboring non-terraced fields made the demonstrations all the more dramatic.

Most of the beginning work had been done on the farm of the Englishman who had first solicited Kincaid's aid, and later on the farms of a few of the Englishman's progressive friends. After the storm, however, many skeptics, including some traditional Chilean farmers, were completely won over. But for the most part, Kincaid's success was greatest among educated resident farmers who made a comfortable annual profit and used as much farm machinery as they could afford.

One might question an approach to Chile's soil erosion problem which overlooked the great number of poor farmers who could not afford even the simplest farm machinery, and which overlooked the most eroded land in favor of the least eroded. But by avoiding these extremes Kincaid reduced the obstacles to introducing soil conservation into Chile. The result? The Chilean ministry of agriculture was so encouraged by the enthusiastic support which Chilean farmers had given this soil conservation program that it established a special soil conservation department. This department would not only continue the work begun in the vicinity of Temuco but would also concern itself with the erosion problems of other areas where government action on a larger scale would be required.

Doubtless Chile would have taken this decisive step eventually without outside help. Kincaid simply acted as a catalyst in speeding up culture change. His philosophy was not to sell soil conservation to people who did not want it, but to help those who already felt a need for it. He was thereby led to work in an area where farmers were best prepared to accept his skills and where he could dramatically demonstrate that Chilean farmers would accept soil conservation measures in sufficient numbers to make a soil conservation training program feasible.

The motivations of the Chilean farmers with whom Kincaid worked were not much different from his own. The farmers were men who took satisfaction in increasing the long-term efficiency and productivity of their farming, for within their own group the successful farmer was awarded considerable prestige. The prosperity of the more successful, reflected in their consumption, also earned them increasing prestige on the national scene. But the fact that they were educated men greatly facilitated their recognition of the usefulness of Kincaid's special skills.

When this case is compared with a study made by Henry Dobyns [2] of a soil conservation program on the Papago Indian reservations of southern Arizona, it can be seen how a similar felt need may result from quite different motivational and cognitive causes. The Papago reservations are located in arid badlands where the annual rainfall is concentrated in a brief period of late summer storms resulting in rapid run-off, frequently in the form of flash floods capable of transporting great quantities of silt. In the past, the Papago unwittingly aided natural erosion by overstocking their range with horses and cattle, thus destroying the natural grass cover in many places. Between 1946 and 1949 a soil conservationist of the Papago Indian Agency worked in two Papago districts, Schuk Toak and Gu Achi, with contrasting results. Although United States government funds were available to support soil conservation work, the Papago of Schuk Toak were apathetic about the program and took part principally to earn wages. At Gu Achi, however, interest was strong and the accomplishments correspondingly greater.

Schuk Toak was selected first because the physical problems there were deemed easier to solve. But because the erosion problems were less severe, the Papago there were less concerned. At Gu Achi, on the other hand, even the buildings were in danger of being swallowed up in the growing arroyo. "People wanted something done to protect not only the school, but also their own houses and fields where one flood could make six-inch gullies or bury bean plants under silt." [3] The Gu Achi villagers not only felt a need for conservation assistance, they actively solicited it, and were much more cooperative than the people at Schuk Toak. Because the erosion problem was more pressing at Gu Achi, the conservation results were more spectacular and local interest was reinforced.

In comparing the Chile and Papago soil conservation programs, we note that in both places the people already felt a strong need for what was being offered. In Chile, however, the program was successful in a region where erosion was slight, whereas among the Papago the program was more successful in a village where erosion was severe. The technicians' felt needs were much the same in each case, but the motivational and cognitive components of the subjects' felt needs were different in the two areas. In Chile the innovator was dealing with literate farmers, men whose range of experience was infinitely expanded through the indirect medium of the printed page. One of the farmers with whom Kincaid began his work was so impressed by literature on the subject of soil erosion that on rainy nights he would toss sleeplessly in bed, wondering which of his fields would be gullied by morning. Although erosion was comparatively slight on his farm, he read a potential danger into each slight evidence. Knowledge derived from indirect experience (from written and oral sources rather than through direct participation) rendered him capable of recognizing as dangerous signs which otherwise might not have seemed so threatening.

Among illiterate farmers like the Papago, learning tends to be limited to direct experience. Here the strength of the felt need for conservation was directly proportional to the size of the threat of erosion. Thus, while the degree of erosion in each case was sufficient to motivate action, in Chile the cognitive factors were more complex. The Chilean farmers could anticipate erosion dangers and worry about them at a very early stage, whereas the Papago became sufficiently alarmed to take action only when their very homes were about to be swallowed up by an arroyo.

Cognition among uneducated, unspecialized people is based largely on direct experience, and in specialized society a great deal of direct experience takes place within occupational specialties where observations are often highly technical. But in both, observations become meaningful and lead to culture change and the accumulation of knowledge through *frequency interpretation*. The operation of this process at both pre-specialized and specialized levels is well illustrated by attempts to introduce improved plant varieties among rural populations.

Frequency Interpretation and Improved Plants

Cognition is that aspect of cultural causality which is most peculiar to it; for it stems from the unique symbolizing ability of the human mind. Cognition as a causal factor in cultural behavior takes the form of probability predictions — frequency interpretations derived from inductive inference. According to philosopher Hans Reichenbach, from whom the term is borrowed, "frequency interpretation" is a probability estimate based on inductive inference from experience.[4] For him it is the basis of the "empiricist philosophy of probability," and to a large extent his own scientific philosophy rests upon it. In this book frequency interpretation is viewed as predictive interpretation based on the observation of repeated events, the dominant cognitive aspect of human action. Experience or observation is the raw material from which frequency interpretations are inductively derived. Tossing a coin, for example, provides experience or observation from which it can be inductively inferred that the frequency of occurrence of each face is the same. It can be predicted, then, that in repeated throws the coin will land heads up fifty per cent of the time. Human knowledge, on which cognition builds, is made up of predictions, which are simply tentative probability statements — never final truths.

Frequency interpretation is not an exclusively human phenomenon. Experiments have shown that birds have a number sense which enables them to select boxes with the same number of spots (never more than seven) as those presented on a cue card.[5] Even in simple trial-and-error learning among animals, certain positive associations are built up when successful choices frequently lead to a reward. The experimental animal is clearly anticipatory in its actions; and as successful responses grow more strongly motivated, one might even consider the animal's behavior "predictive."

The comparison with lower animals can easily be pushed too far, for man, unlike any other known form of life, is a symbolizing creature. His faculty for conceptualizing symbolically makes possible unlimited refinements of frequency interpretation to increase his probable knowledge. This process may be based on either casual or technical observation, but among preliterate, unspecialized people whose observations are almost entirely casual, the process of growth is very slow. Innovations that meet felt needs spectacularly are the ones most likely to be accepted by preliterate and uneducated populations.

In 1951, for example, the Point Four agricultural program in Bolivia introduced Cuban Yellow Corn near the town of Santa Cruz and within two years the local demand for seed far exceeded the supply. The subjects were mostly illiterate farmers, but the advantages of the new seed were inspectional. Cuban Yellow Corn was distinctly better than the local variety because it came up earlier, thus getting a head start on weeds, and because the kernels were harder and could be stored with much less damage from weevils. By 1953, a third of the farmers in the area were planting Cuban Yellow Corn and their production was higher than that for the total area in 1950. The productivity of Cuban Yellow Corn was so much greater than that of the local variety that a quantitative appraisal of its advantages was possible on the basis of casual observation.

As Cuban Yellow Corn was being introduced at Santa Cruz, Bolivia, the Point Four agricultural program in Costa Rica was importing Kennebec disease-resistant potatoes from Maine for trial plantings. This potato proved so resistant to Costa Rican plant diseases that yields increased fifty per cent. Within three years the number of Costa Rican farmers planting Kennebec potatoes had surpassed the number still planting the local variety.

A third example is provided by the experience of the Rockefeller Foundation's experiment station near Medellín, Colombia, which developed an improved hybrid corn by genetic selection early in 1950. The first year that it distributed samples, yields were so much higher than normal that the station was deluged with requests for seed. The farmers' response was so spontaneous and overwhelming that the Foundation had no difficulty interesting entrepreneurs in multiplying seed for profit. In this case, too, the advantages of a new crop variety were inspectional.

In terms of the peso value of Colombia's total agricultural production, sugarcane is that country's second most important crop. Over a period of about a decade — between the late 1930's and the early 1950's — the traditional varieties of "criollo" sugarcane were almost entirely replaced by varieties resistant to the mosaic disease plaguing growers throughout the country. The newer varieties, imported from the Caribbean area and disseminated largely through the initiative of many independent growers, quickly demonstrated their advantage over the "criollo" through greatly increased yields, especially where the disease was prevalent. In a few places, however, where mosaic disease has never been a problem, such as Filadelfia and Salamina in the state of Caldas, the criollo varieties persist because the newer ones offer no advantages. On the contrary, the fact that their tougher stalk required alterations in the pressing apparatus was regarded as a disadvantage from the local point of view.

It often happens, as at Filadelfia and Salamina, that uncontrollable factors cancel the advantages of a new plant variety, especially if the increase in yield is slight even under the best experimental conditions. A new plant variety may result in a fifteen to twenty per cent higher yield on the government experimental farm, but if local plagues, periodic droughts, and other natural phenomena, produce annual fluctuations just as great, it may be difficult for the farmers to discriminate among the possible causes contributing to the yield. Near Jacmel, Haiti, agronomists tried to introduce a new variety of sorghum known as Egyptian Shallu. This new sorghum had so successfully replaced older varieties elsewhere in Haiti as a result of spectacular increases in yields that the agronomists decided not to grow it experimentally before introducing it in Jacmel. Crops did poorly, however, and later experiments showed that the sorghum should have been planted between October and January rather than in March. But by then the local peasantry was prejudiced against it.

These examples show that agricultural technicians sometimes fail to bring about the introduction of a new plant variety in an underdeveloped area because the advantages are not obvious to the farmers. Under experimental conditions, careful measurement is possible not only of the conditions acting upon the plant but also of their precise effect on yield; but the farmers in most underdeveloped areas do not share the background of the agricultural expert. Their observations are casual, without benefit of technical measurements or even of indirect experience. A small increase in yield may not be evident at this casual level, or some misfortune such as a plague or a drought may alter the original experimental conditions and prevent the expected increase.

When based on casual or non-technical observation, frequency interpretations are more readily made if the phenomena in question are spectacular and the advantages obvious. The new corn varieties introduced into Colombia and Bolivia and the new variety of potatoes introduced into Costa Rica resulted in such sizable increases in yields that a casual frequency interpretation favorable to the new varieties was unavoidable. Again it is possible to see why motivation, though an essential part of any causal explanation of culture, is an inadequate explanation by itself. In some cases the motivation of the farmers of Bolivia, Colombia, and Costa Rica was to increase survival margins and in other cases to increase conspicuous consumption, but motivation alone is insufficient to explain the acceptance of the improved plant varieties. In each case a particular improved variety became the special target of this underlying motivation, and the farmers eventually came to feel a need for the plant itself. They assumed that the relation between the higher yield and the new plant variety was predictable, that it would hold true for other farms and succeeding years. The new plant variety was seen as the cause of a higher yield, a cause they felt able to control. This sense of control over the recognized cause was a crucial part of their acceptance of the innovations.

Although the same causes operate in the acceptance of public health innovations as in the acceptance of agricultural innovations, the difficulties in making frequency interpretations by casual observation are much greater in this field than in agriculture. In the first public health program reviewed here, however, frequency interpretation in favor of the innovation was very easy.

Frequency Interpretation and Public Health —
A Yaws Eradication Campaign

In 1950, the Point Four public health programs in Colombia and Ecuador began a simultaneous attack on yaws, a disease very common among the Negro populations on the north coast of Ecuador and the Pacific coast of Colombia. Yaws is a highly contagious disease similar to syphilis though not venereal. The Negroes of this area had become so accustomed to yaws that they considered it as inevitable as measles. Mothers deliberately infected their children in the belief that an early case would increase resistance to the malady in later life.

A campaign to treat yaws with penicillin injections was undertaken by the Point Four program in collaboration with the Colombian and Ecuadorian governments. Teams of doctors and male nurses cruised along the myriads of coastal rivers dotted with the shacks and small villages of the Negro population. At first, many people were afraid, and some hid in the jungles until the doctors had moved on. They doubted the ability of the white doctor to treat this malady — or any other. They had their own native curers who treated all of their ailments with poultices, herbal broths, and magic. Despite this widespread fear and skepticism, thousands of sufferers submitted to treatment, many out of sheer desperation. The results could not have been more dramatic. Ulcers, lesions, and other symptoms responded immediately in nearly all cases. There could be no mistaking the causal connection between the penicillin injections and the cures.

The case of Zatinga, a small village on the Zatinga River of coastal Colombia, illustrates the effectiveness of the program. When the doctors first visited this community, a third of the children were victimized by yaws. Half the male heads of households and two thirds of the mothers were so incapacitated with lesions on their feet and limbs that they were capable of performing only occasional chores. The illness had reduced four unmarried adults to complete dependency on relatives and friends. But by the time of my visit in 1952, yaws had vanished in Zatinga.

Although not all of the Negro communities of this region were in such a desperate condition as Zatinga at the time of the campaign, the number of cases was very high in most of them. Such spectacular results could not be disregarded, and when permanent injection centers were established, people came voluntarily in search of the miraculous treatment. By 1951, these people were convinced that yaws was one disease the medical doctor could cure. Although most were still unwilling to accept modern treatment for other ailments, which they continued to attribute to folk and supernatural causes, even the native curers now freely admitted that the medical doctor's treatment for yaws was far superior to their own. "You cannot deny what you see with your own eyes."

These Negroes did not want to suffer and die from yaws. Their motivations to survive and to avoid pain were demonstrated in their use of folk remedies, however ineffectual. At first they distrusted the medical doctor, who in the past had always tended to belittle what he called their superstitions. But as the yaws treatment took effect, a frequency interpretation in favor of the medical doctor was unavoidable. The cure was spectacular, a fact made possible by the high incidence of the disease and the one hundred per cent efficacy of treatment in many communities.

Preventive Medicine and Indirect Experience — A Water Purification Program

A public health program of a different kind will now be considered. In an Andean community of northern Ecuador, a water purification system was installed in the hope that the new water supply would reduce the incidence of infectious diseases carried by contaminated drinking water. I found in talking with the people in the poorer sections of town that they were enthusiastic about the new plant, not because they considered it an effective health measure, but simply because of the convenience of having water that was not muddy. Previously it had been necessary to let the water stand in buckets until the sediment settled, but now it could be used straight from the tap. As in most of Ecuador, they ascribed to such folk causes as evil eye, malevolent air, and fright sickness the very maladies which might be caused by polluted drinking water. Native curers still maintained active practices in the magical treatment of these ailments.

Since few houses had indoor plumbing, public hydrants were located at regular intervals throughout the town, and housewives and children went several times a day to fill buckets for their household needs. The hydrants were not turned off tightly, and large puddles formed around the bases. Although the puddles were contaminated by animals, the buckets were set in the mud while being filled, then carried home into an unsanitary kitchen. The whole purpose of the purification plant was being counteracted by many sources of pollution.

It is not surprising, under these conditions, that the people failed to associate any beneficial effects with the water purification system. Since they did not understand or accept the germ theory of disease, they did not take the necessary precautions to keep the water pure. Inasmuch as the water continued to be contaminated, there was little likelihood of a reduction in the incidence of ailments caused by impure water. And since there was no spectacular decrease in disease, the people saw no connection between preventing illness and the use of purified water.

The yaws campaign was curative and produced such spectacular results that a causal connection between the modern treatment and the cure was readily made, whereas water purification was a program of preventive medicine. Because it wrought no rapid and obvious decrease in the incidence of any clearly defined syndromes, the preliterate folk had no way to verify its efficacy. Some members of the upper class of this community readily accepted the purified water as a means of decreasing disease. Having had more schooling, they already believed the germ theory, and some had even boiled their drinking water before the new plant was installed. They did not need to test the water or to observe a lessening in the incidence of illness: they were willing to accept the word of the specialist.

Like their yaws-ridden Negro counterparts in the coastal zones, these highland townsfolk wanted relief from physical ailments. But the purported effects of the water purification program were not inspectional. Symptoms which might belong to any number of infectious diseases carried in drinking water were ascribed by these people to quite different etiologies and they had no clear idea what diseases the purified water was supposed to prevent.

In the improved plant and in the yaws programs, the specialist, by virtue of his technical observations, could clearly isolate the variables for public confirmation. His preliterate audience was able to make a causal inference on which to act and thereby gain a feeling of control over the cause itself. In the water purification example the specialist could not "control" all the situations under which drinking water was contaminated. Such preventive "control" would presuppose public acceptance of the very assumptions on which the program was based, an anachronism for a preliterate public with causal assumptions different from those of the specialist. Such acceptance is more characteristic of industrialized society in which the frequency interpretations of the masses are often performed vicariously through statistics collected by specialists.

Preventive Medicine and Direct Experience — A Charity Maternity Hospital

At the Isidro Ayora charity maternity hospital in Ecuador, in 1952, I observed a public health program with both successful and unsuccessful aspects. At that time the hospital was less than a year old, but already about half the births in Quito were taking place there. The fact that care at the hospital was free made it very attractive to lower-class mothers, despite certain hospital practices which were in conflict with their beliefs. They believed, for example, that the afterbirth should be buried in a dry, warm place, preferably under the kitchen hearth. Otherwise *entuertos* — postnatal cramps accompanied by fever and diarrhea and said to be fatal in many instances — might result.

Another source of conflict was the five-day residence limit for most maternity cases. At home mothers would not get out of bed for the first two weeks after childbirth and would not think of leaving the house for the first forty. During this forty-day period, known as the *dieta*, the mother has a special diet and is given laxatives at specified intervals. During the entire forty days she is not exposed to fresh air and is not allowed to bathe, put her hands in water or cut her fingernails. Touching water or clipping the fingernails might lead to *sobreparto*, an illness which follows childbirth, is characterized by headaches, chills, and fever, and is said to be usually fatal.

Since mothers who attended the hospital had no choice about the disposal of the placenta and had to agree to leave five days after the birth, they were obliged to sacrifice their beliefs and customs to get free care. Arguments between women who had attended the maternity hospital and women who had not showed how their beliefs were being changed by the new experience. Those who had gone to the hospital pointed out that despite the improper handling of the afterbirth and their being required to go home in five days, to eat foods inappropriate to a folk diet, and to be exposed to fresh air in the hospital wards, they had suffered no dire consequences. "But what about the mothers who die at the maternity hospital?" the skeptics queried. "Do you know any?" was the retort of those defending the hospital. Once, when two deaths were recalled, it was pointed out that in both instances the women had given birth at home and by the time they were taken to the hospital were already dying of complications. Although the women arguing in support of their folk beliefs knew of no one who had succumbed as a result of hospital care, all knew of many mothers who had survived hospital treatment, and all remembered women who had died in childbirth at home while following traditional practices. Here again we see how new practices are found acceptable when casual observation shows the results to be obviously beneficial.

Some folk beliefs were not being challenged by the hospital experience. When nurses attempted to bathe mothers or to cut their fingernails, many protested so hysterically that they were allowed to have their own way. Staff members also frequently yielded to persistent demands for the traditional postnatal laxative. Since hospital policy vacillated in regard to these folk beliefs, fewer mothers were being convinced of their irrelevance.

Here again the survival motivation is dominant, as evidenced by the anxiety of Quito mothers about the dangers of childbirth. With free care and food during the hospital stay as further inducement, enough women had ventured and survived the experience to bear testimony that "improper" disposal of the placenta, leaving one's bed and room after five days, and breathing fresh air after delivery had no harmful effects. Cognition and motivation were combining to destroy the older beliefs and to increase popular respect for the hospital and its modern medical practices. More and more women were considering the maternity hospital as the cause of a higher rate of survival in childbirth, and they therefore felt a greater sense of control over this situation. But where the staff permitted patients the alternative of refusing to follow hospital routine, no clear or convincing connection was being established between the preferred hospital policy and satisfaction of the mothers' felt needs.

Frequency Interpretation and Probable Knowledge

Motivation and cognition combine to shape the needs people feel. Motivations of survival, sex, and prestige are a partial and basic cause of human behavior, but they take so many different behavioral forms that they cannot be accepted as a sufficient cause of culture and its changes. Motivational cause is very flexible as it fixes on new targets or behavioral forms for cognitive reasons; cognition is the crucial change-producing component of wants or felt needs. Motivation is an action component of cultural causality, but cognition is both active and developmental. Cognition results in a progressive accumulation of knowledge which builds upon past experience.

Cognition derives its dynamic quality from frequency interpretation — the potentiality to synthesize experiences into predictive generalizations. At the preindustrial, non-specialized level, frequency interpretation is based entirely upon casual observation, and spectacularity is important for acceptance of innovations. With specialization, technical observations increase and frequency interpretations multiply tremendously, though they tend to be less inspectional. Communication and acceptance of these frequency interpretations becomes increasingly dependent on indirect experience and vicarious observations, and therefore on the literacy and knowledge of the recipients.

Throughout this book the word "knowledge" stands for "probable knowledge," which is a process and continuum rather than a discrete phenomenon. It is the interpretation of experience, and requires constant revision and correction. In literate industrial societies, frequency interpretations are revised largely by technical observations of specialists, who have greatly accelerated the rate at which refinement of correlations takes place. The growth of knowledge is a continuum of

31

increasing refinement and precision in the interpretation of casual and controlled experience.

Frequency interpretation may be arbitrarily divided into correlation (simple or sophisticated) and the derived causal assumptions that serve as a basis for action. The latter are essentially predictions, which, like probable knowledge, are never final and never foresee all the consequences of action. Man is always faced with new limitations in his interaction with environment — not because the limitations actually increase, but because the growth of knowledge leads to greater awareness of them.

The predictive implications of a frequency interpretation give a sense of control to the observer by providing him with a guide to future action. He assumes the existence of a cause and effect relation by which he can act to increase his expectations. A new "control" is a new alternative of action by which people feel that they can increase their expectations of satisfying wants.

III

Cognition and Probable Knowledge

THE examples of change in the preceding chapter showed that even uneducated and illiterate people are not simply tradition-bound puppets of their culture. Given adequate opportunity to measure the advantages of a new alternative, they act to maximize their expectations. Yet some writers on the subject of culture change are of the opinion that tradition or culture has a kind of determining force of its own. Culture becomes the active agent of its own causality, and man is relegated to passivity.

Francis Hsu's study of a Chinese town's reaction to a cholera epidemic is a good example of this kind of thinking. According to Hsu, the eight thousand inhabitants of Hsi-ch'eng, a town in Yunnan province, were given "adequate proof" that modern scientific measures were more effective than their own traditional magic and religion, yet they held to their old ways and failed to adopt the new.[1] "Magic and real knowledge," says Hsu, are "intertwined" among all peoples, and "man fails to differentiate between magic and science not because he lacks any power of rationality but because his behavior in general is dictated by faith developed out of the pattern of his culture. . . . Given a culture with a traditional material heavily laden with magic, the individual's association and projection will be based more on magico-religious premises. Given a different culture with a traditional material biased toward science, the individual's association and projection will operate in closer accordance with real knowledge. In either case . . . *the culture* and not *the individual* is the determining factor." [2]

If true, we can only conclude that this is a case where a frequency interpretation in favor of a new control was rejected because cultures rather than men maximized their expectations. This contradicts my data presented in the preceding chapter. After pointing out what I consider to be the fallacy in Hsu's evaluation of his evidence, I shall analyze comparative material on folk medicine in Ecuador and Mexico to further demonstrate that people accept new controls when they perceive an advantage, regardless of their cultural traditions.

A Cholera Epidemic in China

Cholera was carried to Hsi-ch'eng down the Burma Road by refugees during the fall of Burma in 1942. Within a month after its onset the epidemic was ended by an abrupt drop in temperature. Because little attention was paid to the epidemic at first, it was a matter of public concern for only three weeks. During this brief period the people of Hsi-ch'eng resorted to many traditional activities to protect themselves from the disease. These traditional activities can be put into two general categories — magical and mechanical. [3]

Magic included both group and individual procedures, the group activities consisting of three different kinds of prayer meetings. In the first kind, supplication was made to all gods who might have ordered the epidemic as punishment for the sins of the populace. The second kind consisted of a ritual parade of an effigy of the God of Epidemics to force the withdrawal of the epidemic-giving spirits. The third consisted of prayers for the dead. Magical precautions taken by individual persons included sexual abstinence, hanging cactus stalks over doorways, stamping handprints on the gates and walls of houses, cleaning up filth and refuse, smoking and sweeping the streets to clean up the area for the gods, abstaining from washing clothes in streams to keep streams clean for the gods, using amulets, and drinking fairy water obtained from temples or other sacred spots. Mechanical activities included observing food taboos as well as employing curing practices once the disease was contracted. The food taboos were connected with ideas about the cold-producing qualities of some foods.

Hsu reviews the possible consequences of these activities in the light of modern scientific knowledge. Group activities concerned with the supernatural may, he feels, have helped to stabilize the community psychologically, but did not prevent the spread of the epidemic. Some of the individually performed magical activities — handprints, amulets, cactus stalks, and sexual abstinence — were neutral, but the cleanliness rituals may have helped. By avoiding the streams in which they had previously washed their clothes and foodstuffs and by cleaning up refuse around their living quarters, the people effected helpful sanitation measures. On the other hand, one magical activity, the drinking of unboiled fairy water at certain public places, may have been harmful.

The mechanical measures could have had both positive and negative effects. One taboo forbade eating fruits and vegetables usually eaten raw or slightly cooked, which could have served as carriers of the cholera bacillus, and such foods as pea curd and bean custard, which were customarily eaten cold and served in the streets. All of these were looked upon as cold-producing foods and their avoidance may have helped to prevent the spread of infection. Popular prescriptions for cholera filled at native drug stores included some drugs which probably had remedial effects as, for example, dehydrated potash, alum, and chlorodyne. Other recommendations, such as blood-letting, may sometimes have been harmful.

Although it is possible, says Hsu, for an outsider to assess the various actions of these people according to their relative scientific merit, the local populace itself was not aware of such distinctions. For them "real knowledge (science) was intertwined with magico-religious practices." [4] Thus, the injections to prevent cholera became intertwined with traditional practices. The new preventive measure was added to the old ones but did not replace them. Although some people submitted to the free injections provided by the local hospital, most were unenthusiastic; and even those who had the injections also took part in the traditional magico-religious activities. "The fact that several large bodies of people, represented by the schools, the refugee college and the hospital, who resorted to scientific precautions and who had as a result become free from the effects of the epidemic" should, argues Hsu, have provided the people of Hsi-ch'eng "with *adequate proof* of the effectiveness of the scientific measures as against the ineffectiveness of the traditional patterns." [5]

But Hsu fails to take into account several reasons why the people of this community could not have made a frequency interpretation in favor of modern scientific practices. He makes much of the fact that "magic" and "real knowledge" are "intertwined" in the community. Most of the people who took the anticholera injections "also supported the prayer meetings and resorted to other age-old safeguards." There was certainly no "control" group here to make possible a frequency interpretation in favor of any one activity. The situation is like that in the water purification study or in those cases in which the maternity hospital vacillated in its enforcement of policy. In both examples the innovators had difficulty demonstrating an inspectional connection between a particular activity and a particular result.

Another obstacle to a frequency interpretation in favor of the injections was the relatively short duration of the epidemic. The situations described in the preceding chapter covered much longer periods, during which the people could digest and discuss the evidence. Although somewhat less than two hundred people died during the epidemic — about two per cent of the town's population — most of these died within the very brief span of three weeks. Finally, as Hsu points out in a footnote, immunity to cholera as a result of these injections was probably "far from being one hundred per cent."[6] It seems remarkable that anyone bothered to have the shots. What percentage of the total population did so is never made clear; nor is it stated whether the daily number of injections increased or decreased during the progress of the epidemic.

Three years after Hsu published his book *Religion, Science and Human Crises*, which deals with the epidemic just reviewed, a greatly abbreviated version was published as a chapter in a casebook on cultural problems in the field of public health.[7] In the newer version Hsu omits his argument that the people of Hsi-ch'eng had "adequate proof" of the effectiveness of the injections. The reason for the omission is apparent in a prefacing comment by the editor, who, in reference to the epidemic says: "At the time, western-trained health personnel assumed the injections were effective; retrospectively the vaccine appears to have been just another kind of fairy water, an unwitting instance of magic offered in a scientific package. This ironic development is somewhat beside the main point of the case, however, since it appears that the people preferred other methods of control for reasons unrelated to considerations of technical efficiency." But the "ironic development" is precisely to the point! Because of this "development" the case loses all the theoretical importance the author originally ascribed to it.

In his earlier version, Hsu disagreed with Malinowski's view that both primitive and modern man distinguish between magic and science. Hsu could not have made a more striking demonstration of his point, for he himself has slipped into a magical explanation by his own definition: he considers science to be "real knowledge" and magic apparently the opposite. But if knowledge is viewed as only probable at best, the difference between "magic" and "science" becomes a matter of degree. The conclusions of Hsu's book were based on a simple error of judgment, an improbability in his own knowledge. The fact that the same conclusions reappear in the later article despite the change in his knowledge in the interim makes him an even better example than the people of Hsi-ch'eng that men are often victims of their own predilections.

If a new alternative behavior offers people no clear reward or advantage, we should not be surprised that they continue traditional activities or add the new practices without rejecting the old ones. Learning and motivation among lower animals is only analogous to human, but experiments show interesting parallels that help in understanding the basic processes involved. A rat in a Skinner box which is rewarded with a food pellet every time it presses a bar develops a close association between bar-pressing and food. One might say it has made a very rude frequency interpretation of a causal connection between food pellets and pressure on the bar. Like most causal interpretations based on a correlation, this would be only partly correct, for the actions of the machine and the experimenter are outside the rat's world view.

What is most interesting about rats' behavior in the present context is the persistence of bar-pressing without reward. Rats consistently rewarded when they make the proper response — pressing the bar — quit very quickly when food is discontinued. But rats irregularly rewarded continue working much longer after the pellets cease.[8] The irregularity of success results in a weaker frequency interpretation, and the animals find it more difficult to distinguish between the reward situation and its termination.

McClelland[9] made an experiment in which he rewarded one group of rats consistently for responding to specific clues in a circular alley, and another group in such a way that they could associate no specific clues with the reward. The specific training of the first group was rap-

idly extinguished when the reward ceased while the more general association between food and the circular alley made by the second group
persisted much longer. These rats showed a tendency to run faster at
a time when animals in the first group were giving up.

Man's linguistic and symbolizing capacities carry him far beyond
the learning limitations of rats, but these experiments with animals are
instructive and help to explain in part why human groups often adopt
new alternative behaviors while retaining the old ones. Replacement or
extinction of old behaviors by newer ones is less likely when rewards are
too irregular for clear frequency interpretation. In the next two sections
of this chapter I shall continue the discussion of folk medical beliefs
to show that even beliefs we might regard as magical and superstitious
may seem to bring rewards. But the irregularity of these rewards makes
the extinction or replacement of their causal interpretations more difficult, especially when a new or conflicting causal interpretation is not
spectacularly successful.

A Health Education Study in Quito, Ecuador

The data in this section were collected while I was investigating public reactions to health programs in Ecuador.[10] I shall begin by describing the nature of popular medical practices and concepts among the
poorer classes of Quito, showing that these popular practices constitute
a folk knowledge which, although much less probable than ours, is a
kind of knowledge nonetheless. I do not distinguish between magic and
real knowledge, for when knowledge is considered merely probable at
best, magic is only a less probable form.

The description of Quito folk medicine will be followed by an analysis
of tests administered to school children and student nurses and nurses'
aides in Quito. We shall see that formal education does not necessarily
lead to the replacement of old causal interpretations if no link is made
between the new symbolic system and the old. But when education
makes the connection, new frequency interpretations can take place
vicariously rather than through direct experience. We shall also note
that change may be greatly encouraged even when it is not understood,
when it is prompted by invidious emulation.

In Latin American cities, there is often a relatively weak middle
class, and the gulf between the lower and upper classes is very wide.
The lower-class city dweller may have more in common with the sur-

rounding rural population than with the upper class of his city. The upper class is frequently a very cosmopolitan society with a culture that is as much urban-international as it is local and national.

In Quito at the time of this study many popular folk beliefs were very strong among the lower classes. This strength is reflected in the volume of sales at the herb stands in the central public market. At intervals over a period of several weeks a record was kept of the purchases of medicinal herbs at the stalls of ten women vendors. These remedies were sought for practically every kind of malady imaginable, but a few illnesses had a considerably higher incidence than others. The six illnesses of highest incidence were malevolent air (nearly all children), cough (children), fright sickness (children), menstrual difficulties (mostly cases of delayed onset, and the cathartics purchased may well have had abortive effects), urinary difficulties (mostly adults with symptoms of blood and pain), and bewitchment (all adults).

In many of the cases of malevolent air, fright sickness, and witchcraft, customers brought prescriptions written out by *curanderos* (professional folk curers). Herbs purchased for these three illnesses were almost always of the magical variety used by *curanderos* for external "cleaning." A few better-dressed customers who appeared to belong to the white-collar or middle class bought herbs for less serious maladies such as stomachache, toothache, and headache. If the number of purchases made at the time of year at which these data were collected was representative of normal conditions, 180,000 purchases of herbs were being made annually at this market alone. Many of the customers undoubtedly were repeaters, but it is interesting to note that the population of Quito at this time was only about 200,000. Nor was this the only source of herbal remedies in Quito. There were many others, including street vendors and the traveling curanderos who sell their own ready-made herbal concoctions.

The information gathered at the herb stalls plus the considerable interview material collected from people living in the poorer sections of Quito demonstrate that here, as in Hsi-ch'eng, the populace has its own traditional explanations for disease and methods of prevention and treatment. These popular causal explanations of disease may be arbitrarily classified as contagion, mechanical causes, and psychological and supernatural causes. The most popular explanation of contagion is bad body humor. The humor is exuded with sweat, and if one does not bathe

39

frequently it may re-enter through his pores and infect his blood. Not only does it produce auto-infection, but it may also be passed to others. It may cause skin diseases, infected wounds, and syphilis. Close contact, sexual relations, or seats still warm from previous occupants are means by which it may pass from one person to another.

Classified as "mechanical" are temperature change, harmful foods, fatigue, and body blows. Exposure to cold air when overheated, being caught in a thunder shower when working in the fields, or drinking cold water when sweating are considered very dangerous. Symptoms include dysentery, menstrual and postnatal cramps, pneumonia, urinary difficulties, rheumatism, measles, partial paralysis, and malaria. Body heat may cause skin diseases, and heat generated in the body by coughing may lead to angina pectoris. Certain foods are dangerous by reason of their heaviness, sourness, acidity, or inherent coldness. Some foods stick to the stomach and others lead to an overabundance of bile which is related to liver trouble. Any cooked food left to stand acquires a quality of coldness which is especially feared. Fatigue from hard work and insufficient food leads to liver and kidney ailments as well as skin infections and inflamed uterus. Body blows can cause meningitis and tumors. Diarrhea with fever is said invariably to accompany the process of teething. For some informants, diarrhea at this age is simply a kind of natural occurrence. Others give a psychological explanation: they say that because the child is irritated he develops anger sickness.

Several illnesses are ascribed to psychological causes. Among these is anger sickness resulting from such causes as quarrels and jealousy. This may cause vomiting, diarrhea, fever, inability to walk, depression, fits, and palpitation of the stomach. Frustration of sexual desire, of the craving of a pregnant woman for a certain food, or of a child's desire for a toy or candy may result in a variety of maladies: fits, syphilis, and urinary difficulties are examples. Sadness resulting from the loss of a loved one, money, or property may also cause fits, as well as palpitation of the heart, fever, lack of appetite, severe headaches, and loss of consciousness.

Among the supernatural ailments, fright and malevolent air are the two most frequent causes and the victims are predominantly children. The cause of fright may be something as natural as a sudden fall or as supernatural as an encounter with a ghost or a spirit. Many persons have a definite feeling that fright produces loss of the soul. Malevolent air may affect a small child if he is taken to a cemetery, too close to a corpse, to solitary places in the mountains, or down into mountain canyons, or if he is exposed to a rainbow or night air. Another children's illness, but one apparently more prevalent in the country, results from evil eye — the malevolent glance of certain adults who have "electrical" or "strong" eyes. Witchcraft is the primary supernatural cause of illness among adults. The methods of the witch include magical poisoning of the victim's food and imitative magic which uses a doll to represent the victim. Symptoms of all ailments having supernatural etiologies are so generalized that they could point to almost any malady in a modern classification, but among those listed for children informants always included fever, vomiting, and diarrhea.

As noted previously, the pains frequently experienced by women after parturition are also attributed to supernatural causes, for they are considered likely to occur if the placenta is discarded in such a way that it comes in contact with water or cold air or is eaten by dogs; this is why they believe the placenta should be buried in a dry, safe place such as the ground beneath the kitchen hearth.

Preventive folk measures may be classified as either mechanical or supernatural. The "contagious" diseases are prevented by such mechanical means as bathing and by avoiding warm seats. The "mechanical" illnesses can be prevented by avoiding sudden changes of temperature or by regularly taking cathartics to keep the stomach clean. Psychological illnesses are considered almost impossible to prevent, since they are brought on by circumstances which a person cannot control or readily avoid. Supernatural ailments may be prevented by both mechanical and supernatural means. Avoidance of those situations in which a child is susceptible to supernatural infections could be considered mechanical. But since avoidance is not always possible, supernatural means of prevention predominate. Wearing certain objects on one's person is the most common type of preventive measure. The beak of a parrot or the wool of a llama will protect against witchcraft. A rosary around the neck of a child will guard it against malevolent air while crossing a canyon. Steel rings protect their wearers against both malevolent air and witchcraft, and a red ribbon will protect a child against the evil eye.

The predominating folk remedy is herbal solutions and broths, with cathartics the most popular. Calmative herbal broths for checking diarrhea and vomiting as well as sudorific herbal broths are, like cathartics, usually taken orally, whereas others are administered as enemas or vaginal douches. Among the external remedies, herbal poultices are often used. Cupping may be employed to extract malevolent air. But the most popular remedy for ailments with supernatural etiologies is that of "cleaning" the patient with special plants, eggs, or guinea pigs. This process consists of slowly rubbing the remedy over the patient's body until the illness is drawn into it.

This folklore of disease is fairly representative of that found throughout Ecuador.[11] Although most of it is no longer compatible with modern concepts of the causes of disease and its treatment, this lore constitutes a body of knowledge, for much of it is undoubtedly based on frequency interpretation. Take, for example, the concept of bad body humor, which is very close to the modern explanation of contagion. It results from a causal interpretation of an observed correlation between the onset of disease and certain situations in which contagion is likely. Although the explanation assumes something not observable, a substance called bad body humor, it leads to predictions of situations in which disease can be contracted or avoided. Bodily cleanliness, for example, is a predictable preventive measure that still holds good under modern explanations of contagion, although the prediction that disease may be contracted from a warm bus seat does not.

According to local belief, cooked food that has been left to stand may acquire a dangerous quality of "coldness." Symptoms resulting from eating such food sound remarkably like those of botulism or enterotoxin-producing staphylococci. The belief resulted from a correlation between illness and cooked food that has been left to stand, and the prediction that illness can be avoided by recooking the food and thus removing the coldness is valid to the extent that in practice it would lead to detoxication of the poison. It must be noted that the preventive measures of cleanliness and storage that would also help to prevent food poisoning are irrelevant according to this view. Unlike bad body humors, the "coldness" of cooked food that has been left to stand is part of casual observation. Since food infected by staphylococci or spores of *Clostridium botulinum* does not necessarily change in taste or smell, the modern explanation is beyond the limitation of casual observation. The modern refinement of this explanation has resulted from technical frequency interpretations which have simply increased the probability of avoiding food poisoning.

A correlation has also been drawn between the symptoms of intestinal infection and the teething stage in the child's development. In this case the explanations add so little that no prediction is possible except that the sickness is inevitable. Since teething children are apt to put things (under conditions of lower class Quito life almost any object on the dirty floor) into their mouths and thereby increase the possibility of intestinal infection, the folk correlation or generalization is both relevant and valid. But it is a very simple empirical correlation. The correlation between the symptomatology and the many diverse activities of the teething child that would be necessary to provide a modern generalization is so complex as to make its observation very difficult on a casual basis.

The supernatural explanation may conceivably be reinforced by partial frequency interpretations in many cases. As a completely hypothetical example, a group of mothers might cross a canyon and stop to give their children a drink of water from a polluted stream. Later, when the children show symptoms of intestinal infection frequently classified by the folk as the result of malevolent air, the mothers might make a correlation between the illness and the trip through the canyon. This correlation would be partly valid despite the irrelevance of their belief in spirits and the fact that they overlooked the relevancy of the stream.

But when a curer attempts to remedy an illness with "cleaning" herbs or guinea pigs it is difficult to see how frequency interpretation enters into the picture. Not all illnesses are fatal, however, and on the average, success is in favor of the curer. This is not so true in the case of modern classifications of illnesses by which we can appraise the relative danger of syndromes with greater exactness. But the symptoms which the folk ascribe to many of their classificatory terms and etiologies are so highly generalized that they may include both fatal and innocent maladies. As long as the law of averages works in favor of the curer, his results are an empirical demonstration that his methods, as well as the theories and explanations on which they are based, are usually valid, though not infallible.

The causes of many "supernatural" illnesses may be psychological. The kinds of partial paralysis that some informants gave as the symptoms suffered by close relatives who had been bewitched, as well as their claims that doctors were unable to find a cause — much less a cure —

for these cases, sounded very much like descriptions of psychosomatic conditions. Furthermore, curers succeeded in relieving the symptoms with a single magical treatment. Of course, this constituted a definite demonstration to the informants that the cure was a proof of the correct diagnosis of the cause as well as the efficacy of the treatment.

Although the popular Ecuadorian explanations of disease and treatment make up a system of knowledge based to a considerable extent on frequency interpretation, the fact that the knowledge is limited to casual observation makes it much less probable than the knowledge of modern medicine. Both the Ecuadorian folk and Anglo-Americans have systems of behavior to help them take action with regard to disease, which shows that people in both groups are motivated to survive and that they are acting cognitively to increase their expectations of survival. But the expectations of the two groups are quite different. For example, the number of deaths among children below the age of five accounts for over fifty per cent of the recorded annual deaths in Ecuador, as compared to less than ten per cent in the United States. Obviously the knowledge of Ecuadorians about disease is much less probable than that of the Anglo-Americans.

After a considerable amount of data had been gathered about the knowledge of Quito's lower classes of the cause, prevention, and treatment of disease, a series of tests was given to schoolchildren, nurses' aides, and nursing students to get an indication of the changes that might be occurring in their beliefs. Three public grammar schools were selected in the poorest sections of Quito and one in a white-collar district that came closest to what might be called a middle-class neighborhood. Students in all schools were eleven or twelve years old and had previously heard some illustrated lectures about public health sponsored by the health education branch of the local Point Four program.

The people of the poor districts of Quito were those shown by my previous investigations to be most dependent on traditional methods of treating disease. This was probably partly the result of an economic limitation, since curanderos and herbal home treatments are less expensive than the medical doctor and his drugstore prescriptions. Students at Roberto Cruz,[12] a small coeducational school in one of the poorest sections of town, were asked to tell their preferred method of treatment — doctor, curandero, or home remedies — for a list of ailments that included both modern and folk names. The results showed that modern names were being associated with the doctor and folk names with folk treatment.[13] Discussions with the youngsters after the testing revealed that although they had a clear picture of the symptoms generally ascribed to folk ailments, they did not know the symptoms of the diseases with modern names. For these children, the diseases the doctor could treat tended to be names rather than recognizable ailments. In any decision to seek treatment, much depends on how the folk classify their symptoms, yet nothing had been done in this educational program to help the children to see that the symptoms they ascribed to folk ailments were also the symptoms of the diseases treated by the modern doctor.

The Roberto Cruz class was also asked to describe the causes of each ailment on another list. Microbes, malevolent air, and bad body humor were the most popular choices of the students, but the cause "microbes" was given predominantly for ailments with modern names, such as tuberculosis, smallpox, and typhoid.[14] Temperature change, including eating "cold" foods in certain "hot" body states, was the folk cause given by most students as the cause of dysentery, coughing with blood, bronchitis, and whooping cough. Microbes were listed as a cause of dysentery, diarrhea with vomiting, coughing with blood, infected wounds, and pneumonia by only two students.

The tests at Roberto Cruz largely confirmed the data already gathered in interviews. It was possible to divide concepts of disease into folk and modern, but the two resulting categories were not mutually exclusive. The new was not simply being added to the old, but was also tending to replace it. But replacement seemed more at the level of treatment than of prevention. The doctor was making gains in the treatment of folk symptoms, but understanding or acceptance of his explanation of disease was lagging far behind. Thus progress in the use of preventive measures was being delayed and symptoms the doctor might be considered competent to handle by some people were being diagnosed as folk ailments by others. Very often the doctor was consulted only after the disease had reached an advanced stage.

At the León Mera and Brazil schools,[15] also in a poor district of Quito, students were asked to explain in their own words the nature and cure of certain folk ailments, why the doctor can or cannot cure them, the nature and danger of microbes, and why microbes can or cannot cause the folk ailments.

Again the results showed an easy familiarity with the folk concepts of disease, with the symptoms and the folk cures. The children also had a fair idea of what a microbe is: it was variously described as something which could be seen "only with a microscope," a "very little animal," "a little insect," and "a thing that lives on dirty hands and under fingernails," and was cited as a cause of "death," as well as "tuberculosis," "typhoid," "smallpox," and other diseases with modern names. But when asked if microbes could cause fright sickness, bewitchment, or malevolent air, the children were practically unanimous in asserting that microbes could not cause these ailments: "a microbe is too small to frighten anyone"; "a microbe is not a spirit or a devil or a person"; "witches do not work with microbes"; "such ailments are not contagious"; "such ailments are not caused by uncleanliness"; "a microbe could cause bewitchment only if sent by a witch"; and "these illnesses are caused by other things."

The students were similarly negative to the idea that the modern doctor might be able to cure such ailments as fright sickness, malevolent air, and bewitchment: "the doctor has not specialized or studied in this field and would not know how to cure by cleaning with eggs and guinea pigs"; "the doctor might catch the ailment himself"; "these are not simple illnesses like the doctor knows how to treat"; "these diseases must be cured by home remedies or curanderos"; "the doctor does not understand such things"; "everyone knows the doctor cannot cure these things."

This test demonstrated even more clearly than the one at Roberto Cruz the split between folk and modern explanations of disease. But as class discussions later showed, the division at the level of treatment was not nearly so mutually exclusive as these results might suggest. Diseases with symptoms considered by the folk to be supernatural or psychological were not always diagnosed as such, and doctors were on occasion being consulted. Once again, modern medical practices were gaining at the level of treatment rather than prevention, because understanding of modern explanations of disease etiology were lagging behind the inspectional frequency interpretations slowly being made in favor of the doctor's cures.

Students at the Eloy Alfaro school came from middle-class families with a higher standard of living than that of the poor students.[16] Each was asked to write a short essay describing the last illness suffered by a member of his family, telling the symptoms, the age and sex of the afflicted family member, the cure used, whether or not a doctor had been consulted, and the cause of the ailment. They were also given the names of certain folk diseases for which they were to provide a definition and an explanation of treatment.

The results of the Eloy Alfaro test confirmed again what interviews had already suggested: [17] that some loss of folk beliefs was occurring in the white-collar class. Replacement of folk by modern concepts had progressed further here than in the poor districts. Since these families were better able to afford doctors and modern drugs, they were making greater use of them; and as they did, their frequency interpretations in favor of the modern methods were increasing. As in the poor districts, however, the influence of modern medicine was greatest in the area of treatment and least in regard to causal explanation, which is so important from the standpoint of preventive medicine. Despite the lag, the understanding of modern concepts of the etiology of disease was somewhat greater among the people of this class than among the poor people.

But a very important influence in the orientation of the Quito white-collar class toward a modern view of its health problems is invidious emulation. The professional and white-collar classes have a tendency to disparage the ways and beliefs of the folk and to look up to those of the upper class. Invidious emulation accounts in large part for the fact that reliance on the doctor and modern drugs for treatment of disease has proceeded faster in this middle class than has an understanding of such treatment or an understanding of the reasons for preventive sanitary measures.

Except for a few health lectures, the grammar school students had not had any special training which would help them to view their folk beliefs critically. The next test, therefore, was given to the nurses' aides at the Isidro Ayora maternity hospital in Quito and to the students at the nearby nurses' training school. [18] The nurses' aides had only a grammar school education, but their participation in hospital life had provided them with some special experience and training. The nursing students, on the other hand, were all high school graduates. Since the school year was just beginning at the time of the test, the first-year students as yet had had no special training other than their high school background.

The tests [19] showed that education was making definite inroads on the folk concepts of disease, despite the fact that not even during the specialized training of the nursing students were the beliefs directly attacked by explanation of the contradictions between folk and modern medicine. When asked later to tell why they thought they made so much better a showing on the test than the other groups, the third-year nursing students admitted that during the second year of training they had begun to question many of their former beliefs, largely as a result of courses in obstetrics and the history of medicine. Until taking this test, however, they said they had not realized how greatly their thinking had been affected.

Of all beliefs, the magical and supernatural were those most altered by both direct and indirect experience. Although belief in psychological maladies showed strong persistence, belief in desire as a cause — the least compatible with a modern point of view — tended to disappear with education. Belief in mechanical folk causes and remedies tended to persist, although here again the greatest changes were the result of education rather than direct experience. The folk concept of contagion was very persistent, but in a form close to the modern concept. Most indicative of the influence of specialized learning through indirect experience were the answers to short-essay questions asking what the subjects would do in certain problem situations with patients.[20] Here empathy with patients seemed to be greatly influenced by education. Although in all groups there were subjects who showed sympathy, the number who were able to combine a desire to help with a sophisticated understanding of the different premises on which folk and modern medicine were based increased with education.

After the testing of the schoolchildren, nurses' aides, and nursing students, two Ecuadorian doctors working in the Point Four health education program gave experimental health lectures before some of the grammar school students previously tested. Instead of the formal, abstract lectures about preventing disease which they had listened to earlier without any significant change in their beliefs, the pupils took part in a discussion of the relative validity of folk and modern concepts. They willingly discussed bewitchment, malevolent air, fright sickness, and other folk explanations of the cause, prevention, and treatment of disease with no fear of being ridiculed for their beliefs. Throughout the discussions the lecturers tried to lead the children to see that the symptoms of the ailments they described were caused by the sources of infection they had previously been informed about in lectures and health films. The primary purpose of the experiment was to link the symptoms of disease with modern causes, preventive measures, and treatment without ridiculing the folk beliefs. The latter were explained as older ways of looking at disease that had now been superseded by newer and more effective measures of prevention and cure.

The objective of avoiding ridicule was not achieved to an equal degree in the two experimental classes. Two lectures were given at the León Mera school to the class of girls previously tested. The lecturer on both occasions derided the students for their frank and unsophisticated responses to questions about their beliefs. This tendency was corrected during the three experimental lectures at Roberto Cruz.

Tests at both schools following the lectures showed that this approach via free discussion was much more effective than the straight lecture method used formerly. The students had been made much more aware of the contradiction between folk and modern medicine and of the point of view that the modern doctor was better qualified than the curandero to cure the symptoms the latter called the result of supernatural or other folk causes.[21] At León Mera, however, where ridicule had entered into the discussion, the new sophistication did not show the same depth of understanding or the same degree of change as at Roberto Cruz. Not only did more of the children at Roberto Cruz now profess a greater disbelief in folk medicine, but nearly a fifth of them were able to answer problem questions as well as the student nurses had. This difference in the results of the two sets of lectures served in corroborating the results of the previous observations and tests among the white-collar class. Invidious emulation can lead to a derogatory attitude toward folk beliefs, but it is not alone sufficient to cause their replacement by a more probable understanding. The latter comes not through ridicule and rejection, but from an appreciation of the alternatives.

Changing Folk Beliefs in Sonora, Mexico

For comparison let us now switch our attention to Sonora, Mexico, the case-study area which will concern us in Part III. Here in the peasant villages along the Mayo River of southern Sonora, Indians and mestizos alike retain a very folk-like view of the causes of disease. Here too rapid change is taking place in treatment rather than in prevention. But here money rather than formal education is crucial.

Rural schools in southern Sonora are not directly affecting peasant belief and practices with regard to illness. Both curanderos and modern doctors are consulted regardless of the ethnic, linguistic, or educational characteristics of the peasant family. A census of recent ailments and their treatment at the village of Mesquital de Tesia showed no appreciable differences between mestizos and Indians, literates and illiterates, monolingual Indian-speakers and bilinguals.

Mestizos as well as Indians believe in the common folk maladies "fright sickness" (*susto*) and "fallen fontanel" (*caída de la mollera*). Only *chíchale* (a mythical bird) sickness is a distinctively Indian malady. All three are primarily children's ailments, although fright sickness sometimes afflicts adults. In twenty-eight cases of these ailments recorded at Mesquital, fifteen were "fallen fontanel" afflicting infants five to fourteen months old, eleven were cases of fright sickness among children three to seventeen, and two were chíchale among infants less than a year old. Five of the twenty-eight maladies (three fright, one fallen fontanel, and one chíchale) were fatal. In all cases the ailments were treated only by folk curers — specialists in the art of curing these particular maladies.

The symptom most frequently mentioned by the parents of the afflicted children for all three of these ailments was diarrhea. Vomiting, eyes deeply sunken, and sleeping with eyes half open were the next most frequent symptoms of fallen fontanel. Vomiting and sunken eyes may also accompany fright and chíchale, although they were mentioned less frequently. Fever and lack of appetite were also mentioned by some informants for all three ailments. Stomachache and swollen abdomen were peculiar to fright sickness.

Fallen fontanel is almost always caused by a sudden fall, as from a stool, bed, or an older child's arms. The folk curer, usually a woman for this malady, treats it by pressing up on the roof of the child's mouth with her thumb and sometimes by sucking the region over the fontanel. The front of the head is usually shaved and a poultice of flour, egg-white, and licorice is applied. Fright sickness, as the name indicates, is caused by a sudden and severe fright, which may result from encounters with ghosts, snakes, mad dogs, and the like. Part of the intestine slips out of place and unless massaged back into position, the misplaced organ may dry out and cause death. Chíchale sickness is caused by a bird no one has ever seen — a flying mammal that crawls into bed with

50

infants at night to suckle them at its breasts. It seeks out children who have not yet been weaned by following tracks left in the dirt outside the house. Toward evening mothers must always erase the tracks of their small children with a broom.

Despite the persistence of these folk beliefs and the idea that there are diseases which are unknown to the modern doctor and must therefore be treated by folk curers, modern medicine is definitely gaining ground among the peasantry. Country people in this area recall that before the revolution of 1910 no one ever visited a medical doctor. To their knowledge there was not even a doctor in Navojoa until after the town was moved to its present site in 1915. The first hospital was built about 1920, but at that time most country people were still depending entirely on folk curers. By 1930, many mestizos were visiting doctors, and by 1940, Indians were doing so as well. Today the inhabitants of even a fairly conservative and predominantly Indian community like Mesquital rely heavily on the modern doctor.

The heads of forty-two households at Mesquital were asked to describe the course of treatment for the most recent serious ailment suffered by any member of their family. While treatment began with home remedies such as herbal broths in 74 per cent of all cases, it ended with them in only 7 per cent. Treatment was initiated by a folk curer in 19 per cent of the cases and in 23 per cent of them folk curers were consulted as an intermediate step. Treatment was concluded by a folk curer, however, in only 10 per cent of the cases. A pharmacist was consulted (pharmacists in Mexico commonly diagnose and prescribe treatment — often from a verbal description of the symptoms) as an intermediate step in 7 per cent of the cases and as a final step in 21 per cent. By contrast, medical doctors, who were consulted as the initial step in seeking treatment in only 7 per cent of the cases and were never an intermediate step, ended the treatment of 62 per cent of the illnesses. In all cases treated by a doctor the patient had recovered. One of those being treated by a druggist's prescriptions was still not considered well, whereas in two of the four cases where final treatment was given by a folk curer the patient died.

The doctor is usually consulted as a last resort, when it becomes obvious that there is no cheaper or more convenient alternative. Household remedies are tried first, then sometimes the folk curer, and finally the doctor. When the doctor is consulted at such an advanced stage that the patient is already near death, the family rarely blames him if the patient dies. "Ya no había remedio" (he was past saving), is the usual comment.

Many deaths could be avoided by prompt medical care, but much of the peasant's seeming apathy and unconcern results from the prevalent attitude that it does not really matter what is done to help a person if his time has come to die. Life, in a sense, is cheaper among many of the underprivileged peoples of the world because they have a much higher expectation of death than we do. If no one is to be blamed or made the scapegoat for illness and death, as is the case in areas where witchcraft is greatly feared, fatalism will probably be common.

But the peasantry's growing reliance on the modern doctor — even as a second and third choice — means an increasing expectation of recovery from illness. When I discussed with peasants, both literate and illiterate, the fact that the rural population of the area is much greater than it was twenty to forty years ago, they explained to me that more children survive today than formerly because of *los doctores* and *las inyecciones de penicilina*. Modern medicine is so effectively lowering the mortality rate even in the villages that many peasants have made a simple frequency interpretation in its favor by casual observation of its results.

The case of Jesús and María Moroyoqui provides a dramatic though not unusual example. This Mayo Indian couple had seven children, three of whom died from illnesses treated by folk curers. They were strongly convinced that doctors and their modern medicines were ineffectual and too expensive, but when a fourth child got sick they bought medicines listed on a doctor's prescription that had been used by a neighbor for a similar illness. On returning home with the remedies, the father found his child already dead. When a fifth child sickened, the couple immediately took him to Navojoa, where the illness was promptly treated by a doctor. Since then the three remaining children have always had immediate medical care when ill.

Today most villages along the Mayo River have both "injectionists" and curanderas. The latter treat such traditional maladies as fallen fontanel and fright whereas the injectionist gives shots according to medical prescriptions. Injectionists are almost always women and usually have had some training from a doctor, although no credentials are required. They keep all the equipment necessary for giving shots except the drugs themselves, and they carefully follow the ritual of boiling their instruments because they have been told that it is dangerous not to do so. In river towns and villages such as San Ignacio, Guaymitas, San Pedro, and El Recodo, I found that the numbers of curanderas and injectionists were about evenly divided, each village having from two to five of each. In more inaccessible areas where people are less likely to go to Navojoa for drugs, the folk curers outnumber the injectionists. At Macoyahue, for example, there were seven curanderas and only one injectionist.

With regard to the unequal progress toward modernization of curative practices and preventive medicine, the situation is much the same here as in Quito. The chief resistance to modern curative medicine is economic: adherence to herbal remedies and folk curers is largely a condition of poverty. Only when it seems certain that there is no cheaper solution does the peasant family seek medical aid. Modern medical treatment has so spectacularly reduced deaths of infants and children that even many of the uneducated country people have been able to make a casual frequency interpretation in its favor and can discuss its effects on population growth.

Preventive medicine is not understood, however, even by many people in the town middle class, among whom the increasing preoccupation with cleanliness and such new sanitary features as indoor toilets and kitchen sinks is more often the result of invidious emulation than of concern with health. When some lower middle-class friends of mine began building their first bathroom and I dutifully commented on the beauty of their new rose-colored toilet bowl, they admitted that it really was not the prettiest color they could have chosen. But they thought this dark shade would be more practical than white or yellow because it would not show the dirt as much. In the towns, most of the current changes in household living that lead to greater sanitation are products of invidious emulation rather than a concern with disease germs. Families are paving their floors, installing indoor plumbing, and keeping their houses cleaner because the "better" people do so. The increasing affluence of southern Sonora, which will be the topic of Part III, has made it possible for townspeople to improve their living standards; and these improvements, attended only incidentally by greater cleanliness, are engendered by status rather than health considerations. Everyone is concerned with keeping up with his neighbors.

Implications

The studies of changing medical beliefs and practices in Ecuador and Mexico substantiated the evidence in Chapter II that people choose new alternatives or "controls" when frequency interpretations make possible a clear connection with reward. Among poorly educated people this connection is made much more readily in the treatment of disease than in its prevention. An understanding of disease prevention in modern terms must come largely through the vicarious experience of formal education, for the relations are so complex that rewards are difficult to perceive inspectionally.

It is not necessary to view culture as *the* determinant of the behaviors in question nor as the active agent of its own persistence and change. In many instances, cultural persistence — the so-called force of tradition — is the result of the generality or irregularity of reward. As I have said earlier, most illnesses are not fatal, so the odds are always in favor of the treatment. This fact can result in the appearance of reward, but reward of a definitely irregular kind. Felt needs for traditional practices with irregular rewards are likely to be strong simply because the specific relations are *not* clear. When such practices are retained after adoption of a new alternative, an additive — rather than a replacement — type of change results.

When additive change occurs, it may be the result of one of three causes. First, the purported rewards of the new alternative may not be clear. In other words, inspectional frequency interpretation in favor of the new may be difficult. There is no real challenge then to the strong felt need already invested in the traditional practice with its own irregular reward. Replacement in such cases is most likely to come about through formal education, the means by which man exercises and expands his capacity to symbolize. As McClelland says, "Our symbolic capacities free us from too great a dependence on external regularities and enable us to produce the same kind of regularities internally as the experimenter produces by control of external conditions." [22] Because of his capacity to symbolize, man can learn vicariously through indirect experience. If all frequency interpretation were limited to inspection, there would be very little cultural development. Preliterate peoples, like preschool children in our own society, are greatly limited in their ability to regularize experience through symbols.

Second, new practices may be adopted, regardless of the clarity or obscurity of the purported rewards, by reason of invidious emulation. For example, turning to new habits of cleanliness or to medical doctors instead of curanderos may arise out of a concern for status rather than health. In underdeveloped areas particularly, an enormous amount of change takes place in this manner. Outhouses and indoor toilets are often built more for status reasons than for either convenience or health. Sometimes people do not even use them, or they maintain them in such unsanitary conditions as to defeat the purpose of health experts. As we have seen, even people greatly preoccupied with the cleanliness of their housing may be motivated by invidious emulation of "better" families rather than by a concern for sanitation. In lower middle-class houses in Sonora the *sala* where guests are received is frequently immaculate and may be mopped and cleaned several times a day. The kitchen in the same house may be contaminated with decaying food, swarms of flies, and the droppings of chickens.

Third, the purported rewards of a new alternative may be very clear, but for lack of opportunity to use it people may cling to the old. Such a situation was illustrated in Sonora, where many country people have made a frequency interpretation in favor of modern medicine but continue to rely on folk remedies for initial treatment as a measure of economy. In this case replacement increases with affluence. Economic development is crucial in expanding opportunities for change through invidious emulation.

When new alternatives are adopted through invidious emulation, the choice is not made with complete understanding of the consequences. The "better" families in Sonora who set the standards of cleanliness understand the germ theory and the consequences for health of sanitary precautions. But most who emulate them do not. Similarly, what a student learns vicariously through the use of symbols is sometimes thought of as acceptance on faith. Since few people look into microscopes to observe germs, they are accepting the word of a specialist as is the primitive man who believes the doctrines of his witch doctor. Both the formal learning and the emulative processes are therefore looked upon by some as evidence that the poor layman in all societies is nothing but the passive instrument of culture. But in a highly specialized society, who is not both specialist and layman? Reciprocity and mutual respect among specialists involve the sanctioning effect of free discussion and questioning; they are not simply a matter of faith. As for emulative change, it does not seem fortuitous to me that in general it proceeds in the direction of more probable — rather than less probable — knowledge.

I have emphasized that culture is not *the* determinant of culture, but I do consider it an important limitative cause. One salient example in this chapter was the limitation of traditional symbolic behavior on Quito schoolchildren exposed to modern health lectures. When no attempt was made to relate the new concepts to the symbolic content of folk knowledge, the lectures made little impression. Here is an instance where local traditions must be taken into account in order to minimize their limitative effect on the understanding of new material. Examples of economic limitation were provided by both the Quito and the Sonoran data. In the first case, change through invidious emulation was being inhibited by lack of opportunity. In the second case, as economic developments increased opportunities and expectations, modern medicine was making inroads through both frequency interpretation and invidious emulation. Limitative causes of culture will be discussed in the next two chapters.

IV

Limitation

I~ THE last two chapters I emphasized the cognitive component of cultural causality in order to demonstrate that man is not simply a passive agent manipulated by his own behavior patterns. But the determination of limitative causes is usually of greater usefulness for applied purposes than is the consideration of motivational and cognitive factors. The latter can generally be taken for granted, particularly by the practical man who is too busy modifying his surroundings to believe that he is nothing but the pawn of historical forces.

Although limitative causes were not discussed as such in the preceding two chapters, they were crucial in each of the cases described. In the Chilean soil conservation project, limitations were both environmental and cultural. The storm, for example, increased the effectiveness of Kincaid's demonstration — an unexpected environmental limitation contributed substantially to the success of the project. Two notable limitations of a cultural nature were also causal in its success: the strength of the Chilean subjects' indirect experience and their ability to finance their own terracing projects.

Environment was a crucial limitation in the Papago case, where the severity of erosion compensated for lack of indirect experience. Capitalization, available to the Papago through federal funds, was another limitation which increased the probability of their accepting assistance in soil conservation. Both environmental and cultural limitations played a part in the successful introduction of improved plant varieties. A new variety had to offer some environmental advantage, and when the crop in question was not a food staple, the presence of a market was vital. If using the new variety required some accompanying technological change, as in the case of mosaic-resistant sugarcane varieties introduced into Colombia, it had to be demonstrably more profitable than the old before new processing equipment was deemed worthwhile.

In Quito, the inducement of free medical and hospital care was a cultural limitation which unquestionably accelerated acceptance of the maternity hospital, but hospital rules which were more persuasive than mandatory constituted a limitation increasing the probability that mothers might control the situation through emotional behavior. The inroads of modern medical knowledge among the people of Quito indicated several cultural limitations. Quito folk, relying mainly on direct experience, were making frequency interpretations in favor of modern medicine in the field of treatment. Higher education was raising those limitations, but educational opportunities were limited in turn by technological and economic factors — the general underdevelopment of Ecuador. The economic plight of the lower classes limited their opportunities to take advantage of modern medicine even for treatment, and as those limitations were lifted by public charity or greater affluence, modern medicine gained more adherents. Finally, a social limitative cause was noted, for because of invidious emulation modern medicine was more desirable than folk medicine to those who could afford it.

As these examples show, limitative causes of culture are situational factors which increase or decrease the probability of the occurrence of some given cultural behavior, without actively determining it.

Technical Observations and Environmental "Control"

The literature on directed culture change in underdeveloped areas yields several illustrations of the importance of environmental limitation. An excellent study by Henry Dobyns [1] concerns a Papago irrigation project during the relief programs of the thirties. A Civilian Conservation Corps administrator who had learned about the *bolsa* type of irrigation practiced across the border in Sonora, Mexico, decided to introduce it among the Papago of Arizona. In this method of irrigation, fields are completely enclosed by low earthen dikes which trap the water and hold it on the fields until they are saturated enough to grow a crop. To conserve moisture, the soil is dust-mulched by brush-dragging after plowing. Sonoran bolsas are filled either by canals that divert flood water from rivers or by ditches made to trap sheet run-off during heavy rains.

This flood or bolsa irrigation was quite different from the traditional irrigation practices of the Papago, who plow and plant on alluvial fans after rains have softened the ground. They make no attempt to impound their irrigation water; instead they divert it from gullies along spreader dikes in order to distribute it over their fields. To the CCC administrator, the Papago irrigation system seemed even less reliable than the bolsa system. If the heavy rains of late summer could be held in the fields to thoroughly soak the ground, he thought, Papago agriculture would be greatly improved. Subsequent planning led to the San Miguel bolsa, which covered 193 acres. The outer walls of this bolsa were approximately eight feet high and the inner dikes, separating basins of fifteen to twenty acres, were about four feet high. (Much of the best topsoil, according to Dobyns, was scraped up into these dikes.)

But environmental conditions here were different from those in Sonora. Normal flow in the San Miguel gully was inadequate to fill the bolsa and thoroughly soak the ground. Yet eventually peak floods washed the bolsa away. Because the Papago country lies at a much higher altitude than the bolsa country of Sonora, frosts there were more severe; yet bolsa flooding in Papago land depended on heavy summer rains that came too late to give a crop before the frosts. Some systematic technical observations before the initiation of the project might have resulted in diverting considerable labor and money into a more feasible project for helping the Papago.

Perhaps the most famous example of inadequate planning before attempting directed technological change is the East African groundnut scheme, also called the Kongwa Experiment. This 3,210,000-acre project for mechanized production of peanuts in an area that eventually proved too dry was based largely on a nine-week aerial reconnaissance without a satisfactory survey of soils, rainfall, or crop yields. Even the assumption that adequate machinery would be available for the project was in error, for World War II had just ended and machines had to be collected from "the salvage dumps of the world." The spectacular failure of this program has long made it an outstanding example of the dangers of "magical faith" in the "power of capital" and "the application of technical power." [2] It has also served the arguments of those who oppose investment in any large technical projects, a view which seems to me as unjustified as the opposite extreme of indiscriminate faith in such projects.

As shown by the examples in the preceding chapter, technical observation of the environment may make possible ready and widespread acceptance of an innovation. For example, technical observation may lead to the selection of a plant variety which is more productive and disease-resistant than the varieties already in use in a given environment, or it may lead to the development of a drug like penicillin which leaves no doubt as to the effectiveness of its curative properties. In such cases technical frequency interpretations permit manipulation of environmental limitations. A new "control" results; that is, a new alternative of action with desired consequences more probable than those that derived from the interaction of previous alternatives with the same environmental causes.

The so-called "controls" which man exercises over his environment are the alternative behaviors which he makes possible by increasing the range and intensity of his technical observations. The bolsa and groundnut projects involved the employment of new actions presumably alternative to those already in use in their respective environments. But these new actions were not new "controls," since their presumed consequences were not borne out in practice. They had been derived from inadequate casual observation, not from technical observation. It would be erroneous to conclude from such failures that technology and the energy it converts for man's use are not important causes of economic development, for these cases do not result from the application of technology but from its misapplication. The planners who thought up the bolsa and groundnut schemes were not introducing new "controls"; they acted with blind faith in something they did not fully understand, much as Juan acted when he put all his hopes in a water pump simply because it was a machine (see Chapter I).

The Market — A Cultural Limitation

Not only does the natural environment include limitative causes of cultural behavior, but so does culture itself. A case illustrating cultural cause — and one which contrasts with the cases of improved plant varieties previously cited — is that of an improved hybrid corn introduced into a Spanish-American community in New Mexico.[3] The author of this study does not name the community, but for convenience it will be referred to here as San Carlos. In the hope of raising corn production in this village, the local county extension agent employed the usual extension procedures to introduce a new hybrid seed corn. The seed chosen had been tested in the immediate area and had been found to be excellently adapted. To make doubly sure, soil from the village fields was tested before the hybrid was introduced. Thus, careful technical observations were made in order to insure "control" over environmental limitations. Meetings were then held with the villagers to convince them of the merits of the hybrid, and they were favorably impressed. A demonstration plot of the hybrid corn set up near the village yielded three times the harvest normal for a plot its size, and the next year half of the growers in the village adopted the hybrid seed. A year later three fourths of the growers planted the hybrid, but two years later nearly all had returned to planting their original "Indian" corn.

The villagers were quick to recognize the advantage of the hybrid seed, for the quantitative difference in yield was obvious. Why, then, did they finally abandon it? According to Apodaca, the author of the study, the women did not like the hybrid. Corn in this community is ground to make tortillas, a flat corn cake indispensable in the local diet. The new variety "did not hang together well for tortillas." [4] Moreover, the flavor was different, and the tortillas were not the right color. As Apodaca presents the case, there was a conflict of felt needs — a conflict between a desire for quantity and a desire for a particular quality. The stronger felt need won out, and Apodaca concludes that had the extension agent taken local cultural patterns into consideration as well as local environmental conditions, he might have introduced a hybrid that would result in good tortillas as well as rich harvests.

Since corn was an extremely important part of the villagers' diet, it was essential to their survival. But their traditional food habits constituted a cultural limitation which increased the probability of the rejection of the new variety. Leaving the story at that point, we have another account of how people cling to arbitrary practices simply because of tradition. Fortunately, Apodaca's study presents enough additional clues to make possible some further cross-cultural comparisons.

The case of the hybrid corn in San Carlos stands in striking contrast to the many cases in other parts of the world where improved plant varieties have been introduced with great success. In the other examples cited, failures resulted when the new variety failed to show a higher yield than the old. Why did traditional food habits or some food processing problem fail to discourage the acceptance of new varieties in the other instances? At Filadelfia and Salamina a processing problem interfered with the acceptance of a new crop variety only because the absence of mosaic disease at these two places canceled the advantages of a higher yield. A similar case is reported by Marriott for a rural village in India;[5] a new variety of sugarcane was successfully introduced despite changes it necessitated in crushing equipment, because the increased yield was great enough to make the investment profitable. Both in Colombia and in Marriott's Indian village, as in other cases of the introduction of improved varieties, the crop was being produced for sale. Although many of the farmers in Costa Rica, Bolivia, and Colombia who adopted the new varieties were peasants or largely subsistence farmers, they were also interested in selling their surplus production to buy clothing and other supplies.

But the Spanish Americans of San Carlos, Apodaca says, grew corn only for their own consumption and fed the surplus to their stock. None of them "complained of lack of market for surpluses" — and small wonder: despite a doubling of production, there had not been "any real surplus over the requirements of people and livestock."[6] The author does not tell us precisely how these people earn their living, to what extent they are dependent on their corn production for their survival, or how much of the additional yield went into tortillas and how much to their stock. He does emphasize that farmers had had no difficulty in getting seed or in producing the new crop and that they did not think the price of the hybrid seed too high. But he notes that the new hybrid was furnished to each farmer the first time in exchange for his old seed. Apparently this exchange was a strong inducement, for the hybrid was dropped once farmers began to pay for it. To demonstrate that the price of the hybrid seed was no deterrent to people raising corn "in small irrigated fields" for household consumption, it would have been more convincing to show that the cost of the seed was insignificant in proportion to the average family's annual money income. This points up an unfortunate inadequacy in the causal analyses of many case studies of directed culture change, largely because the subject is too new and the data too scanty to provide cross-cultural comparison.

The presence of a market orientation can be a decisive limitation in many instances of culture change. Around Cusco, Peru, where improved varieties of wheat and corn both increased local yields by thirty per cent, the new wheat seed sold out every year whereas demand for the improved corn was comparatively moderate. The same farmers planted both crops, but the wheat was for market and the corn for subsistence. Many who bought the improved wheat seed for cash cropping continued to plant their traditional corn for home consumption. The situation is reminiscent of an occasion in Juan's village of Las Bocas when one of his neighbors was butchering a cow with the help of a friend. When the owner of the animal remarked that he was going to make a lariat from the animal's hide, his friend pointed out that he had picked a poor time of the month to butcher the animal, for at this phase of the moon the hide was weak and the rope would be of poor quality. The owner conceded the truth of his friend's observation but added that the lariat was not for his own use but was to be sold in town.

There is also a widespread belief in Latin America that grain crops which are to be stored should be harvested in the waning phase of the moon when the sap in the plant is subsiding into the roots rather than in the waxing phase when the sap is rising. Corn harvested in the waning phase is believed much less susceptible to attack by weevils. Where crops are for the market rather than for the farmer's own use, however, the custom and eventually the belief tend to be disregarded. Thus, the probability that a financial outlay, a belief, or a traditional habit will obstruct change is greater among subsistence-oriented farmers than among those producing for market.

Technical assistance is most likely to be successful when it works with market-oriented goals among peoples producing for market, for in such cases innovators and the people are likely to share the same felt needs. Another case in point concerns the failure of a Colombian program to introduce soya cultivation, a project concerned more with health than with marketing goals. The social planners wanted the peasants to eat soya to make up for deficiencies in their diet, and at first many farmers were persuaded to grow it. But when they discovered that the government did not intend to buy the soya and that the taste was disagreeable, they stopped cultivating it everywhere but in the vicinity of Cali, where a margarine factory provided a market. As in the water purification program previously described, this project had little chance of establishing a frequency interpretation in favor of the needs felt by the innovators, since the people themselves were provided with no spectacular demonstration that the innovation would improve their health. But they were quite able to see a connection between the production of soya and their felt need to increase profits, where this connection existed.

Similarly, when Colombian brewers decided to increase home production of barley, they sent agronomists among the highland peasantry to promise a good harvest price. The richer peasants were usually the first to take the risk, but as confidence in the barley market grew, so did the number of cultivators. As a limitative cause, market orientation is an important consideration in directing culture change. Unfortunately, in the field of public health there is no similar quantitative scale on which the survival value can be expressed in a universally intelligible manner. Profit is a very convenient form of frequency interpretation. The closest parallel to this in public health is a spectacular cure like that effected by the yaws campaign.

A subsistence, rather than a market, orientation offers considerable hurdles to the innovator. Felt needs quite foreign to his own may undo his attempts to introduce change. This is important to keep in mind if the innovator is to avoid highly impractical projects. In the case of San Carlos, Apodaca concluded that the extension agent should have studied the situation more thoroughly in advance, anticipated the difficulties, and avoided them by introducing a hybrid that would not only have yielded a high return but would also have been tasty to his subjects. But since technological and power resources available for development are never unlimited, why not allocate them where they will bring the quickest and highest returns? On anticipating that San Carlos would reject the hybrid for reasons of taste, the agronomist could have left San Carlos and introduced this proven and excellent hybrid among people who grew corn for market.

Formal Education

When one considers the cost of training and maintaining a school-teacher in the United States today, the limitations on lifting underdeveloped areas by means of formal education become apparent at once.

In some states, primary and secondary school teachers must now have five years of college training to qualify for credentials. In the United States the costs of education are greater per capita than the entire per-capita cost of government in most underdeveloped countries. These countries simply cannot afford United States standards of formal education, and the United States has found neither the resources nor the manpower to meet its own educational needs, much less those of the rest of the world.

The difficulties of an educational approach to the problems of underdeveloped areas may be illustrated in microcosm by the quandary of a certain missionary I met to whom I shall refer here as John Smith. Smith was a highly trained agricultural technician who had formerly taken part in foreign aid programs of the United States government, but who had come to feel that the work he was doing was not changing the most important habits of thought and action. At considerable sacrifice to himself and his family he gave up his government job to become a technician and teacher in the education program of a United States Protestant mission group in Latin America. When I met him, he had given four years of dedicated service to the mission and was again a disillusioned man. He had now decided to go back into government service, for he had found it no easier as a missionary to effect the kind of changes he wanted to make than he had as a government technician. Furthermore, he had become more aware of his own minimal requirements as a middle-class American for the comfort and well-being of his family. Not only did the missionary's low standard of living tend to distract him from his high purpose, but he now felt that with the greater operating funds available to a government technician he could use his knowledge to benefit more of his fellow men.

Perhaps John Smith was rationalizing and returned to government service for "selfish" rather than "altruistic" motives. But no matter which of his felt needs we emphasize, we cannot lightly dismiss the underlying limitations illustrated by his case. Production per capita through the capitalization of labor is a limitative cause of culture change which cannot be overestimated.

Population Density and the Limitation of Poverty

The limitations of marketing orientation and per-capita production may be overshadowed in some cases by an even further limitation, that imposed by a disadvantageous land-population ratio. McKim Marriott provides an excellent illustration of this kind of situation in a village in India,[7] doubly interesting because it involves the rejection of an improved plant variety for reasons very similar to the rejection of the hybrid corn in San Carlos. Although this is the same Indian village which accepted the improved sugarcane because of its higher yield and greater profits, not even the profit motive could persuade these villagers to use the improved wheat seed made available at the government seed stores. The improved seed was found unacceptable by the villagers even though it doubled local yields. Three reasons given for its rejection were very similar to those given for the rejection of the corn hybrid in San Carlos — the grains were big and tough and housewives found them hard to grind; the dough made from the flour was difficult to knead and hard to bake into good bread; and finally, the bread made from the flour did not taste the same as the old bread. But in this case other reasons were also important. Cows and bullocks did not like to eat the straw of the new wheat; it would not serve for thatching roofs; it did not even make a good fire. Marriott emphasizes that the new variety would not have been a simple addition; it would have been a substitution of a single-use plant for a multiple-use plant, and the multiple uses of the older variety could not be overlooked by people living as close to the level of bare survival as the people of this village.

To Marriott the assertion by some technical observers that more manure, better seed, and more irrigation would increase India's food production by a hundred per cent seems only partly correct. The farmers are already aware of the importance of these things, but they live where the density of population is high and the level of technology low. They are so conscious of the value of manure that they go to special trouble to defecate in their own fields. But manure is also used as a fuel for cooking. With the forest land gone and very little wood left, less than half the dung available is used as manure. A wheat variety that also provides house thatch, animal fodder, and fuel is indispensable in a community where "there is not now a spare square foot of land to be found," where even the "leaves are stripped off the trees repeatedly" and where "one family of every ten had been compelled to leave the village in this generation in search of food." [8] Under such circumstances as these, survival is the first consideration. Innovations that would bring greater production and higher profits are of interest only if they do not bring with them some new threat to survival. In Marriott's opinion, technical development has reached a kind of saturation point — a state of equilibrium with little room for the spread of new techniques.

There are many evidences that changes have taken place in the village. Several new plant varieties have been adopted, including the improved sugarcane already mentioned. A gasoline-powered flour mill grinds a third of the village's grain, and flashlights and kerosene lanterns now brighten the local scene. But the evidence of change seems small to Marriott in comparison with the overwhelming poverty, the malnutrition, and the inefficiency of a labor-intensive agriculture. By drawing up one bucket of well water at a time, three men and two oxen spend a week irrigating a single acre of wheat. In such conditions of poverty and dense population, the level of production is too close to the level of survival to allow any margin for experimentation, and as Marriott notes, "even improvement requires a minimum of experimentation." [9] Population density, particularly coupled with a low level of technology, can be a serious limiting cause of failure to introduce change.

Haiti is another country with a dense population and a low level of technology. Here, too, the narrow margin between the level of production and the level of minimum subsistence makes change difficult. When an improved breed of chicken was introduced into several rural communities, they soon died for lack of proper care. The Haitian peasants were perfectly cognizant of the virtues of the new breed. They knew they had more meat and laid more eggs than their own scrawny birds. But as they explained it, on occasions when they had to decide between feeding themselves and feeding their chickens, the hardy native flocks could shift for themselves whereas the new chickens died. Improved swine met with the same limitation, as did many attempts to introduce various soil conservation measures. In some parts of Haiti the need for cooking fuel is almost as severe as in India, and as a result the hills are being denuded of their trees and brush. Persuading the natives to take exhausted lands out of production is almost impossible when their subsistence depends on the maximum use of those same tired and eroded soils.

At Fonds Parisien, Haiti, a considerable number of changes were introduced in farming practices and living conditions by increasing the margin between production and subsistence and thereby reducing the limiting effect of labor-intensive poverty. Fonds Parisien had been a comparatively prosperous little farming community until 1909, when the stream it had used for irrigation disappeared in a gravel slide twenty feet deep. The peasants then turned to dry farming with little success, and many began to earn a meager living by selling charcoal made from wood cut on adjoining hillsides. This created a new problem — erosion. Then, not long after the Second World War, the United States agricultural assistance program to Haiti constructed a concrete flume which spanned the gravel bed and returned some of the irrigation water to the farming area. As a result production and living standards rose, and the same farmers who had resisted all previous attempts to change their ways now began trying out many of the new practices and plant varieties suggested by the experts.

Although the Fonds Parisien irrigation project illustrates how the limitations of labor-intensive poverty can be lifted when capitalization increases labor productivity and the workers' survival margin, it was not in all respects a model program. Only twelve hundred acres were irrigated although construction costs amounted to nearly $200,000. That the construction itself was not altogether practical is demonstrated by the fact that two years after my visit the flume was all but destroyed by floods.[10]

An irrigation project at San Raphael, however, has proved sounder, and has also greatly increased productivity, living standards, and receptivity to change. But while such projects alleviate the limitations of poverty, they are expensive, and often — as the Fonds Parisien case illustrates — exorbitantly so. The resources of a poverty-stricken underdeveloped country like Haiti and its inability to invest in capital goods or to get loans and capital transfers from more productive nations are themselves limiting conditions of its development.

Capital Formation and the Limitations of Mechanical and Human Energy

The problems of expanding the quantity of capital goods or energy converters by which man increases his per-capita production are the problems of capital formation. The example of the ancient Peruvian Incas may help to explain the limitations. Although the Incas had only a primitive agricultural technology which depended entirely on human labor, they did accomplish capital formation of a labor-intensive kind.

They constructed irrigation works, roads, and granaries and even fostered industrial crafts to some extent, all by means of taxing labor. Each household was given lands on which to grow its subsistence crops. In addition, each family was required to grow corn on lands belonging to the state. State corn, stored in state granaries, was used to feed laborers working on state construction projects. Not only did commoners pay a labor tax on state lands, but they were also subject to a labor draft. Labor draftees, who were used in construction work, were fed by the state from the corn grown by the labor tax. In addition, certain skilled craftsmen such as weavers and metallurgists were permanently supported from the corn supplies to produce luxuries for the nobility.[11]

The Incas thereby achieved a rudimentary and very labor-intensive kind of capital formation, for when the labor potential of a rural population exceeds what is necessary to produce its own food — a condition true in many underdeveloped areas — considerable rural labor may be diverted into non-food-producing activities for the formation of such capital as roads, dams, railways, and machinery, without reducing farm production. The problem is not only shifting part of the society's labor force, but shifting its food as well. If farm workers are moved into capital formation activities, what is to stop their relatives at home from consuming the extra food themselves or from producing less? In order to continue feeding the laborers taken off the farms, those left on the farm must continue to produce the same amount of food as before, without increasing their consumption.[12] The Incas solved this problem with their labor tax. Production by the commoner for the use of his own household was controlled by the state's limiting the size of his landholdings to a level which curtailed any marked consumption of surpluses beyond subsistence requirements. But by demanding a prescribed amount of work on state lands from each household, the Inca state accomplished the enforced saving of food. This it used to feed that part of the rural labor force it drafted for the formation of "social overhead capital" — for example, roads and irrigation works.

Until quite recently, the Inca system of draft labor was maintained in most of the Andean countries of western South America for the formation of at least one kind of social overhead capital, the building and maintenance of roads. Communities lying along a roadway were made responsible for maintaining certain sections of it or for sending a specified number of men each day to fill work gangs. Within the community, each household was expected to provide and feed its share of the workers. This is an extremely simple case of capital formation peculiar to the construction of transporation systems; it does not require the separation of the rural worker from his source of food, nor does it bring about the development of a permanent non-food-producing class of laborers. The Inca and other *corvée* labor systems of capital formation are much too simple to be used in a money economy with extensive labor specialization, but they illustrate the rudiments of a basic problem of bootstrap capital formation in underdeveloped areas — the problem of shifting rural workers into capital formation on a nationally self-sufficient basis by simultaneously preventing a rise in rural per-capita consumption and a fall in over-all per-capita food production.

A crucial limitation of modern conditions not illustrated by the Inca example, however, is the demonstration effect of the dual society. The self-sufficiency and isolation of preconquest Inca society make it hardly comparable to any present-day society. Modern social structure has a worldwide framework in which the wants and expectations of groups with lower standards of living are being stimulated by increasing knowledge of the consumption patterns of more industrialized groups. The task of restraining consumption and enforcing savings among populations whose wants are rapidly increasing because of such knowledge is far greater than that which faced the rulers of the Inca state. To enforce such a program today would require a despotism stronger than the Incas'. The Soviet Union is such a despotism. To avoid the disrupting influence of the demonstration effect, those in power have, by means of "iron curtain" tactics, isolated the population as much as possible from the rest of the world. By means of its tight controls on land and production, the Soviet state has effectively transferred food along with workers from agricultural labor into capital formation.

Although man can get along, if necessary, without such energy as is provided by wind, water, and fossil fuels, the one source of energy he cannot do without is food. Because of this, some analysts reason that capitalization of labor becomes almost impossible once low-energy, labor-intensive societies have bred up to the limits imposed by the fertility of the land. This reasoning assumes that a high-energy society (highly capitalized) which produces its food by means of high-energy converters (machines) cannot support as large a population on the same land as one which produces its food by means of hand labor.[13] Since hand labor, in this view, will produce more food per acre than machinery, once a population has bred to the limits of a food supply produced by hand labor it cannot change over to high-energy production without eliminating part of its population. This might be called the vicious low-energy circle; for at least two reasons, I believe the theory partly spurious.

First, there is not yet conclusive evidence for the claim that hand labor is necessarily more productive per acre than mechanized labor. Even in the most overpopulated, labor-intensive farming areas of the world, mechanical means may be developed to produce the same amount of food at a great reduction in man-hours. Secondly, hand-labor agriculture does not necessarily imply a low standard of living for the farmer if the labor of the non-food-producing part of the population is highly capitalized and if farm labor is as well rewarded as other forms of labor. The greatest difficulty arises when farms become so broken up by inheritance and population growth that they are nothing more than subsistence plots. No country in existence, however, consists entirely of non-surplus-producing subsistence farmers without a non-food-producing labor component.

Although energy resources are a basic limitative cause in technological development, a dense farming population can be a very real handicap in any attempt to raise living standards through capital formation in industry. In India, for example, it has been estimated that in order to increase the size of family farms to a mere twenty-five acres, thirty million new jobs would have to be created, provided there were no increase in population during the period of industrial expansion.[14] Thirty million is approximately half the number of people gainfully employed in the United States today, which means that tremendous capital formation would be necessary to decrease the size of India's farm population to a point where the size of the average farm would be as much as one ninth that of the average United States farm.

In Puerto Rico, a tiny Caribbean island with a population of more than two and a quarter million, eighty new industries were developed over a ten-year period with the help of United States government benefits and Anglo-American capital investment. Although these new industries provided fourteen thousand new jobs during that ten-year period, the population growth so exceeded the industrial growth that the labor pool was swelled by sixteen thousand new workers each year.[15] Obviously, if capital formation is to have any appreciable effect on living standards in underdeveloped areas, the birth rate is an additional and very important limitation.

Population and the Limitations of Birth Control

In high-energy, industrialized societies, the birth rate is likely to decrease. As old-age security becomes a responsibility of the state rather than the family, as the deaths of infants decrease and parents no longer expect some of their children to die young, and as the length and expense of formal education increases and the economic usefulness of children decreases — developments associated with industrialization and urbanization — the felt need for large families tends to change to a desire for fewer offspring. In addition to this felt need for smaller families, there must also be available some effective means of preventing conception. This is crucial; for even though some preindustrial peoples have recognized a need for reducing the number of births, none have put it so far ahead of the felt need for sexual satisfaction as to choose complete continence.

The Polynesian islanders of Tikopia, a primitive group observed in the late twenties by the British anthropologist Raymond Firth,[16] tried to limit their population by the practice of not marrying, which did not mean sexual continence, but rather coitus interruptus and abortion among the unmarried. The twelve hundred inhabitants of this island were very much conscious of the balance between population and land, for the relation was inspectional in their small insular world. Even during Firth's stay, a rumor circulated among the commoners that the chiefs and their families were planning to join forces to drive the lower-class families from the island,[17] re-enacting a local legend that some islanders had been driven off in years past to make more room for those who remained.

Before the influence of the whites began to break down these mechanisms of population control, an influential chief made an annual address to all heads of households, exhorting them "to limit the numbers of their children by coitus interruptus."[18] The younger males in families with the least land could be ordered by the head of the family to remain single if he thought the elder brothers already had all the offspring the land could support.[19] Since extramarital intercourse was permitted but extramarital birth was not, withdrawal and abortion were practiced by the unmarried.[20] Married partners who wished to limit the size of their family practiced infanticide.[21] Apparently the system was far from perfect if expulsion of part of the population through internal warfare had occurred previously. The fact that chiefs and men of rank with large landholdings practiced polygyny would also indicate that the controls were largely at the family level:[22] observance of these restrictions apparently depended more upon the land or food resources available to the particular family than upon a consideration of the island's resources as a whole, even though all were concerned about the overpopulation of their island world.

By permitting both marital and extramarital intercourse without birth, contraception serves the same purpose in our industrialized society that abortion does at the preindustrial level. Although late marriages are more frequent in industrial than in preindustrial society because of the greater need for formal education and financial independence in the former,[23] contraception has undoubtedly contributed greatly to the lower average age of marriage in the United States since 1945 by increasing young people's expectations of postponing children.[24] Between 1939 and 1955 the proportion of United States Protestants relying on the condom for contraception rose by seventy per cent and the proportion using the diaphragm by forty per cent.[25] About eighty per cent of United States couples[26] have used or plan to use some method to regulate conception (most of the rest are either sterile or semifecund). Today twenty-nine per cent of couples employing contraception use the condom and twenty-six per cent the diaphragm. The closest competitor (twenty-four per cent) is the rhythm method (periodic continence), used predominantly by Roman Catholics.[27]

The mass production of cheap and reliable contraceptive appliances such as the diaphragm and the condom is a result of technological developments peculiar to industrial society, and the use of the first is closely tied to a standard of living which includes the convenience of the modern bathroom. It is not surprising that people in pre-bathroom societies should fear the diaphragm and other contraceptive methods for health reasons.[28] Although their fears may be folk-like in quality, such a device cleaned and reused under their living conditions — as well as jellies and douches applied under the same conditions — might readily produce vaginal infections frequently enough to reinforce the beliefs.

Incentive rather than living standards must account for the failure of condom contraception to spread in underdeveloped countries where it is known and available.[29] Application of the condom, like withdrawal, interrupts the sex act at a moment when the man is least likely to be influenced by other considerations than his satisfaction. For the woman, who must bear and rear the offspring, sex may become a secondary concern. But even if the woman feels a need to limit conception, she must have her consort's cooperation in either withdrawal or the use of the condom. The fact that abortion is entirely a woman's method and one which does not require complicated procedures and hygiene practices on her part help to make it the most common means of preventing births among preindustrial populations.[30] Even in post-war Japan where induced abortions were permitted under the Eugenics Protection Law of 1938, the number of abortions per one hundred births jumped from nine in 1949 to sixty-four in 1954.[31] As a legal means of limiting birth its popularity was further enhanced by its inclusion in health insurance services.[32] During the same period, however, use of the condom spread rapidly in urban areas of Japan, where most parents by 1955 no longer looked on their children as a form of old-age insurance. In rural areas, meanwhile, this traditional view persisted among more than half the parents sampled.[33]

Regarding children as an economic asset and a form of old-age insurance might well deter even the use of an inexpensive oral contraceptive in some populations. Country parents in the vicinity of the Mayo River, an area to be described in more detail in the case study, expect many of their children to die young, and want many offspring to compensate for losses and to be sure of being cared for in old age. These people have difficulty understanding why anyone should want to prevent births. In the towns, however, where reliance on medical facilities is resulting in greatly reduced death rates among infants and children, parents have become more optimistic in their expectations and would be quite content with three or four offspring. But as yet a birth rate just as high as that in the country continues in the towns, and parents are becoming increasingly interested in the possibilities of birth control.

Clearly, attitudes toward contraception are a product of various, and sometimes conflicting, felt needs. In most primitive and peasant societies satisfaction of sex, survival, and prestige motives are complementary. The more children parents have, the greater the security they can look forward to in their old age. Children also become an economic asset in hunting or farming as they grow older and can add to their parents' wealth and prestige. In a primitive society confined to a small island, families may consciously strive to limit births to a number commensurate with the size of landholdings and ultimately, therefore, with food resources. In such a place the desire to survive competes with sex.

In more sophisticated societies where medical facilities have increased parents' expectations that their offspring will survive, economy of numbers and expenses may predominate. If the need is felt more by women than by men, the conflict may be resolved through abortion, or as in Puerto Rico by sterilization.[34] Among the peasantry and lower classes in many parts of Latin America, the male may take pride in the number of his offspring without feeling a deep sense of responsibility toward them. In peasant societies undergoing change, the burden of responsibility is likely to fall heaviest on the woman. Growth and strengthening of the middle class is what helps most to insure men's cooperation in birth control. Increasing opportunities for status mobility and conscious striving for symbols of urban, middle-class success and respectability lead to a greater sense of responsibility in the man and to his greater preoccupation with measures of economy.

Control: Positive and Negative

The increasing "controls" which man achieves over his environment have been viewed here as alternative behaviors made possible by the increasing range and intensity of technical observations. The acceptance of such behaviors is a response to felt needs and to cognitive recognition of the fact that the new alternatives offer a more probable expectation of satisfying those needs. In most of the cases I have cited, acceptance of the new alternative has been voluntary and individual. This kind of control may be called positive. Frequency interpretations in favor of the acceptance of positive controls have been shown to be greater when they are inspectional and spectacular and when they are directly associated with a market orientation.

When frequency interpretations are difficult by casual observation, the expansion of indirect experience through formal education is clearly indispensable. Formal education is not, however, simply a matter of voluntary individual acceptance of a new alternative. Here another kind of "control" becomes important. The educational institutions of a society are limited by the productivity of its members. Labor must be capitalized and teachers trained. Part of the productivity of the citizens must be taken from them and re-allocated for the training of specialists. Individual obligations to the society at large are *negative* controls. Compulsory saving for capital formation is a negative control, because it is the enforcement of savings through taxation. Where such taxation is accomplished through representative government and with the consent of the governed it is a *voluntary* negative control. But all negative controls are not voluntary.

Birth control, as we have seen, has been largely positive, although at the family level it can achieve a voluntary negative quality in some societies. It is difficult to imagine a coercive form of birth control short of a eugenics program in a totalitarian state. But if tax penalties rather than tax deductions were some day multiplied by the number of under-age dependents on our tax return, the legislation would constitute a case of voluntary negative control.

Few attempts at "control" so well illustrate the self-interest which underlies motivational and cognitive causality as do those concerning birth. Though unwilling to abstain from sexual intercourse, people are willing to prevent birth when family resources are so clearly limited with respect to felt needs that additional members would markedly lower the expectations of those already living. Those who employ birth control do so to satisfy their own felt needs — not to alleviate the problems of future generations. This statement should not be construed as an argument against birth control, however; coitus is not performed for the benefit of the next generation either.

———✻———

V

Limitation and Society

THE last chapter emphasized man's cognitive interaction with his environment through his artifacts and technology. In this chapter, we shall be concerned with interaction among men, especially with that between innovators and subjects. The problems discussed will be divided into three categories according to their degree of complexity. First will be situations in which an innovation may be passed, after an initial demonstration, from person to person independently of the innovator. Here the problem is largely one of presentation, as in the case, for example, of introducing improved plant varieties. The second category contains problems of prolonged interaction. Though in these instances the felt need for an innovation may be disseminated by one person to another independently of the innovator, the new alternative itself requires special knowledge and training, which means that there must be continued relations between innovators and subjects. The introduction of soil conservation terraces by trained specialists is an example of this kind of problem. Third are those innovations whose acceptance depends to some extent on group participation and group adjustments. Most so-called community-development programs probably fall in this category.

Problems of Presentation

We have seen that technical observations can lead to innovations which meet a felt need so spectacularly that frequency interpretations in their favor are readily made by casual observation. Furthermore, we have seen that when adopting innovations requires no special training, they practically sell themselves. Technical observation acts to minimize the difficulties of social interaction in cultural change by producing new alternatives or positive controls which tend to be accepted on presentation. The problem in such cases is primarily to demonstrate that the innovation will increase the subjects' expectations.

Yet even presenting or demonstrating requires interaction between subjects and innovators, and difficulties may arise. For example, an agricultural technician wants to introduce an improved plant variety into an underdeveloped area. He first makes sure that the subjects have a strong felt need to produce more of the crop in question and that the new variety will spectacularly satisfy this need under existing environmental conditions. Next, he must present this new "control" to the subjects: in other words, he must provide a demonstration, so that the specific innovation may become a target of the subjects' felt need for higher yields or greater profits. If a government-owned experimental plot is available, the innovator may awaken local interest by planting a demonstration crop to show the merits of the new variety. Very often, however, farmers in underdeveloped areas fail to be impressed by such tactics. Frequently they distrust the government and are inclined to believe that a higher yield on a government demonstration plot is merely the result of the government's having funds and equipment they do not have. But if the innovator can persuade one of the local farmers to plant the new variety, and if the results are spectacularly favorable, his neighbors will usually follow his example the next season.

When a farmer who is well known gets the results promised by the agronomists and makes an unexpected profit as a result, he demonstrates to the other farmers that they too can use the same "control" to increase their expectations. By readily identifying with him they vicariously gain a feeling of control through his success.

This kind of situation usually offers few social difficulties. If the innovation permits a frequency interpretation in its favor it will sell itself with a minimum of promotion on the part of those who introduce it. In such cases the selection of the farmer to try out the innovation first may not be too important. As long as he is friendly enough with his neighbors to provide them with an opportunity to compare his yields with theirs, his status in the community may make very little difference as far as his neighbors' acceptance of the innovation is concerned. Frequently, however, the farmer who consents to make such an experiment is one who has sufficient resources to be able to afford to risk a loss, and because of his affluence enjoys a high status in the community.

Invidious emulation, as noted earlier, is often a very important catalyst in the dissemination of positive controls. During a survey of agricultural extension work in Colombia, I found repeated instances where invidious emulation had led to borrowing from "rich" farmer by poor farmer. By "rich" farmer I mean a man whom the small farmers or peasants include within their social group, not one rich enough to be an absentee landowner living in town and letting his holding out to tenants or sharecroppers. I mean a landowner who farms his land himself and who is known and respected for his astuteness. When this man starts to plant barley, fumigate his potatoes, or use a metal instead of a wooden plow, his poorer neighbors, who ordinarily might not dare take such risks, are immediately attentive. If this "rich" man finds the innovation sufficiently beneficial to be continued a second year, his neighbors begin to copy him; for if the "rich" man were not wise, he would not be "rich."

Results of a rural hygiene program in Colombia provide another illustration of invidious emulation. This program was sponsored by the Coffee Federation of Colombia, an organization originally founded to insure small coffee farmers of a fair and reliable price for their coffee and financed by taxes paid by coffee exporters. In 1952 over three million dollars were turned over to the various state committees of the Federation in amounts proportional to the coffee production of each state. This money was used to finance the Coffee Federation's hygiene program, which consisted of construction projects including the installation of rural water distribution systems, latrines or flush toilets, new houses, and two popular labor-saving devices — coffee driers and coffee hullers. The purpose of this program was to improve the small coffee farmer's health and thereby, it was reasoned, his coffee production.

Actually, this hygiene program was often referred to as a housing program, for each state allocated from half to two thirds of its annual budget to the construction of rural housing. In 1953, I surveyed the results of this program in two of the major coffee-producing states. It was obvious, as might be expected, that a new house does not automatically change a family's living habits. Close to main highways and larger centers of population, the Coffee Federation houses were usually well maintained, and many of the first houses constructed three years before were clean and in excellent condition. But back in the hills, away from the towns and highways, in country accessible only by mule and horseback, it was a different story. Within three months, many new houses had reverted to the same conditions as the unsanitary dwellings they had been built to replace. As before, chickens, dogs, and pigs had the run of the house. In some cases the families had decided that a nice new room with a concrete floor was wasted as a kitchen and tacked an ill-ventilated lean-to against the back of the house to serve this purpose. When the new flush toilets ceased to function there was seldom a plumber handy to fix them, and consequently many were out of repair and most were filthy. The upkeep or cleanliness of the house was not a reflection of the family's understanding of modern preventive medicine. People living in locations accessible to towns had been influenced by the higher living standards they could observe among many of the town dwellers. Their more sanitary living conditions were less a result of the Coffee Federation's housing program than of the invidious emulation of what they had observed in the houses of town friends.

Quite different from invidious emulation in its effect is the practice of invidious sanction. I found this phenomenon to be of considerable concern to agronomists in some remote communities of Haiti where they were unable to get people to make changes in their farming methods or living standards. These people were so afraid of the envy and jealousy of their neighbors that they took great pains not to look richer than the others. Hostility directed toward a person who was more successful than his fellows was usually restricted to black magic, but in some places it might even take the form of willful destruction of his property. The practice of invidious sanction to maintain status quo has a long history in Haiti. Because of it, attempts to colonize freed American Negroes there shortly before the American Civil War were largely unsuccessful. Many of these Negroes were forced to return to the United States when their more successful farming practices caused jealousy and destructive retaliation on the part of their Haitian neighbors.[1]

Today, the strength of this social sanction is quite variable in Haiti. It has persisted in isolated areas far from the influence of cities or where the economic status of members of the community is fairly equal. In urban centers and rural communities where there is more variation in wealth and where there are enough progressive people to find safety in their own numbers, invidious sanction has disappeared or is ineffectual. At Fonds Parisien, mentioned in the previous chapter, incomes and purchasing power have been considerably increased by the irrigation project. As a result, several of the more progressive persons, who found themselves capable of buying new tin roofs for their houses, installed them almost simultaneously. As one of them explained to me, they were no longer concerned about black magic now that so many people were doing well; they were too many to suffer mass bewitchment.

Problems Requiring Prolonged Interaction

When an innovation requires specialists to introduce or administer it, interaction between innovators and public is increased and difficulties are more likely to arise. The innovators must not only provide a demonstration which conveys to the subjects a sense of control over the innovation; they must also make their own behavior as predictable as possible, for unless their behavior is predictable to the subjects, the subjects are not likely to experience any sense of control over the situation and may feel hopelessly frustrated. The predictability of the innovators' behavior depends on the care with which their plans are made and the extent to which they keep faith with their public.

When Kincaid initiated his soil conservation program in Chile, he repeatedly warned farmers that they should consider his initial terraces experimental and should expect some failures until he had had a chance to appraise the rainfall characteristics of the area. And when the rainy season came, he spent hours with his Chilean trainees walking through rain and mud, checking terraces. Chilean farmers came to regard him as a man to be trusted and who would keep faith with them, for he made his behavior predictable.

The kind of program Kincaid was initiating was altogether different from one in which a spectacular new plant variety is to be introduced. In the latter case the acceptance of the new plant increases as more people become familiar with its virtues and decide to adopt it. A soil conservation program, however, demands much more than the acceptance of some technique which can be easily learned and passed on without a direct connection with the original source. The innovators or technicians must deal with each farmer individually, and the continued acceptability of their program will be affected by the kind of relations they have with the people who ask for their assistance. If their results or their behavior are highly unpredictable, relations are likely to grow strained. Kincaid realized this and made every effort to keep faith with the farmers. They, in turn, acknowledged both his sincerity and his skill by supporting his program publicly.

A very different situation was observed at an irrigation project in Haiti, where the agronomists engendered considerable distrust and even animosity among the peasantry because they failed to keep their behavior predictable. On one occasion the peasants were carefully informed that their irrigation water would be cut off for a specified period of several days to permit repairs on a canal. Although the peasants were not advised of any change in plans or offered any explanation, the water continued to run as usual. Several weeks later when a similar warning was given the peasants paid no heed and a crop was lost.

After much cajoling by agricultural extension personnel, peasants at another Haitian project reluctantly agreed to pay for having their land leveled and contoured by machinery, on the promise that irrigation would be facilitated and their yields would be larger. But the preparations did not proceed according to schedule, and the peasants were told they would have to postpone planting until the contouring job was done. For farmers operating close to a subsistence level, this was disastrous news. When, as here, the behavior of the innovators becomes so unpredictable, the subjects may grow completely immune to all further attempts to change their practices. Moreover, the bad name of the project is likely to spread and make further expansion increasingly difficult.

Genuine hostilities and tensions between the people and their local technicians and administrators may often underlie the unpredictability of the latter's behavior in underdeveloped areas. Even where a program is being administered at the top level by foreign advisers, local technicians will have to carry most of the load of daily face-to-face meetings with the public. How this can result in conflict is well illustrated in Colombia, where a class system formerly rigidly based on family background has been changing rapidly into one based on money. Many people are moving from rural areas to take jobs in the cities where industry is expanding rapidly, and in the city, where people come from many different parts of the country and do not know each other's family background, a person finds himself free to seek his own status level. But the new economic statuses are not so clearly defined as the older family distinctions that existed in the towns and rural areas. They make up a kind of gradient along which no one is certain of his position and up which each is forcibly trying to push his way in his daily relations with others.

This general insecurity about status takes extremely aggressive forms. In public eating places, for example, customers are likely to reprimand waiters or waitresses loudly and unmercifully for the slightest mistake in order to show their authority and importance. Taxi drivers scold fares who do not carry small change, and bus drivers belabored for their slowness, rudeness, or bad driving may take revenge by deliberately shutting the doors on passengers as they try to get off the bus. Innumerable unpleasant episodes displaying such hostilities are observable throughout an average day. Many rapidly industrializing countries share these characteristics to some degree, but in Colombia and especially in Bogotá, they seem particularly pronounced.

The preventive medicine program of a Point Four public health center in a poorer district of Bogotá was found to be failing as a result of limitative causes inherent in the social situation just described. Friction between the inhabitants of this district and the staff of nurses and doctors at the center was constant and bitter. The members of the staff had come predominantly from a "middle"-class background with definite status insecurities and were extremely intolerant of behavior on the part of patients that might be interpreted as disrespectful. Interviews in homes within this district revealed that the public felt a great deal of animosity toward the health center personnel for what they considered intolerable treatment. For example, the Colombian doctor in charge of the health center made a ruling that mothers who failed to bring their babies regularly for scheduled checkups on "well baby days" (part of the preventive-medicine program) were to be denied treatment when their children were sick. Since the mothers of the district had no appreciation of the nature or value of preventive medicine and found these visits inconvenient, this ruling in the form of a threat was a source of considerable resentment. But when sick babies were actually denied treatment, animosities flared into bitter hatred. Many of the people interviewed in the district vowed they would never again have anything to do with the health center.

Those who could afford to visit private doctors said they preferred them to the health center personnel because they were treated with more respect. Residents of the most impoverished neighborhoods spoke fondly of their favorite curandero, Don Rojas, a mystic famous in the city of Bogotá for his inexpensive publications on the art of healing — a combination of local folk beliefs, spiritualism, and Rosicrucianism. Don Rojas, they said, was a man of great sympathy and understanding who often would listen to a poor person describe his symptoms and then prescribe an herbal remedy without charging any fee. "He treats us like people," one woman said. "He is better than a hundred health centers."

Status considerations among government workers may lead to their avoiding anything bearing the stigma of manual labor. This is not surprising, for among preindustrial peoples there is likely to be an obvious split between the laboring population and the fortunate few who administer and live off that labor. Even the scribes of ancient Egypt used a comparison of the advantages of a scholar's life with the hard lot of the peasantry to encourage their pupils to master the script.[2] In Latin America, native agronomists and other trained personnel are often more likely to tell farmers what to do than to get out and show them. In Colombia, I have seen highland agricultural extension agents go into the field in a black double-breasted suit with tie, scarf, and black Homburg. They were far more eager to demonstrate their social distance from the farmer than to demonstrate improved agricultural practices.

The social barrier between agronomists and farmers often leads to antagonisms similar to those existing between health workers and their public. In Haiti peasants laugh heartily behind the back of their status-conscious extension agents. "If they knew any more about farming than we do," they point out, "they would be getting rich farming for themselves instead of teaching for a small salary." In Colombia, government agronomists note with chagrin that their colleagues who have opened farm supply stores and sell their services as consultants often get more requests for help than the government agent whose services are free. As the government man explains it to the visitor, the farmers have more faith in a man who charges for his services; they feel he must have more to offer. Correct as far as it goes, this is only part of the explanation. The farmers mention a further difference between the entrepreneur and the government servant. The private expert, they claim, does not treat them like social inferiors; he takes off his coat and goes to work to help them.

When Kincaid first began teaching his Chilean trainees the techniques of soil conservation, they somewhat grudgingly accompanied him in the dirty and arduous task of laying out terraces and then checking them under rainfall conditions — tramping around in deep mud. But what began as a blow to their pride eventually provided them with stronger status satisfactions than they had enjoyed previously. The Chilean trainees suddenly found themselves invited to eat in the homes of wealthy, high-status farmers, who now treated them with new respect. One of the farmers said, "Our agronomists are finally learning how to help us, and they are no longer afraid of getting their hands dirty."

It is easy to understand why people of the lower class in many underdeveloped areas do not always emulate their own government technicians. Foreign technicians often have an advantage on this score; the public can look up to them without being rebuffed for status reasons, and as a result usually directs more respect and less antagonism toward them. One very important form of emulation, however, which cuts across the social difficulties between local technicians and their public, takes place between technicians and children. Most often, children are receptive to the ideas and practices introduced by their local experts even when their parents are not. Moreover, most parents are so pleased by the attention paid to their offspring that they are less apt to object to changes introduced through them. The formation of 4-H and Future Farmer clubs or their equivalents brought excellent results in Haiti, Colombia, and Chile. The local technician is usually more relaxed in his relations with children than with their parents, and the children accept him and look up to him more quickly than do the adults.

Problems Requiring Group Adjustment and Action

Voluntary controls. The examples of social limitation so far presented have all been cases in which acceptance of an innovation or change was basically a matter of individual, rather than group, action. Sometimes the new technique was one which, after presentation, passed to other persons independently of the innovators. In the case of more complex innovations, technical supervision by a specialist is often necessary, even when presentation and acceptance are largely individual. Attention will now be directed to situations where acceptance depends on group adjustments and sometimes group action.

Group action programs that require more frequent meetings between innovators and subjects increase the social problems. It is hardly expedient to attempt changes by group action when this is unnecessary, yet very often this is done by innovators for whom cooperation seems to become an end in itself. Such cases will be discussed first.

In Haiti local agronomists considered the native collective work group or *combite* an institution which justified faith in the cooperativeness of the peasantry and the assumption that Haitian peasants could be organized into whatever kind of rural cooperative organizations the extension agent thought desirable. The combite is a form of reciprocal farm labor which exists in many parts of the world among rural, preindustrial peoples. Very similar to the work-bees common in the United States a hundred years ago, it consists of an informal exchange of labor among neighbors, and often includes some repayment of the guests in the form of food and entertainment. Among subsistence-oriented farmers these reciprocal labor practices meet both social and economic felt needs. But in a money economy, or one that is moving in that direction, the efficiency of such practices usually comes into question as the farmer's felt needs change (see Chapter VIII). The combite had become something of a survival in Haiti when I was there in 1952. Peasants throughout the country described reciprocal labor as an inefficient system still used when farmers did not have enough cash on hand to hire paid labor. The inefficiency of the combite, they explained, was largely the result of the undependability of the workers. Members could not be relied upon to arrive promptly or to do their work well. The guests at such work parties, they complained, acted as though they were doing the host a big favor and were not so easy to control as hired laborers. The wealthy peasants had long since abandoned the combite, for they much preferred to hire labor than to exchange their own or to provide entertainment for undependable work-bees. Poor peasants had come to prefer monetary rather than festive repayment for their services, but admitted that when incapable of paying cash, they reverted to labor reciprocities.

Nearly all the work and production cooperatives organized by Haitian extension agents as a means of introducing changes eventually failed. They ended when the agent was moved to a new locale, when jealousies sprang up among the members, or when members failed to do their duties. Attempts to get groups of peasants to buy animals and tools under a system of joint ownership also met repeatedly with resistance. Most of these extension agents were dedicated men who put a high value on cooperation and collective activity: to them it was more than a means to an end, it was an end in itself. Each of the cooperative ventures they began was the result of great promotional effort on their part to win the peasants to their way of thinking. Each venture, in a way, was like a small messianic movement led by an inspired idealist; and each was consequently very much dependent upon the personal qualities of the particular extension agent and the rapport he was able to establish between himself and the peasantry. A change of extension agents or any serious loss of the agent's rapport with the farmers ended in the collapse of the "cooperative."

One cooperative movement sponsored by the United States assistance program was having considerable success in rural Haiti at the time of my visit. It was a credit union which, unlike the work cooperatives, appealed to the felt needs of a people living in a money economy. The peasants, aware that emergencies requiring immediate outlays of cash put them at the mercy of unscrupulous money lenders, felt a strong need for credit at a fair rate of interest. This "cooperative" involved no reciprocal labor, no cooperative labor, and no joint ownership of goods. Acceptance or rejection of membership in the union was actually an individual matter and the only group activities were business meetings. So-called study clubs of credit union members — meetings to indoctrinate members in the rules of the organization — were used by agricultural extension agents to discuss farming practices. Attendance at these meetings was poor and generally unenthusiastic, for the peasants thought the meetings irrelevant.

Much of the initial success of the credit union movement depended on the personality of the young United States technician who administered the union and was responsible for the funds. He was very idealistic and seemed more interested in the collective aspects of the project than in the economic ones. His major concern was with the "study clubs" at which "democratic" social action could be stimulated. He spoke fervently of the "democratic," "free" discussions which he and his agents "led" at these meetings, helping the peasants to "better understand their mutual problems." However, the social occasion provided by these meetings did not satisfy a desire by any means as strong as the desire for loans at fair interest rates; for most of those who attended the study clubs the meeting was an imposition made necessary by the loan. In fact, going to these meetings was sometimes a considerable bother for the members, who viewed them as social affairs and did not like to go in work clothes. This is a case of a "cooperative" program that was successful in spite of its cooperative aspects because it satisfied a strong felt need and because the necessary accounting duties were performed by foreigners who had little or nothing to gain by dishonesty.

One kind of activity which would certainly seem to justify "cooperation" is maintaining irrigation systems. In rural Japan, for example, small farmers still form cooperative neighborhood work groups to keep up their irrigation systems. In Haiti, however, it has always proved very difficult to get peasants to work at an irrigation system once it has been installed. In fact, the irrigation systems built by the French on their prosperous plantations during the eighteenth century fell into ruin during the nineteenth after the slaves achieved their independence. Present-day Haitian peasants point out the ruins of French irrigation works and realize their importance, but they will not repair or maintain them. In some cases where new irrigation systems have been built, the problem of upkeep has been solved by the formation of a water-user's association which collects a tax from each beneficiary and hires a man to keep the system working.

Haiti is not the only place where it has proved difficult to get farmers to cooperate in keeping up an irrigation or water distribution system even when the benefit to each person is perfectly clear. When Panama disease attacked the banana trees on one large section of a plantation owned by an American fruit company in Colombia, the land — along with its expensive irrigation system — was presented as a gift to the local government. The acreage was promptly divided up into ten-acre plots and distributed among a group of small landless tenant farmers who proceeded to grow corn and cotton. But because the peasants could not agree on an arrangement for maintenance of the irrigation system, it soon fell into disrepair.

In a similar case, the Coffee Federation of Colombia, as part of the hygiene program previously mentioned, installed a number of rural water distribution systems. To save small coffee farmers the chore of going long distances to springs and to prevent the use of contaminated sources of water, the Coffee Federation built a great number of small reservoirs, each to provide water for ten to two hundred and fifty small farm homes, and piped the water directly to each farmer's house. These programs were extremely popular with coffee farmers, who were only too glad to share part of the construction cost. Yet when the Coffee Federation left it up to committees composed of water-users of a single reservoir system to maintain these systems, inadequate maintenance invariably resulted. This was just as true of systems serving fewer than fifty houses as it was of the larger ones. But the Coffee Federation found the farmers perfectly willing to pay a monthly water bill for the service of permanent caretakers.

These cases illustrate a misconception very common among technicians in underdeveloped areas that people are "naturally" cooperative or that they will automatically take collective action if they are only shown the need for it. Even though people want to accept an innovation and cognitively recognize a need for it, social limitations may obstruct the acceptance if group action is required in the absence of group sanctions. This may be made clearer by comparing irrigation maintenance in rural Japan with the three examples just mentioned. In Japan, where rural irrigation systems have been in use for hundreds of years, a villager still faces ostracism for failing to do his share of the work. In times past, the deviant and his family might even be exiled from the community. Today, as well as in the past, the felt need on the part of rural Japanese for village cooperation in marriage and funeral ceremonies provides a powerful group sanction.[3]

Although the irrigation systems in Haiti before the uprising of the slaves had been built, maintained, and operated largely by slave labor, the slaves themselves had been deprived as much as possible of any social organization strong enough to threaten their French masters. Plantation owners deliberately selected their slaves so that there would never be very many from a single tribe together on one plantation. When they first gained their freedom, the former slaves were still controlled for a brief period by such strong men as Toussaint, Dessalines, and Christophe, who kept them working on the plantations by force. But after Pétion divided up many of the larger landholdings in the south and redistributed the land in smaller lots, the former slaves were content to grow subsistence crops by dry farming methods rather than an export crop such as sugarcane which required irrigation. Coffee soon replaced sugarcane as the leading export crop, for it needed no irrigation and would continue to grow in an unattended, almost wild state.[4] Since the population of Haiti after the slave rebellion was only about a tenth of Haiti's modern population, a more extensive type of agriculture than that practiced by the French could readily support the population without any need for complicated irrigation systems or the well-knit local social organization that would have been necessary to maintain those systems.

When the diseased banana lands, as mentioned above, were turned over to Colombia by the American fruit company, the peasants who were awarded plots on this irrigated land were, for the most part, strangers to one another; they had no social organization embodying sanctions for the maintenance of an irrigation system. Similarly, the Colombian coffee farmers who shared the same water distribution system were united by an engineering convenience rather than by common residence or community bonds. Usually the engineering system included far more families than those who lived close enough together to see each other daily. Where there were no group ties providing sanctions for cooperative maintenance of an irrigation or water distribution system, taxation for upkeep and administration of the system by the government were much more acceptable to the beneficiaries than a system of maintenance which would have required the creation of sanctions by an artificial social group. Even in rural Japan, the sanctions for cooperative work on irrigation systems weaken when outsiders come into the local group. During World War II, many people who owned land in the country moved out to their farms to escape the American bombing. Lacking the countryman's vital interest in local marriage and funeral ceremonies, the city people felt no compulsion to attend irrigation work groups either, and local farmers had to be content with payments to hire the necessary labor replacements.[5] Moreover, marked differences in social status everywhere weaken sanctions supporting cooperative work groups. The Japanese villagers who work together to keep up their irrigation systems do not vary greatly in status and affluence. But the beneficiaries of the irrigation and water systems in the other cases did not all regard themselves as social equals. Many would have felt it degrading to cooperate with people whom they looked upon as having lower social status.

The tendency of many social planners to expect what they consider a need for cooperation to be sufficient to produce a social organization capable of effecting cooperation is hardly realistic. Furthermore, if such a social organization does not exist and the planners are also trying to encourage market-oriented production, the attempt to introduce both may be inconsistent. Market production and its incentives are more likely to accompany socially limitative factors compatible with state supervision (formal voluntary controls) than those factors compatible with the mutual reciprocity sanctions of small groups. When small-group "cooperation" is expected or fostered among people whose attitudes of independence are already compatible with the market economy in which they are becoming increasingly involved, "cooperation" has ceased to be a means of innovation. It has become merely an end desirable to the innovator, and quite apart from the felt needs of the people.

The results of land reform programs that introduce collective ownership and operation show some of the discrepancies between the need for cooperation felt by innovators and that felt by the people. Collective ejidos in Mexico are an example of this and will be discussed in Chapter X.

Cooperation takes many forms, but it is easier to find than to create. If Colombian coffee farmers or Haitian peasants prefer to pay a water tax to the government to maintain their water distribution or irrigation systems, this is an acceptable form of cooperation if maintenance is the objective. But if getting people to work together is the objective, then the felt needs of the innovators for this idealistic form of cooperation must be transferred to the people. And if, as is usually the case, the same objective could be accomplished by some other form of cooperation, it is very difficult to persuade the people that "working together for the common good" will be to their advantage.

If some projects have been unnecessarily handicapped by a preoccupation with collective action demanding small-group sanctions among people who are already adapting to state controls, other projects have been equally handicapped by a failure to solicit the cooperation of all concerned.

Anthropologist Allan Holmberg has described what happened in the Viru Valley of Peru when the introducers of a well-drilling program failed to give sufficient consideration to the community as a social group.[6] They concerned themselves with the people's desire to obtain more water for irrigation, but not with other wants important to the outcome of the project. Although the village of Viru had no adequate, dependable water supply, and although the villagers had asked for aid from their government, the project was finally abandoned because of the villagers' unfavorable attitude. Unfortunately the innovators did not explain to the villagers the reasons for some of their procedures, nor did they attempt to consult with them in any way. This angered important persons in the community, who felt their status threatened and either failed to support the project or spoke out against it. Worse still, the first well was drilled on the property of a large landowner widely disliked by the other villagers, who suspected that he was going to derive an unfair advantage from the project.

Failing to consider the status needs of the influential members of the community and the fears and hostilities of the rest, the innovators did not get the expected collaboration. The villagers, in effect, felt no "control" over the situation: they had not been consulted and had no basis for fairly appraising the intentions of the innovators. Communication with the villagers before initiating the project might have made the innovators aware of other important village needs and would have apprised the villagers of the innovators' true intentions.

Oscar Lewis has described a similar happening in the community of Tepoztlán, Mexico, in 1944.[7] Because the people there had repeatedly expressed the wish that those who came to study them would also do something to help them, he decided to collaborate with the health and welfare department of the federal government in setting up a medical clinic. Research was to be coordinated with this service, for the government was interested in learning more about the nature of the rural public's resistance to modern medicine. The clinic was short-lived, however, because it conflicted with the interests of certain powerful local figures. One of these was a professional curer known in the village as Don Rosas, who had a lucrative curing practice using a combination of herbal lore, folk beliefs, and Roman Catholicism. The clinic was a major threat to this man, whose power and prestige derived from folk curing.

In addition to Don Rosas, some of the local politicians were also annoyed by the clinic. Since they had not been instrumental in its introduction and could claim no credit for it, it served as a reminder to them of their own past failures to help their fellow townsmen. Their feelings were intensified by the fact that the clinic was introduced not long before election time, and by the fact that people were saying that members of Lewis's project were doing more for their welfare than their own local government officials.

These influential persons who saw the clinic as a threat to their own interests seized upon one part of the research as a means of indirectly attacking the health program. The researchers had been administering Rorschach tests to the schoolchildren, so Don Rosas cannily bought a set of pornographic pictures in Mexico City and showed them to village parents as examples of what the researchers were showing to their children. When parents began to object to the testing program, the local officials eagerly joined the attack on the project, which they portrayed as a menace to the morals of the community. Condemnation by the officials and by an active minority of villagers whom they rallied to their support led to the permanent closing of the clinic and a temporary lapse in the testing program. Had the local officials been encouraged to identify themselves with the program in such a way that the clinic met their felt needs for social status as well as the public's felt needs for a health service, the clinic's history might have been different. Even Rosas might eventually have been embarrassed by his attempt to undermine the project if local officials had not been so ready to join his opposition.

In both of these cases, the innovators failed to give full consideration to certain important felt needs not directly related to the projects but which, in the end, imposed important social limitations on their success. As these examples also suggest, however, there may be a conflict of felt needs within a group which cannot easily be resolved, and then the question arises as to whose felt needs are to be given precedence. When a sly and nefarious folk curer is the villain, the choice seems dramatically clear. But very often innovators feel that there is some justification for compelling even the majority of a group to make changes "for their own good." At this point, of course, the controls become coercive rather than voluntary.

Coercive controls. Little attention has been given to coercive controls because they are not compatible with the objectives of our society, but they sometimes come up unexpectedly. For example, S. C. Dube has reported that in many of India's "community development" programs which have been widely praised for the accomplishment of construction projects through "voluntary" collective labor, the work has actually been done by the lower castes under the direction of powerful upper-caste men who "use pressure — often bordering on coercion — on the lower castes to make them undertake the hard work." [8]

Dube's observation brings to mind an occurrence which I witnessed in 1952 in Tota, a village in the Colombian Andes. At that time there was no road between Tota and the highway several miles away, so the local priest organized a collective community project to construct one. Although this was no simple task, for the terrain was mountainous in the extreme, a road finally was constructed by work parties composed of the able-bodied men of the community. Superficially, this would seem to be a perfect example of a voluntary, cooperative, self-help project by which a community interested in its own advancement had collectively acted to improve its economic situation without direction from outside. Actually, the situation was not at all as it appeared.

In this backward, isolated community, the priest still collected tithes at harvest time. He did this indirectly by "selling" the right to collect tithes to the highest bidder. The man who won the bid then went to each poor farmer — never the rich ones — and demanded every tenth row of potatoes. If a farmer failed to comply, he and his family would be denied rights to burial, baptismal, and marriage services until he conformed. For the poorer people of backward, mestizo Tota, this was a very effective sanction, which placed them very much in the power of the priest and the local political bosses in league with him. The priest was eager to build the road in order to win approval from his superiors because he hated the cold, isolated village of Tota and was hoping to win a better parish in a milder climate. Thus the men of the poor families of Tota actually built the road while members of the upper-class citizenry supervised the work.

Even when the intentions and motives of the administrators seem above reproach there are sometimes suggestions of coercion. These reveal much about the personal objectives of the administrators. Let us take, for example, a report on community development programs in India, Iran, Egypt, and the Gold Coast sponsored and published by the Community Development Division of our International Cooperation Administration.[9] This report begins with a brief sermon on the virtues of community development, saying that these programs are a democratic method of helping people to help themselves and are based on the philosophy that people have the right to choose their own objectives. Yet a few pages later the same authors express interest in "shock therapy" which makes sharp breaks between a people and their traditional methods and customs. How this "therapy" is to be accomplished without some form of coercion the reader is left to guess.

The same impatience is evident in this report at the international level, when the Iranian and Egyptian responses to community development are evaluated. In Iran, where the community development program is solidly entrenched but where the reception of community development has not been all that its United States promoters could desire, the authors flex their dollar muscles. "The Iranian government must . . . attempt to create that climate which will foster a widespread community development program," for "Only such action will demonstrate a commitment to . . . the worthwhileness of continued United States aid." But in Egypt where the internal development program "is more nearly determined by the nationals than in any other country studied," and where there is little emphasis on "self-help principles" the authors step much more softly. Here they recommend that the International Cooperation Authority "set an example of organization, planning, and coordination of activities for community development." The policy underlying the recommendations is clear and consistent — to expand job-markets everywhere for personnel in the Community Development Division of the International Cooperation Administration.

Much of the talk about self-help and self-determination and "leading" people to formulate their own objectives for self-improvement is actually as unrealistic as it sounds. Negative and even coercive controls are to some extent unavoidable in the internal development of preindustrial areas. McKim Marriott poses the question of control in describing the administration of new irrigation works in India.[10] When some peasants did not want to use the new irrigation facilities, their land taxes were increased to the point where they had to grow sugarcane, a cash crop requiring more water than could be provided from an old-fashioned well. Then, since canal agents could not resist taking bribes, jealous quarrels soon sprang up between neighbors over the distribution of water. But no farmer would complain to higher authorities, for each feared reprisals from the petty officials in charge. Marriott concludes that large centralized projects will continue to result in peasants' antipathy toward the projects unless some means can be found to give the people enough control over operations so that they will not be left completely at the mercy of outsiders.

What are the consequences for foreign aid of Marriott's conclusions? How is control to be given to peasants? Are we to take over the governments of underdeveloped countries in order to eliminate corruption and enforce honesty and democracy? Obviously such behavior is unthinkable. Yet the question of control raised by Marriott is one which can be asked about most underdeveloped areas. Corruption in government at the peasants' expense has a long history as well as a wide distribution. But I am not so pessimistic about graft as Dr. Marriott is, and I will try to show why in Part III.

In most underdeveloped countries, government service provides one of the few opportunities for rapid economic and social advancement. In a preindustrial society, the potential entrepreneur is likely to become first a crafty bureaucrat. It is not difficult to understand why the peasant tends to distrust his government, because in the underdeveloped country satisfaction of felt needs in government circles may depend more upon the restriction of public expectations than upon their expansion. With few avenues open to increase consumption and living standards by entrepreneurial methods, the intelligent person may join the ranks of the select few who are able to enjoy a higher standard of living through graft or totalitarian privilege.

The totalitarian government, through confiscation of property, restriction of consumer goods, and coercive manipulation of labor, can effectively and rapidly capitalize its labor potential without dissipating its capital in the consumption of luxury goods — particularly luxury goods imported from more advanced countries. Russia is the best example of this totalitarian solution to the problems of economic development, but totalitarianism alone does not explain Russia's rapid development during the past fifty years. Many totalitarian governments have had no directed development. The deleterious effect which many Latin American dictators have had on the economies of their countries as a result of quixotic projects, lavish consumption, and the flight of capital is enough in itself to bring the above assumption into serious question.

"Rational" totalitarianism is dependent in large part on a country's natural resources and its potentialities for development. Insofar as this is true, it is an open question whether Russia's development would not have been even more impressive without such extensive employment of coercive controls; there seems little doubt that her standard of living would have been higher. But the objective of Russia's ruling political class has been to compete with the West in the struggle to dominate the world, not to provide the masses with a high standard of living.

PART II. CULTURAL DEVELOPMENT

VI

Conspicuous Giving and Closed Societies

The word "culture," as used in this book, refers to observable phenomena — the muscular, vocal, and symbolic behavior learned by men as members of social groups. So defined, culture is only a means to understanding culture capital or knowledge, the basis of all forms of human capital. We know of culture capital and "observe" it indirectly through the written and spoken word. Although the stream of symbolic consciousness of which culture capital consists is not directly observable, it increases man's control over his environment and himself in ways which are observable.

The material category of culture I have excluded by this definition. Artifacts are regarded here as a cultural product only to the extent that they can be fitted into a context of meaningful human behavior appropriate to the situation in which they are, or were, used. What we normally speak of as capital goods — the material labor-saving devices which convert energy for us and make possible, either directly or indirectly, the incrementation of knowledge — are indispensable for development, but they are only a reflection of culture capital. If our capital goods were destroyed, we would still have know-how to rebuild them; but if our knowledge and cognitive faculties were destroyed, our capital goods would be powerless to help us. For this reason true capital forma-

101

tion should not be looked upon simply as the expansion of material goods but rather as the expansion of probable knowledge with maximum utilization of mankind's indispensable resource — his cognitive faculty.

In two ways, man takes control of his world in a gradual but ever accelerating fashion. First, he adds to his probable knowledge about his natural environment through technological refinements in his observations. This progressive knowledge-building process I have called "positive." New and improved controls are behavioral alternatives by which man increases the predictability of the consequences of his acts. Man's positive controls accumulate in the fields of greatest specialization, as he increases his technical observations. The cumulative growth of positive control thus has an evolutionary or progressive quality.

Second, man takes negative control of his social environment through law and social sanction. As positive controls progress through the process of specialization, social reciprocities are expanded and altered, and new restraints grow up to define them. Unlike positive control, which evolves progressively, negative control is best regarded as an additive process which depends for its growth upon the expansion of reciprocities. Changes in the two realms of control are interdependent, for specialization depends upon reciprocity, and the growth of probable knowledge depends on specialization.

In Part I, I stressed man's active role in cultural causality and the passivity of those limitative causes to which culture itself belongs. In so doing I opposed extreme cultural or historical determinism, without denying the importance of culture, society, and tradition as limiting causes of human behavior and its development. No "force" or final cause outside man is necessary to explain human development, but this does not mean that man has planned its course. In the short run man's goals and plans may result in the expansion of culture capital, but in the long run his inability to foresee all the consequences of his acts makes his behavior seem random and indeterminate. The limiting causes which circumscribe development loom so large in the long-run view of history that it is not surprising that some have seen these limiting causes as active determinants and final causes.

Part I was concerned with short-run problems; this part will present a long-run view, one in which the active nature of man's contribution will not be totally eclipsed by limiting causes. Man's wants, particularly those through which the prestige motivation seeks expression, will be the center of attention. We shall see how self-interest in the form of prestige motivation sparks the activity necessary for development and how it takes the form of conspicuous giving, conspicuous ownership, and conspicuous production as specialization and knowledge increase.

This chapter will deal with the "closed" societies — those in which specialization and probable knowledge are poorly developed. Four primitive groups will be compared to show why conspicuous giving is the prevalent form of prestige motivation in closed societies. Again, and in more detail, we shall see how a limited degree of capital formation may take place in closed societies through coercive negative control of large quantities of unskilled labor rather than through the development of specialization and knowledge. Before making these cultural comparisons, however, I wish to digress long enough to clarify further my position on the nature of culture, particularly with regard to "material" culture and technology.

The Nature of Culture

According to the view adopted here, culture consists of all behavior acquired by men as members of social groups. This is an abbreviated version of E. B. Tylor's famous definition of culture as "that complex whole which includes knowledge, belief, art, morals, law, custom, and any other capabilities and habits acquired by man as a member of society." [1] Tylor's definition is much more inclusive than mine; it includes material artifacts (art) as well as behavior (habits) and what I call culture capital (knowledge). I am restricting the term to that behavior learned by men as members of societies. By behavior I mean any meaningful human activity whether it be technical — as in driving a car — or symbolic — as in speaking and writing. What has commonly been referred to in the past as "material culture" is not "culture" per se. Automobiles, houses, bridges, and the like, are cultural only with reference to the human behavior associated with their creation, manufacture, and use. I shall explain why I find this distinction useful.

Not long ago, an archeologist digging near San Diego, California, found some stones he considered artifacts of the third interglacial period, a very early date for New World artifacts. These stones he assumed were unspecialized tools resulting from simple percussive flaking. The find, however, has met with skepticism in professional circles because the percussive flaking is so simple as to be indistinguishable from that produced by nature. Archeologists do not agree, therefore, that the finds are really cultural, that is, that they show evidence of meaningful human behavior.

Elsewhere in California, an object known as a charm stone is frequently encountered in archeological sites. These stones are not only convincingly hand-ground but are found in association with other artifacts and are so similar to one another in appearance that their recurrence cannot be mere coincidence. They are therefore considered bona fide artifacts — products of human manufacture or culture. But from the shape of these ground stones it is very difficult to guess the use they were put to. On the other hand, the purposes of the fishhooks and weapon points found in the same sites are obvious from their shapes, because the wide occurrence of artifacts very similar to these among living primitives or primitives known to us in historic times provides a behavioral context in the observable present on which to base an explanation. The explanation, of course, can never be fully tested, since the past cannot be directly observed; but on the basis of indirect evidence, the explanation may become widely accepted. Since the shape of the charm stones is not nearly so diagnostic as that of fishhooks and weapon points, several explanations of their use may be offered on the basis of modern comparisons. Until some way of weighing the logical probabilities of the various explanations presents itself, it is more convenient to give the artifact a tentative name such as "charm stone" or "religious object." Later, some new indirect evidence may lead to a consensus concerning the most logical explanation of the object's use. It is extremely important, then, that the behavioral context of a relic be explained even though it is generally conceded that the relic is a product of culture.

The case of Juan and the water pump in Chapter I provides another illustration of the usefulness of a behavioral definition of culture. The artifact in this case was a gasoline-powered water pump, but Juan had not completely absorbed its behavioral context into his own behavior patterns. He only partially understood its use, and knew next to nothing about its maintenance. To the extent that the behavioral context of the pump was unknown to Juan, it was for him simply a manmade artifact much like the charm stone is for the archeologist. And so, in Juan's hands, the pump became a useless and to some extent inexplicable object, a mass of rusting metal perched beside a well.

A more dramatic example is the British groundnut (peanut) fiasco in East Africa already mentioned in Chapter IV.[2] To alleviate a shortage of fats at the end of the Second World War, the British government sponsored a scheme to clear and cultivate 3,210,000 acres in parts of Tanganyika, Northern Rhodesia, and Kenya for the production of groundnuts. The plan called for a highly mechanized form of agriculture that would require a permament labor force of only 32,100 Africans and 749 Europeans for the entire area, without any need for additional seasonal labor. Only a small fraction of the proposed area was actually cultivated before the impracticability of the project became self-evident. Among the many causes for its failure was the fact that the African natives had had no experience in maintaining and operating machinery. In fact, when they first saw the machines, they ran in fright. It was necessary to import such a great number of highly paid European technicians that the resulting labor costs were completely out of proportion to the value of the crop. Again, machinery outside its behavioral context was a useless artifact.

As a result of mistakes like the one just described, we frequently come up against the attitude that construction projects and mechanization are somehow the wrong approaches to development. As I pointed out in Chapter IV, however, if technical artifacts are separated from technical observation, the misuse of the artifacts is not the fault of technology. In other words, the behavioral context of energy-converters is part of technical observation or technology, but energy-converters alone do not solve problems of development. They are only artifacts; they must be employed intelligently.

Unfortunately, the idea of a "material" as opposed to a "nonmaterial" culture has resulted in a popular conception of culture which often handicaps constructive thinking on the subject of cultural change. Two short stories illustrate this popular conception.

In one of the stories a young galactic administrator from Earth is assigned the job of managing the economic development of a distant planet inhabited by an intelligent form of humanoid life with a very simple technology. Despite the technological simplicity of the inhabitants of this underdeveloped planet, the new administrator and his staff experience a vaguely uncomfortable feeling that something about these natives is not primitive at all. The first clue is the mature behavior of the children, who are never subjected to any of the humiliating punishments by which Earth parents reproduce in their children their own emotional immaturities. But the full revelation comes after the discovery that the planet possesses a valuable natural resource, which, if exploited, would permit rapid technological advancement and a very high standard of living for its inhabitants. The natives shock their Earthman administrator by rejecting on rational grounds his offer of economic development. They point out to him that there is not always intrinsic value in the material things Earthmen want, but simply the prestige value of conspicuous acquisition and display of goods which conveys the impression of wealth. Although they themselves do not understand why they have so much insight into the motivations of Earthmen, they are clearly a race of superior social psychologists who live a much healthier and happier life than Earthmen despite their primitive technology. Even the new Earthman administrator learns to relax as he realizes that technological advancement and the neurotic hustle and bustle of life on Earth are not the most important things in the galaxy after all.[3]

Much the same sort of culture-consciousness is reflected in a well-executed story by Shirley Jackson called "The Lottery."[4] The setting is implied indirectly by clues presented as the plot unfolds. Mention of a village square, a post office, Halloween, a safe in the coal company office, tractors, and a teen-age club indicates that events on this fine June morning are taking place in a contemporary rural community somewhere in Anglo-America. The villagers have gathered for an annual lottery which has been traditional on this date for so long that the meaning of much of the ritual has been forgotten. The lottery box itself is very old and according to local lore was made from pieces of the original box constructed when the first people settled there. As the villagers — gathered in the square between the post office and the bank — wait their turn to draw lots from the old box, they seem tense and uneasy. In answer to one man's comment that in a neighboring village there has been talk of giving up the lottery, the oldest man in town snorts in disdain that young people do not know what is good for them these days. He repeats an old adage: "Lottery in June, corn be heavy soon." After all the heads of families have drawn lots and it is determined that one, Bill Hutchinson, has the marked slip, his wife, Tessie, complains fretfully that the drawing was unfair. A neighbor kindly admonishes her to be a good sport since they all took the same chance.

Each member of Bill Hutchinson's family must now draw again from the box; first the three children, then Tessie, then Bill. Tessie is the last to show her slip of paper; her husband has to force it from her hand. On it is a black spot. All the villagers, children as well as adults, pick up stones from a pile previously placed in readiness. Someone even gives a stone to little Davy Hutchinson. In the center of a cleared space Tessie screams.

The story of the backward planet poses a question often raised about underdeveloped areas. Does technological superiority in the material sphere necessarily imply moral superiority in the non-material? In bringing technological and material "improvements" to underdeveloped areas, are we not perhaps destroying non-material aspects of local culture which may even be superior to our own? In the second story, the power of tradition to keep alive a harvest sacrifice in a modern world of banks and tractors is given a kind of horrible plausibility by this same division in our thinking.

To understand the origin of this relativistic conception of culture we must go back to the latter half of the nineteenth century, when expanding colonialism coincided with the spread of Darwinian views of biological evolution. The survival of the fittest became a handy rationalization for colonialism. The strongest cultures and "races" were those most fit to rule — those with the most developed technologies. Concurrently with the birth of anthropology as a profession about the turn of the century, a reaction against this view began to take hold. As primitive peoples came to be studied by professional anthropologists, earlier reports by travelers and missionaries were decried for their emotional and usually uncomplimentary comparisons between the immoral, ignorant savages and the superior habits of their Caucasian observers. Physical and cultural anthropology were much more closely related in those days, and questions of race were bound up with questions of culture. American anthropologists in particular opposed social darwinism. Other races and cultures, they argued, were not to be judged inferior to the white race and to Western civilization by virtue of the latter's superiority of arms. Perhaps it could be grudgingly admitted that some development was needed in technology, but certainly in religion, art, marriage practices, and other non-technical parts of their cultures the peoples in colonial areas could not be called inferior to westerners. How could anyone rate these manifestations of culture on a quantitative scale?

In some ways the new profession of anthropology became a kind of inspired creed, its members champions of the racial and cultural underdog — all in the name of science. Anthropologists began to describe what they saw dispassionately, as scientists supposedly do, without injecting their own personal values. They viewed and analyzed each culture in its own value context, not in relation to any other. But something more than dispassionate description has resulted from the movement against social darwinism. Today, particularly at the popular level, there is a tendency to look upon technology as something quite distinct and separate from "non-material" culture. Some regard these two kinds of culture as almost mutually exclusive, to the extent that they believe changes in one occur independently of changes in the other. The resulting picture may be either one of extreme culture-lag in which social change is far outstripped by developments in material technology, or one of an idealized Rousseauan picture of the happy primitive life in which the only thing that is primitive is the technology. In either case there would seem to be an inference that technological development is something not quite nice, or at least something completely apart from really important changes in culture.

In both of the short stories we find evidence of the influence of this split in people's thinking. In the first, a society with a simple technology and little specialization is gifted with an innate social psychology — innate because it could hardly be a product of knowledge and learning: knowledge grows through the division of labor and the extension of man's powers of observation by means of continual refinements in the technical equipment with which he makes his observations and measurements. The insight of the backward natives into the conspicuous consumption of the Earthmen was really owing, of course, to the insight of an Earthman named Thorstein Veblen, who died in 1929 but whose ideas either directly or indirectly influenced the writer of this story. Veblen was the product of late nineteenth- and early twentieth-century terrestrial civilization which even then had become sufficiently specialized and sophisticated to make possible the existence of satirical social philosophers such as he. The natives of this story supposedly did not know how to account for their social maturity in the face of their technological simplicity; but their sophisticated awareness of the problems of the emotional development of the child was really a reflection of the author's awareness of twentieth-century psychology. It is no wonder that the author had to locate this anomalous primitive culture in another world.

In the second story, a shocking practice is found persisting in what to all appearances is a modern American rural community. This story is so cleverly done that one would almost suspect it of being an ingenious satire. The author tricks her readers. Without emphasizing the cultural situation and without giving any indication of the story's macabre denouement, she carries them unsuspectingly through the description of a curious tradition without seriously straining their credulity, for that has already been amply stretched by their cultural "sophistication." The finish comes as a shock rude enough to awaken the perceptive reader from his relativistic complacency.

But the story of the lottery is also influenced by the idea of cultural determinism, because in it tradition — the weight of the past — becomes sufficient explanation of ritual in the present. A sacrifice is performed because it has always been performed and because it is the thing to do. People may sense that something is wrong, but they are powerless to act; they dance on puppet strings manipulated by tradition. Since his ability to create new technologies is limited by what he has been given to work with by the past, man may come to be viewed as culture-bound almost to the point where he becomes the passive recipient and culture the active agent. Ritual is always a favorite example of those who favor this deterministic point of view, for ritual seems so senseless and yet so compulsive. But human sacrifice is not in the same category as a harmless liturgy, and immediately we are struck by the cleverly conceived disharmony; for in matters of life and death, people are not mere puppets and never have been.

I once heard a professor suggest in all seriousness to a class of undergraduates that human sacrifice is not found in Anglo-America today because it is not a part of Anglo-American tradition or culture, but that if native Mexican civilization, for example, had been left to develop without interruption from the Old World there might very well have grown up in the New an advanced (technologically) civilization which practiced human sacrifice. This statement was made almost twenty years ago, and I doubt that many anthropologists would take such a point of view today even for sake of argument or explanation. But the effects of this extreme form of relativism are still very much alive in popular thinking. Implicit again in this example is the mutually exclusive division between material and non-material culture, a relativistic dichotomy which precludes any possible causal relation between the occurrence of human sacrifice and the degree of technological development. Instead, the presence or absence of human sacrifice in this hypothetical argument is explained as a product of tradition or history, in other words, as a product of its own prior existence. If culture is restricted to human behavior, however, and the distinction between "material" and "non-material" culture is eliminated, it is difficult to divide culture into such independent categories; for the behaviors of any individual human unit of culture are to some extent meaningfully interrelated within that individual. It is possible to speak of behavior which is technical and performed in relation to artifacts or things as compared with behavior which is social or symbolic and has to do with other human beings. But when both kinds of behavior are viewed as stemming from the same cognitive source, it seems unjustifiable to make them mutually exclusive. Besides, the growth and application of technology is itself a social phenomenon to the extent that it depends upon human interaction through discussion of the findings and explanations of technical observations.

Of human sacrifice in ancient Mexico it could be argued that *if* technological advancement had continued independently as it had in the past, there would have been a correlative increase in the division of labor, commerce, and the size of the state. Since the sacrificial victims of the Aztecs were largely prisoners of war, warfare for the sake of plunder and tribute would have become less profitable than commerce, and prestige through warfare and the capture of prisoners would eventually have been replaced by prestige through the conspicuous consumption of goods. Sacrificial victims brought in from outside the group would have become fewer as the feuding tribes were drawn closer together by economic and political ties. But equally important, the technological advancements would have amplified New World man's technical observations and increased the probability of his knowledge of himself and nature far above that to which unspecialized man is limited by purely casual observation. Consequently, many of the causal interpretations of nature on which his religious rituals were based would eventually have been replaced by more probable knowledge. This replacement would in turn have led to behavior which we today would be more likely to view as "rational." [5]

History as a Model

The developmental sketch which follows is heuristic and might properly be called a "model," or rough hypothesis.[6] Many kinds of model have been used to organize and clarify cultural behavior. Durkheim, as we shall see in the next chapter, used an organismic model, which was analogic. But an analogy is based on a likeness between two different things, and the differences between them may lead to the exclusion of relevant factors. The cells or different parts of an organism do not interact cognitively, so Durkheim's human units played no cognitive role in the causal structure of the division of labor.

History provides a very useful model for interpretation of the cultural present. The picture of cultural development in time which history makes possible is heuristic, but it is of the same substance as the phenomenon it is being used to interpret. Such a model is not anthropomorphic, but legitimately anthropomorphous.

Those who consider history a scientific discipline may object to its being referred to as a model. But science involves the testing of theories open to public confirmation: for example, a prediction that preliterate groups are likely to accept innovations which spectacularly meet their felt needs is a theory open to testing. The subject matter of cultural science is human behavior, which can be observed again and again under similar conditions.

History is not open to public confirmation in the same way. Scholars may debate the veracity of historical documents and devise ingenious means of cross-checking different sources, but none can go back in time and recheck original observations. All the descriptive studies of primitive and rural peoples made by anthropologists are historical, for they are not completely open to retesting; the original situation cannot be duplicated. Explanations of human behavior which the anthropologist draws from his observations are scientific only if they can be retested against the raw material of human behavior.

A history-bound explanation cannot be retested. Explanations of ultimate origins are the most obvious illustration, but all antecedent explanations tend to be history-bound. An antecedent explanation is a causal explanation of some cultural behavior based on phenomena preceding it in time. "Cause" as it has been used in this work implies not only antecedence but also covariance or correlation. Cultural causes do not cease to function once the behavior they have caused comes into being, but occur along with it until that behavior is replaced by another. Antecedent explanations are history-bound when they rely on unique preceding conditions which cannot be retested in the present.

An illustration may help to clarify this distinction. In the last chapter we learned that collective labor was effective in maintaining irrigation systems in Japan but was not effective in parts of Haiti and Colombia. We decided that lack of group cohesion and concomitant group sanctions were the causes of collective labor failures and that the presence of these factors was the cause of successful collective action in Japan. This generalization and the additional one that water taxes and government administration are more likely solutions to maintenance problems in places like Haiti and Colombia are history-free theories that may be tested by further observation of similar situations. But if someone chose to, he could explain each case separately by emphasizing its historical antecedents. In Haiti, for example, the slave trade, the French practice of dispersing members of a tribe among plantations, the breakdown of the plantation system under Pétion, and the preference of the freed slaves for subsistence cropping rather than sugarcane cultivation constitute a history-bound explanation of the collapse of the irrigation system, and as such one that could not be rechecked by first-hand observation.

Such a history-bound explanation can, nevertheless, help make a history-free theory clearer by providing a narrative of heuristic value. Furthermore, history-bound events or explanations can be used to substantiate history-free causal generalizations. The antecedents of the breakdown of the French irrigation systems in Haiti all point to conditions which one might expect to result in a fragmentation of Haitian social organization. The history of the colonization of the fruit company land and the installation of rural water distribution systems by the Colombian Coffee Federation also shows reasons for social fragmentation. Though the history of each case cannot be re-observed, the repetitive pattern of social fragmentation adds some verification to the history-free explanation. As the precision of documentation increases, history adds considerable opportunities for verifying causal explanations even though observable behavior will always provide the raw material for testing purposes. But the more inferential the historical subject matter in the history-bound explanation, the less becomes the justification for using it in other than heuristic fashion.

Conspicuous Giving in Closed Societies

Comparing two very primitive peoples, the Eskimo of the frozen North and the Siriono Indians of the tropical Amazon jungles, will illustrate some of the limiting causes of closedness where per-capita production is very low and the margin of survival very slim.[7] The Eskimo are hunters and depend primarily on sea mammals for their subsistence. Despite the ingenious technology which they have adopted to survive in their environment — snow goggles, the dog sledge, the kayak skin boat, and the snow house — their technology is primitive and the environment extremely severe. The margin of survival is so narrow that Eskimos on occasion find it impossibly difficult to support the unproductive members of society. Not only are the old and infirm often killed — frequently at their own request — but even infanticide is not uncommon if the newborn arrives before the preceding child is ready for weaning.

Because of the paucity of the food resources, Eskimo bands seldom exceed a hundred persons. Usually these bands hunt over such large areas that meetings among bands are very infrequent. Although the Eskimo of one local group do not claim hunting rights over any given territory to the exclusion of others, although they share food in time of famine and permit a hungry man to take food from the storage cache of another if in need, and although a winter house after being abandoned in the summer becomes the property of whoever claims it first the following winter, they feel a strong sense of ownership over the tools and weapons they manufacture and a strong individual claim to a fair share of any kill in which several have cooperated.

It is difficult for any one Eskimo to accumulate great wealth. Not only would the accumulation of goods be inconvenient to a nomad, it would be hard to accomplish when the margin of survival is so narrow. An Eskimo with more goods than he can use is more likely to distribute than to hoard them, for an Eskimo is not admired and respected for the amount of his possessions but for the extent to which he distributes food and goods to others. The skillful hunter is likely to be a giver more frequently than a receiver, and so is more likely to be prestigeful and a leader.

If an Eskimo does not distribute his wealth, he may become the victim of invidious sanction, a mechanism for maintaining redistribution and the status quo mentioned in Chapter V as operating in modern

Haiti and a phenomenon common in many parts of the world among equals living close to the bare level of survival. At the time of Edward Nelson's four-year stay (1877–1881) in the Bering Straits region of northern Alaska, trading posts had been established among the Eskimo of the region, and some had found it possible to accumulate considerably more property than their fellows. But to assure good will, they distributed food and other presents within the community, which enhanced their prestige and leadership. If a successful trader did not distribute his goods, his fellows might force him to do so at a special feast or they might simply kill him and divide up the spoils. (Nelson cites a case of the latter.[8]) Although the skillful hunter and prestigeful distributor of goods may become leader of opinion in his local group, he never becomes a formal leader with authoritarian powers. His influence is persuasive rather than coercive. Internal control is accomplished largely by means of reciprocity, as in the case of murder by blood revenge.

In their tropical forest environment in northeastern Bolivia, the Siriono Indians live mainly by hunting supplemented with agriculture, fishing, and collecting palm cabbage and wild fruits. Monkeys, wild pigs, and anteaters are the principal game hunted by men, who also help their womenfolk cultivate small gardens of corn, manioc, and sweet potatoes. The technology of these people is very simple. The digging stick is their only agricultural tool and the bow and arrow their only weapon. Their pottery is poor and their houses are mere lean-tos. They make hammocks of fiber bark string and know how to weave baskets; but they have no knowledge of how to make fire and must carry a brand from camp to camp. Unlike the Eskimo, the Siriono can roam naked in their environment without endangering their survival, and their technology lacks the ingenuity of the Eskimo's in many respects. But as part-time horticulturists the Siriono possess an important alternative not available to the Eskimo in their frozen wastelands.

The Siriono are also nomadic, and their bands are not separated by definite territorial divisions. Because the area they live in is poorly drained, they must migrate to higher land during the annual inundation when most of the area becomes a great swamp. It is on these high spots that they plant their small gardens. Siriono bands, like those of the Eskimo, are small, usually with fewer than a hundred members, and meetings among bands are very infrequent. The Siriono like the Eskimo find it difficult to support persons who are too sick or old to keep up with the group, and such people are abandoned to die by themselves. Here, too, feelings of individual ownership are apparently strongest for tools, weapons, and other personal property. The environment exists to be exploited equally by all. But while a person may own the garden plot he has cleared and planted, the wild fruit trees he has discovered, and the animals he has slain, he has little real opportunity to accumulate any great store of material goods. The nomadic life, the simple technology, the amount of time consumed by the quest for food — all these are severe limitations which decrease the opportunities for individual ownership of goods. The Siriono do not attempt to accumulate property, and as among the Eskimo, the prestigeful person and the leader of the local group is the most successful hunter, for he is the most able provider of food. One indication of a chief's status is the number of his wives, for a poor hunter may not be able to support even one.

Although the Siriono share food, food is a subject of constant ingroup conflict. People are always accusing each other of hoarding it and failing to share it. But, despite the quarreling and the obvious reluctance, sharing takes place all the time. People share and expect to get food in return when they ask for it, even though the reciprocity is more likely to be provoked by hostile demands than to be volunteered out of a feeling of generosity. Chiefs are more likely than others to receive favorable responses to requests for food because a chief, as a good hunter, is likely to have occasional surpluses with which to reciprocate, and a man who gives him food has a high expectation of being repaid. The sanctions of reciprocity are therefore definitely in favor of the better hunter, since in the long run he gives more than he gets. Like the Eskimo, such a leader has no coercive control over the group, but because of his prestige as a "big man" he exercises persuasive influence.

Both the Eskimo and the Siriono have a low margin of survival — that is, a very small amount of food production above bare subsistence requirements. For both, this marginal subsistence results from a combination of environmental and technological limitations. The small food supply, the primitive technology, and the proportion of time devoted to the quest for food limit the amount of non-food production and the opportunity to accumulate permanent individual advantages in durable goods. Since a hunter's luck is frequently uneven, there is obvious benefit to a system of reciprocity whereby he distributes his surplus on good days and helps consume others' surplus when his own luck has been bad. But hunting is not all a matter of luck; skill is also important. Those who most frequently make a kill will distribute more than they receive in return, but in compensation they win respect and prestige from their fellows. Among both the Eskimo and the Siriono the prestigeful leader was a skillful hunter. But he was also a man who distributed his surplus. One who hoarded did not arouse admiration, but jealousy and hostility. Invidious sanction operated in both groups. Among the Siriono it was openly and constantly a part of the bickering of daily life, and among the Eskimo it took the form of the group's retaliating against the person who amassed wealth without distributing it. The Siriono illustrate how the giving which earns prestige and respect in primitive societies is not necessarily synonymous with altruistic generosity.

Two primitive societies which enjoy a more dependable food source than either the Eskimo or the Siriono will now be compared. These people are the Haida, who live along the northwest coast of North America, and the Ifugao, a Philippine tribe inhabiting the mountainous interior of Luzon.[9] The Haida were the aboriginal inhabitants of the Queen Charlotte Islands which lie off the northwest coat of British Columbia. Like their neighbors on Vancouver Island and the coast of British Columbia, these people enjoyed an environment rich in marine fauna. They were fishermen, and salmon and halibut were their staple foods. The men also hunted sea mammals such as otters, seals, and sea lions, and the women gathered shellfish, birds' eggs, roots, and fruits. Great quantities of berries and fish were gathered and dried during the busy summer months and stored for the long winter, when the people took part in ceremonies and feasts or worked at non-food-producing activities.

The Haida no longer live the life described here; accounts of their aboriginal way of life were based largely on reconstructions from historical sources and the memories of older informants. In fact, none of the groups still lives exactly as it did when the accounts were set down. All but the Haida, however, will be described in the present tense, and for convenience all comparisons will be in the present tense.

The Haida lived in permanent villages with as many as five or six hundred inhabitants. Their houses were large rectangular structures occupied by a large extended family of thirty or more under the leadership of a house chief. Although the Haida had no unified government, the tribe was divided into moieties or halves, each of which was further divided into about twenty clans. There were one to a dozen households in each clan and the most prominent household chief was chief of the clan.

Although Haida technology was the simple technology of an unspecialized society, nature gave them an abundance of food and other goods. With stone tools they fashioned smooth cedar planks for their houses and large elaborately ornamented dugout canoes. They carved ornate dishes and spoons, wove watertight baskets, and made rectangular boxes for storing skins and foods. Each family produced its own goods, which constituted its private property. The available food supply was sufficient to free the Haida and their neighbors from the quest for food long enough to permit many time-consuming manufactures not strictly essential to their survival, and to permit social activities among several villages at a time. Among the Haida, old people were never killed or abandoned but were respected and well cared for by their families.

Among the Haida a person's reputation and prestige were measured directly in terms of the quantity of goods he had distributed in the form of giving ceremonies known as potlatches. By means of a funeral potlatch the heir to a chieftainship validated his claim to office and to the deceased chief's house. The house-building potlatch was very important, for it enabled a married couple (who had worked diligently for some ten years or more to accumulate sufficient wealth for distribution) not only to acquire prestige for themselves but ascribed status for their children. A man's ascribed status might be high as a result of the potlatching efforts of his parents, but his own prestige and influence would be low if he had never shown the diligence necessary to distribute goods himself. George P. Murdock, who studied the Haida, has compared such men to the black sheep in one of our aristocratic or upper-class families.[10] In contrast, a man whose unambitious parents bequeathed him a low ascribed status could, through a house-building potlatch, lift himself to the position of a house-chief and win respect and prestige; but because of his low birth, he would always be looked upon, says Murdock, as the equivalent of the nouveau riche in our own society.

Two other potlatches brought destruction rather than distribution of goods. In the face-saving kind, a man of high standing who had suf-

117

fered some embarrassing incident in public invited all members of the opposite moiety who had been witnesses to the event to a destruction of property in their presence. From that time on, they could never again mention the incident. In the more extreme vengeance potlatch, a man of high rank would disgrace an enemy who had insulted or wronged him in some way by destroying more property than his opponent was able to gather together and destroy.

Haida chiefs could not command or punish; their influence was persuasive and depended upon their prestige and personality. There were no state or tribal controls, and murder was avenged by the clansmen of the victim. Compensation might be made in goods, however, with chiefs of neutral clans acting as mediators in arranging the negotiations.

The Ifugao farmers of northern Luzon are not blessed with an environment abundantly stocked with wild food. But in their deep mountain valleys they produce a fairly secure food supply by careful and arduous farming. The terraced rice fields which scale the sides of their mountains are supported by stone walls often twenty feet or more high, although sometimes the field behind such a wall may be only eleven feet wide. On these terraces the Ifugao grow wet rice irrigated by streams and springs which depend on a heavy rainfall of about a hundred to a hundred and twenty-five inches a year.

Because their terraces are irrigated by rain-fed springs, long irrigation ditches and the cooperation requisite to build and maintain them are unnecessary — an important limitative factor, inasmuch as the Ifugao, like the Haida, have no tribal organization and no village chiefs or village councils. As among the Haida, kinship is the important social tie, and murder is a cause of action by the victim's kinsmen rather than by his fellow villagers.

Like the Haida, the Ifugao produce sufficiently to permit the accumulation of property. Here, too, a man achieves prestige by giving away wealth, but an Ifugao does so in the form of pretentious feasts to which he invites the whole district. Having given a series of such expensive feasts, he wins the rank of *kadangyang* and is eligible to build a special bench in front of his house known as a *hagabi*, which symbolizes his status. The prestige of a kadangyang is similar to that of the chiefs of the other groups. He may become an influential leader of opinion and a mediator in disputes, but again his influence is more persuasive than coercive.

As among the Haida, a great deal of work and diligence is necessary in order to accumulate the wealth to finance the ceremonies in which it is given away. As farmers, however, the Ifugao go about this accumulation a little differently than the Haida. Here the ownership of rice fields is vital: a man must not only produce enough rice to sustain his family, but he must also produce a surplus which he can lend out in times of scarcity at high rates of interest. In addition to rice, people often borrow livestock for funeral or illness ceremonies at interest rates of one hundred per cent in kind, even for short periods. With luck the ambitious man may accumulate enough wealth to buy more rice lands, and these will provide him with ever more capital for making loans at high interest rates.

Both the Haida and the Ifugao potlatchers may expend all their goods in the ceremonial distribution of accumulated wealth, but the Ifugao, unlike the Haida, retains a valuable property in the form of rice lands and with luck may remain a wealthy man the rest of his life. But since a man may borrow on his lands to finance his kadangyang ceremonies, a few misfortunes may cause him to lose much of his land as an indirect result of these ceremonial feasts. Moreover, as his children marry, the land will be divided among them, and as his health begins to fail, he will often sell land in order to buy the sacrificial carabao with which to appease the gods who are afflicting him. Although the son of a kadangyang cannot inherit his father's rank and must gain the rank himself, he is more likely than most to inherit enough land to make his start easier.

In contrast to the Eskimo and the Siriono, the Haida and Ifugao enjoy greater food supplies and security. These supplies are the product of a favorable combination of environmental and technological limitations. The Haida are favored with abundant marine fauna and the Ifugao with sufficient rainfall to make wet rice cultivation possible on their irrigated terraces. The Haida accumulate surplus wealth in the form of a redundancy of consumption goods of a very limited variety. The Ifugao accumulate it in the form of land capable of producing more wealth. Both peoples attain prestige by giving, which tends to reduce the differences between wealthy and poor, and the wealthy and prestigeful families in both groups bequeath some advantage to their descendants. It would seem, however, that the inherited advantage is greater among the Ifugao, inasmuch as giving away wealth would not necessarily result in reducing the kadangyang's wealth in land. But even a Haida who potlatches away all his goods is not permanently stripped of his greater advantage in wealth, for the distribution of goods at a potlatch is not an equal one. Those guests who have acquired greatest prestige through potlatches of their own are the ones who receive the largest gifts. And thus the man who distributes his wealth is likely to get much of it back. The giving away of wealth among the Haida and the Ifugao, then, is as much a way of displaying ownership as of equalizing it.

In all four societies prestige is sought by giving, although the limitative factors produce variations. Among the simple hunters whose food surpluses are small, opportunities for the production and accumulation of durable goods are few. Acquiring goods is too difficult and unusual to become an acceptable means of winning social approval. The prestigeful person is likely to be a successful producer who gives away more food than he receives. Where unusual circumstances permit one man to accumulate much more wealth than his fellows, invidious sanction acts to maintain its distribution. Distribution of wealth at this level is a form of conspicuous giving. This is not an altruistic phenomenon divorced from acquisitive designs, but stems from individual motivations of survival and prestige.

The Siriono are very possessive about food and share it only with great reluctance. They live so close to minimal subsistence that survival and prestige conflict at every reciprocal sharing of food. But here cognition takes a hand, for reciprocity takes place out of individual recognition of the fact that one must share a temporary abundance of food with his fellows if he is to expect to share their good fortune when his own luck has been poor. And the good hunter is usually willing to help support the group for the social approbation he receives. But even in a very primitive economy, there may be some opportunities for another kind of conspicuous consumption, that of conspicuous ownership. Such an opportunity is provided among the Siriono by the practice of polygyny. The more successful hunter can attract and support more wives by virtue of his greater production, and they become in a way a conspicuous form of property which helps to mark him as a big man.

The Haida and Ifugao, with their greater production, are able to achieve more ownership of goods in the process of acquiring prestige than the Eskimo and Siriono. While the distribution or giving away of goods reduces inequalities of ownership, it also serves to display them. An Ifugao kadangyang, for example, keeps an advantage in the number of rice fields he owns and a Haida house chief retains the right to expect larger gifts at other peoples' potlatches. Among the Haida, destruction of wealth at a vengeance potlatch is a means of reinforcing one's prestige — an alternative to conspicuous giving, though apparently not so popular. It has the same effect, however: displaying inequalities in the ownership of wealth. Despite the fact that a greater abundance of food increases opportunities for conspicuous ownership, the means of acquiring prestige are characteristically via conspicuous giving.

The basic limitative cause for this form of prestigeful behavior among societies like these is the restricted amount of durable goods. Although the Haida are able to produce a great amount of consumption goods during the winter months, the variety of these goods was limited by the lack of specialized production and the relatively minor importance of regional trade. Since each family produces the same things, beyond a certain point the quantity of durable goods means endless redundancy. Even destruction of such supplies in vengeance potlatches would not necessarily threaten either the survival or the normal standard of living of the Haida. Inasmuch as the variety of durable goods owned by the members of a primitive society is limited by its unspecialized labor, conspicuous giving overshadows conspicuous ownership as a means of displaying prestige. Mere quantity of goods ceases to provide any further satisfaction when the utilitarian needs for which they were made are satisfied. When the felt need for the acquisition of goods becomes social, what disposal is made of the goods may be unimportant so long as it meets that social need. If the prestige motivation can be satisfied more readily by periodically distributing wealth than by accumulating it indefinitely, conspicuous giving will be the predominant form of consumption which the motivation takes.

An outstanding characteristic of cultural closedness as illustrated by these four societies is the limited number of methods for acquiring prestige. Each method involves activities participated in by nearly everyone. A person may get social approval for his skill at hunting, farming, or some craft pursued by the members of many other households, or he may be respected and admired for his willingness to distribute wealth or for his prowess as a warrior. But since the number of occupations in the primitive society is small, many of man's potential aptitudes and skills go undeveloped. The variety of activity is small and the range of experience and observation narrow. Within the limitations of a primitive technology, frequency interpretations are based almost entirely on casual observation and most of the predictions derived from them are of low probability. Among societies in which knowledge and prediction have a low degree of probability, actions designed to meet the same felt needs may vary considerably from group to group. This characteristic of closed societies I shall call random tolerance.

Random Tolerance

The discussion of Ecuadorian folk medicine in Chapter III gave an idea of the potential range of explanations of and actions with regard to disease where knowledge has a low probability. The Siriono attribute most ailments to evil spirits, although they also believe that disease may be caused by the absence of the soul, when it has left the body during dreams. Entry into the body by the disease-causing evil spirits is facilitated by the violation of food taboos and breaches of tribal customs. Few herbal remedies are known to the Siriono and they have no special medical practitioners. Consequently very little treatment is even attempted. In one case observed by Holmberg,[11] a man sick with diarrhea was attended only by his wife, who gave him no medicines but chanted at his side for about an hour each day to drive away the evil spirits. When this did no good, she stuck six arrows in the ground near the head of his hammock. He eventually died.

The Eskimo have shamans, each of whom has some control over a special spirit, such as a human ghost or an animal spirit, which can be summoned to do the bidding of the shaman. During a very dramatic dance the shaman commands the spirit to find and bring back the lost soul of the sick person he is treating.

The Ifugao believe in special "pathogenic" deities such as "dysentery deities," "boil-and-abscess producers," and "liver-attacking deities." The spirits of ancestors may also cause disease by calling away the patient's soul. Animals are sacrificed to appease these supernatural agents of disease.

The Haida have shamans who breathe on the patient to blow out an ailment and who prescribe treatments while possessed by supernatural helpers. Here, too, loss of the soul is considered a cause of illness, for the Haida also believe dreams to be evidence of nocturnal wanderings of the soul. They use a great many herbal remedies, but when a patient fails to respond to such ordinary measures, sorcery may be suspected and a shaman called to prescribe treatment.

Though the variety of beliefs and treatments associated with sickness among primitive peoples is very great, it is not entirely random. The possible association of ideas has certain obvious limitations. Losing the soul, being possessed by spirits or objects, sorcery, and punishment for wrongdoing are quite understandable. That they should recur frequently is not surprising.

Many other aspects of life also show a great range of variability among primitive and preindustrial peoples, although in all cases some non-random factors act as limitations. The Siriono, for example, have no marriage ceremony whatsoever; the Eskimo practice mock abduction of the bride; the Ifugao marriage transaction requires four ceremonial feasts, including sacrifices of animals and the exchange of gifts; among the Haida there is a wedding ceremony in which the bride is showered with many practical housekeeping gifts. Wealth is another obvious limitation: the elaborateness of the marriage ceremony as a social event is undoubtedly limited by the group's productivity.

The same variability is true of death rites. After placing the corpse on a platform in the house in which the person died, the Siriono shoot arrows through the walls to drive away evil spirits and then abandon the house without any further ceremony. Later, when the body has decomposed, they may return to bury the bones. The Eskimo inter the corpse as soon as possible, build a stone cairn above, and place all the person's belongings beside it. Relatives gather to mourn and praise the deceased, and no one hunts or fishes for five days. The Haida dress the corpse in ceremonial garb and display it propped up by the fireplace for four days. Each night certain kinsmen keep a vigil by the body, and after the corpse has been placed in its coffin and deposited in the clan burial hut, a final feast is provided for all who assisted at the funeral. Among the Ifugao, who also display their dead, the corpse of a man of rank may be displayed for as long as two weeks, until partly decomposed. Until burial, there is a wake each night at which songs are sung and stories told. Sometimes as many as two thousand people make up the final funeral procession.

The amount of food produced is a major determinant of the size of social gatherings and the amount of feasting at funerals. As for methods of disposing of corpses, these are, as George P. Murdock has pointed out, variable within a range limited by what is possible.[12] The corpse can be abandoned, exposed to carnivorous animals, buried, thrown in the river or the ocean, put in a tree or on a scaffold, cremated, mummified, or embalmed. Among the four peoples described here there were as many different means employed for disposing of corpses, but all within an expectable range of possibilities.

This great variability of some cultural behavior among societies with a low degree of probable knowledge constitutes random tolerance. Usually social and often ceremonial, these behaviors vary within the range permitted by their own limiting possibilities. It would almost seem that the choice of customs made by a society from alternative possibilities is entirely random. This is not altogether true, of course, for many limitative causes act selectively in each case. Some environments may favor certain methods of corpse disposal over others; and certainly the social organization of a group, which is itself related to the group's size and economic productivity, will have a selective or limitative effect on the kind of marriage or funeral customs most likely to be practiced. A particular custom is not determined in the sense of being necessitated by the limitative causes inherent in the situation; rather, the limitative causes simply make its occurrence more or less probable than the occurrence of other behavior possible under those same circumstances.

The Siriono Indians, for example, could bury their dead; but it would be very difficult to dig a deep grave with a digging stick. It would be even more difficult for them to hold an elaborate wake at which guests would be fed. Similarly, there are no limitative causes which necessitate the Haida custom of showering the bride with gifts. But in a society which enjoys a considerable surplus of household goods and in which gift-giving and prestige are so clearly linked, it is certainly not an improbable custom. The Ifugao practice of displaying corpses for several days in a tropical climate seems a highly improbable custom, for the Ifugao are not immune to the stench and have special words to indicate five recognized stages in the progressive decomposition of a corpse and the disagreeableness of its odor. But the Ifugao place a great emphasis on prestige and wealth, which they display at this time, and they have a strong belief in the supernatural powers of the deceased.

Random tolerance has been responsible in part for tradition-directed and organismic viewpoints with regard to primitive culture. But even if inaccurate, there is some justification for them, for among primitive societies the cognitive component of cultural causality is weak — weak in that the alternatives of random tolerance are not "controls" resulting from technical observation, but variations within a range of tolerance and probability set by limiting possibilities of the circumstances. Much cultural behavior at this level is the result of interaction between basic motivations and limitative causes. It is understandable that tradition is so often viewed as guiding primitive man's behavior and that primitive societies are conceived of as organisms composed of non-cognitive cells.

Negative Control in Closed Societies

As suggested by the preceding discussion, leadership among primitive peoples is more persuasive than coercive and likely to be associated with conspicuous giving. The good hunter will probably distribute more than he receives, but in groups which enjoy sufficient production to allow the development of a permanent advantage in favor of a few members, conspicuous giving may bring prestige to the leader who receives more than he redistributes. Giving by the leader may then reflect a permanent advantage which can become his instrument for coercing his fellows.

Under exceptional environmental conditions such as those enjoyed by the Haida, even hunting or fishing people may lead a relatively sedentary life. More often, though, the practice of agriculture makes possible a more sedentary existence and a greater number of man-hours for non-food-producing activities. With the development of farming, the density of populations and the size of local groups increases.

In a recent comparative study of three different farming areas in contemporary Mexico, anthropologist Angel Palerm has demonstrated quantitatively some relations between farming limitations and population characteristics.[13] At Tajín, Vera Cruz, where a tropical slash-and-burn agriculture is still practiced, each family cultivates at least three and a half acres at a time; but because of the long periods of fallow necessary between plantings, each needs at least thirty acres in all. Settlements in this area are small, dispersed, and migratory. In the rainy but temperate climate of Eloxochitlán, which lies in the mountains of Puebla, farmers also practice slash-and-burn. Although here the average family plants six acres, the periods of fallow are much shorter and a family requires a minimum of sixteen acres in all — about half that at Tajín. Settlements here are small but stable. At Tecomatepec, in the state of Mexico, where irrigation is practiced in a temperate climate, plots are cultivated continuously without fallow periods and the minimum amount of land necessary to sustain each family is only about two acres. These are kept under continuous cultivation and yield two crops per year. This last, of course, is a much more thickly settled area. Judging from these statistics of Palerm's about sizes of farms, the number of families per square mile (figured for an area in which half to all the land was cultivable) might vary from ten to twenty families under tropical slash-and-burn conditions, twenty to forty families under temperate slash-and-burn conditions, and one hundred and fifty to three hundred families under irrigation agriculture.

Given a favorable environment and intensive farming, the potential non-agricultural labor supply — either seasonal or permanent — may be considerable. Sylvanus G. Morley's calculations of the non-agricultural labor potential of present-day and ancient Maya Indians [14] can help in estimating what such potentials are for primitive farmers in general. According to Morley, the modern Maya Indian farmer, to support an average-sized family of five, works at food production only a little more than half the working hours available during the year. Since even in that time the modern Mayan produces a surplus enabling him to buy cloth and other goods — needs the ancient Mayan did not have — Morley calculated that the ancient man might have had as much as nine to ten months in each year to devote to non-food-producing activities. But the food production of the ancient Mayas — due possibly to local soil conditions — may have been unusually large in terms of the amount of labor rather than the amount of land which it required. Allowing for environmental differences and for the performance of farm and household chores not directly connected with food production, the labor of one adult male for a four- or five-month period would probably be a conservative estimate of the disguised unemployment (non-agricultural labor potential) of a family of five among many modern and ancient primitive farmers. If this estimate of disguised unemployment is multiplied by the number of average family farms which might be contained in a square mile of farm land under various farming conditions, it is possible to get some idea of the number of surplus man-days of work available under these conditions during a single year. Where slash-and-burn agriculture was practiced and settlements were sparse and migratory, one to two hundred thousand man-days of expendable labor would have been available within a five-mile radius of a population center. The same space in an irrigated area would have yielded two to four million man-days of labor expendable for other than mere subsistence activities. When coercive rather than persuasive leadership was combined with a large farm population, new forms of conspicuous consumption were made possible, forms peculiar to the highest development of the closed society. The concentration of the population need not always be crucial if the area under control is big enough to include large numbers of people. Some idea of how persuasive leadership became coercive may be obtained by comparing aboriginal New World farmers in three different agricultural areas: the Amazon, the Caribbean, and the highlands of South America.

The tropical Amazon basin was a region of fairly primitive farmers, some of whom, like the Siriono, were actually more dependent on hunting than on agriculture.[15] They were slash and burn agriculturists who moved at regular intervals within a fairly definite area. Composed of several large families, their semisedentary villages sometimes had as many as six hundred inhabitants. Partly as a result of differences in natural resources and partly as a result of random tolerance, some villages specialized in producing such articles as bows, arrows, pottery, flutes, and necklaces, and carried on an informal barter with other villages. Most Amazonians had a more secure food supply than did the primitive hunters who lived south of them in Patagonia. They had time to produce a greater variety of artifacts and to enjoy a more extensive ceremonial and social life than the hunters.

Warfare was an important pastime and a major way of achieving prestige. Amazonian chiefs were usually more persuasive than coercive, and if they were not "generous" men they would lose their following. Among the Tapirapé, all village, ceremonial, and household heads were shamans as well as secular leaders, and possessions accumulated as payment for successful cures were redistributed at annual ceremonies. The Tenetehara collectively tilled large plots which were nominally the property of the head of the family, in addition to their own individual gardens. The head of the family lived off the produce of these communal plots on which he also worked, and he was responsible for the distribution of the surplus. Presumably, where special fields were collectively cultivated to provide food surpluses for ceremonies, disposing of the surplus was supervised by the chief. In many tribes, chiefs assigned work in the fields, organized collective work parties, led war parties, and arranged feasts and ceremonies.

Sometimes ceremonies were attended by several villages which reciprocated in extending each other invitations. Among the Carajá these ceremonial units composed of several villages formed a kind of insurance group which aided a member village in time of crop failure. Although many chiefs in this region obviously performed their organizational and redistributive chores largely as prestigeful persons sensitive to majority opinion, some apparently had an advantage in goods not equally redistributed. Some chiefs clearly derived an advantage in food supplies over and above what they redistributed. Manasí villagers, for example, tilled two large fields for their chief and gave him a share of all game and fish. He kept order in the community by personally thrashing those who disobeyed him or by assigning a subordinate to do so. Houses of important shamans or priests were built by the community and served as assembly halls. Chieftainship was apparently hereditary. A Bauré chief was supposedly provided with everything he needed. If he wanted to get rid of somebody, his wish was complied with immediately. Tacanan tribesmen are also said to have been obliged to work for their chiefs.

Agriculture must have been more productive in some parts of the Caribbean and the areas bordering upon it, for communities were apparently larger there than in the Amazon. Although the reasons for this are not entirely understood, they must have been largely environmental, for the agriculture in most of this area used the same slash-and-burn technology as in the Amazon basin.

The Taino, an Arawak tribe of special interest because of their extensive irrigation, inhabited the southwestern part of Hispaniola.[16] Their settlements were large — perhaps three thousands inhabitants. The island of Hispaniola was divided by the Taino into five provinces, each with its own chief. Under each chief of province were some thirty subchiefs who controlled local districts made up of one or more villages, each governed by a headman. Chiefs, subchiefs, and village headmen administered the villages in which they lived; they organized the daily work routine and the storage and distribution of food supplies. They also were leaders of ceremonial and social affairs and of public worship. Since they could order the death of their subjects, they had achieved considerable coercive authority. Chiefs and subchiefs also had the power to draft the manpower of subordinate villages for agricultural labor and military service. This power, however, apparently varied with the personal influence of the particular chiefs and subchiefs. Chiefs were entitled to wear special dress and ornaments and to live in special dwellings built along a rectanglar ball court. On land they were carried about in a litter and on the water in canoes large enough to hold as many as seventy or eighty men.

Beneath the chiefs was a social class apparently regarded as a kind of nobility, the members of which acted as the chief's assistants. They supervised communal labor and had certain judicial functions. The provincial, district, and petty village chiefs controlled the storage of supplies produced by the draft labor of the commoners, and owned their own storehouses. After providing for the maintenance of their own households, surpluses were probably redistributed to support the "nobility" and the local ceremonial life.

The Maya Indians of the Yucatán Peninsula [17] provide an example of sociopolitical organization somewhat comparable to that of the Taino of Hispaniola. Yucatán was also divided into provinces directed by hereditary rulers under whom town and village chiefs served. The provincial rulers appointed these chiefs from a class of hereditary nobility, and both rulers and chiefs were supported by commoners who tilled their fields, constructed their houses, and served as their domestic servants. If men came back from a hunt with meat or fish, the local chief always got a share. In addition, the ruler received a "light" tribute of corn, beans, and cotton cloth from each village and town in his province, and one of the chief's duties was to see that his community paid its tribute when due. Both the rulers and chiefs were attended with great ceremony by many people wherever they went. Rulers were carried in litters followed by large retinues of attendants, and chiefs were protected from the sun by fans of bright-colored feathers. Among the duties of the chiefs was to see that the people kept their houses in good repair and planted and harvested their crops when the priests decided that the time was propitious. They also commanded soldiers in war, performed judicial duties, and presided over the local council of elders. Rulers and chiefs governed through their overseer assistants, who were also of the nobility but dealt more directly with the people. Warfare between towns of different provinces was carried on to get slaves and sacrificial victims as well as for glory.

The puzzling thing about the Mayas has always been their crude slash-and-burn agriculture, necessarily shifting, and probably requiring the dispersal of much of the population in scattered hamlets. Apparently the soil yielded harvests sufficiently rewarding in terms of man-hours, though not necessarily high in terms of land area, to make a considerable labor force available at slack periods in the farm cycle. At periods of peak labor load, however, there was not even time for warfare, a fact which finally made easier Spanish conquest of the peninsula.

We may now consider some of the motivational and limitative causes which facilitate change from persuasive to coercive control in the closed society. In the simple farming community, the leader is persuasive, but his powers of persuasion depend considerably upon public opinion and his reputation for generosity. Persuasion suffices to elicit the collective labor of the group on lands nominally the chief's to produce a surplus which is distributed during festivities and as aid to needy individuals. But when under a coercive political structure, the produce of the collective work done on the chief's land is not equally redistributed to the workers. Their work becomes more like an obligatory labor tax rather than a voluntary work party. Formal "generosity" is no longer a necessary persuasive device for controlling the labor supply.

Where leadership is persuasive, the people have a powerful control over the chief's distribution of the surplus, for they have allocated to him the right to redistribute part of the product of their own labor. Any flagrant display of conspicuous ownership by the chief which results, to his advantage, in marked inequalities of redistribution, may cause him to lose followers. Conspicuous giving is required of him if he is to perpetuate his prestigeful position as distributor of group surpluses. Where environment or technology leads to considerable "disguised" unemployment, however, either in a fairly concentrated farming population or in a fairly dispersed population like that of the Mayas with its long seasonal periods of unemployment, the potential supply of food and labor at the chief's disposal may become exceedingly great. If this happens, inequalities in the redistribution of food may increase without appreciably curtailing the expectations of the group at large, for in the relatively unspecialized society with its limited range of both perishable and durable goods, consumption expectations are more readily saturated. Some of the produce may now be used not only to support the chief's household, but also the families of favored kinsmen. Thus a hereditary class of nobility may develop, which is dependent on the food produced by commoners. Such a group will have a vested interest in preserving their chief's control over his unequal redistribution of corvée-produced food. They can become, in effect, the chief's coercive arm, by means of which he can make collective labor an obligation of the group and simultaneously free himself of the old reciprocal obligation to give conspicuously.

Another kind of conspicuous consumption can take the place of conspicuous giving among the ruling members of a coercive, closed society. This form Thorstein Veblen called "conspicuous leisure," which, in effect, is a conspicuous consumption of labor. Even among simple farmers a symbol of a chief's status may be the number of his wives, whose economic activities may provide him with both leisure and services. Chiefs, as among the Taino, may wear special ornaments and other insignia of rank and live in bigger houses, but there conspicuous ownership is limited by the monotony of perishable and durable goods in an unspecialized society. The conspicuous consumption of labor takes the form of servants, litter bearers, and attendants. The man with prestige enhances his standing by using the unspecialized manual labor of others in a great variety of trivial services.

The Inca civilization [18] mentioned previously with regard to capital formation is a remarkable example of the extent to which the closed society was able to develop through coercive control of unspecialized labor. Moreover, it probably illustrates better than any other "ancient" civilization, past or present, the centralization of the gathering, storing, and redistribution of goods in societies where writing and accounting are either rudimentary or non-existent. Such "centricity" [19] simplifies the redistribution of goods in all closed societies. In the small primitive community, centricity takes the fairly direct and simple form of collection and redistribution through the local chief, as has been shown. But in Inca society centricity was attempted from modern Chile in the south to modern Ecuador in the north. This great empire was divided into quarters, each of which was subdivided into several provinces corresponding to the native states and tribal areas which the Inca found in the various regions they conquered. Each province included two or three sections containing not more than ten thousand taxpayers in each. These sections were further subdivided into groups of five thousand, one thousand, five hundred, and one hundred taxpayers. At the top of this hierarchy was the emperor, with his many wives and children and his court circle of kinsmen who comprised the cream of Inca nobility and from which he picked his top administrators.

With the empire organized in this chain of command, labor and production resources could readily be controlled. In each community the largest share of farm land was divided among the commoners and worked by them for their own subsistence. Collectively, the commoners also worked special plots for the support of the state, the church, and the curacas. All land was nominally the property of the emperor, and the people were deemed to have only rights of use to their fields. Community lands were reassigned annually, and each family received a plot proportionate to its size, presumably only large enough to insure subsistence. The produce from the state lands was stored in local granaries throughout the empire and was used to feed the army and the corvée or draft labor which built the state buildings, roads, and irrigation works and worked in the state mines. All able-bodied men were eligible for draft labor, and although the annual amount was not fixed, enough men were always left at home to tend the fields. The centricity of this system greatly facilitated the calculation and collection of taxes and made possible the organization of corvée labor parties for any job anywhere in the empire. Because of the wide distribution of state granaries it was possible to depend on local labor and local food reserves for most projects. Yet, if they so desired, the Inca could deploy their corvée labor or their armies over an enormous area, a remarkable organizational accomplishment considering that these people had no writing and only a tally system of accounting known as the *quipu*. Instead of developing an elaborate accounting system which might have made it possible to leave the tax and labor organizations more flexible and redistribution easier, the Inca apparently tried to accomplish the same result through a pyramidal command organization.

Although goods were not equally redistributed in the Inca empire, the common people reaped many rewards and satisfactions. The state stores were distributed in time of famines and disasters and were used to support widows, old people, and the infirm. When the storehouses grew too full, surpluses were doled out among the commoners in such a way that products of different provinces and climates were interchanged. Wool from government herds was distributed to all families, and copper was apparently in general use. Irrigation works built with draft labor fed from state stores benefited commoner and nobleman alike. Thus it might be argued that centricity and negative control afforded the common people a great measure of security. In exchange, they gave the central authority the power to enforce the means of assuring this security, no matter what conflicting felt needs had to be suppressed in the bargain.

The redistribution of goods within the empire was to the nobility's advantage; it was an unequal redistribution. By means of it the higher nobles were freed from direct participation in the quest for food and became administrative specialists. But they enjoyed many additional privileges — more wives, fine cloth, and gold and silver ornaments. In short, the emperor and the nobility indulged in a certain amount of conspicuous ownership, largely of luxury goods produced by full-time craftsmen supported by the state. Metal workers, tapestry weavers, and so on, specially chosen for their skill, were maintained from the state food supplies in order to manufacture objects for the emperor, who distributed them as gifts and rewards to his nobility. According to one student of the Inca, the lesser nobility also financed craftsmen and specialists and made presents to the emperor of their articles of production.[20] Perhaps the emperor in turn redistributed many of these gifts.

Leisure and labor were also consumed conspicuously by the controlling class. The emperor, for example, had serving women just to hold his plates while he ate; he traveled in a litter accompanied by a great entourage of attendants and servants. Bravery in combat was also a means of acquiring prestige in Inca society, just as it so often was even in simple farming societies. Not only were nobles given special rewards for bravery, but commoners might be raised into the lower nobility or given extra wives for valor.

One of the most interesting facets of Inca redistribution was the support of the full-time specialists who produced merchandise for the nobility. Regional specialization in the production of foods and handicrafts, and bartering among commoners at organized markets, existed within the Inca empire — apparently on a much larger scale than among such simple farmers as those of the Amazon basin. But the regional specialization was still within households consisting of the surplus manufacture and production of family labor dedicated primarily to subsistence farming.

The growth of specialization is the growth of the open society and is the subject of the following chapters. Despite the appearance of some full-time specialists among the Inca, their society was far more closed than open. Inca society, with its low degree of probable knowledge, relied on the control of great quantities of undifferentiated labor, as did most other early or primitive civilizations. Through centricity of redistribution, labor was controlled so as to make its employment and production as fixed and predictable as possible. Instead of favoring the specialization of labor, this kind of redistribution restricted it. The full-time specialists were supported only to meet the felt needs of a very limited market — the favored class. The specialists constituted, in a sense, conspicuous consumption of labor, for they produced the household articles which every commoner made for himself but which the nobility no longer produced once leisure and service became a privilege of rank and power.

Specialization did not expand rapidly in the closed society. Instead of gaining new controls through the division of labor, people of the closed society gained a sense of predictability over their environment by controlling human behavior at an undifferentiated level. In the closed society, security against old age and disaster and the construction of irrigation projects to reduce the uncertainties of dry farming were the product of coercive negative controls. Development depended on the knowledge and experience of a few rather than upon the comparison and synthesis of the varied experiences of many. In the closed society the limitations were enormous on man's greatest resource — the combined cognitive potential of men interacting to discuss, question, observe, and create.

VII

Conspicuous Ownership and the Opening of Society

In the last chapter conspicuous giving was related to the lack of variety in durable goods, a limitation of closed societies where the division of labor is rudimentary. This chapter deals with the growth of "acquisitiveness," which parallels the increasing abundance and variety of durable goods made available by the division of labor. The strictures of invidious sanction weaken as the opportunities to possess goods spread within a population. Men become more interested in emulating each other's consumption habits than in pressing for redistribution. As invidious emulation takes precedence over invidious sanction, the importance of conspicuous ownership grows, while that of conspicious giving decreases.

Conspicuous ownership never completely replaces conspicuous giving. In our society there are wealthy philanthropists who draw attention to themselves by means of conspicuous gifts for the public welfare, and many well known entertainers make a conspicuous display of their support to charities. At the opposite end of the social scale, leaders of slum gangs operate very much like the persuasive leaders of primitive groups. In his study of the Norton Street Gang, William Foote Whyte found that the leader is much more constant in meeting the demands of reciprocal aid than other members are — one reason why the rest feel dependent upon him. By means of his social contacts outside the gang the leader becomes a distributor of favors within it. When the gang's support is requested for local political reasons, the leader is directly rewarded. This puts him in a position where he can consistently give his followers more than he receives from them. They repay him by acknowledging his leadership.[1]

Though conspicuous giving never disappears, conspicuous ownership tends to predominate in societies where many kinds of goods are produced through the division of labor. As we shall see in Part III, a sudden increase in consumption expectations leads to competitive buying. Neighbors begin to emulate each other in buying new stoves, refrigerators, and indoor plumbing. In our own society we have long called this process keeping up with the Joneses, and we have given unique expression to it in our ownership of big, chromium-plated automobiles.

In the small, highly personal society where every man knows his neighbors and where nearly all daily associations are with persons who know each other well, there is no need to display wealth. When disparities exist in such a society the affluent person prefers to hide them rather than arouse jealousy. In the specialized, urbanized society, relations among people are more casual. Many daily meetings are with strangers or persons who see each other infrequently, and symbols of status and wealth gain importance. The man who drives a new Cadillac into a gas station is likely to receive more deference and service from the attendants than one who drives an older, cheaper car — unless the latter is a well-known customer. In some countries, anyone with a car is treated deferentially. In Colombia, for example, an automobile owner who meets people in service, or lower-class, occupations is automatically addressed as "Doctor," the local term of respect.

In discussing the social limitations affecting the change from conspicuous giving to conspicuous ownership, I shall deal with peasant or rural rather than urban society. In their early discussions of the division of labor in pin and carriage factories, respectively, Adam Smith and Karl Marx were concerned with intra-industrial specialization in manufacturing. Although Adam Smith felt that "The man whose whole life is spent in performing a few simple operations . . . becomes as stupid and ignorant as it is possible for a human creature to become," he was generally optimistic about the division of labor in society.[2] As he saw it, the "consequence of the division of labour . . . in a well-governed society" is "universal opulence" which "extends itself to the lowest ranks of the people." The division of labor creates this opulence first by improving the dexterity of the workman, second "by saving the time commonly lost in passing from one sort of work to another," and third by applying "proper machinery." As a result, the working force of a society has a greater quantity of goods to exchange than if each man worked singly.

Marx, the great pessimist, carried Adam Smith's reservations to their logical extreme when he claimed that the division of labor in manufacture was but a "refined and civilized method of exploitation." To become rich, the capitalist makes each of his laborers "poor in individual productive powers" and converts each "into a crippled monstrosity." [3] It would seem that history has justified the optimism of Adam Smith more than Marxian pessimism.

To a certain extent, Adam Smith also grasped the importance of specialization for the growth of culture capital. Comparing differences among members of human society to differences among members of animal species, he wrote: "The strength of the mastiff is not in the least supported either by the swiftness of the greyhound, or by the sagacity of the spaniel," because "for want of the power . . . to barter and exchange, . . . the effects of those different geniuses and talents . . . do not in the least contribute to the better accommodation and convenience of the species." Before discussing the interaction between the desire for prestige and specialization, I shall briefly compare the famous explanations of the division of labor in society by Emile Durkheim and by Adam Smith.

Emile Durkheim and Adam Smith

Durkheim began his causal analysis of *The Division of Labor in Society* (1893)[4] by comparing the structure of society to the structure of an organism in which the various parts or operations perform functions or services for the whole. Just as the function of lungs and respiration, for example, are to introduce "necessary gases into the tissues of an animal," so the function of the division of labor is to create solidarity in the society. In a simple society with no marked division of labor this function is unnecessary, because solidarity is achieved through sameness: all the members are united by common beliefs, sentiments, and experiences. In the simple societies, however, breaking away of segments is more common and takes place more readily, since the economy is not so disrupted by the losses and gains of members. The higher societies, marked by a greater division of labor, are made up of many differentiated and mutually interdependent parts, so that new elements cannot readily be added or old ones taken away without altering relations on a wide scale and upsetting the social equilibrium. Thus, the complex society is bound together by specialized and mutually interdependent parts rather than by the homogeneity of its segments. Turning the analogy around, this is very much like saying that the greater structural complexity of more developed organisms functions to hold them together. The result of Durkheim's functional analysis is not an explanation of social phenomena but a spurious description framed in terms of an organismic analogy.

Durkheim asked what it was that made the division of labor increase, and because his causal analysis was secondary to his functional one, he got into trouble immediately. Since the function of the division of labor is to hold society together, he reasoned that it could not have preceded the existence of a society large enough to need its binding function. Although he admitted that the division of labor itself increases the concentration of populations, he dismissed this as unimportant: to uphold his organismic analogy the division of labor must be the derived fact. What, then, he was led to wonder, are the conditions which activate the division? He dismissed what he considered *the* psychological explanation — man's unceasing desire to increase his happiness — because such an explanation would not conform with his analogy. Since the parts of an organism have no cognitive ability to determine their functions through deliberate action, the cognitive abilities of individual men are not to be given causal weight in explaining social phenomena. Cells do not realign themselves into higher forms out of a conscious desire to progress toward a more ideal state. The explanation of the division of labor must therefore be "sociological," not "psychological," because the latter implies cognitive action.

The tendency of societies to become greater in volume and density results, according to Durkheim, in greater concentrations of population, a fact which not merely permits the division of labor but actually necessitates it by making more acute a struggle for existence in which the greatest conflict is between like functions. While a judge and a businessman, for example, are not in direct competition, a brewer and a winegrower are. Among competitors satisfying the same needs, the weaker must either disappear or transform their functions. If they do the latter, the result is more specialization, and thus the process of specialization becomes more rapid as the competitive struggle for existence becomes more acute.

Durkheim then asked how the new functions resulting from the transformation of weaker competitors are able to survive. The individual members of society, he reckoned, must feel a need for these new things, and thus he returned to the problem he began with. Now he attributed these felt needs for new things to the struggle for existence because the latter, he reasoned, depletes the forces of the human body and results in greater fatigue. To restore organic equilibrium, a more abundant sustenance is necessary. Moreover, cerebral life develops as competition becomes keener, and as the brain thus becomes more refined it needs more complex stimulants. In this fashion the depletion of forces produced by the struggle for existence results mechanically in needs for the new functions which have also resulted from the struggle.

But, said Durkheim, the aptitude alone would not provoke the desire. Then why *does* man turn to these new enjoyments? To be consistent with a purely sociological explanation based on the organismic analogy, the needs should not be consciously felt. What then impels a person to taste new pleasures? At this point Durkheim fell back on a psychological explanation which he called "the attraction of novelty." This is a kind of instinct which drives men to try the new things created by the struggle for existence and which their systems unconsciously crave as a result of fatigue produced by the struggle. Because of its non-cognitive nature, this psychological characteristic does not conflict with the organismic analogy, and so Durkheim found no difficulty in including it in his "sociological" explanation. By employing an automatic psychological factor as an efficient cause, he avoided cognition. But cognition is implicit in a part of his arguments that is glossed over — the creative ability of the individual cells of society to transform their functions in time to survive the competitive struggle. In fact, the very struggle he discussed is based on an organic analogy of another order from that with which he began — a struggle among individual forms of life rather than a system of functioning parts within a single organism.

Ingenious as it is, Durkheim's explanation of the division of labor is inadequate. In his desire to avoid an explanation implying that man consciously acts to create his behavior patterns in anticipation of all the consequences of those acts, Durkheim went too far. He warped his causal explanation to fit the weft of an analogy and in so doing left out of his explanation the ingredient most peculiar to cultural causality — symbolic cognition.

Over a century before Durkheim, in *The Wealth of Nations* (1776), Adam Smith gave a much more acceptable explanation of the division of labor. He did not use an organismic analogy; on the contrary, he dealt with man in very anthropomorphous fashion, for his model was Mr. Anthropos himself.

Motivated by "self-love" and a natural "propensity" to "truck, barter, and exchange," Adam Smith's man pools his special talents with those of his fellows to provide himself with "all the necessaries of life which he has occasion for." For when a man is certain of exchanging those products of his labor which exceed his own consumption needs for the surplus of other men's labor, he is thereby encouraged "to apply himself to a particular occupation, and to cultivate and bring to perfection whatever talent or genius he may possess for that particular species of business." The certainty of exchanging products is related to "the extent of the market," which thereby limits the extent of the division of labor. When the likelihood of exchange is small, one is not encouraged "to dedicate himself entirely to one employment." The extent of the market was dependent initially on the development of "water carriage" along sea coasts and navigable rivers. As exchange became more important, the older bartering process grew increasingly inconvenient. Metals, because they were durable and could be divided into convenient units, became the common medium of exchange.

All three kinds of causes are either stated or implied in this explanation of the division of labor. Motivation is explicit, as are such limiting factors as market size, transportation, and the use of money. Cognition is implied in the capacity to barter and to develop latent talents.

The principal weakness in Adam Smith's explanation is the quality of the motivation: "self-love" is too general and the "propensity to truck, barter, and exchange" too specific. But he was aware of the problem; he wrote: "Whether this propensity be one of those original principles in human nature, of which no further account can be given; or whether, as seems more probable, it be the necessary consequence of the faculties of reason and speech, it belongs not to our present subject to enquire." Of one thing he was sure: "It is common to all men, and to be found in no other race of animals."

Against the picture of Economic Man which grew out of Adam Smith's few brushstrokes, anthropologist Bronislaw Malinowski strongly rebelled. In 1922 he wrote that the "notion . . . of the Primitive Economic Man . . . must be exploded, once and forever." [5] To Malinowski this "Primitive Economic Man" was "an imaginary . . . savage, prompted in all his actions by a rationalistic conception of self-interest, and achieving his aims directly and with the minimum of effort." He then showed that the Trobriand Islanders, among whom he had lived, "are not directed towards the satisfaction of present wants, or to the direct achievement of utilitarian purposes . . . work is not carried out on the principle of the least effort. On the contrary, much time and energy is spent on wholly unnecessary effort . . . from a utilitarian point of view." Trobrianders produce more food than they need in order to give it away and to win distinction as excellent gardeners.

Although objecting to the "misconception" that the "passion of acquiring . . . is the fundamental and most primitive element in man's attitude to wealth," Malinowski ascribed to man a "natural acquisitive tendency." He believed, however, that social convention overrides this tendency among primitive peoples, for the wealthy Trobriander is conventionally a generous man who accumulates in order to give away.

Most modern economists do not hold that man is "utilitarian," for they are aware that there is no absolute measure of utility. They now speak of the maximization of satisfactions, and thus leave room for social conventions that reward generosity as well as those that reward acquisitiveness. This reduces the problems stemming from Adam Smith's indecision.

The one objection to the Primitive Economic Man concept which Malinowski did not pursue all the way is his objection to self-interest. Apparently satisfied that he had contradicted it by showing that acquisitiveness is not universal, he then supported the idea by showing how Trobrianders derive status satisfaction through non-utilitarian gardening and giving away wealth. He failed to note that self-interest is obviously still present as prestige-seeking, of which acquisitiveness may be only one expression.

Since prestige motivation can take either the giving or the acquisitive form, it is obviously not a sufficient cause of either one. Having looked at the limiting causes of conspicuous giving in the preceding chapter, let us turn now to the causes of conspicuous ownership.

Transportation

Even in the Old World, early civilizations followed the patterns of closedness.[6] Irrigation and other public works were constructed by labor parties of drafted commoners. Directly by means of a harvest tax or indirectly by means of a labor tax, grain produced by the commoners was stored by the central authorities to be redistributed through support of corvée labor on public works, through support of a limited number of full-time specialists producing for a privileged class, and through giving food to the public in emergencies. But the Old World had certain environmental advantages over the New which led to the early and rapid development of specialization. The absence of these advantages in the New World had greatly restricted the opening of society there by the time of the conquest. These New World limitations demonstrate very well the importance which Adam Smith so correctly gave to transportation and particularly "water carriage" for "the extent of the market." Because of these limitations, the New World was foredoomed to conquest by the Old, for it could never have overtaken the Old in time to have discovered and conquered it first.[7]

Transportation in the New World was extremely labor-intensive as compared to that in the Old. The dog and the llama were the only New World draft animals, and although some believe the sail was being used in the Caribbean in aboriginal times, the data are inconclusive. Even if the sail had been invented in the New World, the conditions were not highly propitious for its rapid development as a means of commercial transportation. The early civilizations of the Old World were admirably situated around inland waterways in a temperate region where seafaring provided an invaluable boon to commerce. There the sailing ship was in use six thousand years ago. The aboriginal civilizations of America, however, were stretched across tropical latitudes along a mountain chain connecting two continents. Even today there is no continuous land transportation between Central America and northern South America. In much of this area, air transport has played a vital role in the development of modern commerce. The sailing ship might some day have become a valuable aid to commerce in the Caribbean and in the Gulf of Mexico, especially if intensive farming had ever developed in the Mississippi Valley, but much of the best land in this latter region would have required cultivation with the plow, and plowing also failed to develop in the New World, for lack of suitable draft animals.

Facilitation of transport through the domestication of animals and the use of the sail were vital to the development of commerce and specialization in the Old World. As noted previously, specialization of production began on a regional basis, primarily as a consequence of two factors: sufficient food production to permit periods of non-food-producing activity, and regional differences in natural resources. Farmers or even well-fed hunters with enough time on their hands between periods of peak labor load can manufacture household items in excess of their own needs. If the product is affected by local resources which make it seem superior or in some way more desirable to neighboring people than a product of their own, there is a basis for trade so long as transportation difficulties are not great enough to discourage it. This is just as true of differences in food production as of differences in manufactured goods.

The way in which animal- and wind-power facilitate transportation can be illustrated by computing the proportion of a grain cargo consumed in transit under different methods of transport. Suppose a man is the beast of burden and he carries an eighty-five-pound sack of corn over Andean or Sierra Madre mountain trails for about two hundred miles. If he averages twenty miles a day, he will cover the distance in ten days; but during that time he will have consumed one fourth the cargo or the equivalent. If, however, four men are outfitted with a pack train of twenty-five burros and sent over the same mountain trail with sixty-five hundred pounds of corn, they can make the trip in five days; since the burros graze along the trail at no expense, the cost of the trip in food consumption amounts to only 1/150 of the cargo. The beast of burden, especially when it can forage for itself, permits a great reduction in the amount of food energy consumed in transportation. Although the Incas built highways to facilitate communications and troop movements within their empire, they were greatly handicapped by the labor-intensive quality of their transportation, for the llama is a sorry beast of burden. The Aztecs of Mexico were not even so fortunate as to possess llamas. Based largely on manpower, New World transportation was hardly of a kind to stimulate commerce among primitive food producers, for trade would mean the direct consumption of a large part of their annual food supply. This fact becomes even more apparent when labor-intensive transport is compared with the sailing ship.

Professor Fred Cottrell has estimated that an Egyptian sailing ship had a cargo capacity of 150 tons and a crew of thirty-five to forty men.[8] These ships could have gone a distance equivalent to the circumference of the earth in 112 days and at a cost of only 1/33 of a cargo of grain. A Roman sailing ship, according to Cottrell, had a cargo capacity of 250 tons and a crew of only ten or twelve men. It could have gone the same distance with the same cargo in about the same time as the Egyptian ship, but at a cost of only 1/222 of a cargo. The use of the sailing ship greatly increased the distance over which trade was economically feasible and consequently the diversity of products that could be exchanged. As exchange and commerce increased so did the intensification of inter- and intra-regional specialization. Standards of weight, measure, and value became increasingly necessary, and as money came into common use, full-time specialization was freed from dependence on a highly centralized form of redistribution. The emancipation of the specialist, owing to the use of money, from a centralized dependency on food surpluses produced by undifferentiated labor was an important step in the development of the open society, a step not taken in the New World before conquest.

Conspicuous Ownership and the Expansion of Labor Reciprocities

Once the specialist could exchange his services or merchandise for money, it became easier for him to separate commercial from social reciprocities. Take, for example, the case of a specialist among the East African Hehe, a pre-money society with some incipient specialization. If a tribesman required a spear, a stool, or a pot, he went to the appropriate artisan, taking twice the amount of raw material required, and during the manufacture of the product he either assisted the artisan or cultivated his fields.[9] Thus unskilled labor was exchanged for the product of specialized skill. The "profit" to the artisan lay in the accumulation of raw materials from which he made gifts for the chief, who might respond with gifts of cattle. In this case political control had obviously become sufficiently centralized for the surplus production controlled by the chief to be redistributed to support a somewhat cumbersome system of diversification of labor.

Full-time specialists among the Inca were the product of a stronger and more centralized system of redistribution than that of the Hehe. But it is most unlikely that anything approaching our high degree of labor diversification would have been possible without the full development of a money economy. The laborer or craftsman who is paid in money is free to choose his own reward at his own convenience. The development of his special skills is not hampered by direct exchanges between primary producers or by direct exchanges of skilled for unskilled labor. Nor is the diversification of labor necessarily restricted by a small number of consumers who are privileged to occupy a controlling position in a stratified society with a highly centralized system of redistribution.

Two further developments are made probable by the emancipation of the specialist. First, each man has a much greater chance of achieving prestige and status through the development of his own special skills and talents. Second, as a greater variety of durable goods are produced and become available for consumption, conspicuous ownership can take precedence over conspicuous giving as a means of gaining prestige. An illustration of these changes can be found today in the modification of rural labor patterns that accompanies commercialization and the use of money.

This change did not come about easily, even in the development of Western commerce. Considerable resistance arose against the idea of gain, particularly in the Church; capitalists and moneylenders were very nearly social outcasts. Pirenne relates an amusing anecdote in the life of St. Gerald of Aurillac (tenth century) which suggests something of the moral conflict induced by the rise of commerce in medieval Europe. Returning from a pilgrimage to Rome, where during his stay he had bought a pallium, he was complimented by Venetian merchants on his excellent bargain, for they assured him it would have cost much more in Constantinople. "Gerald, reproaching himself for having defrauded the vendor, hastened to forward him the difference, considering that he could not take advantage of it without falling into the sin of avarice." [10] Even as late as the thirteenth century, St. Thomas Aquinas wrote: "He . . . who derives great advantage from something received from another, may of his own accord pay the seller something in addition. This is a matter of honor." [11]

The spirit of capitalism, however, was certainly taking root in medieval times, and St. Godric of Finchale, who lived and prospered in the early twelfth century, is an excellent example of how strongly older social values were conflicting with the new.[12] The son of a poor peasant, Godric began his business career as a beachcomber, selling goods washed ashore from wrecked ships. Next he became a peddler and finally a professional merchant who traded along the English, Scotch, and Danish coasts, buying goods cheap and selling them for large profits where they were scarce. Although he transported his goods in sailing ships, he negotiated much as the independent truckers do today in many parts of Latin America where roads are joining inland markets together. But once he became wealthy, Godric gave away all his wealth to the poor and became a monk. Conspicuous giving won out in the end.

Though the medieval attitude toward gain has often been ascribed to the Roman Catholic Church's influence and domination, it might as easily be argued that the Church merely voiced the sentiment of the times. The opening of Western society took place slowly, and older attitudes of conspicuous giving did not give way easily to the new. For one thing, there were many impediments to commerce that had to be gradually overcome, impediments that do not exist today when commerce, full-blown, comes to an underdeveloped area. Vehicles for transportation were crude, and money was limited in circulation and importance. Business transactions took place almost entirely in local markets, and the coin in use was restricted to local districts. A king or emperor gave coinage rights to individual lords who found it to their advantage to debase their own coin. The prevalence of counterfeiting added to the confusion. Although credit facilities were rudimentary, usury was a great problem by the twelfth century, and loans were sought mainly in emergencies. The major impetus to commerce in the medieval period was export trade rather than local trade, and, not surprisingly, an export trade primarily of luxury goods. Spices, raisins, perfumes, dyes, and silks were being imported into Europe by the thirteenth century; woolen cloth was the principal export.[13]

The importance of a luxury export trade in early medieval times is again a reflection of the rudimentary nature of the commerce. The fact that the market was still largely restricted to a privileged class reflects the transition from closed to open society that was coming about. Trade goods used by the common people were too heavy and too inexpensive to justify costly long-distance shipments. The same was true of the "ancient" civilizations. Even the commerce carried on by the Aztec pochetca traders was largely in such things as jade and the colored feathers to be made into robes for the nobility.[14]

Perhaps we shall never reconstruct the precise steps by which common men and the peasantry eventually became involved in the expansion of commerce and the consumption of greater and greater varieties of manufactured goods. But it is not unlikely that their felt needs grew first along primarily utilitarian lines, as seems most usual among peasants today where I have had an opportunity to observe the process. I mentioned earlier (p. 79) a program sponsored by the Coffee Federation of Colombia to raise the living standards of coffee farmers. The federation stood ready to finance new houses, coffee hullers, and dryers and to pipe water to farmers' houses. The hullers, dryers, and water services were requested far more often than the houses. The same is true of northwest Mexico: such useful things as sewing machines, bicycles, and farm tools seem to take precedence over improved housing or conspicuous luxuries. Only families which have enjoyed some very unusual rise in their fortunes begin to spend on luxuries like expensive phonographs. More often a man will spend conspicuously on much more machinery than he needs, and as a result one often sees expensive tractors or trucks proudly parked beside tarpaper or mud and wattle shacks. The dominant consumption tendency seems to be utilitarian, until the incomes of enough families reach a point safely beyond subsistence requirements; then invidious emulation pushes consumption toward both luxuries and the kind of practical goods that serve as much for the display of ownership as for actual use.

Today, the consumption wants of peoples in retarded areas can increase much more rapidly than during the opening of Western society. Now that industrialization has taken such a prominent place in the world, the variety of goods that can become available in any one place depends mainly on a rise in local purchasing power. Where rapid rises are going on, it is possible today to observe the transition from old ways of life, which were directed toward giving, to new ways of life, directed more toward conspicuous ownership. What happened to the institution of reciprocal farm labor mentioned in Chapter V with reference to

Haitian cooperative labor practices shows how this transition works. After my interest in reciprocal labor had been aroused by my experiences in Haiti, I began gathering information about it in Colombia, Ecuador, Peru, and Chile, as my duties with the Point Four program provided opportunities. The results of my observations illustrate the change from conspicuous giving to conspicuous ownership and the change from personal to impersonal reciprocity, both of which accompany commercialization and the wide establishment of a money economy.[15]

As in many other parts of the world, reciprocal farm labor in South America takes two major forms which I shall call festive and exchange. When a host invites his neighbors to help him with some urgent farm chore and repays them with festivities, usually in the form of food and liquor, the labor is festive. Since he repays his guests for their labor with food and drink, the host is not strictly obligated to attend the work parties of his guests, although he probably will if they are given by kinsmen or close friends. In other words, in the festive form the host most often reciprocates with festivities rather than with labor. In the exchange form the host must reciprocate with labor, and there are usually no festivities. If a man cannot repay an exchange labor obligation when requested because of some extenuating circumstances such as sickness, he will send a replacement to whom he will owe the day's work instead. Exchange labor is a contractual arrangement in which sanctions to maintain attendance and work standards are strong; the man who does not fulfill his obligations will find no one willing to exchange with him. Exchange work parties usually have fewer than ten men, whereas festive work parties are generally much larger.

Both forms are used at times of peak labor load. The fact that such peaks are usually seasonal does not prevent reciprocal aid among neighbors, for the loads need not be simultaneous on neighboring farms if seasonal changes in the locale permit some flexibility in individual farming cycles. Even if two neighbors plant the same crops, they do not have to plant the same day or week. Yet once either man begins to plant, he must finish the job quickly if the crop is to be uniform and if weeds are not to grow back on part of the land while he prepares the rest.

In its pure form among subsistence farmers, festive labor requires conspicuous giving. The festive labor host most likely to get a large response to his invitation is a man known to be generous, a man who gives his guests lots of food and drink. The festive labor host who is entirely or almost entirely a subsistence farmer may produce a surplus of food as a result of his work parties which he cannot consume himself. This surplus, however, can be redistributed within the local group in the form of more festive work parties, which reinforce the donor's reputation for generosity and reinsure the success of future work parties and future food surpluses. By virtue of their confidence in his generosity, the workers allocate to the conspicuously-giving entrepreneur the right to entertain them with the fruits of their own labor.

Where surpluses are large enough to permit a permanent advantage to the upper classes, only a small part may be redistributed among the labor force. In such cases the host, as a member of the upper class, has acquired some control over the land and through it controls his labor force independently of his reputation for generosity. Workers attend the festive labor parties out of necessity in order to receive certain perquisites, such as the right to collect firewood in the landowner's forest, to graze livestock in his pastures, or to have use rights to a subsistence plot. As was true in feudal England [16] and is still true today in some haciendas in the highlands of Ecuador and Peru, the festivities accompanying a work party become merely a token of good will on the part of the lord or the owner of the hacienda, but the workers' attendance is compulsory. Conspicuous ownership and the conspicuous consumption of leisure and labor are in these cases the outgrowth of centricity and coercive control.

Throughout most of the parts of western South America that I visited, I found that festive labor had disappeared within the last decade or two; where it was still practiced it was fast losing ground. With its disappearance everywhere came the greater commercialization of agriculture and the greater use of money. But even where it was no longer practiced, people still remembered it and had the same strong negative opinions about it. They compared it unfavorably to wage labor because of the poor quality of the work, the high cost, and the difficulty of controlling the worker-guests. All three criticisms partly reflect a change in the form of prestige satisfaction from conspicuous giving to conspicuous ownership. Where the practice had disappeared or was disappearing, farmers were marketing more and more cash crops and were buying a great new variety of durable goods. Their increasing desires for consumption goods often resulted from the opening up of new communication and new transportation routes into once inaccessible areas.

Nothing suggested that the quality of work at festive labor parties had gone down in recent times; measured by cash-cropping standards, festive labor had always been uneconomical. Damage to crops during weeding or hoeing and unevenness of work in clearing, plowing, planting, weeding, and harvesting were apparently common enough even when the custom was popular. But in earlier days, when farmers were largely subsistence-oriented, their neighbors' good will and the enjoyment of the social occasion were more important than the quality of the work. Hosts were not worried by the fact that the workers came as guests and could not be scolded when their work was careless. As long as production was sufficient to insure the farmer his subsistence and provide him with enough surplus to meet next season's festive labor requirements and his own felt needs for a very limited number of manufactured goods, he was satisfied. Greater efficiency than this would only have conflicted with his social obligations as a conspicuous giver.

Moreover, the host of the festive work party was not so worried about relative "costs" before he began to produce more intensively for a money market. As a subsistence-oriented farmer, the host provided his guests with food produced on his own land, and he did not measure the cost of the labor in terms of the food consumed. He was glad to give if he could afford to, for his generosity as a festive work host was important to his prestige. But the farmer increased his production of a market crop, especially one like coffee, at the expense of his subsistence crops. Gradually he began to buy more of his food, and as he did so he became more conscious of its money value. The food necessary for a festive work party represented a cash outlay which could be directly compared with the cost of hired help from whom he could demand care and efficiency.

Today, wage labor has replaced festive nearly everywhere in western South America. The farmer produces for a market to get money to buy the increasing number of consumption goods available. Conspicuous giving has been largely replaced by conspicuous ownership, a different form of conspicuous consumption made more probable by the expanding diversity of consumption goods resulting from the division of labor. As long as his surplus was perishable food, the farmer could most easily satisfy his desire for social status through conspicuous giving. But when it became easier for him to convert his food surplus into a great variety of durable goods, he began to acquire prestige through the display of wealth he did not distribute — through conspicuous consumption in the form of ownership rather than of giving.

As an illustration, let us consider the influence of some recent changes on the Negro peasant farmers living along the Cayapas River of coastal Ecuador, a tropical region lying on the equator. Living scattered along both sides of the river, these people plant food crops of corn, manioc, and plantains. Change has come slowly to this part of the world and the Cayapas Indians who still inhabit the upper reaches of the river have managed to maintain their aboriginal way of life. About 1948 two fruit companies began fomenting the production of bananas among the Negro population. Previously a few bananas had been grown by each household, mainly as feed for pigs, but as the fruit companies began to buy them at good prices, they rapidly became a cash crop all along the river. This sudden boom in banana production was made possible only by the organizational efforts of the fruit companies. Regular purchasing trips were started, using shallow-draft boats which stopped at specified loading points along the river about twice a week. Two or three days before the arrival of a river boat, its schedule was announced by an employee of the banana companies who traveled the river in a fast motor launch, cutting his engine in front of each farm shack and village while he shouted the arrival date of the next boat. Farmers then loaded what bananas were ready for market on balsawood rafts or in canoes buoyed with balsa logs and floated them to the nearest loading points downstream. Farmers who lived above that point where the river becomes too shallow to be navigated by the banana boats had to carry their bananas much farther and were much slower to cultivate them as a cash crop.

Near the coast, where people have been cash-minded for much longer, festive labor was abandoned even before the banana boom, although many older people still remember it from their youth. But further inland, particularly in the upper reaches of the river, festive labor was still being practiced at the time of my visit in 1954. Even here, however, as people began planting bananas on a larger scale and their cash incomes increased, conspicuous ownership was replacing conspicuous giving to the detriment of festive labor. In the past, farmers had been accustomed to spending four or five days in the jungle shooting meat before a work party. In addition, they raised their own plantains and other foodstuffs, grew their own sugarcane, and even distilled their own rum. Festive work parties required no cash outlay because all the materials for the feast were at the host's disposal.

Entrepreneurs from the coastal region, however, were providing a catalyst for local change. These young men had moved inland to find unoccupied lands on which to establish banana plantations, and were not interested in growing subsistence crops or in establishing conspicuous giving relations with their new neighbors. For them festive labor would have required a greater cash outlay than would wages for the same amount of work, so they preferred to hire their labor. Influenced by their example, even the local Negroes were beginning to figure relative costs. As they began planting bananas in place of subsistence crops, they had to buy the supplies for a festive work party at a price substantially greater than that of wages for labor. And the new cash income was greatly increasing their consumption expectations. In one small village, for example, men proudly compared their new clothes and wristwatches and bragged about the price they had paid. Only a few months before, some of these same men had been boasting about the size of their festive work parties. Nor were they by any means unconscious of the rapid change that was taking place: "We have new aspirations (*aspiraciones*)."

Although exchange labor is outlasting the festive form nearly everywhere in western South America, it too is gradually being replaced by the payment of wages in money. Unlike festive labor, exchange of labor is considered superior to wage labor both for its high quality and for its low cost. Sanctions, though informal, are strong in the exchange form since participants know that the quality and quantity of effort expended on a neighbor's chores will determine the return. Moreover, when the workers agree to provide their own food, none of them has any expense when it comes his turn to be the beneficiary.

Ultimately, wage labor also replaces exchange labor, despite all its virtues, because it is inconvenient. Labor obtained by exchange is not free; it must be returned in an amount equal to that received. Working out exchange arrangements at a time when extra help is needed is not always easy, for others must be found who are willing and able to exchange. Again the Cayapas River area can serve as an example, for at the time of my visit even exchange labor had recently been abandoned by many of the new banana growers. Motivated by new standards of conspicuous ownership made possible by the greater abundance of cash, these growers were trying to expand their holdings and their production. As a result, their labor needs began to grow out of all proportion to those of their neighbors. Initially these entrepreneurs exchanged their labor as they always had in the past, but as their operations grew larger and the management of their own enterprises took more of their time, they found it more and more necessary to hire replacements to fulfill their exchange obligations. At this point, they said, it became easier to pay their own laborers directly and circumvent the dependence upon the convenience of others. They had, in effect, become specialists in management, and their management functions had become too time-consuming to justify their doing unskilled labor in order to maintain labor reciprocities.

When a recognized specialist such as a carpenter is employed at work parties in western South America, he usually receives some money in addition to that of festive or labor reciprocity, for the most outstanding characteristic of reciprocal labor is the unspecialized nature of the work performed. The use of money frees the entrepreneur and the specialist — often one and the same — from dependence on others' convenience.

This change coincides with what some have referred to as the process of individualization. As commerce, specialization, and the use of money increase, a man in a sense acquires new freedom. He finds new avenues for acquiring prestige by exercising special aptitudes that might never have been tested — much less developed — in the unspecialized society. And this greater freedom to develop his potentialities is directly related to the circumvention of two limitative cultural causes. One is the limited variety of durable goods in the unspecialized society, which increases the probability that prestige motivation will take the form of conspicuous giving. Through conspicuous giving the social entrepreneur is limited largely to a reinvestment of his surplus in highly personal social reciprocities rather than in more impersonal commercial reciprocities. The second limitative factor is the nature of the reward. Money permits the reward to be both delayed and differentiated. The specialist who is paid in money does not have to depend upon barter with other direct producers nor does he have to accept unskilled labor in exchange for skilled. He can choose from a larger variety of rewards and at a time convenient to himself. He is freer to select his rewards independently of others' convenience.

153

Now we begin to see the outlines of the development of the open society, a development closely tied to increasing specialization. First, increases in population density resulting from favorable farming conditions or the development of irrigation made possible the advent of full-time specialists without any necessary concurrent development in commerce, writing, and the use of money. In these closed societies, the specialist was part of the conspicuous consumption of labor enjoyed by a privileged class capable of enforcing negative controls to insure the unequal redistribution of surplus. The development of specialization under centricity was limited largely to the needs and expectations of a privileged market. The division of labor derived its initial impetus from developments that facilitated transportation between areas of regional specialization. The domestication of animals and the development of the sailing ship contributed importantly to the growth of commerce, which, as its complexity grew, increased the need for a portable standard of value. Once money became common, the potential market for the specialist's goods and services was limited only by the size of the population. Felt needs in turn became progressively more elastic.

Major limitative causes of the division of labor, then, were the increase of food production and population density, improvements in commercial transport, and the use of money. Motivational causes included, first, the widening of prestige satisfactions through the increasing number of new avenues for self-expression and, second, the change from conspicuous giving to conspicuous ownership made possible by the increasing variety of durable goods.

Because he failed to face up to the cognitive implications of his argument, Durkheim explained the development of new specialties by means of a purported struggle for survival among like functions, institutionally rather than individually motivated. As we view it here, the expansion of specialties results from a combination of cognition and motivation — in other words, of creativity and the desire for prestige. Market competition is just one of the limitative causes that offer fertile situations for change, given the other two causal components as the active ingredients.

Cognition is causal in the growth of specialization not only in the individual act of creativity, but also in the individual act of acceptance. The change from festive to wage labor, for example, is partly impelled by a cognitive causal component. The people concerned are faced with these alternatives: to employ wage labor or to entertain festive labor.

What are the probable losses and gains of each method? Festive labor affords the host some prestige if he is generous: this is a very important potential gain. But if the host gives freely, using produce to get good will, he thereby diminishes the amount he has to sell or trade. If he has felt needs which could be met by sale or trade, using festive labor means a loss. If, however, he can save produce by hiring labor and still derive prestige from the ownership of goods accumulated through trade, he gains twice, without any loss. He has gained prestige, and in addition he has acquired goods which he did not have before.

I do not mean to imply that people who give up festive labor for wage labor cognitively choose between alternatives in just this way. They may be very much aware, as are many farmers today in western South America, that the monetary cost of festive labor is high relative to wage labor and that this cost represents a loss in purchasing power. But they do not consciously analyze their own prestige motivations. A man may be keenly aware of the attention he receives for conspicuous giving or conspicuous ownership and may knowingly struggle to reinforce the satisfaction it gives him by further activity of the same kind, without necessarily conceptualizing his actions in our terms.

A discussion I had with five Peruvian Indians in 1953 may help to illustrate the cognitive nature of the choice. When I met these five on a road not far from Cusco, they were on their way back to their isolated mountain community some distance away. My inquiries disclosed that in their community they held the festive work parties common in this area and that they did not employ wage labor among themselves. I asked them to give me detailed estimates of the amount of food and liquor they would have to provide at a festive work party, and they did so very readily. I then asked them to give me the market value in Peruvian money of the various commodities consumed in the festivities. This provoked considerably more discussion than the previous request, but the prices they agreed upon were reasonably accurate for the area. (By comparison, people living near the highways and closer to towns gave much quicker responses to questions about prices.)

After they had estimated the quantity of food dispensed at a festive work party and the monetary values of these commodities, I asked the five to compute the cost of a festive work party and compare its cost to that of wage labor. This they were unable to do without help, for they were not accustomed to figuring relative costs in monetary terms.

When the computations showed that festive labor was more expensive in money than wage labor, they expressed considerable surprise and interest and said that they had never made this comparison before; but when I asked if they would now use wage labor instead of festive, they laughed. No, it was not their custom to use wage labor, they replied. They enjoyed their festive work parties and did not care if they were more expensive.

These people were sufficiently familiar with money economy to understand the comparison, but they were not sufficiently integrated into the money economy to have made this comparison for themselves as the Negroes along the Cayapas River of Ecuador had. They did not yet feel the needs which would lead them to make such a comparison. Nothing would be gained by cutting costs in terms of money when the social relations of festive labor were still of great importance to them. In a community like theirs a person who becomes too acquisitive in his consumption habits is likely to be very lonely. A change to wage labor and all the additional changes it would bring in local production and consumption patterns would cause a loss rather than a gain in the individual's satisfaction of prestige motivation. These Indians did not analyze their decision in terms of felt needs or motivations, but certainly their answers showed cognitive activity within the limits of their situation. They had not yet entered into the local money economy to the point where they had unlimited wants for manufactured consumption goods. They would derive no immediate gain from increasing production for market at the expense of their traditional social satisfactions. Invidious sanction was still stronger than invidious emulation.

VIII

Conspicuous Production in Free and Coercive Societies

Wɪᴛʜ the opening of society through the development of transportation and the use of money, commerce and specialization increase and with them the variety and abundance of durable goods. Conspicuous ownership can then predominate over conspicuous giving. Even in primitive closed societies, of course, there is always some conspicuous ownership. Often it is in the form of the sumptuary privileges of important personages; such persons have the largest and most imposing dwellings in the village or the most wives or the exclusive right to wear certain ornaments. Invidious sanction and the relative absence of durable goods tend nevertheless to limit conspicuous ownership. But as goods increase through the division of labor, a wider consumption of durable goods becomes possible, and invidious sanction gives way to invidious emulation. Persons capable of the greatest displays of ownership provoke emulation rather than sanction and enhance rather than sacrifice their prestige and influence.

Even at the most primitive level, though, prestige is sought in still another way. The expert hunter, for example, is likely to be a conspicuous giver, as we have seen; but his skill itself brings him admiration, as does the skill of the successful warrior, the able farmer, the expert craftsman, or the savant of ritual. In all such cases the person enjoys popular acclaim for excellence. The ability to manipulate others is another such skill: the "big" man in a primitive band is not just a good hunter; he must also know and practice persuasive leadership. Among the Nootka (neighbors of the Haida) the children of chiefs were taught to walk away from arguments rather than quarrel, to take care of others, and to provide them with food and gifts, so as to win the good will and affection of people, because "If your people don't like you, you are nothing." [1] From what we know of leadership in other societies, many of the rules for social manipulation are as widespread as man himself.

In coercive society the leader who can manipulate vested interests to his own advantage may be despotic as well as successful, but his social skills, power, and influence are still a source of prestige. Successful conquest may become a creative activity to which he applies his skill in social manipulation. The nouveau riche capitalists of the late nineteenth century were not hesitant to display their wealth. They enjoyed their conspicuous ownership by wearing diamonds and lighting cigars with hundred-dollar bills. And many, in their declining years, became conspicuous givers just as did St. Godric of Finchale. But there was a point in the activities of these men, and possibly in St. Godric's as well, after which conspicuous ownership had diminishing returns. The motive that carried them past that point was the one we have alluded to: the desire for conspicuous production. [2]

Conspicuous Production

By conspicuous production I mean prestige motivation that takes the form of creative, productive, or manipulative activity. Again, it is a general form of prestige-seeking, one that under certain limitations becomes so important in a society that it characterizes it more than does either conspicuous giving or conspicuous ownership. In some of the primitive Amazon tribes, for example, conspicuous production through headhunting and warfare may have been as characteristic a form of prestige-seeking as conspicuous giving. Usually, however, conspicuous giving seems to best characterize closed societies, whereas conspicuous ownership seems strongly characteristic of the opening process, when the division of labor takes place through free commercial expansion. Only to this extent do the concepts have a developmental or sequential implication.

CONSPICUOUS PRODUCTION

Conspicuous production comes into prominence in open — or opening — societies when the demand for goods is either restricted or saturated. Restriction, as in Russia, occurs in the coercive, catching-up society; saturation, as in the United States, is well summed up in John Kenneth Galbraith's apt term, "the affluent society." [3] So far, conspicuous production has been most congenial with the coercive society, for in the affluent society conspicuous ownership still predominates.

In the coercive, catching-up society, conspicuous ownership is deliberately curtailed by concentration on forming capital rather than on producing consumer goods. The controlling elite establishes production goals for itself and the rest of the society, and makes ability in skilled labor, industrial management, and science the supreme virtues. Status depends upon one's position in the state bureaucracy rather than upon one's ability to display wealth. In fact, the privileged class tries to conceal its advantages and to present an outward appearance of austerity and frugality. Publicly the controlling elite must be a model of conspicuous production, for invidious emulation of their own higher consumption standards would defeat the major purposes of the society.

Although conspicuous consumption is still predominant in our affluent society, it has achieved for many a saturated quality — a kind of variation within monotony. Mass production by its very nature produces a leveling effect within the various degrees of conspicuous ownership. After the Cadillac, what? But the greatest leveling effect has come through negative controls in the form of income and inheritance taxes. The middle class has grown larger at the expense of the rich as well as the poor. Even the suburbanite who buys a fairly expensive new house may find it annoyingly similar to every other house along the street. And so at the magazine rack in the corner drugstore he buys a periodical featuring an article on how each owner of a house can make his different. He then attempts by landscaping and interior decorating to "express" himself through his home and give it his individuality.

Citizens of the affluent society are engaging more and more in creative and competitive activities, many carried on in their leisure, in an attempt to conspicuously express their individuality. Some choose photography as a form of self-expression. Others may join a club of old-car fanciers who rebuild American "classics," cars of the 1930's and before which they carefully restore by hand on evenings and weekends. People who live near the sea may develop a knack for selecting and arranging driftwood that wins the admiration of their friends and associates. Some men and women become part-time authors. Nor should we forget the housewife who joins a ceramics or painting club or the man with the unimportant job who is nevertheless the most important man on the office bowling team. Finally we should mention those people earnestly trying to become conspicuous intellectuals. Some take night-school courses at local colleges, read paperback classics, and attend plays, opera, and ballet. Guests at reciprocal cocktail-hour contests often find themselves propelled into an intellectual potlatching of knowledge about plays, art, and music, in which each participant tries to show how much more widely educated he is than everyone else.

Two limitative factors are vital in the increasing importance of conspicuous production. First, the leveling of consumption norms resulting from mass production, mass installment buying, and negative controls in the form of income and inheritance taxes have reduced the status value of many forms of conspicuous ownership. There is still enough variation and expansion in consumption goods for conspicuous ownership to be important, but the leveling effect of high expectations widely shared within the population is circumscribing the variation in a framework of opulent monotony. Secondly, the growth of specialization has provided an endless number of activities and a technology which affords members of society more time in which to "express their individuality." It has also led to innumerable professional and interest groups within which members can seek social approbation according to their aptitudes and skills. Two pertinent examples are conspicuous administration and conspicuous scholarship.

Neither the government administrator nor the college professor earns enough money to indulge very competitively in either form of conspicuous consumption. But the sums of money for which they may be responsible in administration or research are often very great, regardless of their salaries. Both seek prestige as producers and in both cases there is frequently strong invidious comparison. Invidious promotion is the form of invidious comparison most characteristic of conspicuous production. Although sanction and emulation also take place among conspicuous producers, the emphasis is on promoting oneself through competitive creative activities, skills, or social manipulations.

The university professor promotes himself mainly through his publications, for his rank and the quality of his university post depend largely on his "bibliography," the score-card of his professional achievement. According to a joke among university people all of a professor's articles and books are piled up and weighed at promotion time; the implication is that the evaluation of the scholar's production is quantitative rather than qualitative. His works are not read; they are simply measured. There is some truth in this cliché. At least one university I know annually publishes what might be described as a scholastic coup-count.

Counting coup was a serious game played by the Plains Indians before they were confined to reservations. A warrior achieved prestige by leading successful war parties, stealing enemy horses, and being the first, second, third, or fourth to touch the enemy in an encounter.[4] Men ranked themselves according to the number and variety of valorous acts which they had performed. The modern scholastic coup-count consists of a printed bulletin listing each member of the faculty and the title of each book, article, and book review he has published during the year.

Much invidious comparison takes place when the coup-count appears. An important professor in one department became greatly incensed when he was mistakenly left out one year, although he had published several articles. He accused his department chairman, a low coup-count man, of deliberately failing to submit his publication list because of jealousy.

In a social science department of another university which does not use this system, a longstanding status feud existed between two of the senior professors. One man had published very few books but was internationally known for their quality. The other had never written anything of note, but in sheer volume had greatly outproduced the first. The latter urged the printing of a staff bibliography in which all the publications of each faculty member would be listed. The problem was solved when the quality producer received such an outstanding salary offer that he willingly moved away, leaving the volume man undisputed coup-chief.

Obviously, as this case shows, quality is rewarded too. But the amount of scholarly material published today is so great that the bulk of it can be scaled quantitatively much more easily than qualitatively. This has unfortunate consequences, for its creates a sense of urgency and a pressure to produce which often lessen the quality of the product.

With the growth in number and size of universities, the memberships of most disciplines are now large enough to form their own reading publics. Each discipline has one or more professional journals subscribed to by most members and most college and university libraries. Since members also publish in these journals, they in effect help support this major publication outlet themselves. In a sense professional journals are informal cooperatives for conspicuous scholarship. But some men learn to operate better in this system than others, for the more a man publishes — even through an outlet he may partially control such as a university monograph series — the better he becomes known; the better he is known, the more receptive editors become to his contributions. Obviously there is feedback in the game of conspicuous scholarship.

Another avenue for conspicuous production is editing books. Instead of writing their own books, some conspicuous scholars work up anthologies or solicit contributions on a single theme from several authors. The advantage to the contributors is the opportunity to publish an article in the form of a chapter in a book. The advantage to the editor is the listing of a book after his name on his scholastic coup-count. This technique achieves its greatest elaboration under the "hacendado" scholar. This gentleman must be prominent enough to acquire large sums of research money with which he can support the research of other scholars — preferably graduate students over whom he exercises the sanction of awarding or denying the Ph.D. degree. He may then publish jointly with the graduate student or edit the research results of several in a single book. In either case he manages to display his own name to maximum advantage. The perquisites accruing to his scholar-serfs are the opportunities to do research and to publish the results. In return they contribute their labor to the joint or combined project designed by the "hacendado" and for which he receives the major credit.

Feedback also works for the "hacendado," for the more publications he gets to his credit the greater are his chances of obtaining research funds for future "cooperative" projects. Foundations that want to reduce administrative headaches by getting rid of money in large amounts find it convenient to do so by financing these big scholars and letting them disburse the funds among collaborators of their choice. Past projects of a "hacendado" are his financial sponsors' best guarantee of getting a competent publication display for their money. Most everyone is pleased by these operations, but occasionally someone is dissatisfied. A scholar who got funds to support an assistant for writing up his research submitted one of the resulting articles to a prominent scientific journal under his own name and "with the assistance of" his aide. The journal wrote back saying that they had no precedent for this kind of authorship and that the second man would have to be listed as co-author or not at all.

The way invidious promotion operates among conspicuous government administrators has been superbly diagnosed by scholar C. Northcote Parkinson in his conspicuously excellent essay modestly entitled *Parkinson's Law*.[5] He claims that bureaucratic expansion via the elasticity of paperwork, has two "motive forces" which he states as axioms: (1) "An official wants to multiply subordinates, not rivals," and (2) "Officials make work for each other." Foreign-aid administrators illustrate these rules as well as any officials.

The ideal so often heard expressed among foreign aiders that in a good technical assistance program personnel work themselves out of a job (that is, they indoctrinate the nationals to perform their specialties so well that the United States personnel can soon return home) is seldom if ever realized. Were such an ideal to be fulfilled in practice it would refute Parkinson's Law that work expands to fill the time available. The fact that practice differs sharply from the ideal is a clear substantiation of Parkinson's axioms.

A country director is the man in charge of all United States technical assistance in a given country, and beneath him are the chiefs of the various field parties in agriculture, public health, public administration, housing, and so on. Among country directors and even chiefs of party there is considerable invidious comparison of budgets and staffs. Each man is conscious of the size of other countries' programs or field parties and in most cases tries to promote his own operations by expanding the number of his subordinates. The foreign-aid administrator is clearly a conspicuous producer engaged in invidiously promoting his influence and position in the bureaucratic hierarchy.

To increase the number of his subordinates, the administrator must make work for them. In most countries the official policy is to supply only those technicians requested by the local governments. And this policy is followed officially, but the needs usually originate with the United States officials. Few chiefs of party or country directors wait for requests. They have their own ideas of how they can best expand their programs in the foreign country to which they have been assigned, and they adroitly and diplomatically pressure officials in the host country to accede to their requests. As paying guests in foreign countries, able country directors hold out the carrot of financial aid, for even in countries paying a large percentage of the costs, a collaborative program means the spending of some United States funds. Moreover, the interest and concern for a country's problems which are generated by technical assistance programs often lead to the substantial construction loans in which the host governments are primarily interested.

An illustration of how technical assistance administrators seize opportunities to make work for others is provided by the results of a housing program study I was assigned to make in a Latin American country. The United States was not aiding this program in any way, but an official in the Washington office had heard it was a model program and wondered if anything could be learned from it that might be applied in other housing programs with which the United States was cooperating. When my report disclosed that this was not a model program, the official was delighted. He had two housing men on his hands whom he wanted to get located, so he urged the country director to make the necessary overtures to the host government to ask for two housing specialists. Although the country director in this case was unenthusiastic about housing programs, he recognized an opportunity to help another division get men into the field and simultaneously expand his own staff.

How technical assistance administrators seek subordinates rather than rivals is illustrated by another occasion, when I was investigating public health programs in a certain Latin American country. In this instance the chief of the field party for public health had been by-passed for promotion to country director and a new man brought in for the top post. An intense animosity soon developed between the two men. Although the public health director had previously been interested in my investigations, he now viewed them as a potential threat, for he was afraid the information might be used against him by his rival. To avoid complicity in this administrative rivalry, I had been extremely careful to discuss only the successful aspects of the public health program with the country director and its shortcomings only with the chief of field party. The latter, however, felt so threatened by the rivalry that he began calling on the carpet all the host country's personnel under his jurisdiction who were responsible for mistakes uncovered by my investigations and so thoroughly intimidated them that my rapport with the lower echelons was completely destroyed. He sacrificed help in improving his program in order, he thought, to remove a potential source of danger to himself. This story illustrates another "law" which could be added to Parkinson's in the same vein — to wit: A do-gooder works for the general good in inverse proportion to the degree of conflict between the general good and his own good (as he sees it).

I have emphasized some excesses of conspicuous scholarship and administration to show the importance of the prestige motive even at this high level. The stereotypes of the dedicated scientist in pursuit of knowledge for the sheer ecstasy of learning truth and the loyal public servant working at all costs for the benefit of his fellow man are only partly correct. The quest for prestige courses through human development at all levels. Yet I do not want to obscure the fact that conspicuous production intensifies the specialization of labor leading to the growth of knowledge. It makes possible the accumulation of culture capital at a much faster rate than is possible among people motivated only by conspicuous ownership.

The conspicuous producer often seems impractical to men caught up in the goals of conspicuous consumption. Why search for knowledge just for the sake of learning? Surely the knowledge must be useful in the sense that it will produce consumption goods. And what justifies the salary or existence of a bureaucrat either at home or abroad? He is not helping to make a soap which will more effectively kill underarm odors, nor is he helping to design the non-functional adornments of next year's automobiles. What possible good can *he* be? Though it is true that many soap salesmen and automobile manufacturers are to a certain extent conspicuous producers too, they are more directly linked to the conspicuous ownership goals of their society. And to these men money and the prestige symbols it buys are usually more important than they are for the conspicuous producer who can get social approval for his creative activity. Members of a scholarly profession may look for their social esteem in each other's eyes and largely disregard the values of the greater society they live in. Their publications or their popularity as teachers may give them more satisfaction than a big house and car or expensive clothes. And to the administrator, the size of his program and the amount of his accomplishment in office may be far more important than his relatively small salary.

As conspicuous production increases in our affluent society, the public view of "the practical man" is changing. The change is even becoming evident in advertising as it switches from "The Man of Distinction" to "The Man Who Thinks for Himself." The first associates a product with the wealth and class symbols of conspicuous ownership, the second with the skills or intellectualism of conspicuous producers — the postman who paints pictures on weekends or the milkman who turns archeologist during his vacations.

As society's view of the practical man alters and conspicuous production comes more and more into the foreground of public consciousness and esteem, the man who seeks knowledge for its own sake or administers for the reputation of being a good administrator will seem less and less impractical. And the more our society's reward system swings toward conspicuous production, the greater will be the activity in those specialties that increase our culture capital. But we should not forget that there are detrimental aspects to conspicuous production, a subject to which I shall return in the final chapter when we consider how scholars and administrators may be of reciprocal benefit to one another in curbing the excesses of their prestige-seeking.

Foreign Aid and Invidious Sanction

In the preceding chapters we saw how the "big man" in the small primitive group was a conspicuous giver and how invidious sanction operated to restrict his acquisitive tendencies. Events at the international level are to some extent parallel today, although we must be careful not to attribute basic motivations to whole societies and nations, but rather to the people active in determining their foreign policies.

The people of the United States have been aware for some time that their standard of living is much higher than the rest of the world's, and many have known that in other countries they were envied for this fact. After two world wars Americans have become self-conscious about their high standards of living. The world has grown smaller and the possibility of foreign invasion is now considered a real danger. Americans are more uneasy about their enemies and more concerned with keeping their friends. We note with more interest and sympathy the desire of other peoples to have a standard of living closer to ours. United States foreign aid is largely a consequence of invidious sanction at the international level, for the United States has become like the "big man" in the hunting band, a conspicuous giver and persuasive leader among the "free" nations of the world. And the sanctions are still much the same. Just as the members of the band might leave the stingy leader in preference for a more generous one, the smaller countries can threaten to make closer ties with Russia as a sign of displeasure with the United States.

Here the parallel ends, for at the international level the order has been reversed. During her industrial expansion and isolationist period the United States was largely insensitive to poverty and suffering in other parts of the world and cared little who envied her her wealth. Americans freely boasted that they were the biggest and best. Thus here, in a sense, conspicuous ownership can be said to have preceded conspicuous giving at the international level.

There is no question, however, that in the very process of giving aid the United States creates more envy. For this reason some observers seem to feel that foreign aid is actually detrimental to good will abroad. But at this point one must be careful to distinguish among kinds of help. I have seen technical assistance programs act as a stimulus to local envy, which sometimes became hatred. The reason for this is the personal nature of technical assistance and the fact that conspicuous giving by this medium is usually overshadowed by conspicuous ownership. The United States technician takes his higher standard of living with him wherever he goes. In fact, his standard of living in foreign countries is often higher in many ways than that he enjoyed at home. For example, because he is able to buy an American car for use abroad without the United States federal excise tax (and often at a big discount besides) and because the government ships it to his post along with his household furniture free of charge, he can afford a more expensive car than he would ordinarily buy. And since the middle class is at best an incipient phenomenon in underdeveloped countries, the American technician usually lives in housing which is upper class from both the local and the United States point of view. The most backward countries — where housing is often difficult to find — are likely to be considered hardship posts and the technician is given a special supplement to his salary to meet the expenses of the luxurious housing which he must rent if he is to have any at all. Although the high living standards of the American technician abroad are not necessarily a conscious attempt on his part to consume conspicuously, conspicuous consumption is frequently thrust upon him.

Most host countries accept technical assistance for the limited financial aid that accompanies it and with the hope that by accepting technial assistance the country will have a better chance of getting loans or grants for development projects which are more important to them. Widespread among Latin Americans is the attitude that loans (or, even better, outright grants) for developing public power, irrigation works, and roads are the primary need and that the countries themselves can either provide or hire the necessary technicians.

It does not seem to me that conspicuous giving by the United States (and I am considering long-term loans here, as well as outright grants, as gifts) engenders the envy of the beneficiaries. Unwitting conspicuous consumption seems to me to be a major cause of envy, one stemming from American technicians' and government personnel's inability to lower their accustomed standard of living when they go abroad.

But we should not expect gratitude and affection in return for actions we perform out of self-interest and national interest. Foreign aid is getting desirable results even though it has not made us a Mecca toward which the rest of the world bows in worshipful adoration. The fact that reciprocity has taken place is evidenced by our influence as a persuasive leader among free nations.

In Russia, conspicuous ownership is deliberately kept to a minimum, while conspicuous production (of certain kinds) is rewarded. Even the members of the ruling political class and oligarchy are frequently portrayed to the rest of the world in clothing conspicuous only for its drabness. Russia may not be envied as much as the United States, but she is feared, and that is to our advantage.

Knowledge and Ethics

I do not intend the difference between the closedness and openness of society to signify a moral or ethical difference. The open society is not necessarily a good society: it is a highly specialized one in which knowledge is rapidly becoming more probable. Those who like to find some evidence of moral progress in the transition from primitive to modern life usually point to the savagery of the primitive and his disregard for the lives and feelings of others. Constant warfare among small groups, taking body parts as trophies, the torture of prisoners, human sacrifice, cannibalism, and mutilation as a form of punishment are considered inhumane, immoral practices no longer condoned in civilized society.

It is interesting to note that many who deny that moral progress accompanies modernization do so on similar moral grounds but with somewhat different evidence. They point to modern warfare and claim that man's inhumanity to man is greater today than ever before. They may even disparage the growth of knowledge itself by pointing to the amorality of German scientists who experimented on living human beings.

In both primitive and modern society man has tended to perpetrate his socially sanctioned "immoral" acts against men in other societies. Members of the closed primitive society look upon themselves as men and upon those outside their group as something less. Much of the propaganda against the "Huns" in World War I and the "Japs" in World War II worked on a similar social psychology. When life is cheap *within* a society, however, whether it be open or closed, that society is coercive and the redistribution of power and wealth within it favors the exploitation of one group by another, more privileged group.

In general, my position on the subject of ethics and morality is that taken by Franz Boas thirty years ago.[6] According to him, "There is no evolution of moral ideas. All the vices that we know, lying, theft, murder, rape, are discountenanced in the life of equals in a closed society." He saw only a growth in the size of the social groups to which the same ethics apply. The same moral ideas, he felt, took different behavorial forms in different societies "according to the extent of knowledge of the people."

The existence and the importance of morals cannot be denied, but they are not cumulative in the same sense as probable knowledge is. They are a part of the cultural behavior we call social, which is an involutional rather than an evolutional phenomenon: that is, social behavior is bounded by limiting possibilities which make variation and change additive or substitutive rather than progressively cumulative.[7] In technology man interacts with his artifacts and power sources to increase his controls by building on those he already has. Knowledge accumulates in the sense that it increases in probability by refinements which build upon past knowledge.

In the realm of social interaction the variations are limited. Even in large factories and in government and business bureaucracies men arrange themselves in informal groups within which they interact in much the same ways. Kinship and the family have long been of particular interest to sociologists and anthropologists because of the limitations on the number of ways in which the members of kinship groups can build their behavior.

Because social behavior is not basically a cumulative phenomenon, ethics are not cumulative or evolutionary. They are the product of self-interest (or basic motivation) and reciprocity, and changes in ethical sanctions reflect changes in forms of self-interest and reciprocity. The Golden Rule, "Do unto others as you would have them do unto you," expresses very succinctly the basic compromise between self-interest and reciprocity in human ethics — an ethical compromise between each person and his society. It is not necessary to view the compromise as selfishness versus altruism. Shaped by cognition, self-interest becomes the positive activator of all cultural change and growth. And reciprocity, as we saw in the last chapter, is not synonymous with altruism.

We have seen how the growth of commerce and the development of money increased opportunities for impersonal reciprocities, and how the realization of these opportunities was motivated by the desire for conspicuous ownership. Specialization was freed from the bounds of personal reciprocity as it became possible for labor to exchange delayed and differential rewards in a more impersonal way. The doctor can choose his barber and the barber his doctor, each according to his own convenience. It is possible for a doctor and a barber to employ each other's services, but a direct exchange would be unusual in our impersonal system of reciprocity. They would not put an equal value on their services and it is unlikely that the doctor would need a haircut at the same time that the barber needed a doctor. Instead, the barber receives money which he can use later to buy a doctor's services when the need arises. Thus is the reward delayed and differentiated.

As a consequence of the widening sphere of delayed and differentiated reciprocities in the open society, the same underlying ethic of reciprocally balanced self-interests is applied in a larger and more impersonal social context through additive changes in negative controls. If this did not happen, a person would have no sense of positive control over the consequences of his social relations. Without even this small sense of predictability in human relations, the large impersonal society could not exist.

Formal negative controls — presupposing the existence of the state — provide sanctions which make possible the predictability of impersonal social reciprocities. The development of formal negative controls, or law, is a cognitive phenomenon and is affected by the increasing probability of knowledge. Recently, in discussing a Supreme Court decision, a certain widely read periodical criticized the Court for basing too many of its civil rights decisions on sociology rather than on the "solid substance of the law." According to this view, the law is immutable and absolute. Actually, law is a process in which the reciprocal balance of self-interests is continually being adjusted either directly or indirectly (although often very imperfectly) to the growing probability of knowledge. The periodical's criticism is an acknowledgment of the fact that the social sciences are making a contribution to knowledge which our courts are taking into account.

Open Societies — Free and Coercive

Just as the open society is not necessarily a "good" society, neither is it necessarily a free society. But the coercive open society is regarded here as part of a transitional phase. It has not been my intention to construct ideal types of societies, but to consider the change from closedness to openness. The process of opening leads, I believe, to free society; but this long-range view is not intended to be a guide for action in the immediate future.

Russia best exemplifies the coercive open society and is the model used throughout this discussion. She is by no means open in the same sense as the United States, for she retains many closed characteristics. But she is highly specialized and at least certain parts of her population are on a high level of probable knowledge. Her controlled economy, however, is highly centralized and strikingly similar to redistributive centricity in a coercive closed society. In some ways the collective farm or *kolkhoz* closely resembles the Inca system of labor taxation. According to the description of the Ukrainian kolkhoz by Belov,[8] a former kolkhoz chairman, each member family is given a small homestead plot on which to grow produce for the household, although even part of the income from this source is taxed. These plots are cultivated intensively and the yields per acre are much higher than those from the fields of the collective farm. (This difference in work incentives parallels what we shall find later for individual versus collective ejidos in Mexico.) The threat of the loss of the homestead plot is used as a coercive mechanism for enforcing work on the kolkhoz. The yield from the kolkhoz

171

land goes to the state, but all men, women, and children receive grain and a small amount of cash in payment for days of labor. Although this payment is considered the principal income, the peasants rely heavily on the income from their household plots to tide them over periods of scarcity. Each household also has to deliver eggs and meat to the state, and milk if it owns a cow. In addition to the food products turned over to the state the kolkhoz has to provide labor for public work projects such as building and repairing roads and bridges, cutting and hauling lumber, preparing and transporting stone, and reforestation. Every year several men from each kolkhoz are drafted to serve two or three years in industry or the mines and a certain number of boys are sent away to state schools to be trained as permanent factory laborers.

Money is used in Russia, but free commerce is held to a minimum and is often clandestine and extralegal. The state effectively controls its farm labor and, through a centralized process of redistribution, it removes food from the farms in order to support non-agricultural labor deployed into capital formation. The period which Belov describes for his Ukrainian kolkhoz was the particularly difficult time of reconstruction after World War II, but there is an undeniable parallel between the Russian and Inca states in the control and taxation of agricultural labor and the redistribution of food. Unlike the Incas, the Russians do not have a hereditary class of conspicuously-consuming nobles. But the party leaders are a privileged and dominant group with coercive control over the masses. The most significant difference between the Russian rulers and those of the coercive closed society is the difference in the forms of prestige satisfaction: the nobility in the coercive closed society were conspicuous consumers, whereas the Russians emphasize conspicuous production.

If one can imagine the Inca state in a twentieth-century world with twentieth-century knowledge and technology at her disposal and the freedom to adopt and adapt that knowledge at her own discretion, one can form a hypothetical picture of development very close to the Russian state today. It seems extremely improbable that a coercive open society like the Russian would have developed anywhere but in a nation that was catching up with developments already achieved elsewhere. Facilitation of transport, the expansion of commerce, and the use of money permitted the acceleration of entrepreneurship, specialization, and probable knowledge in the Western world. This opening process took place faster in some nations than others, but invidious emulation has helped to close the gap. The coercive open society is a transitional catching-up phenomenon, an example of highly controlled invidious emulation on a national scale.

In the long run, free society is the most congenial matrix for the opening process. The coercive society is eventually doomed by the cognitive element of cultural causality. Although cognition is psychological, it cannot in practice be readily separated from knowledge, whose development is social. Even the most individualistic scientist, reporting on some new theory or discovery, anticipates the criticisms of colleagues as he works and writes. The very act of creativity is social to a large extent. Nor does the scientist or technician work for long in isolation. The ideas exchanged through critical discussion lead to innovations and refinements — toward increasing probability of knowledge. It is in the free society, where self-interest is balanced against self-interest through reciprocities regulated by voluntary negative controls, that the greatest opportunities exist for the fullest use of man's cognitive resources. In the coercive society where one group satisfies its felt needs by subordinating the felt needs of other groups, much of the potential cognitive force of the society goes unused.

But even more important than the give and take of free social discussion for the persistence of voluntary controls in the open society are the changes produced by the creative aspect of cognition. The ability to make frequency interpretations is a human faculty which cannot be coerced out of existence, a fact which makes culture change inevitable. Change, however, is not necessarily disruptive to the coercive society if change is kept within channels regulated by its coercive controls. The coercive society feeds on changes which increase the power and influence of those in command. But the coercive society bent on competition with free society must industrialize and expand its technical observations, both of which necessitate the training and education of vast numbers of specialists and scientists. When the intensification of cognitive activity through frequency interpretation which this education involves become too widely dispersed within the coercive society, it can overflow the channels of control.

The spectacular and surprising popularity of a book published recently in the Soviet Union suggests that the creative faculty in that coercive society is already leading to at least some intellectual unrest.

The book, *Not by Bread Alone*, by Vladimir Dudintsev, somehow passed the party censors.[9] The hero is a schoolteacher and engineer who asserts his creative individuality even though it means clashing with the state bureaucracy. He invents a new way of casting iron pipe that can result in enormous savings of labor and materials. But in his attempt to introduce his invention he is blocked by a bureaucrat who eventually has him exiled to Siberia on a trumped-up charge of revealing state secrets. Eventually the hero is pardoned and his invention put into use, but the conflict between hero and bureaucrat and the conflict it symbolizes between individual creativity and state coercion are left unresolved. On the face of it, Dudintsev is attacking what we might call the "organization man." But to question the propriety of an organization man's activities in a centralized coercive state is to question the state itself. In training the personnel necessary for her industrial and technological competition with the West, Russia has inevitably created a growing educated class eager to ask and ponder the kind of questions that create new felt needs and expectations.

Felt needs, growing out of cognitive activity and inevitable culture change, are a constant threat to coercive social control. No one man or group of men will ever satisfy the felt needs of a whole society as well as that society itself does when individual interests are reciprocally balanced through the growth of voluntary negative controls. A group with the power to decide for all, even when imbued with the best intentions for the good of all, cannot help but decide in favor of its own self-interests when these conflict with the felt needs of the governed. For "good" has an elastic meaning which changes with the growth of knowledge and felt needs and simultaneously varies with individual self-interest. The basic conflict is inevitably with authority — the right of those in power to their position and its perpetuity. As rulers concede to the governed in conflicts of interest, their rule in effect becomes the persuasive and managerial rule of a free society.

Persuasive rule must eventually prevail even in the Soviet Union. But optimistic long-range predictions like this are of little help for the problems of the immediate future. Our free society has never before been in such danger of extinction. Critical discussion may be a social requisite for the growth of knowledge, but in a short-run race for survival against a competitive coercive rival, the free society cannot count on its greater freedom of discussion to automatically provide it with a scientific and technological advantage. Even in a free society, the critical discussion and social interaction leading to scientific and technological advancement take place within specialized professional groups which could not use all of the society's cognitive resources. In the coercive society technicians and scientists can be trained in sufficient numbers not only to catch up with advanced nations but to provide the critical discussion necessary for the development of a knowledge in some ways even more probable than that in the free society. This is accomplished by concentrating developments in fields of knowledge which strengthen the coercive controls, for thus the coercive society not only increases her chances of dominating her competitors but simultaneously accelerates her developments in those fields. In the free society where felt needs are permitted a more unlimited and rapid expansion, the cognitive resource can flow into innumerable channels of productivity which in part contribute to our high standard of living. Though in the long run this provides a wider creative base for development, in the short run it distributes much of the cognitive resource into developments not crucial to our competitive race with the coercive society.

Although there is good reason, as we have seen, to be optimistic about the long-range effect of education on the coercive open society, there is much less reason to expect any sudden alteration in the coercive structure as a result of "enlightenment." Such a hope rests on the assumption that an educated person or a scientist is somehow more moral or freedom-loving. The assumption that knowledge necessarily leads to greater morality was questioned in the previous section. As for freedom, if a scientist finds sufficient reward in his conspicuous production, why should anyone suppose that his self-interest would be better served by opposing the government which rewards his efforts? If scientists raised and educated in a coercive society are an honored and privileged class, why should they transfer their allegiance to another society in which they would not even be second best?

There is an inherent weakness, however, in the system of rewards to a privileged class through a centralized system of redistribution. When the scientists and highly educated groups are few enough relative to the total population, they can be treated as a privileged group and made to feel a vested interest in the coercive government. But as their numbers increase in the process of industrialization, the strain on the centralized system of redistribution to keep these educated groups especially rewarded becomes progressively greater. Three methods are used to reduce the strain as much as possible. First, to curtail the growth of felt needs, knowledge of the outside world is kept from all groups. Second, rewards to the specially privileged are kept quantitative rather than qualitative as much as possible, in order not to engender too many new felt needs and invidious comparisons by persons on the lower levels. Third, education is restricted to the technical and scientific requirements of an industrial machine directed toward world supremacy rather than the expansion of felt needs and their satisfaction through mass production for mass consumption.

It seems highly improbable that the Russian coercive society will open into a free society in the immediate future. Meanwhile there is plenty of time for her to continue concentrating manpower and resources on the task of winning her scientific and technological race with the free world. Free society cannot afford to let her get ahead in this race. We often hear the opinion that the Russian oligarchy is too smart to start a war. Wars, it is argued, are not profitable any more because both sides lose. Of course the rulers of Russia are smart, but so were Hitler, Napoleon, and Alexander the Great. As for wars no longer being profitable — in what terms were they ever profitable? Warfare was never carried on simply for economic gain, whether among headhunters or Plains Indians or in nineteenth- and twentieth-century Europe. Where acquiring wealth was an incentive, it was but part of the desire for prestige and greatness. Can we possibly take seriously the suggestion that the rulers of the Russian coercive state would not make a play for world dominance if they thought they had a chance — that they would refrain out of concern for the loss of life and destruction that it would entail? Can we impute reverence for human life to the men in the Kremlin?

Reverence for human life is a universal characteristic of mankind to the extent that each man reveres his own life. But reverence for human life which is plural or social depends upon a reciprocal balancing of self-interests. In the small closed society of equals the balance is accomplished face to face. In the larger impersonal society, if it is free, the reciprocal balancing of self-interests is accomplished by voluntary negative controls largely in the form of written law. But in free as well as in coercive societies there have been occasions when the distribution of power or influence has served the self-interests of some men more than others, with consequent cheapening of life. Even in our own society a young Negro boy can be brutally killed for winking at a white woman and his murderers allowed to go free. But the more the self-interests of some men outweigh those of their fellows, the more coercive is the society and the less human life is revered.

The coercive open society shows no more reverence for human life by virtue of its greater knowledge than does the coercive closed society. Where probable knowledge becomes the tool of privilege it can be used to strengthen the unequal distribution of power and rewards which favors those in control. In such a society life can become cheaper than ever before, and thousands — even hundreds of thousands — can be killed at a despot's whim. It is not impossible that in such a society a man might come into control who preferred to achieve immortality by giving his subjects freedom rather than by achieving conquests. But this would be a poor frequency interpretation of past and present evidence on which to act in defense of the free society.

Dual Societies

The underdeveloped countries of the world, which direct invidious sanction against our affluent society to force a wider distribution of the material benefits of culture capital, are dual societies in the sense that they tend to combine characteristics of both openness and closedness within the same population. They show great contrasts in wealth and poverty and there is little prosperity in the middle range. The elite is cosmopolitan, educated, specialized in knowledge and skills, and prosperous. Reciprocities with them are more delayed and impersonal and prestige-seeking is more individualistic and acquisitive than among the backward citizens. The latter are illiterate, impoverished in goods and knowledge, and exist primarily by means of unskilled and semiskilled labor. They are only casually or indirectly caught up in the world's industrialization and its infinite expansion of consumption wants and expectations.

Every society is dual to some extent, for contrasts exist in all. The underdeveloped countries merely accentuate universal extremes. Everywhere, the opening up of backward components has become a competi-

177

tion between free and coercive forms of government. In coercive society the extremes are reduced by limiting the growth of consumption wants and by directing conspicuous production at all levels of society toward capital formation in the tools of industry. The elite must set the example of conspicuous production so that invidious comparison will support, rather than destroy, the major orientation of the society. In free society the extremes may be reduced or controlled by income and inheritance taxes and by gradually drawing all levels into the expansion of consumption wants and expectations through free industrial and commercial growth. The elite in such a society sets an example of conspicuous ownership that predominates over conspicuous production, and invidious emulation becomes the chief stimulus to a rising standard of living. As a giver of technical and financial assistance, our own free society is chiefly concerned with those dual societies which qualify as "free" in this broad sense of the word.

But two major administrative problems arise in aiding these countries through governmental channels. First, governmental personnel in the dual society are much more concerned with owning symbols of status than with goals of conspicuous administration, for invidious comparison is focused primarily on emulation of ever higher consumption standards. Since the large mass of illiterate and impoverished people in the backward component have only weakly developed sanctioning power over the elite, the government bureaucracies of these countries are usually shot through with graft. Dual society is a two-headed monster, for graft is the main alternative to coercion. In either case reciprocity between the elite and the backward is unequally balanced in favor of the former. As it commands most of the culture capital of the society, the elite has a tremendous advantage over the backward sector. If it cannot actually coerce the backward population it exploits them through graft.

Second, the United States bureaucrat administering his country's funds abroad is far removed from the customary sanctions of his own country. Too few of his countrymen, including even his immediate superiors in Washington, know exactly what he is doing. Though this situation rarely leads to graft — for in most cases the American government administrator does not feel sufficiently separated from the sanctions of his own society — the desire to achieve stature as an administrator through the size and influence of The Project may lead him to sponsor costly adventures later demonstrated to be inappropriate and wasteful. This unfortunate combination of circumstances has resulted in considerable distrust among intellectuals and others of costly development projects requiring large investments in the construction of such capital goods as roads and dams. But even when the economic feasibility of such projects is unquestioned, the social repercussions may be. Some will argue that most of the benefits will go to the privileged elite while the poor benefit little if at all.

The most often mentioned alternative to such "bigness" in development programs is the self-help, community-development kind of project which uses techniques of extension and "fundamental" education. Not only are people supposedly taught to lift themselves by their own bootstraps, but they supposedly accomplish this modern loaves-and-fishes miracle at very little expense. These programs seem to me most open to the promotional excesses of conspicuous administration. The very reason that these programs are so popular among foreign-aid personnel is that they permit an almost unlimited expansion of subordinates. Staffs can continue to increase and always with the same justification: they cost less than construction. But do they?

In Chile I once studied a rural extension program where costs included the salaries and travel expenses of six staff members and the maintenance of two cars and two offices. Regular dealings were being maintained with some two hundred and fifty people belonging to fewer than a hundred and fifty different families. Ideally, the six staff members should have dealt with more people than they did, but ideal conditions usually differ markedly from practice in fundamental education programs. The same program extended on a national scale to all the poor rural families of Chile would have cost more in one year than all the construction costs for the dams and irrigation works on the Yaqui and Mayo Rivers of Sonora — about which we shall have much to say later — or for comparable construction projects in Chile. Since the results of this pilot Chilean extension project were surprisingly negligible, the only consequence of a similar program on a national scale would have been the enlargement of Chile's already badly bloated bureaucracy. In Sonora, on the other hand, the rapid changes and developments which have taken place within the past decade have come about without benefit of fundamental-education, self-help, extension programs.

Disillusioned with what I had seen of promotional assistance programs while working for the Point Four program in Latin America, I was anxious to return to Sonora and study the developments taking place in an area where construction projects were harnessing new energy and facilitating transportation. In the fall of 1957 I returned, and for eighteen months studied the remarkable changes taking place. Part III tells the story of what I found.

PART III. A CASE STUDY OF CULTURAL DEVELOPMENT IN NORTHWESTERN MEXICO

IX

Introduction to the Area

I$_N$ THE story of Juan in Chapter I, I told of seeing him again seven years after his trip to California. This was during the summer of 1955 when I made a quick reconnaissance of southern Sonora to appraise the changes. As a result of that preliminary visit, I had four major reasons for wishing to return to Sonora, in the fall of 1957 when the opportunity arose.

First, technological developments had been happening very rapidly during the ten years since I had lived there; I wanted to see what effect they were having on the people and their way of life. Paved highways and irrigation projects had been opening up the area, and agricultural production had increased enormously. The towns had grown rapidly, and their inhabitants looked much more prosperous. A substantial middle class seemed to be growing up between the social extremes. Many private farmers were eagerly seeking improvements in their farming methods, some even by subscribing to agricultural journals; and none of this interest was being deliberately fomented by extension programs. The agronomists busily driving about the area in pickup trucks giving advice to farmers were not government extension agents but representatives of insecticide and fertilizer companies.

Secondly, I was curious as to why, in spite of the rapidly increasing prosperity of the towns, changes seemed to be taking place very slowly among the peasantry. I wondered what accounted for their different rate of development.[1] Certainly overpopulation could not be blamed, for the area had long been characterized by immigration rather than emigration. It seemed that here was a chance to dip beneath problems of population density and observe other basic problems of control. For example, if invidious emulation was leading to rapid changes among the townspeople as opportunities increased, why wasn't the same process affecting the country people? Was the more static position of the country people the result of fewer opportunities or fewer expectations? Could it be possible that there is a segment at the bottom of every population — no matter how spectacular the expansion of opportunities — that needs the direct stimulus of community development programs to draw them into the over-all development of society?

Third, this was an area which, like all of Mexico, had been subjected to a great social experiment in the distribution and redistribution of wealth. From 1918 on, but principally during the administration of President Lázaro Cárdenas (1935–1940), the large landholdings of the hacendados had been broken up and redistributed in small plots to many ejidatarios. As a result, much of the land was owned by ejidos, groups of people who had been the beneficiaries of grants of land from the Mexican state. Yet through graft and other extralegal means, large farming operations had persisted, and in some ways the illiterate peasantry was still being exploited. The masters had changed, of course, for now bureaucrats rather than feudalistic landowners were reaping the spoils.

The results of this land reform program give us considerable insight into the workings of dual society. They show how graft becomes the alternative of coercion and that the basic problem is not the unequal distribution of natural resources or manmade artifacts but the unequal distribution of culture capital. The illiterate, backward component of a dual society fails to exercise a sanctioning effect commensurate with its size and potential strength. Consequently, the unequal distribution of wealth and rewards remains much to the disadvantage of this component, despite reforms. Reforms may help to equalize the distribution of culture capital in the long run, but the process is slow and the reasons for its slowness must be taken into account.

Fourth, I was interested in studying a transition from conspicuous giving to conspicuous ownership as it was taking place. The Indian population still preserved ceremonial practices which had traditionally included conspicuous giving and a considerable investment of effort. These practices were changing in such a way as to minimize conspicuous giving but to preserve opportunities for conspicuous production. A study of the breakdown and persistence of these customs became another objective of my revisit. I did not find conspicuous ownership so important as I had expected, however, for reasons related to the different rates of development in town and country. And conspicuous giving, it turned out, had been waning for a long time. People here were dropping older conspicuous giving patterns without yet being caught up in the invidious emulation characteristic of consumption patterns in the towns. Their felt needs were changing, but their expectations were not changing as fast. Yet there was apparent here no vicious class system to keep the Indian strictly in his place. The slow growth of expectations among the peasantry seemed largely the result of their own humble self-image. Although there was no severe problem of anomie in this population, the emotional distress that existed was most intense among peasants who were losing their old prestige system but did not have the confidence, the background, or the opportunity to take part in the new one.

This and the following three chapters discuss the results of my study in northwestern Mexico. The present chapter introduces the area, the people, and the class structure. Chapter X considers the effects of the land reforms, Chapter XI the consumption patterns and class mobility in town and country. Chapter XII deals with the major characteristics of "Indianness" in the area — the ceremonial patterns. It discusses why conspicuous giving is declining even though ceremonial production continues to be supported by many Indians.

Recent Technological and Commercial Developments

The prosperity and rapid rise of living standards in southern Sonora during the past ten years has followed upon government investment in irrigation projects and road-building. Since 1949, the area irrigated with Yaqui River water has grown from about a hundred and fifty thousand acres to almost six hundred thousand acres, at a cost of approximately thirty-three million dollars for dams, canals, and drainage ditches. During the same period, the area irrigated with Mayo River water has been increased at a cost of about ten million dollars from approximately one hundred thousand to two hundred thousand acres.[2]

The annual value of agricultural production in the irrigated areas of the Mayo and Yaqui River valleys has jumped from about thirteen million dollars in 1948 to about fifty-eight million dollars in 1958. Most of the expansion has been in wheat and cotton, the two major crops of the region. During 1957, eighty-seven per cent of the cultivated land in the Yaqui River valley and ninety per cent in the Mayo irrigation zone was devoted to these two crops.[3]

Since cropping practices are highly mechanized in all irrigation districts, peak labor loads occur during irrigation and cotton picking which require the most hand labor. Although no figures are available, I estimate that less than ten per cent of the cultivated land in the irrigation zones is still plowed with draft animals. Today even farmers with only a few acres of land pay for contract plowing.

Other crops planted in the region include chickpeas, tomatoes, peas, chile peppers, sesame seed, corn, beans, linseed, and alfalfa. Tomatoes, peas, chile peppers, and melons are exported to the United States and Canada in refrigerator cars by wealthy growers, a highly speculative business which pays its biggest rewards in years when Florida crops are damaged by frosts. Small farmers who plant perishable vegetable crops must depend entirely on local markets which are very quickly saturated. Partly because of this marketing limitation, most farming is extensive and mechanized.

This is an agricultural, not an industrial, area, and the most prosperous farmers are invariably townsmen. They may commute daily to farms nearby, but they live in the larger towns and are members of the highest class. Towns are service, banking, and retail centers with relatively little manufacturing. There are a few very small furniture manufacturers, several pop-bottling concerns, a processing plant for cottonseed oil, and several cotton gins. A brewery was being built in Obregón when I left in the spring of 1959. With the exception of two of the bottling concerns, all of these industries were less than ten years old.

Retail outlets have multiplied very rapidly in the past few years. Of the sixteen clothing stores in Navojoa in 1958, ten were less than ten years old and fourteen less than thirteen years old. Twenty-eight of the thirty-one largest grocery stores in Navojoa were less than fifteen years old and twenty of them less than ten. All but one of the five auto-supply

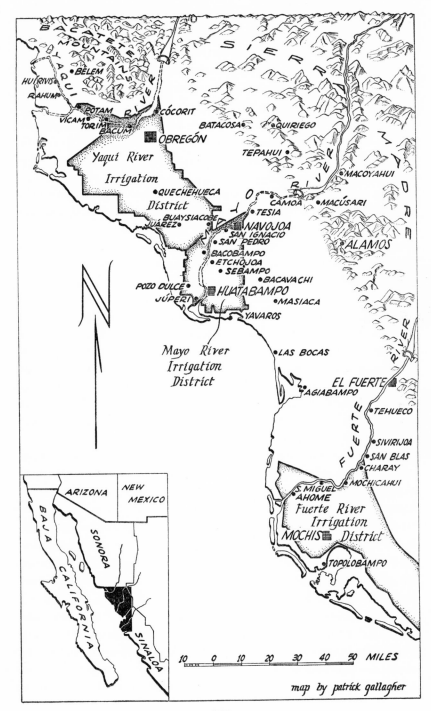

BACATETE MOUNTAINS

SIERRA

YAQUI RIVER

HUIRIVIS
RAHUM
•BELEM
POTAM
VICAM
TORIM
BACUM
•CÓCORIT

BATACOSA•
•QUIRIEGO

MADRE

OBREGÓN

Yaqui River

Irrigation

•QUECHEHUECA

District

•TEPAHUI

•MACOYAHUI

O

R I V E R

•CAMOA
•TESIA
•MACÚSARI

BUAYSIACOBE
JUAREZ•
NAVOJOA
•SAN IGNACIO
•SAN PEDRO
BACOBAMPO•
•ETCHOJOA
•SEBAMPO
•BACAVACHI

ALAMOS

POZO DULCE•
JÚPERI•
HUATABAMPO
•MASIACA

•YAVAROS

Mayo River
Irrigation
District

•LAS BOCAS

RIVER

EL FUERTE
AGIABAMPO•

•TEHUECO

•SIVIRIJOA
•SAN BLAS
•CHARAY
•MOCHICAHUI

Fuerte

S. MIGUEL•
AHOME•

Fuerte River
Irrigation
MOCHIS District

•TOPOLOBAMPO

ARIZONA
NEW
MEXICO

BAJA
CALIFORNIA
SONORA

SINALOA

10   0   10   20   30   40   50   MILES

map by patrick gallagher

187

shops and three of the seven hardware stores were less than ten years old. Also less than ten years old were six of the ten drugstores, two of the three gas stations, four of the six furniture stores, and all of the five tractor and farm implement agencies.

The west coast highway, which passes through Obregón and Navojoa and just east of Mochis, was completed about the middle of the last decade and has greatly speeded up the area's commerce. Many new consumption goods previously unobtainable are now trucked in from the south. During the last two years small "super" (self-service) markets have opened up in Obregón, Navojoa, and Los Mochis. Though still a long way from their Anglo-American counterparts, these stores represent a minor revolution in production, transportation, and merchandising; the products sold are made in Mexico and include a multitude of canned goods, baked products, packaged delicatessen meats and cheese, and so on, most of which were not available in the area ten years ago.

The same changes are evident in the selling of other lines of merchandise. Furniture stores have increased greatly in number and size and are stocked with such a variety of Mexican manufactured goods that one returning after ten years is amazed by the contrast. Gas stoves and electric refrigerators are no longer novelties. Both have become common in Obregón, Navojoa, and Huatabampo, where they symbolize the rise of the middle class. The market for electrical appliances has grown spectacularly with the extension of the thermoelectric and hydroelectric system which will eventually join the river valleys of southern Sonora and northern Sinaloa into one great network. This electrification program ranks in importance with irrigation and highway improvements.

The rapid increase of buying by consumers in the towns during the past few years is a healthy sign for the Mexican economy. This increase represents an important growth of the internal market for the many new manufactured goods being produced by Mexican industry. Of great importance in motivating consumers within the local class system has been the expansion of credit buying. Although ten years ago it was possible to buy furniture and clothes on time, down payments were never less than ten per cent and usually much higher, depending on the retailer and his confidence in the buyer. Now credit buying is urged on the public by advertisements like the road sign of one Obregón store which invites customers to "buy like a rich man and pay like a poor man." Today in Navojoa and Huatabampo a resident owner of a house can buy furniture and electrical appliances on time without any down payment. Farmers are allowed to make time payments seasonally at harvest time, and if they have a bad year their payment period is usually extended.

The reason most often given by merchants for this increase in credit is greater competition. With the increased population, many new stores and other businesses have sprung up and each has had to make credit buying easier in order to keep up with his competitors. The greater number of stores not only reflects the increase in town population as a result of migration from other parts of Mexico but also the greater abundance and accessibility of goods. As the west coast Pan American Highway neared completion some five years ago, shipping of merchandise from southern Mexico began to shift from rail to truck with a great increase in volume. Now even bakery products and ice cream are brought in from Mexico City and Guadalajara.

A large store in Navojoa provides an example of the changing business tactics of the past few years — changes resulting mainly from the opening of the highway. This concern used to buy up local food crops of corn and beans at harvest time to sell them later at inflated prices. After the highway was completed, food prices remained more stable through the year, because truckers on the lookout for regional price differences carried food from areas with surpluses to areas with shortages. No longer able to corner the market on local food staples, the store has successfully entered the highly competitive field of furniture, appliances, hardware, and household supplies and now offers the consumer the easiest credit terms in town.

The irrigation project is partly responsible for the relaxed credit situation because it created more work and increased the region's productivity. Not only have the merchants gained confidence in the people's ability to pay, but the public itself has more self-confidence and is less hesitant about assuming debts of two or three years' duration.

The Area and the People

The area we are concerned with lies along and between the Yaqui and Mayo Rivers where these cross the narrow coastal plain of southern Sonora. The climate of this desert region alternates between mild winters and hot, humid summers. Hot weather begins in May and lasts well into October, and the season of sporadic but heavy rain extends from July through September. October to January is the period of winter rains and January to July is the usual dry season. The annual rainfall is about twelve inches. The natural vegetation, which still flourishes outside the irrigation districts, is a thorn forest abounding in mesquite trees and many varieties of cactus.

As the two largest communities in the area, Obregón and Navojoa are referred to locally as cities. Their populations are about seventy-five thousand and forty thousand respectively, and each is the head of its *municipio* or county. Three municipios (Navojoa, Etchojoa, and Huatabampo) lie along the lower course of the Mayo and three (Cajeme, Bacum, and Empalme) along the lower Yaqui. In addition to the head town (*cabecera*) of each municipio there are smaller towns or *pueblos*. Each pueblo is head of a *comisaría*, the jurisdiction of a *comisario* or sheriff. Within each comisaría the town has several satellite hamlets or villages usually called *rancherías*. Each hamlet has a deputy sheriff (*delegado de policía*) responsible to the comisario.

Within the three municipios bordering the lower course of the Mayo River there are 266 of these smaller towns and hamlets. Of these, sixty-four per cent had fewer than two hundred inhabitants in 1950 and ninety-two per cent fewer than five hundred. In 1950 the population of the three Mayo River municipios of Navojoa, Etchojoa, and Huatabampo totaled about eighty-five thousand and that of the Yaqui River municipios of Cajeme and Bacum around seventy thousand.[4] Today the population of the Mayo River area may come close to a hundred and twenty thousand and that of the Yaqui River may be as much as a hundred and fifty thousand.

The population along the Mayo River has not grown so rapidly as that within the Yaqui River irrigation zone, for much less new land has been brought under cultivation there. Many towns in the Yaqui River area doubled or even tripled their populations in the course of the past ten years.

Excluding the towns of Navojoa, Etchojoa, Bacobampo, and Huatabampo (populations of about forty, four, five, and ten thousand respectively), I estimate that roughly half of the Mayo River population west of the municipio of Alamos is Indian. That would mean a total Indian population of about thirty to thirty-five thousand. I classify as

Indian persons who consider themselves Mayos and who speak the aboriginal Cáhita tongue.[5]

The Mayos live predominantly in the hamlets or rancherías around the towns, but there is no sharp break in the settlement pattern to differentiate Indians and "whites." Though in general the largest communities have the smallest proportion of Indians, the rancherías are by no means exclusively Indian.[6] The prevailing pattern here, as in all of Mexico, is for rural families to live in small towns and villages and walk or ride to their fields.

The Yaqui Indians live on the northern bank of the Yaqui River, some forty-five miles north of the Mayo, in a *comunidad indígena* (indigenous community) similar to a reservation. Although some "whites" live in the reserve, particularly at Vicam Station, the population is predominantly Indian; the Yaqui do not live so interspersed with "whites" as do the Mayos. A recent publication estimates that there are two thousand heads of families in the reserve.[7] If true, this would put the Yaqui reservation population at about twelve thousand, but I believe the estimate is high.

The Yaquis formerly irrigated their farm plots with the river's flood waters and manufactured mats from the wild cane that grew along its banks. As the construction projects diverted the water into irrigation canals to the south, the river bed dried up and the cane disappeared. The Yaquis were forced to support themselves by selling firewood cut in the thorn forest still covering most of the one-million-acre reserve. To alleviate this situation, the Mexican government has been increasing the amount of Yaqui land under irrigation. By 1959 some thirty thousand acres had been opened up, and by 1961 the total area under irrigation was expected to reach fifty thousand acres, the maximum the government planned to irrigate north of the river.

Except for the thirty thousand acres north of the river in the Yaqui reserve, the bulk of the Yaqui River irrigation district lies to the south, where it stretches across the coastal plain to within a mere three miles, at one point, of the neighboring Mayo River. This is the area of greatest population increase, for over two thirds of it has been cleared within the past fifteen years and many of the communities here have sprung up in that time. Although Mayos and a few Yaquis are encountered in this area, the population is predominantly non-Indian. Many people are from other parts of the country. For example, of the original one hundred and fifty families which "colonized" Villa Juárez — grown to a town of about six thousand since its founding in 1942 — all but one were from other states. All laborers on the Angostura dam, they were given the opportunity to colonize twenty hectares apiece upon its completion.

Judging from data collected in towns and villages in the Mayo River area,[8] immigration there has been much greater in the towns than in the rural communities. Some new lower-class districts of Navojoa, for example, are largely inhabited by immigrants from states further south. Both Obregón and Navojoa (on its present site) are only about forty years old. Many families have moved into these centers of population from older communities, such as Quiriego and Alamos and the numerous mountain villages between them. Even the Yaqui villages were thriving communities early in the century, and Potam, which is the largest today (about two thousand people), had at least eight thousand inhabitants in 1914.[9] While great numbers of people have unquestionably migrated to the major towns from the Sierras to the east, large numbers have entered from far outside the boundaries of the accompanying map (p. 187). In a sample of some two hundred and fifty male family heads in Navojoa upper and middle classes I found that almost a third had moved there from outside the area. About the same number had come from other communities within the region, but especially from around Alamos and Quiriego.

As in the rest of Mexico, the high birth rate also contributes to population expansion in Sonora. A history of births was collected from a hundred and thirty-three married women in four villages.[10] The average age of these women was thirty-nine, yet they had averaged 6.1 live births apiece. Those forty mothers in the sample who were over age forty-five at the time of the census had averaged 8.3 live births. However, mortality in childhood is also very great. Of the children born alive to the mothers in the sample, thirty-five per cent died before the age of eighteen. Of these, over half died during the first year of life and over seventy-five per cent below the age of three. But modern medicine is beginning to cut down the deaths of children, as the difference between two villages would suggest. In the Biacusi sample forty per cent of the children died before the age of eighteen and in the Buaysiacobe sample twenty-six per cent. Buaysiacobe has a resident nurse, and a doctor visits the town regularly. This medical help is provided by the national social security program because Buaysiacobe is an ejido working with credit from the Ejido Bank. Biacusi, on the other hand, lies several miles upriver from Navojoa where medical aid is less available, and is composed of poor farm families not enrolled in the social security program.

Family histories of a sample of fifty-six middle-class Navojoa mothers showed a total of 383 live births, an average of 6.8 per mother. The average age of mothers in this sample was forty-three. The average number of live births among the twenty-seven mothers in the sample who were over forty-five was 7.5. Only nine per cent of the children in this sample died before reaching eighteen. Apparently there is no great difference in the maternity ratio (average number of live births per mother) in town and country, but a much lower infant and childhood mortality ratio (average number of dead offspring per mother) prevails in town due to the greater availability of modern medical attention.

Even in the first or wealthiest class one encounters families with as many as eight or ten children, although they seem to be somewhat fewer at that level. Some wealthy farmers are anxious to have many children because of the agrarian law which limits the size of individual landholdings in irrigated areas to one hundred hectares (247 acres), for holding land in the name of children can be a legal means of expanding the farm's operations.

The peasants look upon children as a form of insurance for old age. Among those families I came to know very well and with whom I could discuss the subject without embarrassment to anyone, there was a real lack of interest in birth control, aside from curiosity about customs in the United States. Children are definitely wanted among the peasantry, but middle-class town women are eager for information about birth control. Middle-class parents are becoming increasingly concerned about educating their children, and they feel they cannot provide adequate opportunities for more than a few. Many claim that for this reason they would prefer "only three or four children." But peasants expect some of theirs to die, a reason they frequently give for desiring many offspring, whereas young town parents no longer share the peasants' fatalism in this regard.

Contraceptives for women are not available in local drugstores, and doctors — "because we are all Catholics here" — prescribe only the rhythm method. Local doctors have told me, however, that it is practically unheard of for a woman to solicit such information from a physician: "They would be too embarrassed." But according to informants in Obregón, it is becoming common for married women of the first class to go to Tucson, Phoenix, or Los Angeles to be fitted with diaphragms.

Here, as in many areas undergoing rapid economic development, greater reliance on modern medicine is reducing infant mortality in the face of a high birthrate. The peasantry, especially in the more isolated villages, exhibits the high growth potential found in areas where the infant mortality rate is high but where marriage is early and children are considered an economic asset. Among town people and those country families who rely on modern drugs and medical practitioners, the high birthrate continues and the mortality drops, with consequent increase in the size of families. The economic pressures of a large family on many middle-class parents anxious to raise their living standards and their level of education is awakening an interest in birth control. Thus it is that a dual society may embody the entire cycle of population growth with all the related attitudes toward the size of family that changing felt needs within the family give expression to.

Social Classes

Even in complex societies there seems to be a limitation of possibilities in the structuring of classes; three principal divisions are usually found and described. At the top are people with some hereditary advantage and at the bottom are those who work hardest for the least return. Those in the middle look invidiously toward the top, and usually the distribution of goods provides them with enough to make them aspire to more. In the United States, five and six class systems have been described by subdividing the major three. Thus, the upper, middle, and lower classes may each be divided into an upper and lower subclass. For describing New England class structure, W. Lloyd Warner uses a six-class system, whereas in the more "democratic Middle West and Far West" he distinguishes only five classes.[11] In the latter areas he does not subdivide the upper class, for where communities are insufficiently large or have grown very rapidly, the "old" or "good" families at the top are "not recognized as superordinate to the new families." The "old" and the "new" families regard each other as equals. This is very similar to what is taking place in the rapidly growing urban centers of Sonora.

My observations of the Sonoran class structure were confined primarily to the Mayo River area, and especially to the towns of Navojoa, Huatabampo, and Etchojoa. The inhabitants of these towns distinguish three classes and clearly label them first (*la clase primera*), second (*la clase segunda*), third (*la clase tercera*). Since public attention and interest is directed toward the top of the ladder, the first and second class terms are those most frequently heard in use, and people draw the line between first and second class membership much more clearly than they do between second and third. Dwellers in Navojoa districts regarded by some as third class and by others as a mixture of second and third class families often deny the existence of class distinctions in their neighborhoods. "We are all equal here," they say. Yet the more ambitious and affluent of these families try to strengthen their social connections with members of the second class and to acquire the goods and living conditions associated with that rank. Although some families on the borderline between second and third may deny the existence of class distinctions in their own neighborhoods, they are very much aware of the class divisions and can name the important families in the upper two categories. Many third-class townspeople, however, are reluctant to place themselves in the class system. Those at the very bottom, usually Indian families, admit that people of the first and second classes look on them as third class; the fact is that some second class persons look on them as "even lower than third." The defenses of people in the lowest stratum with regard to class distinctions seem much like those encountered in the United States.[12]

The most important single criterion of class affiliation in the Mayo River area is club membership. In both Navojoa and Huatabampo the first-class club is known as the Casino. Here first-class men may gather at any time of the day to drink and talk, and on weekends dances are held for "the society" (*la sociedad*). Etchojoa has no Casino, and only a few families known as the "real first" (*las meras primeras*) belong to the Huatabampo Casino. The rest of the Etchojoa first class is made up of satellite families who are invited to social affairs at the homes of the "real first." It is widely conceded that most of these satellite "firsts" in Etchojoa would be considered only second class in Navojoa.

Within the first class families of Navojoa and Huatabampo three general categories may be distinguished on the basis of their origins. First, there are the "good families" who are descendants either of local hacendados — who owned most of the land before the agrarian reforms —

or of "good" Alamos families. Although today Alamos is only a picturesque ruin, it was the most important city in the area before the turn of the century. Most of the prominent families have moved out of Alamos, and many have settled in Obregón, Navojoa, and Huatabampo.

Second are the families who have moved here from more distant parts of Mexico, equipped with capital or good educations. If a man has enough money to set himself up well in business or has been educated as a doctor, dentist, engineer, lawyer, or architect, he is accepted at once into the Casino and first-class society. Holders of important managerial jobs are treated in the same fashion. Heads of government bureaus and bank managers, for example, are often transferred about the country and are readily accepted into Casino society here. The family background of these professional men and managers is not always well known, but many were educated at considerable sacrifice by second-class parents or have risen to managerial office from second- or third-class beginnings through their own efforts and ability.

Third are those local families which have risen from second or third class within the past forty years. Most of these are families which have become wealthy during that period.

Although people in the upper classes give considerable attention to family background, the "good" families have had to share the dominant position in the class hierarchy with the newer arrivals. In the upper ranks of Casino society the newly rich and the members of old families treat each other as equals. There are several reasons for this. First, as already noted, population growth has been too rapid to permit any entrenched group to dominate the class system. The steady influx of people with money or professional competence but with questionable family background has undoubtedly helped to keep the system open. Secondly, the revolution and the agrarian reforms weakened, and in some cases destroyed, the economic advantage previously held by the hacienda families. Third, many of the old hacienda families in the immediate area were "little hacendados," more like the "rancheros" or small ranchers of today, and were looked down upon to some extent by the better Alamos families of an earlier period. Fourth, the shift in population and commerce from the mining industry of Alamos to the agricultural development of the plains dispersed the top families of Alamos and broke the continuity effect which recognition of a "good family" might have preserved in a single community over time.

In a sample of forty-one millionaires in the Navojoa first class, half were of good family background, a fourth were from outside the area, and somewhat less than a fifth had moved up from a lower class. (A millionaire in Mexican pesos would have been worth about $125,000 in 1959.) Of a hundred and thirty-four male family heads in the Navojoa first class (including the previous group), about a third were descendants of good families, somewhat more than this were immigrants to the area, and slightly more than a fifth had worked their way up. In a Huatabampo sample of sixty-one first-class family heads, the portion descended from good families was again about half; but over a fourth had worked their way up, and only an eighth were from outside the area.[13] Among the seventeen Huatabampo household heads who qualified as millionaires, only eight were descended from good families.

In Navojoa two millionaire heads of families in my sample were not considered members of the first class and did not attend the Casino. One was Japanese. It is often said of Orientals in this area that "they have no class," a disparaging way of saying that Orientals are beneath the class system entirely, an attitude which stems from the early thirties when the Chinese merchants, who had come to dominate so much of the commercial life of Sonora, were driven out of the state. Despite the prejudice against Orientals there are quite a few mestizo offspring of Chinese and Mexican unions now in the first class. In most cases these are women married to first-class men. The Japanese family in question is accepted into second-class society because of its considerable wealth.

The other millionaire who is not a member of the Casino is said to be too rustic to be comfortable in first-class society. Some second-class persons classify him as first class and as one of the few exceptions to the rule that first-class membership depends upon acceptance in Casino social circles. They are rating him on the basis of his wealth. They sometimes explain that he could be a Casino member if he wished, but he prefers not to join. Some members of the first class laugh at this explanation and claim that he would not be accepted.

This case of the rustic millionaire is duplicated in Huatabampo; in both instances the men are said to be *muy ranchero* — very ranch-like in their behavior. This means they dress very commonly, sometimes even wearing old-fashioned *huaraches* or sandals. They prefer the typical straw hat worn by the country people to the felt sombrero copied from the Texas model, and their language tends to be ungrammatical like that of the peasantry. Both men are also called "Indians." As we shall see, the term "Indian" is as much social as ethnic. Actually, both men are mestizos, like most Mexicans, but their Indian ancestry is known. None of these characteristics is a permanent bar to mobility, however, for the grown children of both men have been completely accepted into the first class. They have had good educations by local standards, thus acquiring the breeding which their fathers lack; yet they benefit from their fathers' affluence.

Education and good manners plus affluence or good family background are the principal requirements for membership in the first class. One family in Huatabampo and two in Navojoa who have Indian names are fully accepted in Casino society. All three families are pointed out as illustrations of the openness of the local class system. Even Indians can join the first class, it is said, when they are well educated and have good manners. These families are mestizos, however, and not very Indian in appearance.

Some professionally trained persons are found in the second class, but they are exceptional. A doctor in Navojoa who is very untidy in dress and personal appearance and treats only the lower classes is considered second class, as is a certain drunken architect.

The situation in Etchojoa, as has been noted, is somewhat different from that in Navojoa and Huatabampo. Since the "real firsts" are so few, there is no Casino in this town, and the inhabitants extend the designation of first class to families invited to social functions at the homes of the "real firsts." The latter group is composed entirely of good families descended from local hacendados. Actually the class system in Etchojoa most closely approximates the situation in this area before the 1910 revolution when the hacendado or large landowning families formed the core of the upper class and decided which of the commercial and small landowning families they would allow to be their satellites. If members of the core group for any reason disapproved of the behavior of a satellite first-class family, they simply stopped inviting it to social functions, which in effect, reduced it to second-class status.

Even today, however, the first class in the larger towns consists of a core group of rich influential families and a satellite group of less rich, less influential families which enjoy membership in the Casino and the first class by virtue of the beneficence of the core group. Although no terms are used to distinguish between these two groups in Navojoa and Huatabampo, the difference is recognized. Many people are aware that the satellite families must be more careful of their behavior and appearance than the wealthy core group. As some people expressed it, "Money removes the stains," but among less wealthy families the stains must be avoided altogether. The truth of these remarks is patent, for the satellite first-class families are undoubtedly those most sensitive to class distinctions.

Further justification for distinguishing between core and satellite groups within the local first class is provided by the attitude of some people within the first class itself, particularly men in managerial posts who have lived in other parts of Mexico. These men have a much more cosmopolitan outlook on the class system than most local persons and do not regard themselves as "real firsts." They place themselves near the top of the expanding national middle class, for to them the local second-class view which lumps all Casino people into one class seems oversimplified. One might be justified, therefore, in thinking of the local "first" class in the larger towns as consisting of two subclasses — an upper of both "good" and newly wealthy families and a lower of less affluent but educated families with good manners (*buenas costumbres*). Thus, from a cosmopolitan rather than a local point of view, this lower first class might be combined with the local second in a larger middle-class designation.

Second-class people are also very conscious of the class system, and they have their own clubs. The most prominent second-class club in Navojoa is the Hispano-Americana and in Huatabampo the Club de Gatos. Unlike the first-class Casinos these clubs hold their functions in rented buildings, and are open only for scheduled dances. Although there is considerable overlap between the first and second classes in the wealth of members, the first class is generally much richer. Farmers of the first class usually work more than a hundred hectares (more than two hundred and fifty acres), whereas those of the second class usually have less than a hundred. Members of the first class engage in other businesses in addition to farming: own car or tractor agencies, hotels, houses, stores, or motion picture theaters. A few doctors and some holders of managerial jobs own or rent farms in addition to their regular duties. First-class members who do not farm at all own the largest businesses in town — the big hardware, furniture, clothing, dry-cleaning, drug, and auto supply stores. Usually the first-class businessman is an employer, while the second-class businessman is merely self-employed. In addition to operating small family-run stores the second class run various kinds of repair businesses; drive their own taxis, buses, or trucks; or work as barbers and the like.[14]

Employees in the first class are usually managers of stores, granaries, banks, and so on, or are the chief accountants for the larger businesses. Men in responsible positions like these are paid much more than ordinary employees and also get generous year-end bonuses. Graft is so prevalent in Mexico that a businessman's only defense is to pay his managers and accountants well. Some managers are members of the impoverished branches of "good families"; other managerial jobs seem to be hereditary; and still other managers have worked up from menial jobs. Working up, however, seems most common in government and bank jobs where managers have been shifted to branch offices outside their home towns. Second-class employees include schoolteachers, policemen, government and private office workers, and clerks in the best stores.

The line between the second and third classes is very nebulous even to the local people, and those closest to the line are most uncomfortable about collocating themselves. The Mutualista Club epitomizes this confusion. Said to have been the important second-class club in Navojoa and Huatabampo a few years ago, it is now considered mixed second and third. In Etchojoa, however, the Mutualista is still considered second class, but there the second class includes families which many people in Navojoa would consider third or on the borderline between third and second. It would seem that in the larger towns where the living standard of many second-class families has been rising rapidly, the second class has become increasingly heterogeneous. Second-class expectations have been growing, and the lower limits of this class are now being viewed differently by different members of the class.

Families clearly designated third class by everyone do not even belong to the Mutualista. They attend imitation clubs which are actually privately owned, open-air dance arenas where beer and soft drinks are sold. These are called "clubs," however, in imitation of the upper classes and bear such names as Club Verde, and Club Balerina. During seasons when the first- and second-class clubs are electing queens to preside over their festivities, the owners of these third-class dance arenas sponsor similar elections among their clientele. Heads of families which everyone definitely assigns to the third class are predominantly landless, unskilled day laborers. Also in the third class are many ejidatario farmers living in town who also work a large part of the year as manual laborers in agriculture and construction. Most of the Indian families living in town fall in the third class; less than five per cent of my secondclass samples for Navojoa and Huatabampo were classified as Indian. Only in Etchojoa did lists of second-class persons contain as many as twenty or twenty-five per cent Indians, and almost all were farmers rather than merchants.

We come finally to the country people and their place in the class structure, and it should be noted that first-class families in the Mayo River area rarely have their permanent homes in the country. They prefer to live in town where they can send their children to private schools. However, some families living in the smaller villages have become sufficiently prosperous for members of the second class in Huatabampo and Navojoa to consider them their equals. Most of the country people are equated with the town third class, although, as I said earlier, some assert that "Indians" and those who live in mud-and-wattle houses are even "lower than third."

Although the country people or villagers are equated by members of the first and second class with the town third class, they are usually referred to by the more descriptive phrases *la gente campesina* (country people) or *la gente ranchera* (ranch people). Like people in some thirdclass or borderline second-third-class neighborhoods in Navojoa, villagers characteristically deny the existence of class distinctions among them. One hears again and again in the villages and small towns that "We are all poor here." Country people do not deny that classes exist, but they consider them peculiar to the larger centers of population. Among themselves they stress the equality of poverty.

This attitude is strongly held even in some of the newer small towns in the Yaqui River irrigation district, where an appreciable amount of economic differentiation has already taken place. At Quechehueca, for example, the ejido families are considerably better off than the landless families who have moved there to work as day laborers, but no class distinctions have evolved as yet. The ejidatarios remember very well that they were day laborers themselves not long ago. At Villa Juárez one again meets with this attitude of equality, and even greater economic differentiation has taken place there than at Quechehueca. Though all social affairs and public dances at Quechehueca are community events attended by everyone, the more prosperous families at Villa Juárez have begun to hold separate social functions. The difference results primarily from the fact that Villa Juárez was not formed by ejidatarios but by *colonos* (colonists) — persons given plots by the government of twenty hectares as small private landowners. Their abilities varied, and without any agrarian law to forbid the transfer of ownership, the holdings of some of the original colonos have grown in size as others have sold out. Colonos who have increased their holdings, built new brick and cement houses, and bought pickup trucks now form an incipient upper class. Those who are solvent show the strongest tendency to feel themselves somewhat better than the rest. They look back on their success and the failure of their neighbors, who started with the same opportunities, as clear proof of their own superior ability. They do not brag, for this would be considered poor taste, but when asked why they have done so well and others so poorly they answer modestly that not everyone knows how to take care of money: some spend it foolishly. When one suggests that intelligence and managerial ability also play a part, they quickly agree and marshal evidence to prove the point. The less successful who are greatly in debt are much more equalitarian. They blame the government and their creditors for their trouble and are still firmly on the side of "the poor."

Despite the country people's disclaimer of class distinctions among them, they recognize a difference between Yoris and Yoremes. These terms for whites and Indians respectively are from the native Cáhita language of the Yaquis and Mayos, but have been adopted into southern Sonora Spanish. "Yori" literally means "white," but it signifies a distinction more social than racial, for many Yoris are as dark-skinned as their Indian neighbors. One is a Yori if he does not speak Cáhita as a household language and does not take an active part in the traditional Indian fiestas and ceremonies. Members of a family of known Indian background who now speak Spanish almost exclusively and have given up Indian religious customs may be called *indios civilizados* — civilized Indians. Or it may also be said of them that they are *yoremes que quieren ser yoris* — Indians who want to be whites.

The term "mestizo" is little used, and actually both Yoris and Yoremes may be mestizos in a racial sense. I once heard several Mayos discussing the problem of differentiating between Indians and Yoris when addressing strangers on the road. To address a stranger in Cáhita and have the stranger reply in Spanish, or vice versa, was, they agreed, embarrassing. "It is better not to talk to strangers," the men concluded.

Another local term for Yoris or non-Indians is *gente de razón* — people of reason. The term is not opprobrious to the Mayos, and they sometimes use this phrase themselves in referring to their Yori neighbors. "People of reason" refers to those who are "more civilized" — confident of their ability to get along in Spanish and not overly self-conscious and ill at ease in the presence of Yoris. Indians who have had some schooling or have had continuous close relations with Yoris through jobs or intermarriage are sometimes referred to as *más de razón ya* (more rational now). Antonyms of *gente de razón* are *indios broncos* or *indios cuatreros*. "Indios broncos" literally means "wild Indians" but is now used to refer to Indians who avoid relations with Yoris. These may also be called *indios desconfiados* — distrustful Indians. "Indios cuatreros" refers to those Indians who speak Spanish with errors of grammar and pronunciation. For this very reason they often prefer to avoid situations in which they must converse in Spanish because it causes them to feel shame.

Although the peasants recognize a difference between Yoris and Indians, for townspeople these distinctions are usually unimportant. Many members of the first and second class in the larger towns classify country Yoris as *indios blancos* (white Indians) or simply Indians. Sometimes this failure to distinguish between the two groups results from a genuine confusion, for the country Yoris often live in a manner indistinguishable from the Indian. The houses and standard of living of the two groups are much the same from the townspeople's viewpoint and very often along the Mayo the native Yori can also converse in the Indian tongue. Sometimes, though, the townsman may call a country Yori an *indio blanco* for the very reason that he knows the person's background. For example, Ramón C. is light-skinned and speaks Spanish like any Yori, but he converses just as well in the Indian tongue and his mother is known to have been an Indian. Though he is married to another country Yori, speaks Spanish at home, and does not take part in Indian ceremonial life, some townspeople who know him consider him a "white Indian." One man who told me this was considerably darker than Ramón.

Some peasant Yoris when irritated or amused by the behavior of a close relative will say *Así son los indios* — "That's the way Indians are." If one points out to the speaker that his relation to the man in question makes him an Indian too, he invariably smiles or laughs good-naturedly. "Of course I am an Indian," he is likely to say. "Why should I lie to you? We are all Indians here. We all have Indian blood. But some are more Indian and more *duros* (thick-headed) than others."

On the other hand there are a few Indians who resent being called "indios." The Yoris refer to these as "Indians who want to be Yoris." These men deliberately try to associate with Yoris and often avoid other Indians. They are inclined to brag a lot, exaggerating how much money they have, the size of their crop yields, and their close association with Yori "friends" in town.

Very little real hatred or prejudice is directed against the Indian in this area. Certainly there is nothing approaching the discrimination practiced against the Negro in the southern United States nor that practiced against the Indian in the Andean countries of South America. If there is anything approaching real racial prejudice in this area it is felt by Indians, especially the Yaquis. Their hatred is based on the long history of Yaqui-Mexican wars that lasted until quite recent times. Older people still remember and discuss the bitter fighting between Yaquis and Yoris and have kept some of the hatred and horror alive in the minds of the younger generation. The Yaquis fought to retain their tribal lands and finally were formally conceded their present reserve in the thirties. Jealousy over their land is still the Yaquis' major concern and the major inspiration of their continuing tribal identity. Friction between Yaquis and Yoris is greater on the reserve than anywhere else. Off the reservation, Yori prejudice against the Yaquis seems slight today. There are a few old men in Obregón who remember the Yaqui wars and have no great love for the Indian, but the Mexican population of the Yaqui Valley has been so diluted with immigrants from other parts of Mexico in recent years that there is now a different Yori population with no tradition of hatred for the Yaqui. As a consequence we have here a case where surviving prejudice is stronger in the minority group.

In the Mayo area, Yori and Indian peasants mix at all social gatherings. This is not so true of the Yaqui, whose social affairs are mainly sacred, with ceremony and ritual of both Roman Catholic and aboriginal origin. Although Yaqui women do not engage in secular dancing, unmarried Mayo girls attend public dances along with their Yori neighbors. Public dances are the most common and popular form of entertainment among Mayo and Yori peasants, just as they are among the various classes in town; they are usually sponsored purely for profit by anyone who gets the necessary permission from the local authorities. In this respect the dances are most like the third-class "clubs." An electric phonograph with badly worn records and scratchy needles, amplified at full volume over a squealing public address system, provides the usual music, and the dancing is on ground sprinkled with water to keep down the dust. These pay-dances also accompany most of the larger religious fiestas in the Mayo area. Since there is free dancing for couples at weddings, they are always well attended.

Both Indians and Yoris attend wedding dances. Food, coffee, and beer are served to Yori and Indian guests alike, but the former are usually served first when the host is a Yori. As in town, boys and girls attend dances separately, the girls always accompanied by chaperones. Girls sit on benches set up around the dance arena and as each dance piece commences, the boys approach their favorites and invite them to dance. Usually Yoris dance with Yoris and Indians with Indians.

Theoretically a girl never refuses an invitation, for to do so is considered extremely rude. But by her attitude she can clearly suggest her unwillingness. Some Yori girls do not like to dance with Indians, and few Indian men have the courage to invite them. Sometimes, though, an Indian boy finds courage in his tequila bottle and asks a Yori girl to dance. In such circumstances the girl would be afraid to refuse, for it is said that "some Indians are very mean," (*algunos indios son muy malditos*). Everyone has heard of cases where even sober men have struck girls who spurned them at dances. No retribution is demanded of the spurned man either by the girl's sweetheart or by her relatives, for "all girls should dance when invited," and "men do not fight over women." But once a Yori girl has complied with custom by dancing once or twice with her Indian pursuer, she may retire from the arena and take refuge in the dance "owner's" house. Yori men sometimes dance with the Indian girls, but it is generally said that the Yoris do this "to laugh at" the Indians.

Although both Indians and Yoris most often prefer to marry their own kind, mixed unions are common, occurring in twelve to twenty-seven per cent of the marriages in different villages. Of thirty peasant

Yori heads of families whose opinions about mixed marriages were solicited, all but three felt it made no difference whether one married an Indian or another Yori. Three women believed that Indians should marry Indians because they understand each other better. Of forty Indian families questioned, twenty-two thought the choice was immaterial or a matter for each person to decide for himself. Eighteen objected to mixed marriages, always for the reason that Indians understand each other better. Two Indian women added that mixed unions are undesirable because Yori men abandon Indian wives.

Most heads of families in the country work a good part of the year as day laborers whether or not they have land.[15] In villages like Las Bocas or Vicam, which are outside the irrigation area and a considerable distance from the large towns, men are often self-employed instead of supplementing their farm incomes by hiring out as laborers. Such self-employment usually consists of selling firewood, weaving maguey fiber bags or reed baskets, or manufacturing lime powder from rock or shell. Men who support themselves entirely by farming usually have fifteen acres or better and several head of cattle. Actually, the number of a peasant's cattle is a better index of his independence than the amount of his land, for many peasants with several acres of land rent them to others. Those with cattle are financially able to pay the water taxes, buy seed, and sustain the various costs of planting, for they can always sell one or two head to raise cash if necessary.

Living standards vary considerably with class, as differences in housing clearly show.[16] Houses of Navojoa first-class families range in value from twenty to five hundred thousand pesos, and average about a hundred and forty thousand pesos (about twelve thousand dollars) in value. Because of lower labor costs, both materials and construction are very cheap in Sonora, and local people are able to build at least twice as much house for the money as one can in the United States. Second-class housing in Navojoa averaged about fifty-five thousand pesos or about forty-five hundred dollars in a sample skewed toward the richer members of that class. The average value of second-class housing in the smaller town of Huatabampo was only half that in Navojoa. There is a very big difference between the second- and third-class housing or between second-class townsmen and the country people. Most housing in the country villages as well as much of the third-class housing in town is simple cornerpost construction with adobe or mud-and-wattle walls and dirt floor and earth roof, and costs less than two thousand pesos or under a hundred and sixty dollars.

Another clear indication of differences in wealth among the classes is the automobile.[17] The small pickup truck is the most popular vehicle in the area, for it is the least expensive and of obvious usefulness for farming. Many first-class families (between a fourth and a third) in Navojoa and Huatabampo own both a pickup and a passenger car (called *carro de lujo* or "luxury car" in Sonora). About the same number own a passenger car only and somewhat fewer a pickup only. The pickup is definitely the most popular second-class vehicle (owned by a third to a half of the families in my sample), but both the cars and the pickups of second-class families tend to be more than four or five years old and those of the first class less than four or five. Country people very infrequently own cars — usually not more than one or two families in a village, or less than five per cent. By contrast, ninety per cent of first-class families and two thirds to three fourths of the second class have automobiles of some kind.

W. Lloyd Warner has estimated that the upper class in the United States contains three per cent of the population, the middle class thirty-eight per cent, and the lower class fifty-nine per cent.[18] The Mayo River upper class would probably be limited to the wealthy core of the local first class, including both "good" families and the newly rich. My estimates are only well-informed guesses, but I believe this upper class would account for less than two per cent of the local population. The middle class, in which I would include the satellite families of the first class and all members of the second (based on Navojoa and Huatabampo standards) may account for as much as a fourth to a third of the population. At least two thirds of the population is lower class, consisting of the town third and the country people. The proportions of the classes do not seem strikingly different from those in the United States, but our people have more money and are better educated. It is my impression, however, that the middle class in this area has grown considerably over the past decade in absolute numbers, but whether it has grown larger relative to the third class I cannot guess without knowing to what extent the third class has been increased by immigration during that same period. Certainly the middle class is much more prosperous than it was ten years ago, and this prosperity has given it a definite new strength and a new optimism about the future.

The country people have not enjoyed the same striking increase in wealth. We have here a society in transition, with three clearly distinguishable major classes, yet still preserving the marked extremes characteristic of dual society. Obviously it would be a mistake to think of a dual society as simply a bifurcated one. A three-class system is old in Sonora, and unquestionably dates back to a time when contrasts were even greater than they are today, and when social mobility was much less. I strongly suspect that all urban societies, even preindustrial societies, could be — or could have been — divided into at least three classes. And some degree of mobility was probably present in all. Even in ancient Egypt, skilled craftsmen could rise from humble beginnings to positions of considerable importance and status. The crucial division within a dual society results from most of the people's being deprived of power and culture capital.

Technological growth and concomitant increases in the mobility of the labor force would seem to be most closely associated with any gradual straightening of the convex gradient between the contrasting extremes of dual society. But simple redistribution within a dual society tends to favor asymmetrically those who already have power and knowledge. Attempts to redistribute material wealth equally within such a society, without an equalitarian distribution of power and culture capital, will tend to cause a retreat again toward asymmetry. Such redistributions may not lead to technological growth: they may only shift the distribution of wealth around the same mean.[19] This weakness in simple redistributive measures explains in large part why the Mexican land reforms have failed to lift the peasantry as far as some had hoped they might. It is appropriate, then, that we turn now to a consideration of land reforms.

X

The Land Reforms

In the discussion of exchange labor in Chapter VII we saw that a strong ethic reinforced by sanctions of reciprocity guaranteed the equivalence of the work exchanged. In these very simple cases where man-days of unskilled labor are reciprocated, the so-called labor theory of value, associated with Adam Smith, David Ricardo, and Karl Marx seems applicable. But in even the rudest societies, when goods are produced by special skill some additional reward accrues to the specialist. As such rewards become more and more delayed and differentiated with increasing specialization, the labor investments in the various goods, skills, and services exchanged become more obscure for each participant. Labor investments can no longer be directly compared, and the delay of impersonal reciprocities (exchange) leaves relative price open to fluctuations caused by changes in supply and demand independent of changes in labor costs.

Modern economists find a normative and ethical concept of value rather than an empirical one like relative price in the writings of Smith, Ricardo, and Marx, when these three men concern themselves with the labor theory.[1] The strong ethical sanctions in exchange labor, a case where the theory applies, agree with the modern view that the labor theory is an ethical concept. But the normative nature of labor theory by no means eliminates its importance for understanding human society, for the ethic is as universal as the invidious comparison on which it is based.

Despite the difficulty of equating labor investments by casual inspection as the division of labor increases, when the distribution of rewards within a society becomes so asymmetrical that those at the bottom of the hierarchy feel exploited or unfairly used, they act to increase the exchange value of their labor. The limits of endurance are highly variable, but apparently they can be reached in any human group. The acceptance of Marx's ideas in so much of the world, the rise of the labor union movement in our own society, and the expropriation and redistribution of land in many countries all testify that there are limits of tolerance, however variable, on the minimum exchange value which people are willing to accept for their labor.

The people of Mexico reached their limits with the revolution of 1910. The subsequent land reform movement, which has persisted up to the present time, has been a deliberate attempt to make the distribution of income more symmetrical within the population by redistributing agricultural lands among the peasantry. This situation provides us with an opportunity to examine the effectiveness of a land reform program as an instrument of invidious sanction for the redistribution of wealth. But to put the land reforms in perspective, it is necessary to consider briefly the preceding hacienda conditions. Only fifty years ago this was a coercive society for many of the country people. Now old and growing fewer in number, the men who worked as peons on the pre-1910 haciendas help to keep alive through oral tradition the memory of the legendary injustices of that period. For no matter how poor they may be, peasants seldom fail to derive some measure of satisfaction from a comparison of the present with that time so recently past when parents or grandparents were "slaves" of the hacendados.

The Haciendas

Apparently a few "free" villages managed to survive along the rivers during the hacienda period before 1910, but most of the Indians and poor mestizos were forced to work from sunup to sundown six days a week — and sometimes Sundays as well when work got behind. All the haciendas operated stores (*tiendas de raya*) where the workers could get food and clothing on credit. Hacendados also loaned food or money to sponsors of fiestas and weddings and to the "free" farmers whose small plots failed to maintain them in bad years. Once in debt, a man was obliged to work as directed until he had paid his debt in full. It is said that a good worker never had trouble getting credit; consequently debts tended to increase. Many owed between two hundred and eight hundred pesos apiece at the time of the revolution. With wages of only eight pesos a month the prospect of repaying debts was hopeless once a man owed more than a hundred pesos.

Some freedom was made possible by the practice of "buying" laborers. A man dissatisfied with conditions where he worked could appeal to another hacendado to "buy" him by paying his debt. Between 1900 and 1910 when only a few "tame" Yaquis remained on the Yaqui River haciendas, many Mayo Indians were "bought" in Navojoa in this fashion and taken north. Some of these Mayos remained in Yaqui territory, while others returned home after the revolution or later took up residence in towns and villages in the irrigation district south of the Yaqui River. At haciendas where women worked as laundresses, cooks, or as field hands at weeding and harvesting corn, they too were extended credit. If a man from another hacienda wanted to marry such a woman he would persuade his *patrón* (boss) to "buy" her for him by paying her debt where she worked and adding it to his own. When a man grew old, a son might assume his debt to spare him the hardship of working in his old age.

If a man failed to show up for work at dawn muster, a *sobresaliente* (hacienda policeman) went in search of him. Sickness was not an acceptable excuse if the local curer in whom the hacendado had confidence pronounced the man well. Escape was difficult, for hacendado owners cooperated in catching runaways. Even if he was willing to abandon his family, there was no place a man could readily hide, for he was suspect wherever he went. A stranger was asked his means of support and if he had none was considered a thief and put in the army. Peons could also be put in the army for refusing to work or trying to escape.

Others were punished in various ways. They might be locked up without food for twenty-four hours and then made to do a full day's work. Some were enclosed in a room in which lime powder had been thrown into the air. Another favorite punishment was to tie a man's arms under his knees and suspend him from a horizontal pole in the sun until he fainted, while his wife and children looked on, crying. After begging the patrón's forgiveness three times, he might be cut loose. Some were made to work with a *niño* (literally "child"), which meant being chained by the ankle to a heavy log. These men were assigned chores requiring considerable movement, such as weeding, so that they would have to shift the "child" periodically as they moved down the field.

The worker could appeal to no higher authority than his patrón, for all local government was controlled by the hacendados. Local police aided the sobresalientes in hunting down runaways, and when the owner of hacienda San Ignacio was mayor of Navojoa, he used municipal police for sobresalientes, and the municipal jail became his hacienda prison.

Workers had few perquisites. They could collect firewood on hacienda land, but in most cases were not allowed to keep livestock or to cultivate subsistence plots. Within the hacienda itself land was set aside for growing the corn and beans necessary to feed the workers. The commercial crops were primarily wheat and chickpeas, exported from Yavaros and Agiabampo, and some corn and beans were also sold locally. Peons who owned small parcels of land could not work them on Sundays without their patrón's permission and on some haciendas they were expressly prohibited from doing so at any time until their debts were paid — a rule obviously intended to make repayment more difficult. Only on the cattle ranches in the sierras were peons given seed and loaned mules and plows to plant small subsistence crops, but even these men had to work their plots on Sundays.

In 1910, debt slavery came to an end when Madero's followers rode from hacienda to hacienda burning the debt records of the hacienda stores and telling peons they were free. Private capital continued to develop the land, however, and the size of the farms increased until the late thirties. Before the revolution the haciendas of this area were primarily cattle ranches, although some had short canals to irrigate a few hundred acres. Hacienda Chucarit had the largest irrigated area on the Mayo River before 1910 — about a thousand acres. But by the late thirties several landowners on the Mayo were irrigating over two thousand. The small size of farming ventures before 1910 seems inconsistent with the legend of "slavery" so strong in the oral history of the region. But as one old man explained it, "Less land was cultivated then, but there were much fewer people too. Besides, it was the tyranny that was great — not the size of the farms."

The Ejidos

Actual redistribution of large landholdings or *latifundios* got off to a slow start after the revolution and did not reach its peak until the administration of President Lázaro Cárdenas (1935–1940), who is still idolized by the Mexican poor. It was he who reinterpreted the reform to include resident peons on haciendas; previously the beneficiaries had been members of independent villages whose traditional village lands had been absorbed by the hacendados. The earlier and more limited purpose of the reform was to restore communal village land tenure, an aboriginal form of ownership dating back to pre-conquest times.[2]

The lands expropriated from the hacendados were turned over to *ejidos*. An ejido is a group of no fewer than twenty beneficiaries of a grant of farm land, sometimes including pasture and woodlands as well, received from the federal government and owned in accordance with the national agrarian code.[3] That code specifies that members must work the land personally and can lose their right to membership if they fail to work it for two consecutive years.[4] No ejido member has the right to sell his land; sharecropping and renting are permitted only to ejidatarias with small children, persons under sixteen who have inherited ejido rights, and the physically incapacitated.[5] An ejidataria loses her ejido membership by marrying a man who is an ejidatario,[6] and no ejidatario can name another ejidatario as his heir.[7] There can be only one heir; ejido rights cannot be divided. These last regulations prevent accumulation of ejido plots by an individual and division of plots through inheritance.

Ejidos are of two kinds — individual and collective. In the individual form, which is by far the more common, the cultivable land is divided among the members and each works his own plot. In collective ejidos, the profits are divided, but the land itself is worked as one large farm, without being subdivided into individual parcels. The agrarian code favors the collective form for agricultural zones producing crops for industry, where it can be shown by economic studies that the collective system will result in better living conditions for the peasants, and where the individual form would be uneconomical for the kind of crop produced or for the employment of farm machinery.[8] Once common in the Yaqui Valley and in the sugarcane zone around Mochis in northern Sinaloa, the collective form has all but disappeared. Its main support came not from the ejido membership but from the government lending agency known as the Ejido Bank. It is much more convenient and economical for the Bank to deal with an ejido as one collective unit than with a great many ejidatarios individually. The collective form reduces paper work, supervisory duties, and the Bank's financial risks.

Each kind of ejido has a board of six directors (*mesa directiva*) divided into two committees — the *comisariado ejidal* (executive committee) and the *consejo de vigilancia* (vigilance committee). Each committee has a president, secretary, and treasurer, although in the vigilance committee the latter two offices are non-functional. Officially the term *comisariado* applies to the entire executive committee, but it is widely used in this area to refer to the president alone; the president of the vigilance committee is generally referred to simply as the *vigilante*. The president of the ejido is its administrator and in the collective form he controls all the planting and work schedules and acts as general overseer. He directs ejido meetings, represents the membership (with power of attorney) in all dealings with government officials, and receives and acts on all official correspondence. He is assisted by his secretary and his treasurer. The vigilante's job is to keep close watch on the president to make sure that his actions square with the agrarian code and that his monthly accounts are in good order.

Officers of the ejido are elected every three years by a majority vote of the membership. Before an election meeting, ejidatarios in this region usually divide informally into two groups to support the candidates of their choice. Each candidate, by agreement with his supporters, picks his own running mates for the jobs of secretary and treasurer. The winner becomes president and the loser vigilante.

In the larger individual ejidos the president, vigilante, and secretary receive a daily wage of fifteen or twenty pesos. (The daily wage of a peon is twelve pesos — about ninety-six United States cents.) The officers of a collective ejido are paid for their working time like any other member of the ejido, except that they work the year round whereas other members work seasonally. A five per cent harvest tax is usually collected to pay land taxes and to meet all the operating expenses of the ejido — rental of office space and equipment, the salary and travel expenses of the officers, and the upkeep of the ejido truck for the president's use.

Collective ejidos are all financed by the Ejido Bank, which determines the crops to be planted, oversees the work, and sells the harvests. The Bank may buy farm machinery for a collective or pay contractors to clear, plow, plant, and harvest. In this area it seldom finances anything but mechanized operations. To maintain members of collective ejidos between harvests, the Bank advances them a daily wage later deducted from the harvest profits.

Today approximately thirty-four per cent of the land in the Yaqui River irrigation district and forty-one per cent in the Mayo River district is ejidal. Much of the Yaqui River area developed in very recent times has been turned over to colonos, small private farmers, rather than to ejidatarios. Although it has almost three times as much irrigated land as the Mayo, the Yaqui River zone has fewer landowners (8,867 as opposed to 9,609 in the Mayo district). Forty-three per cent of the Yaqui River land is owned in holdings of from 125 to 250 acres whereas only twenty-three per cent of the Mayo holdings falls in this category. Thirty-three per cent of the Mayo district is held in plots of twelve acres or less as compared to only one per cent in the Yaqui River district. The average size of holdings is three times as great on the Yaqui as in the Mayo zone — sixty as compared to twenty acres. The ratio for ejido lands is the same — thirty-five acres in the Yaqui River zone and twelve and a half acres in the Mayo.[9]

A major reason for the larger average size of holdings in the Yaqui River zone has been the faster rate of expansion of the Yaqui irrigation district. Many ejidos, for example, began with very little cultivated land but considerable thorn forest. As the irrigation system developed and the thorn forest was stripped away, some ejidos ended up with fifty to seventy-five acres of irrigated land per member. Since the area was not so crowded that people were agitating to get into ejidos already formed (as was the case on the Mayo), the ejido farms grew while their memberships remained fairly constant.

Ejidos vary considerably in size. On the Mayo the smallest (Bocano) has only 20 members and 207 acres; the largest (San Pedro) has 1,134 members farming 13,500 acres. The membership of an ejido is seldom confined to a single ranchería or pueblo, and even when it is, members usually share the community with *vecinos*, or non-ejido neighbors. Of the thirty-five ejidos I visited in the Mayo irrigation district (all but two or three of the total number), seventeen had memberships distributed among two to ten different communities. In the other eighteen ejidos, better than three fourths of the members lived in one community, but always with vecinos. Of these eighteen communities, nine were populated predominantly by the families of the ejido, and in the other nine cases half or more of the community was non-ejido or of mixed ejido membership. For this part of Mexico, the ejido should be thought of as an association rather than as a community.

In twenty-two of these thirty-five ejidos ninety per cent or more of the members spoke Cáhita as well as Spanish. In three ejidos ninety per cent or more spoke Spanish only. In the remaining ten the monolingual Spanish-speakers were slightly in the majority. For the Mayo, ejidos are no more ethnically isolating than villages.

Of the thirty-five ejidos I visited, two were formed in 1920, seven during the early thirties, and twenty-five during the late thirties. Twelve began as collectives, all formed in 1937 or 1938. The life of these collectives varied from one to nine years and averaged about five years. The number of peasants who favor the collective system is small. Almost everywhere, public opinion is overwhelmingly against it and nowhere more strongly than in those ejidos which have experienced it. (One notable exception will be discussed below.)

One very common objection to the collective ejido is aimed at the inefficiency of its management. The work foremen were fellow ejidatarios and often friends, relatives, or compadres of the men they bossed. Most found it difficult or impossible to reprimand workers, and when they did so they were accused of feeling self-important and of treating their men like peons. A foreman who tried to get a normal day's work out of his crew was laughed at. "We are no longer living in the days of Porfirio Díaz," they reminded him. The fact that so many ejidatarios did not do their fair share of the work was the most persistent criticism of the collective system encountered among the peasantry. "Most workers went out to the fields to report for payment, but did no work." The more industrious members soon grew discouraged, for they felt that by working hard they merely helped support the loafers.

Members of collectives never really felt like farmers, much less like owners of their collective enterprises. They were still peons; only the bosses had changed. Besides, in the ejidatarios' opinion, the Ejido Bank was even more impersonal, unpredictable, and inefficient than the hacendados. The Ejido Bank, as we saw, is a government lending agency established to provide ejidos — especially the collectives — with the farm credit necessary to carry on their operations. The Bank's funds are provided by the government, and appropriations are usually delayed.

The ejidatarios' credit often is approved so late in the planting season that crops are inferior as a result. The Bank, which collects and sells the harvests, may delay liquidating accounts from six months to more than a year. These long delays in payment have hurt the Bank's reputation among ejidatarios more than anything else.

To most ejidatarios the Bank seems like a very cold and impersonal sort of patrón. "The Bank does not care if we starve," is a common complaint. A man fairly regularly employed by a rich landowner can always get a loan of money or food when his family is hungry. In contrast, the Bank's practice of taking an entire wheat harvest and not even leaving the ejidatarios enough for their tortillas seems unwarranted and heartless. And complaining at the Bank's offices does no good. "They (the Bank personnel) are just employees. They get paid no matter what happens, so why should they care about us?"

As we saw earlier, the Ejido Bank advances a daily wage to members of collective ejidos when they work. But since this is officially considered a loan rather than a wage, the Bank is not obligated to make the payments meet the minimum wage laws. Consequently, members of collectives often earn less than the average hired hand.

Related to all these problems is the very basic one of rewards and incentive. In a collective ejido there is no clearly measurable relation between individual effort and returns for that effort. Dividing profits according to the number of days each man works provides an incentive to show up for work but does not affect workers' productivity. Working for a wage below the minimum because it is not officially a wage might be easier to bear if annual profits were high enough to stimulate interest. But in nearly all collective ejidos most of the profits go to pay off debts incurred during bad years when the ejido lost money or from investments in machinery, land clearing, leveling, canal construction, and so on. Because they never seem to get out of debt to the Bank, ejidatarios sometimes compare it to a *tienda de raya* (the old hacienda store). They feel that costs are deliberately piled on them to keep them in debt and under the Bank's thumb. Since members are usually illiterate and do not know or understand the Bank's transactions, they quickly become discouraged and believe that all their profits are being unjustly taken from them. Members — and frequently even their own ejido officials — do not know the exact size of the harvest, the costs of production, or even the price at which the crops were sold. There is no limit to the suspicions and recriminations that can arise under these unpredictable conditions.

Ejido Bank officials now prefer a modified collective system which preserves the three chief advantages of the collective and avoids its major fault. The three advantages are more economical deployment of farm machinery, cheaper administration, and reduced risks. The chief fault is the lack of individual incentive. The modified collective is not necessarily an ejido but a credit society within an ejido, and consists of fifteen to fifty persons. These smaller groupings allow ejidatarios to associate themselves with others of similar work habits and goals. The local Bank officials believe that a thousand acres is about optimum for the economical use of farm machinery. In an ejido which has fifty acres per member the credit societies would consist of twenty men each. In ejidos with smaller holdings the Bank cuts the work area to five hundred acres so that the associations will not be too large. By working land in large blocks the Bank also reduces its accounting and the records it must keep.

The modified collective differs from its predecessor in that the land is actually divided among the individual members and the individual plots are harvested separately. Plowing and planting continue to be done collectively across ownership boundaries, but each member must attend to his own irrigating and other manual chores on his own plot and is in charge of his harvest. The Bank keeps individual records of harvests, but other costs are figured collectively and divided equally. Harvests may differ considerably as a result of individual differences in skill and diligence, especially with regard to irrigation. Lazy and irresponsible members may go into debt, but the Bank makes up their deficit from the profits of the other members in the same credit association, a practice which greatly reduces the Bank's risks. Strong pressures are brought to bear on lazy members by their fellows, and when one gets too far behind, the association may expropriate the debtor's plot and work it collectively until his debt to them is repaid.

Under this system ejidatarios sense a much closer relation between reward and effort; their incentive is consequently greater. Furthermore, since each member has his own accounts, he has a better understanding of what is going on and does not feel so completely at the Bank's mercy. The failure of the earlier collectives and the trial-and-error development of the modified form has an interesting parallel in the collective preparation and planting of land once commonly practiced by primitive slash-and-burn farmers throughout the world. Except for lands cultivated for the support of chiefs or ceremonial feasts, these collective farms were divided after preparation into plots cultivated separately by individual families who owned the crops produced on those plots. Recognition of the causal relation between the effort and skill of the farmer on the one hand and the size of his yields on the other is probably as old as farming itself. It is also noteworthy that even primitive farmers did not own their tools collectively. The collective ownership of tools and machinery was another failure of the collective ejidos, for the common attitude toward such property was that it "belonged to everybody" or "to the government" and no one felt any responsibility for taking proper care of it.

In relation to incentives, Bank officials now think it inadvisable to allow their credit associations to assume too many long-term debts. They prefer that associations do not invest so heavily in machinery and improvements that profits will be absorbed by a vast array of time payments. Ejido Buaysiacobe is an illustration. When the new irrigation system was extended into this area, most of the ejido land was still virgin thorn forest. The new lands were cleared with Bank credit and were to be worked on the collective system until the clearing costs were paid. But, for the usual reasons, the ejidatarios soon grew dissatisfied with the collective system, and the Bank changed to the modified collective system. Meanwhile so much machinery had been bought that most of the harvest profits continued to be used to pay off long-term loans. Discouraged and demoralized, the ejidatarios revolted against the Bank and many began renting out their plots illegally. A new Bank director took charge, and the debts were reduced by selling most of the machinery. Their confidence won back, most of the ejidatarios are again working with the Bank.

At present most collectives are the modified kind, and almost all of the true collectives that still exist are considered temporary working arrangements for repaying the costs of clearing new lands. The members look forward to a division of the land into separate parcels. All the newly cleared lands in the Yaqui reserve are being worked on this basis. The Yaquis are very much dissatisfied with the collective system and have submitted to it only with the expectation of changing to the modified form in the near future.

Land Tenure, Land Management, Credit, and Graft

Although the agrarian code limits the size of private holdings on irrigated land to one hundred hectares (247 acres), many persons within both irrigation districts farm areas well over a thousand. In some cases these farms are several times larger than any of the areas irrigated on the pre-1910 haciendas. Some are held legally in the names of various relatives and thus constitute family farms. A married man with six children, for example, can operate a farm of eight hundred hectares (about two thousand acres) by holding one plot of a hundred hectares in the name of each member of his family. Those with even more land usually hold plots in the name of trusted employees. The deeds to the plots are mortgaged to the full value of the property. An employee who is the legal owner of such a plot is usually given a substantial bonus each year in addition to his salary.

Men who control these large farms are branded as *latifundistas*, and the threat of expropriation is always in the air. The labor unions and particularly the communist Partido Popular (Popular Party) endeavor to incite ejidatarios and landless farm laborers against these "modern hacendados," demanding investigations and expropriation for the landless. Although he may work within the letter of the law, the large farmer is uncomfortable about its spirit. As part of his operating expenses he must pay off those agitators who can be bought, including the local press.

Not only does the size of private farms, in practice, pass the limit imposed by the agrarian code, but even ejido lands tend to consolidate so far as their management is concerned. Some estimates say that half of all ejido land within the Mayo irrigation district is either rented or sharecropped. Sharecropping of ejido land theoretically requires an equal division of expenses and profits between landowner (ejidatario in this case) and tenant. In practice, the tenant finances and manages the entire operation. He buys the seed, rents farm machinery (or uses his own), and pays for all labor including that of the landowner. Here the tenant is the capitalist or financier and the landowner is the impoverished sharecropper. After the tenant has deducted that part of the harvest corresponding in current market value to his expenses, he divides the rest equally with the ejidatario. Tenants generally prefer to rent ejido land rather than sharecrop it; but they must be extremely careful, for they have no legal right to their harvests if the ejidatarios should decide to claim them, as occasionally happens. To protect themselves against such tactics, the tenants in some cases sign an illegal contract with the president of the ejido which, by implicating the president, serves to insure against his treachery later on. The president, naturally, is paid for his cooperation.

Because renting is illegal it is difficult to get statistics about its frequency. But my investigations of one Mayo River ejido convey some idea. This ejido has about two hundred members and approximately twenty-five hundred acres of irrigated land. At the time of the study two private farmers were renting from 250 to 375 acres and another four were renting from 100 to 175. About 250 acres more were being rented by several small farmers and ejidatarios accustomed to planting from one to three plots to supplement their own holdings. All these rentals together accounted for about sixty per cent of the total acreage of the ejido. By and large, the practice of renting shifts land management from Indians to non-Indians while the work force remains the same. The ejidatario is always given first consideration when hired farm labor is needed, so, in effect, many Indians hire out for work on their own ejido plots.

A strong tendency for independent parcels of irrigated land to be consolidated through sales, renting, and sharecropping persists in spite of the land reforms and the agrarian code. A major reason is the increasingly high cost of planting. Although ejidatarios have recently been exempted from paying their share of the dam and canal construction costs, private landowners are taxed for these improvements. In addition, all must pay water charges and buy their seed. Most small farmers rent plowing machinery. A few rent mules, but within the irrigation zone the soil has become difficult to till with animals and requires heavy tractors. Since all of these costs come at planting time and require a considerable outlay of cash, farmers, both large and small, get credit to meet them. Only a few finance their own operations: even most wealthy farmers prefer to invest their cash in other businesses with the hope of realizing a higher return than the one per cent monthly interest they pay on borrowed money. Keeping cash in the bank "where it does no work" is considered poor policy, partly because of the fear of inflation.

Wealthy and middle-class farmers usually have no problem in getting credit. Most join credit unions which borrow several million pesos each year from private banks. Each member can borrow from the union up to the full value of his land, which is normally figured at five thousand pesos a hectare (one hundred and sixty dollars an acre).

Poor farmers must get credit from government lending institutions or from private moneylenders. The Ejido Bank is specifically for ejidatarios, and the Banco Agrícola for small private farmers. The personnel of both agencies do not consider them banks in the business sense, but rather as a form of government aid for developing Mexican agriculture. This is one way of justifying the losses, which have been heavy. In the Mayo zone alone the Ejido Bank has written off over twenty million pesos in bad debts. Although the Banco Agrícola works with small farmers who own their land, it never forecloses on anyone.

The government "banks," for the reasons mentioned earlier, are unpopular among the farmers. The Ejido Bank has been working hard lately in the Mayo zone to regain the confidence of ejidatarios, most of whom prefer to rent or sharecrop their land rather than work with the Bank. Others get credit by selling their crops *al tiempo* — in advance and at a price so far below market value that the interest in some cases may amount to as much as fifty per cent. Families with draft animals and plows and enough cattle to sell one or two head a year to pay water taxes and buy their seed can farm independently, but such families are comparatively few.

The major reason for popular distrust of the Ejido Bank is its reputation for graft, which is managed in innumerable ways. For example, Bank officials may get a percentage on all purchases of insecticide, fertilizer, and farm machinery ordered for ejidos. This is undoubtedly one reason why some collectives were so overloaded with debts that they were never able to show a profit. Fertilizers have been used on newly cleared lands without any preliminary soil tests and ejidatarios have often been encouraged to buy unnecessary farm machinery. One ejido was induced to dig a great many wells and install expensive pumping equipment only two years before the area was to receive water by gravity from the new irrigation system. Graft was involved in the construction of the wells and in the purchase of the equipment. A popular pun sums up the Bank's reputation: *Banjidal,* a common abbreviation of Banco Ejidal used in newspaper captions or painted on Bank equipment, is often read *bandidal* or "bandit gang."

Graft extends down into the ejido itself. Only too often the president, secretary, and vigilante of the ejido come to an agreement with the Bank inspector during a friendly drinking session at a bar in town. From then on they may find many ways to graft ejido funds. Part of the harvest, for example, may never be entered in the accounts. Ejido members may be credited with more days of work than they are paid for and the difference pocketed by the officials. Expenses may be padded, especially for repairs to equipment. Several ejidatarios told me that they had learned to read, write, and calculate since becoming ejidatarios so that they could defend themselves against the *mordilones* (grafters) within the Bank and their own ejidos. But even those who are able to read and write do not always get the chance to defend themselves. Members of several of the new Yaqui collectives complained that they never were told of ejido expenses or even the size of harvests. They had no way of estimating for themselves what profits should be, and when they asked their credit society officials for an accounting, they were rebuffed. Some of the heads of ejidos were illiterate and did not understand the accounts; others acted insulted and accused their questioners of impugning their integrity.

Collectives have been a failure, as has been shown, and where they still exist, as among the Yaqui, it is with the expectation of changing to the individual or modified collective form after land clearing debts have been paid. That the failure of the collectives has been due in large part to dishonesty and poor management is attested by the one exception that proves the rule — the case of the Quechehueca collective. This collective is named after the small town of some four thousand inhabitants where its members live. The town and ejido lie in the Yaqui irrigation zone. About a fourth of the town's inhabitants are ejido families and the rest are families of day laborers. The three ejidos found today at Quechehueca are fragments of what was once a single large collective formed in 1937 with 183 members. One group split off in 1948 and another in 1952 to form individual ejidos. They were disenchanted with the collective system for the usual reasons. Since 1952, however, the last remnant of the old collective — shrunken now to forty-two members — has enjoyed considerable success. Its morale is high and all the members enthusiastically support the collective system.

The current success of the Quechehueca collective has several causes. First, the membership is now smaller and more homogeneous than before. It includes those people in the town most firmly convinced of the virtue of collective principles; its leaders are active members of the Communist-influenced Popular Party. Secondly, the number of hectares per member — about twenty-seven — is much above the average for the area. Third, the land owned by the collective is some of the best in the Yaqui valley and yields have been above average. These last two facts alone mean a relative level of prosperity that would not be possible in most other ejidos. But the success of the association as a *collective* undoubtedly results from the fourth and fifth facts — the honesty and the ability of Bernabé Arana, the collective's leader.

At Quechehueca there is no longer any secrecy about the accounting system. Records are on display in the office and any member can come in at any time and get information. The collective also runs a cooperative store where members may buy up to thirty pesos' worth of food a day on credit. A member's debts accumulate until harvest time when they are automatically paid from his share of the profits. The collective also pays members' butane gas and electric light bills and similarly deducts these expenses from their profits. Profit-sharing, as in all collectives, is figured on the basis of the number of days worked. Some jealousy is aroused by the fact that the ejido officials work all year round whereas the rest of the members are unemployed at certain seasons, with the result that the officials draw a larger share of the profits. The officials have tried to compensate for this by crediting field workers with overtime when they work more than eight hours.

According to Arana, good management of the cooperative store and attention to such details as paying the electric light and butane gas accounts are essential to the collective's success. Otherwise members would spend all their profits when harvests are sold and would be unable to buy provisions or pay for utilities during most of the year. Arana also sets aside part of the ejido's land for the planting of food crops, such as corn, and distributes the harvest to members. Chicken corn is also planted to provide grain for members' fowls and pigs. In addition to a wage of twelve pesos for each day's work, plus food and utilities on credit, members receive a substantial sum of cash when harvests are sold. Arana has slowly accumulated three million pesos' worth of machinery and parts, but without so swamping the ejido with debts that annual profits would be consumed by time payments. Members have been getting between twenty and thirty thousand pesos a year in addition to their wages. None has ever been so well off before in his life.

The success of this unusual collective has depended on the exceptional management ability of Arana, who is proud that all his associates depend upon him, for he is a conspicuous producer — so much so that he is even willing to deny himself the pleasure of consuming conspicuously. Several members have bought new cars and trucks with their share of collective profits, but when Arana bought a new car, people in Quechehueca began to say he was *mordiendo* (grafting), so he replaced it with a used pickup truck. He would like to have a new house, but he has continued to live in the same old adobe and tarpaper shack to avoid criticism. He is trying to interest the government in financing new houses for all the members of the collective. Then he could have one without being conspicuous.

Arana is an unusual man, and very few collectives and ejidos have had his kind of direction. He is proud of his accomplishment. The fact that his is one of the very few successful collectives in all Mexico has brought him attention and respect. Most Mexicans do not seek this form of recognition, for the rewards are less tangible than those of conspicuous ownership. The common tendency among men in responsible government positions is to exploit their offices for their own advantage. The public expects this. I have heard Mexican businessmen joke that bureaucrats in Mexico are considered corrupt if they take more than half of an appropriation; they should leave at least half "for the people."

During the presidential election campaign in 1958, a street crowd in Mochis was responding warmly as PAN (Partido de Acción Nacional) candidates bitterly criticized the incumbent all-powerful Revolutionary Party for the many forms of graft and corruption in the area. Onlookers were nodding and whispering, "True, true," to each other. One old man smiled broadly at his friends and said, "Yes, it is true. But if these were to gain office they would do just the same." Everyone who heard laughed in hearty agreement. The incident is typical of a general attitude, an almost hopeless distrust of government personnel, but an attitude never completely divorced from the Mexican sense of humor.

One day a group of people in Huatabampo were discussing their last three mayors. The most recent one was considered the best, for he had done much for the town and had stolen nothing. In contrast the first of the three was a poor mayor because he had done nothing and had stolen besides. But the second was really the worst of the three, for he had not only been a very poor administrator, he had stolen nothing either: "He not only did nothing for the town, he was too stupid to do anything for himself." This not only illustrates the general tolerance of graft in spite of the fact that it is publicly disapproved of, but it also demonstrates the ambivalence with which graft is viewed.

A friend of mine frequently criticized the existence of the mordida "institution" in Mexico and its purported effects on the country. One evening, passing the local mayor's new house, we remembered that the mayor had been a mere peon twenty years before. My companion chuckled as he intimated how his friend the mayor had continued to improve his finances since entering office. When I mentioned mordida, he hastened to explain that the mayor was not taking a great deal and was not a rich man. He must think of his family, for he might never get such a chance again. He would be a fool, my friend said, if he did not help himself a little. It is worth noting that my friend had hopes of becoming mayor himself someday.

Graft is by no means confined to the Ejido Bank; it is common in all branches of the government. Tax inspectors, police, state, and municipal administrators, and men in charge of the irrigation systems are just a few of the many who practice the mordida. On the Mayo River where the irrigation water is sometimes insufficient, graft is much more common in administering the water distribution than in the Yaqui River irrigation zone where the supply is more than adequate. Although limits are placed on the number of hectares that any one farmer can irrigate during water shortages in the Mayo zone, the large farmers always manage to have enough. One method is to rent ejido lands to get their water rights. By paying a mordida to those in charge of the irrigation system, the large farmer may have these rights honored for his own property. Sometimes inspectors are sent from Mexico City to investigate rumors of graft, but they find nothing wrong. Before the investigators arrive, the local irrigation officials advise the wealthy farmers of the area, and the mordidas are prepared.

Partly in reaction to this state of affairs, a new religious fiesta "for God" spread from the Fuerte River area to the Mayo River peasantry during 1958. In a surprisingly short time it diffused to twenty-four communities along the Mayo River. According to one popular account God had told the young man who founded this messianic movement that he would send rain to fill the dam reservoirs. Speaking in the Indian tongue and wearing Indian sandals, God said he was displeased by the fact that when water was scarce the rich farmers always got their full share while the poor farmers had to make do with less than enough. He would remedy the situation by filling the dams. Coincidentally, as the Indians danced, the summer rains were the heaviest in several years, and the water shortage was temporarily ended. (More will be said about this religious movement in Chapter XII.)

Although it is probably true that the poorer people are the ones who directly or indirectly suffer the most from the mordida system, I do not believe that this system is entirely detrimental. In this region at least, the grafters are not responsible for any large flight of capital. The grafters are too small, for one thing. Naturally, it would be impossible for an outsider to verify the disposition made of mordida funds. Nevertheless, after carefully checking the histories of various ex-mayors, tax officials, Ejido Bank officials, federal police officers, and irrigation project officials, I concluded that the objective of most grafters — particularly those who get away with it — is not to graft and run but to graft and invest. Although most improve their living conditions fairly rapidly, it is usually the ones who are too greedy and who consume their fraudulent gains too conspicuously who provoke legal sanctions. The objective of most successful grafters is to accumulate enough capital to become independent of their government jobs. This means going into business, usually farming, for themselves. The successful grafters who stay in this region buy farm land and become independent farmers. Even allowing for the invidious distortions of informants, the weak economic position of these persons at the time they entered office and their relative prosperity afterwards can be verified by cross-checking community knowledge.

Usually the small, successful grafters who manage to become independent farmers are men of better than average ability, and they tend to be good, progressive farmers. The institution of mordida provides one means for ambitious and able men to accumulate the necessary capital to go into business for themselves. Not all grafters save and invest, however. Some spend their fraudulent profits, and if they are grafting on a big scale, this procedure will quickly tax even the limits of tolerance of the Mexican mordida system. On the other hand, if they are petty grafters, no one pays much attention, and the money goes quickly back into circulation.

Many people consider the mordida serious national moral turpitude, but the fact that Mexicans themselves are very much concerned about it would suggest that its existence results more from lack of sanctions than from lack of ethical or moral standards. In fact, the mordida, as I see it, is not really a moral problem at all in Mexico, for although ambivalent attitudes toward it are common, few people openly condone it. Amusingly enough, wealthy men who got their start via the mordida are often its most bitter critics.

Most Mexicans blame "the government" for the present state of affairs, an attitude especially common among the country people, who often say that what Mexico needs is "a good government." For most critics, "a good government" means an administration of honest bureaucrats and politicians who "want to help the people." And in this regard Sonorans almost always refer to federal rather than state or local governments, not because they consider the latter less corrupt or more altruistic than federal government, but because they regard the local situation as so bad that the only hope lies with central authority.

When I had an opportunity to discuss politics informally with groups of peasants, I suggested that *they* were the government because they were living in a democracy and that it was up to them to improve their political administrations. Though they quickly warmed to the beauty of this idea, it obviously was not the way they thought about their situation. Their own view was much more realistic. As one old man expressed it after some reflection, "Yes, we were the government once — during the revolution. But again we have become like sheep." The more common reaction was, "No one pays any attention to a poor man." The poor feel that they are helpless and that they need a strong benefactor.

The ideals of the Mexican revolution are still very much alive, and the federal government seems very sensitive to the wishes and well-being of the people. The labor parties, too, play a large part in keeping the government liberal. The feeling of helplessness and political ineptness among many Sonorans is a corollary of their lack of education, their general feeling of inferiority, and their inexperience. When any group or part of the population becomes sufficiently aroused over an issue to take action, it contributes funds to send a representative or delegation to the capital to speak with the highest federal authorities — if possible with the president of the republic himself. Far from being a last resort, this is usually the first plan of action. The opinion is generally held (and apparently with justification) that to get anything done, to cut through

all the red tape, and to circumvent the vested interests of local authorities, it is necessary to go straight to the top — to Mexico City.

Ejidos trying to get water or financial assistance, committees of landless peasants petitioning for lands, even the Yaqui Indians, are examples of groups which frequently send a representative to Mexico City
to plead their cause. One of the most sophisticated or acculturated members of the group is always chosen to represent it, for most people in the
lower classes and particularly the peasantry are ashamed to deal directly with the authorities, especially at the local level where their station in life is most likely to be known. They feel that even their clothes
are a mark against them. "If I were to call on the (local) authorities,"
says the peasant, "do you think that they would take me into account?
In these clothes they would know that I am a poor man. Do you think
they listen to the poor? No, señor, *this* is what governs!" and with
thumb and forefinger meeting in a circle he forms the Mexican symbol
for money.

At first I was puzzled as to why local newspapers in Sonora did not
function to curb graft. In the United States, where dependence on advertising tends to make them predominantly conservative, newspapers
are a potent and useful instrument for uncovering graft and corruption
in government. Mexican papers, on the contrary, tend to be pro-govern-
ment and strangely uninterested in the serious problems of graft. When
they make accusations and complaints it is usually against local businessmen. The reason for this is that the small-town paper often depends
more on its mordidas than on its advertising. In fact, it often solicits
its advertising through libel and blackmail. When one of the three open-
air motion picture theaters in a certain town refused to advertise in
the daily paper, it was attacked in front-page articles which called it a
corral, unsanitary even for animals. The attack ended abruptly the very
day the theater resumed its advertising. An article appeared praising
the remodeling, which consisted of a light whitewashing of one inside
wall.

Prominent persons may also be attacked in terms that would be considered nothing short of libelous in the United States. In Mexico, however, libel suits are rarely even brought to court, for the judges themselves are said to be afraid of the newspapers. One wealthy farmer in
Navojoa was repeatedly attacked in a local paper as a latifundista, and
insinuations were made that he had financed the murder of a prominent

labor leader in Obregón. The victim was approached but refused to pay blackmail. Instead he and other local businessmen banded together to finance their own newspaper in self-defense. The same thing was attempted by local businessmen in Los Mochis. But in both towns the newspapers had heavy losses as bad as the mordidas, if not worse.

Occasionally papers do attack graft in government, but only when they are not getting their cut. Mayors and other officeholders often pay local papers a monthly retainer as a public relations expense, but a local grafter who is not paying his public relations money is fair game. For several days one federal highway policeman was attacked unmercifully by a Navojoa paper in an exposé of his bribery techniques until he finally made the necessary arrangements with the newspaper's publisher.

Eventually, as more people buy and read papers and newspaper advertising becomes more profitable, the press's civic-mindedness will undoubtedly increase, for the trend is already in that direction. But the way in which the mordida system extends even into journalism shows that the problem of graft in dual society is basically one of sanctions. The expansion of the middle class and education at all levels are the worst enemies of graft in dual society.

Implications

The Mexican land reform program actually began as a popular revolution against a coercive government which permitted exploitation of farm labor that often approached slavery. So strong still is the reaction against this earlier unequal distribution of power and wealth that even many wealthy Mexicans confuse modern large-scale farming with the labor-exploiting haciendas. Both are grouped together as latifundios (large landholders), but latifundios can exist without exploitation of labor, as farming conditions in the United States show.

One thing necessary, of course, to counterbalance the power potential of large landholders is a strong labor movement. There is every indication that between the time of the revolution and the beginning of Cárdenas' extensive application of the ejido plan in 1936 the Mexican labor movement had gained considerable strength among agricultural workers on corporation farms. The United Sugar Company at Mochis, Sinaloa, provides an interesting case in point.

By 1932, through strikes, the five thousand farm laborers and the twelve hundred factory workers of the United Sugar Company had made their labor union independent of company control. Working hours had been reduced from twelve to eight, wages had been raised, and working conditions were being improved. But because of the continued strikes fomented by the Mexican Communist party, which wanted the lands expropriated, President Cárdenas finally expropriated them in 1938, and the United Sugar Company's cane fields were turned over to its five thousand field hands in the form of collective ejidos financed by the Ejido Bank. At this point the workers became nominal landlords but in actuality continued to work as peons of the company without any working contract.[10]

As landowners, the workers could no longer strike for higher pay and better working conditions; theoretically they were their own bosses. SICAE (Sociedad de Interés Colectivo Agrícola Ejidal), the local collective ejido organization, took the place of the workers' union and through it the workers became dependents of the federal government. The leaders of the collective organization replaced the union leaders as intermediaries between the workers and the company. The workers still grew cane for the company on the land it had previously owned. But instead of receiving individual salaries from the company they were paid collectively for the cane they produced. The individual worker's reward now depended upon the integrity and business acumen of the collective leaders as well as upon the integrity and business acumen of the company's management.

Suppose, for the sake of example, that the workers in a United States factory were organized into a collective and paid through its leaders in amounts based on the volume of their combined production. Suppose also that it was up to these leaders to distribute to each worker his share of the total earnings and to act as foremen and work bosses in organizing and administering the work. Through such a system the collective — or union — bosses would not only be taking over part of the functions of management, they would have the entire earnings of the workers at their disposal, instead of the usual union dues. The opportunities for graft would be unlimited. Suppose further that this collective or workers' union had the official approval of the federal government, but no government curbs on mismanagement, abuse of power, or graft. Like all analogies this one is imperfect, but it conveys some idea of the situation in which the Mochis sugarcane workers found themselves after the

231

land reforms. Considering the amount of corruption that takes place in United States labor unions, one can easily imagine the results under this system in Mexico.

Today the older sugarcane ejidatarios around Mochis look back on the pre-ejido days when they were laborers as a golden era by comparison with what followed. SICAE was bankrupted by graft and inefficiency, and in 1958 the collective was in the process of being broken up into individual ejidos. Some former SICAE administrators who started out as peons are now well-to-do.

Perhaps if it had not been for the ejido land reform, the peasantry today might be more self-reliant and politically united — closer to being a rural proletariat. In effect, the ejido system divides and conquers the peasantry for the bureaucrats and "biters." Although most ejidatarios in this area continue as part-time day laborers, their interests are concentrated largely on the problems of their particular ejido association rather than on the problems facing them as members of a nationwide class of farm laborers. Though the land reforms have changed the form of labor exploitation, they have not ended it.

The debt slavery of earlier days has not persisted, of course; but through the mordida system the peasant is still directly or indirectly the victim of labor exploitation. For example, the graft system may work directly to keep his wages below the lawful minimum when wealthy farmers pay local "work inspectors" to disregard complaints. It may also buy the wealthy farmer irrigation water when there is too little to go around among the poor. It also operates when the members of collective ejidos work for years at wages below minimum and all their harvests go to pay "debts," while the government officials in charge buy their own farm land and build new houses. But the new post-revolutionary variety of exploitation is much less centralized and coercive than the old. It results in a much wider redistribution of the fruits of production. And so far as this region is concerned, the grafter tends to invest his ill-acquired capital in farming and business ventures.

To protect the ejidatario from himself, he is not permitted to sell or rent his ejido plots. Thus, thousands of farm laborers have been converted into permanent managers of small farms on the unformulated assumption that all men are created equal in ability — not just in their political rights. To the extent that the program is successful, it has the effect of "protecting" Mexico from the most productive and competent management of its farm land. But farm management tends to slip back into more able hands anyway, through illegal renting facilitated by the mordida system: those who can best exploit the land will be best able to pay the graft taxes necessary to circumvent the letter of the law, a circumstance which helps to protect Mexico from some of the more unhealthy consequences of its own reforms.

The conviction that the ejidatario must be protected from himself is very strong in Mexico and provides the principal argument for continuing the ejido system, even among the intellectuals and peasants who recognize the many faults of this tenure system and would prefer to replace it with private ownership of the individual plots. Though nearly all of the many ejidatarios I asked claimed that they would prefer to own their land outright in order to avoid the administrative entanglements of ejido membership, many thought the system was justified in preventing members from selling their holdings. None of these thought that they themselves would sell, but they felt sure that most others would.

The distribution of village lands at Sebampo (near Etchojoa) provides a test case of what might happen if ejidatarios were given title to their parcels to work or sell as they saw fit. In 1903, a foreign company owning land between Etchojoa and Huatabampo sold out very cheaply to various buyers. A block of some eighty-seven hundred acres of uncleared land was bought by a small group of Mayo Indian families living at Sebampo. They and their heirs owned it collectively until 1947. Each family had a few head of cattle, and some dry-farmed small clearings in low spots that were flooded during summer rains. By 1947, irrigation canals were pushing toward the Sebampo area, and Yori farmers became interested in renting or buying land there. An Indian by the name of Yucupicio, who had been given power of attorney to represent the rest, began selling and renting parts of the Sebampo common without the permission of the other owners. Uniting against him, they petitioned the federal authorities for an equal division of the land among all the heirs.

Some thirty-eight primary heirs were recognized by the government. It was left up to them to further divide their shares among their brothers, sisters, and children as they saw fit. Since some heirs were delinquent in their land taxes, fractions of their shares were divided equally among the rest. Twenty-seven of the heirs received some two hundred acres apiece and the rest smaller amounts. Sales already made by Yucupicio were honored as legal. Soon after the division, the land became a part of the expanding Mayo irrigation district, and by 1958 all but some six hundred acres had been cleared and was under cultivation.

The resulting changes in the ownership pattern over the ten-year period are especially interesting in view of the fact that the size of the plots was much larger than that usually granted to ejidatarios. The rent alone from two hundred acres could provide an annual income six times as great as a farm laborer could earn in one year if employed steadily. Most of these people were farm laborers but none had steady employment. Simply to have kept the land would have assured the heirs of an income enormously greater than anything they had ever known.

Yet by 1958, sixty-one per cent of the land had been sold to thirteen Yori town farmers, all of whom already owned land elsewhere. All the land purchased by these thirteen was in full production and was being farmed entirely by machinery. Two of the new owners were considered wealthy, but none of them was among the richest in the area. All were men who had considerably improved their economic situation by their own efforts.

After ten years, a fourth of the original Indian owners had sold all of their land, having spent most of the proceeds for liquor. Of that thirty-nine per cent of the land still retained by seventy-five per cent of the heirs, about a fourth was being rented. Only half was being worked by the original owners and the relatives with whom they had divided their shares. The size of the plots being worked by these primary and secondary heirs averaged eighteen acres per farmer. Only four men (a tenth of the original Indian owners) had kept their entire two hundred acres. One of these had his land cleared and was working it himself with machinery. This man had moved to Huatabampo to put his children in school and had adopted middle-class living standards. A second man had cleared most of his two hundred acres by loaning it out on the customary three-year, rent-free contract to tenants willing to clear land at their own expense. The contract had expired and he was living comfortably off his rent. Another had divided his land with his five brothers. Together they had cleared sixty-four acres, which they farmed collectively with mules. The fourth man had divided his share among his six sons and together they were working about sixty-four acres with draft animals. The rest of their land was being loaned for three years on a land-clearing contract.

Within a ten-year period, then, over half of the land had passed to Yoris, who were managing it efficiently and productively. The less responsible Indian beneficiaries were working as day laborers as they had before. Very few had shown the foresight and patience to keep all of their land. Most had preferred to sell parts of it as they felt the need for cash, keeping only what they considered necessary to maintain their minimum living standards.

Doubtless most ejidatarios, if allowed to do so, would sell their lands either to spend the money on liquor or to pay for medical treatment in the event of a severe illness. Debts incurred during illnesses are one of the chief reasons for the renting and selling of land among the poor. (A man who becomes a regularly employed laborer is enrolled in the national social security program and is eligible for free hospitalization and medical care for himself and his family.) But as this example shows, most of those who would sell their land would be day laborers who usually rented it anyway. The change would be greater in legal ownership than in actual managership.

Land ownership and management tends to shift from Indian to Yori hands whenever the law permits, and it would seem that this shift is toward more efficient and profitable management and greater national production. The land reform laws that attempt to keep the use-ownership and management of farms fixed form a policy to protect the Indian but not necessarily the economy at large. As has been shown, the mordida system facilitates the circumvention of the land reform law to the benefit, I believe, of national production. Protecting the land tenure of Indian and poor Yori peasants does not insure the most productive use of the land. The poorest-looking fields are almost always those of ejidatarios, fields that are not being managed collectively or by renters. The peasants, especially the Indian peasants, do not have the know-how or are not sufficiently aggressive. They have limited ambitions and give precedence to immediate felt needs. Only a few are inspired to save and plan ahead for future benefits on any sizable scale.

The fact that exploitation can continue in the very face of benevolent reform is a limitative condition of dual society. When a large proportion of a society is impoverished, illiterate, and withdrawn from active participation in the affairs of government, the sanctioning power of the total society may be diminished at the expense of the more backward part. This does not mean that the backward part is totally powerless.

Far from it; the land reform was a popular reform, just as the welfare state is a popular government. The old peasant who said, "We were the government once — during the revolution, but again we have become like sheep," was not far wrong. But those in power have retained a great deal of respect for their flock; the revolution has not been forgotten. Yet the dual situation itself permits exploitation and graft, even though such acts are never openly condoned.

In the dual society, neither the disapproval of corruption in government nor the approval of honest service is strong enough to give force to moral consensus. Only as the lower classes absorb much more of the culture capital and as the social reforms are made more feasible will social sanction effectively curb graft. In the meantime, many of the rising members of the middle class are the worst offenders in their competition for the conspicuous ownership of goods. Mexican society has not achieved the opulence of ours. It is still a dual society with marked differences in ownership but with considerable mobility in status and wealth. In such a situation it is quite unremarkable that status motivation should flow primarily toward conspicuous ownership. Where conspicuous production does occur, it is usually part and parcel of the desire for conspicuous ownership through expanding a private business or farm and the personal fortune that goes with it.

When the middle and lower classes have grown much stronger and many of the present differences in wealth and ownership are erased, prestige through conspicuous production will become more important. Until that time, vast welfare-state programs will continue to be vehicles for the pursuit of individual advantage through bureaucratic corruption. This does not mean that *all* government officials are, or will be, corrupt. I am speaking here of the predominating tendency. One frequently hears it said of some Mexican politicians that they are not "biters" because they are already rich. And it is true that successful businessmen who are already conspicuous owners of modern houses and expensive cars take pride in being honest political administrators. Navojoa had such a mayor when I left in 1959. But by and large the importance to prestige of durable goods in a rapidly expanding market and the tolerance of graft (first, because of the ignorance and apathy of the retarded part of the dual population, and second, because of the impracticality of much protective social welfare legislation) combine to make the bureaucrat and the elected official a conspicuous consumer first and a conspicuous producer last.

The collective ejido is a good example of the susceptibility to corruption of welfare-state programs in a dual society. I encountered only one successful collective, and there the manager was definitely oriented toward conspicuous production — even to the point where he deliberately curtailed his normal consumption tendencies when they threatened his position as a conspicuous producer. This one success shows that conspicuous production is possible in this free, dual society but improbable on a scale sufficient to justify making it the basis of public policy.

Under the Communist regime, farming collectives have apparently never been completely voluntary. The Russian leaders make a great show of conspicuous production, and among some members of the party there is unquestionably a strong *esprit de corps* and messianic concern for putting conspicuous production ahead of conspicuous consumption. But the emphasis on conspicuous production within the society at large, including the farm collectives, is largely the result of coercion.

The kibbutz of Israel is a voluntary organization with strong *esprit de corps*. These farming collectives approach messianic movements in tone, and perhaps nowhere does conspicuous production more completely replace conspicuous ownership than here. The "most important ideal upon which the entire kibbutz culture is based . . . is the moral value of labor," [11] an ethic of the renunciation of private ownership and the idealization of conspicuous service to the group through productive physical labor. But these societies are not government-instigated and government-managed. They are the spontaneous creations of a rejected people, many of them migrants to Palestine from Europe.

Conspicuous production may be successful for indeterminate periods as the dominant motif of small ingroups with a strong messianic sense of purpose. Within a large state it can be the by-product of a coercive bureaucracy. But in free dual societies with great internal inequalities in culture capital it seems unrealistic to expect it to take root widely. The prestige-seeking most likely to be stimulated on a broad front is conspicuous ownership, since the emulative form of invidious comparison is most likely to precede those promotional varieties which require a fairly sophisticated population. The next chapter will be directly concerned with the operation of invidious emulation as a stimulus to development in Sonora.

XI

Mobility and Emulation

T HE Mexican land reforms did not end all exploitation of the lower classes, but sudden reforms seldom work permanent miracles in a dual society, especially where the lower classes themselves hold a weak sanctioning position in the creation or enforcement of the negative controls. The land reforms have, however, certainly helped to open the social structure for greater mobility. The breakup of the large landholdings and the new ownership limit of one hundred hectares did not terminate latifundios, as we have seen; but they have helped to shake up the established order of vested interest and keep it flexible. The large landowner is now more like a manager than an owner, for if he does not "own" the land in the name of members of his family, he owns it extralegally in the name of employees. Such holdings tend to break up upon the death of the manager and often are sold. The ejido system, however, is an aspect of the land reforms which has probably decreased the mobility of many families by tying them to land they cannot sell. Men who might have moved permanently into town to join the working proletariat have remained in rural areas working sporadically as day laborers.

Recent technological improvements in Sonora have also accelerated social mobility by expanding opportunities for emulative buying of consumption goods. Again the effects seem to be more marked in the first and second classes than at the bottom of the social ladder. This chapter deals with the emulative changes taking place first in the towns and second in the country.

The Townspeople

In a sample of two hundred first-class Huatabampo and Navojoa male heads of families, between a fifth and a fourth had apparently moved from second to first class in their own lifetime.[1] The line between second and third is not so finely drawn and the amount of mobility within the second class is not easily estimated on the basis of informants' opinions. Most members of the second class have appreciably raised their living standards within the last ten or twenty years. This general rise in affluence has increased the difficulty of deciding which have actually crossed the line, for in retrospect people tend to assign second-class status rather generously. Occupational changes are not decisive unless the person has moved up from the hired-hand category to become a businessman or a farmer with land of his own. Apparently there have been few such. Usually, the rise in class status has resulted from an expansion of farming or commercial activities from small beginnings rather than from a major occupational shift. No attempt was made to get information about shifts in occupation between generations. The expansion of opportunities has been too recent and the variety of occupations too few in this predominantly agricultural society for such shifts to be very significant as yet. In this respect I believe that by far the greatest occupational shift between generations is represented by members of the various professions and managerial positions, particularly those who have moved into this area from other parts of Mexico.

Of forty-five male heads of families who had definitely moved up into the first class while in the area, apparently none had begun life as a peon or a day laborer. There is little doubt that nearly all had at least second-class status to begin with. More than a fourth (twelve) had inherited a small amount of capital to start their farming or business operations with. Another twelve married women whose families were able to advance them enough capital to get off to a good start. Six men had got financial backing from wealthy men while working for them, usually in managerial positions. One had been loaned money by a relative to make a beginning. Five, a tenth of the total, got their start through the

239

mordida system. Only six (thirteen per cent) had become wealthy enough to enter the first class purely on their own saving ability. These started variously as peddlers, mechanics, or employees, and then began some very small business operation such as a *taniche* (a store with an inventory worth as little as fifty dollars) with accumulated savings. Each built up his business first and eventually bought farm land. Only three had entered the first class without greatly improving their financial status; these three were employees with responsible positions, two of whom had married women of the first class and a third who had moved up entirely because of his personal appeal and respectability. Among those second-class men who improve their financial status, many more than in the first class seem to do so through their own ability to accumulate savings.

It is easy to understand why Sonoran townspeople, despite their class consciousness, place such a high value on social equality; for in contrast to the country people, who always stress the equality of poverty, the townspeople put great emphasis on the equality of opportunity. They can always point out an example to prove that any man, no matter how humble his origins, can rise to the top of the social ladder through his own ability. It is certainly possible for a poor man to climb a long way in Sonora, but among societies which share a strong ideal of equal opportunity for all, Sonora is not unusual in its discrepancy between ideal and practice. By far the majority of all marriages, for example, are intraclass, and very few Indians reach positions anywhere near the top of the social ladder. Ejidatarios who gain social stature have usually expanded their operations by buying or renting more land, and there are few. Nevertheless, mobility is considerable, and it provides an effective demonstration to support the ideal.

In general the descendants of hacendado families have tended to maintain the status quo and have profited more from the inflation of property values than from entrepreneurial ability. Persons who have risen in social and economic status or have migrated to the area usually make the most inspired farmers and businessmen. There is considerable resentment in some quarters against many of the hacendado descendants — the feeling that they not only fail to make the most of their opportunities (the farms and town properties which have inflated enormously in value), but retard developments in the area through their conservatism. These hacendado families are likely to oppose civic improvement measures out of fear of taxes, to refuse either to develop valuable town properties or to sell them to people who want to buy them for business purposes, and often to operate their farms with far less than model efficiency. Leadership in civic improvement and business acumen most often comes from the newly rich and the immigrants.

Members of the first class, as we have seen, have the largest, newest, and most expensive houses. Because construction labor is so cheap, a twenty-five-thousand-dollar house is the equivalent of one two or three times as expensive in the United States. But it sometimes costs nearly as much to furnish a house as to build it, particularly if it is filled with all the latest electrical appliances, which are very expensive in comparison to building costs. Yet even air conditioning is common now in the first class.

The consumption habits of the Navojoa second class are a smaller-scale version of those of the first class. Many have built new houses of brick and concrete and others are remodeling their old brick or adobe ones. They are installing metal-frame windows, laying tile on their concrete floors, adding modern bathrooms, buying new furniture, stoves, refrigerators, and even washing machines and air conditioners.

Third-class families feel less compulsion to buy and to improve their living standards, though those on the borderline between third and second, with young unmarried women who occasionally attend second-class dances, definitely follow the buying pattern. But the families of the unskilled day laborers, who may work alternately in town as construction workers or as loaders and on nearby farms as day laborers, barely manage to make a living. Families of Indian descent in Navojoa and Huatabampo usually belong to the third class and work at unskilled and semiskilled jobs.

The tendency is growing even in the smaller towns toward emulative buying of goods with the aid of generous credit facilities. Refrigerators and stoves are becoming so common that some families buy them even before paving their kitchen floors. To keep it off the dirt, a section of floor is cemented to accommodate the new appliance. The reason furnishings in the poorer second- and better third-class homes are often more elaborate than the housing is that furnishings can be bought on time, whereas families must save cash to construct or remodel their houses.

It is in families of the second class and the managerial, professional, and small business families of the first class that one encounters the greatest preoccupation with conspicuous ownership. These are the families striving to improve their status and the ones most preoccupied with appearances. When a family rebuilds its house or buys a new refrigerator, the neighbors frequently stop in to look: the owner shows off his improvements with pride, but the visitors are often critical. The bathroom ceiling should have been concrete to avoid the unsightly beams supporting the tile. And the new kitchen sink or refrigerator is nice, but the one *they* are planning to buy is much bigger and has additional features.

The preoccupation with acquiring consumer goods is increased by the very fact that they are the principal symbols of status. The occupational structure in this farming area is so relatively undifferentiated as yet that it provides no clearcut measure of class. More important than whether a man is a farmer, merchant, or manager is how big, successful, or important he is within these categories. Being in one of the professions is one of the best criteria of class status, as is employment as a day laborer. But most of the dividing lines are gradients rather than black and white distinctions, and a family's wealth as displayed in house, furniture, car, dress, and education is the best measure of its status in other people's eyes.

Much of the buying in the towns, especially in the middle class, is done by or for the young unmarried women in the family. Time and again one encounters families of very modest means — those of schoolteachers, for example — who are remodeling their houses and buying new living-room furniture, refrigerators, and big gas ranges. And invariably when one asks the reason for all this spending one hears, "There are young ladies in the house." Beginning when they are in school, town girls of the same age form cliques within which very strong emulative comparisons are made. Girlfriends regularly visit each other, often in groups, and are extremely conscious and critical of each other's living conditions. As a consequence, they are constantly striving to improve the appearance of their homes. Girls of seventeen or eighteen may mop the floor six or seven times a day just in case unexpected visitors should arrive. They nag their parents continually to buy new furniture and appliances on time or to install modern plumbing where they have not done so.

Many girls find work as store clerks and secretaries in order to help their parents pay for such improvements. Sometimes even very modest middle-class families have been able to make striking improvements in their living conditions when several unmarried young people were working and helping to meet the family's time payments. Often families competing in this new conspicuous ownership race try to save money by subsisting on the peasant diet of tortillas and beans. On several occasions I heard people jokingly depreciate the household improvements of another family with the comment, "But they do not eat."

The tendency for invidious, emulative consumption within the middle class to center on the young unmarried girl is in large part a product of the great attention paid to the courtship pattern of social dancing in which she plays the leading role. This dancing is the most popular social activity in the towns and is a focus of interest at all levels of society. It is at these dances, moreover, that the middle-class girl finds her greatest opportunity for upward social mobility. Only among the Yaquis, for whom dancing is a purely ceremonial activity performed by males alone, is courtship dancing absent.

Except among the Yaquis, social dancing accompanies religious fiestas, weddings, and birthday parties, or it may be sponsored solely for secular entertainment, for benefits, or for profit. Because girls are carefully chaperoned and guarded at all times, a dance is the one socially accepted occasion when young people can meet eligible prospective mates. Most people meet and begin their courtship at dances. This is especially true in the country, where dances bring together young people from neighboring rancherías who would otherwise have little opportunity to meet. In all but first-class circles, where United States dating customs are beginning to be copied, boys attend these dances separately from the girls, who go in the company of their chaperones. At country dances the girls sit on log benches around the dance arena and at clubs in town they sit on benches or at tables. During the evening, as each dance begins, boys approach the girls of their choice and invite them to dance. This is practically the only time a young couple can talk together in private.

In the towns the dances are more formalized and institutionalized than in the country, for in town they take place in connection with the clubs. In Navojoa young people of the first class attend Sunday afternoon dances quite regularly. Members also sponsor frequent Saturday night dances at the Casino which are attended by married couples as well as young people. Groups of unmarried first-class girls may form small temporary clubs of their own and sponsor occasional benefit dances at the Casino. The benefit, often for the church, is an excuse to hold the dance and justifies the girls' activity in publicly arranging it.

No girl who attends or hopes to attend second-class dances would be seen at the third-class "clubs," and many clearly disdain even Mutualista affairs. Upward mobility in the dance pattern takes place principally through friendships with other girls of higher social status. Since dating is unusual here, attendance by girls at social dances depends on invitations from other girls. Friendships between girls of different classes are often formed at school or in places where they work as clerks, stenographers, or bank tellers. Often a girl from a marginal third-class family who has a good reputation and is attractive, personable, and well dressed is invited by her office friends to second-class functions. This usually results in increasing pressure on her family to bring their living standards closer to those of the girl's second-class friends. Similarly, second-class girls are often invited to Casino dances by friends in the first class.

A first-class boy interested in a second-class girl may attend second-class functions to be with her; or, if he has female relatives who know her, he can persuade them to invite her to Casino dances. Such procedures are uncommon, however, since most first-class men marry within their class. Although the girl who moves upward in the social dance pattern may hope for a better marriage as a result, she also claims to be interested in the move upward for its own sake. Her parents, too, are interested in her rise in the club system, for their own status is thereby enhanced. In classifying others in the local class system, an informant invariably gives considerable weight to the position of their daughters in the social dance pattern. This has become a handy reference, and one which occupies everyone's attention, for gauging status.

Middle-Class Ethics

The social dance pattern also demonstrates the greater preoccupation with ethics and especially with sexual morality in the middle class. The burden of the system again falls on the girl because of the double standard of sex morality in most of Latin America. Men of all social classes are expected to be promiscuous, but women are carefully guarded, especially the *señoritas*. (*Señorita* literally means "Miss," but in certain contexts it is a polite way of saying "virgin.") This is true at all levels of society. Even peasant and Indian women travel in pairs or groups when they leave the house without a male relative to accompany them. In town, women now have considerably more freedom than they did ten years ago, and today many drive about in cars and pickup trucks. But even in town no young girl of good reputation ever goes far from home without someone to accompany her.

It is not surprising, therefore, that the second class has taken a very dim view of the recent adoption of Anglo-American dating patterns by some first-class families. The fact that boys are allowed to pick up their sweethearts alone in cars to take them to the movies or to a dance at the Casino is a sure indication to many people in the second class that premarital chastity is becoming a thing of the past among first-class girls. For a second-class girl to enter a car alone with a man would be unthinkable at any time.

The middle class certainly worries more about the whole question of women's virtue than either the upper first families or those in the third and peasant categories. (I am here, as on pages 199–207, using the phrase "middle class" in the cosmopolitan sense to include not only the local second class but those first-class families who hold their status because of education or managerial position rather than wealth.) Because the middle class feels less secure about its status and is more concerned with rising, the ethics of the society at large seem intensified at this level.

In Navojoa today a second-class girl's loss of her virginity does not necessarily pull the other members of her family down with her into disgrace as it might have a few years ago and still does in towns like Etchojoa. Cases of first-class men seducing second-class girls as a result of liaisons arranged at dances are growing rare. Nevertheless the widely held attitude is that when men go down the social ladder to attend social dances they do so with dishonorable intentions. While mobility for girls within the dance pattern is upward, for boys it is downward. It is much more difficult for boys to attend dances of a higher class than for girls. But though girls would not think of going to dances of a lower class, boys frequently do so. Attending dances of a lower class does not carry the stigma of lower status for boys as it does for girls. Girls attempt to move upward to make a better marriage or to gain status; boys move downward seeking a premarital conquest. If a boy seduces a girl of the second class, her indiscretion usually becomes known when he brags of his conquest, and she is henceforth barred from attending second-class affairs. One pretty Huatabampo girl who was asked to leave a second-class dance became the mistress of a rich old man a few weeks later.

Although such seductions are growing more uncommon in the larger towns, second-class girls are still very suspicious of the intentions of first-class men who attend their dances. When invited to dance by a boy of the first class, a second-class girl sometimes accompanies him as far as the dance floor and then abruptly returns to her seat, leaving the boy standing alone. The girls do this "to laugh at" the first-class boy who, they believe, attend their dances only "to laugh at" them. By such behavior a girl shows her indifference and asserts her virtue, which the courtship system simultaneously idealizes and jeopardizes.

In the middle class, where status anxieties are greatest, the double standard of sexual morality is intensified, and the burden of the family honor continues to rest principally on the woman, especially the marriageable girl. Although common-law unions are prevalent among peasants and third-class townspeople, no woman can gain or keep second-class status as a common-law wife. A man's status, however, is not changed by such a relation. There are cases of prosperous common-law unions in which while the man has gained second-class acceptance because of his business acumen and affluence, his mate has remained third class. But in one instance where the couple registered their marriage with civil authorities after living together for many years, the action automatically raised the wife to the second class.

Common-law marriage has no official recognition in Mexico nor does a church ceremony by itself. To be legally married a man and woman must register their union with the proper civil authorities. Among the peasantry and the town third class a civil union does not really give the woman any greater security than a common-law union, however, for the man's income is neither substantial nor regular enough that authorities can effectively force him to support his family after separation. Common-law unions are no less stable than civil unions at this level, and they even have a certain legitimacy within the lower class since they are frequent enough to be a normal and expectable phenomenon. Civil registration of a union some time after the couple have taken up residence together is common in the lower class, but is not the most respectable form of marriage at any level. Couples frequently register their unions after conception "for the sake of their children." Civil registry accompanied by a church service and a wedding party before consummation and residence together is the most respectable form of marriage, and the usual form in the middle and upper classes.

People are very conscious of each other's marital status, and in all but first-class homes, wedding pictures hang in some conspicuous place, usually the room where visitors are received. Even peasants go to considerable expense to have a well-framed picture made of bride and groom together in their wedding finery. Not only is this picture a public reminder of the woman's marital status, but it is said to be a reminder to her daughters. A father can point to it and admonish them to follow her example, saying, "Su madre salió bien de su casa; salió bien casada" (Your mother left her home honorably; she left properly married).

When a girl elopes with her lover, as happens in most unions of country or third-class people, the girl's parents are always greatly distressed and the mother weeps as though the event were a great tragedy. The reason most often heard for elopements is that weddings are expensive and a waste of money. Upper- and middle-class couples, however, look upon the wedding as a very necessary expense.

Investigations I made at Buaysiacobe and Biacusi [2] showed that only twenty-two and thirty-five per cent respectively of the unions counted had been accompanied by a wedding and in several of these cases the bride was already pregnant. Thirty-three and forty per cent legalized their unions at various times after taking up residence together and forty-five and twenty-five per cent never legalized their unions. For twelve and eighteen per cent of the samples this was the second or third union.

Out of a small sample of twenty-eight Indian couples in the third class of Huatabampo, only thirteen were legally married. Six persons of each sex (twenty per cent) had lived with one or more spouses previously. Among fifty-one households in the Rosales district of Navojoa on which information was secured, a fourth of the unions were common-law. No information was collected about the number of remarriages in this group, but in eight of the households there were women of varying ages who were separated from their husbands.

Only one first-class girl was found who had entered into a common-law union, as a result of an elopement several years ago. Such unions are now rare in the middle class of Navojoa. Sometimes, however, second-class girls in Huatabampo and Etchojoa become the mistresses of first-class men, but in these towns many of the families considered second class would be only third in Navojoa. Thus, some of these girls are so poor that an irregular connection with a wealthy man seems desirable. For this reason, a wealthy married man looking for a mistress among second- and third-class girls gives special attention to girls from families where the father is dead and the widow has several children to support.

Since first- and second-class unions are usually accompanied by both legal and religious ceremonies, remarriage is much more difficult, for it presupposes the formality and inconvenience of divorce. If a man enters into a union with another woman without divorcing his first wife, the new spouse is his mistress and he cannot hope to have his new family accepted at his own class level. Divorce is very unusual in the middle and upper classes, although men in both may keep mistresses or have occasional affairs with other women. Both men and women are so confident that men are by nature promiscuous that a man who is faithful to his wife is often said to be dominated by her. While some men of first and second classes can afford the luxury of maintaining or partly maintaining a mistress or a second wife, peasants and third-class males, who usually can afford only one family at a time, abandon one woman and take another when it suits them.

Although it is true that the burden of a family's virtue rests upon the woman, and that the man who indulges to some extent in extramarital affairs is doing a natural and manly thing, an excessively amorous man is criticized. Only moderation in women and liquor is socially approved. Again and again it is said of the man who is considered a failure or who has not made the most of his opportunities that he is "very drunken" and *muy mujeriego* (very much addicted to women). In contrast, most men who have been successful and have moved upward are said to be *muy trabajador y muy serio* (very hard workers and very serious). Time and again people tell you that anyone who works hard and does not waste his money foolishly on frivolities is bound to "go up."

This firm local belief that hard work with little or moderate indulgence in "the vices" will automatically bring its reward is altogether justified, for there are endless examples to demonstrate the rule. Local prosperity has carried many people along with it. Any number of small storekeepers and other businessmen, for example, have worked hard — though not necessarily brilliantly — and invested earnings in businesses, houses, or land. Such men have prospered with the growth of the towns, the commercial life there, and the inflating value of town property. And where hard work and a serious temperament have been combined with intelligence and good business judgment, men have become wealthy. But those who inherited farm land or other property and did not work hard or were not careful in their spending have either remained at the same economic level or have gone down. There is no doubting, then, the practical wisdom of the local ethic of work, temperance, and frugality. These local values are not confined to any class nor to the townspeople any more than is the concern for women's chastity, but all are emphasized more by the middle class.

For those successful men who *do* indulge "vices," there are always extenuating circumstances that make them, in the eyes of the local people, exceptions which prove the rule. One prosperous man who often drinks heavily on weekends is said to be cold sober every Monday morning, an example of praiseworthy self-control. As for the successful man whose *vicio* is women, it is said, "He can afford it."

Oddly enough, I once heard the ethic of hard work and temperance very earnestly proclaimed by a Mayo Indian fiesta sponsor. This surprised me because fiesta sponsors are a favorite target for criticism from Indians who have joined local Protestant evangelical sects. This man, one of the current sponsors of the Holy Trinity fiesta in Júperi, said that the expenses of ceremonial office were not a worry to him because he could afford them. As he explained it, he was not the kind of man who wasted money on drink. Some men, he said, "invest" their earnings in liquor and so never accumulate anything. But he had always worked hard and had cleared more land whenever he was financially able,[3] so now he could shoulder the economic burden of this religious duty.

To the Indian Protestant evangelists, the traditional Indian Catholic fiestas and all their attendant expenses are foolish and wasteful. The fiesta sponsors, who carry the major economic burden of supporting certain annual religious ceremonies, are among their chief examples of wasteful improvidence. But in a house-to-house survey of peasant evangelists in one district along the Mayo River, I found that they did not really differ significantly from other peasants. They included the same range of racial, economic, and personality types generally found among the peasants of this area. They were not saving and not progressing materially more than their neighbors, although many of the men professed that they and their families were living better since they had given up drinking and going to fiestas. But infidelity and separation from spouses persists. In most respects the Protestant ethic of this group has not made them substantially different from other peasants. Usually the Indians who join the movement are already prejudiced against the expense of the traditional fiestas.

It can be said that this region is developing what might be called a Protestant ethic which draws most of its strength from the most mobile part of the population — the growing middle class. The strengthening of this middle-class ethic is not just independent of any Protestant religious movement, it is taking place in a thoroughly Roman Catholic environment. Many more middle-class men than third-class men and peasants go to Mass. As a group, they are much more devout than lower-class males with the exception of the Indian; most peasant and lower-class males are unbelievers who frequently joke about the Church, the saints, and the Roman Catholic clergy and proclaim their disbelief. Although wives often laugh at their husbands' shocking statements, they always defend the Church. It is an accepted fact that women at all levels of society are more religious (*más católicas*) than their menfolk. But there is little doubt that the most devout men are in the middle and upper classes. Some of the most energetic businessmen in Navojoa are so constant in their church attendance that their lower-class employees consider them *fanáticos* (religious fanatics).

Though envy here often takes the form of accusations of dishonesty (mordida), throughout the society invidious emulation has become much more characteristic than invidious sanction. Envy is still strongest among the peasantry, particularly the Indians. When a Mayo Indian has some financial success and begins to buy expensive clothes and fix up his house, he may still be spoken of depreciatingly by his neighbors as an Indian who is trying to become a white man. But even this mild rebuke seemed to me to be heard a great deal less often in 1958 than in 1948.

Another and even milder form of envy which still persists is to explain a neighbor's success as the result of having found buried treasure. Throughout the area and especially among the peasantry there is a belief that great quantities of gold coins lie buried in the ground. Local folklore has it that the inhabitants of this area in previous eras kept lots of cattle and were very rich. But since they had no banks to put their money in, they buried it for safe keeping, and then often forgot about it. Although even some townspeople put great stock in these stories, the majority laugh at them as greatly exaggerated. They argue that the ranchers of old could not possibly have been rich enough or buried enough money to account for every instance of improved finances. Instead they will tell you that these men are rich today because they worked hard and used their heads. This attitude is an interesting contrast to that more common among the peasantry. Many times I was told that such and such a man — be he a peasant or storekeeper or small businessman who has had remarkable success in improving his business and living standards — could not have done what he has done without luck. "I can remember when he was just as poor as I," the speaker is likely to say. "He works hard, yes, but so have I. No, señor, I am sure he uncovered treasure." It is difficult and to some extent distasteful for the poor and unsuccessful person to credit his more successful neighbor with greater ability. The treasure stories provide a very handy way of explaining these differences in a fatalistic fashion that absolves the speaker of any responsibility for his own lowly station and that shows little malice toward the successful man.

At the other extreme is the growing tendency to admire the successful man openly, particularly when he has done nothing to harm others on his way up. One millionaire who lives in Huatabampo but has business interests all over Sonora is generally well liked along the Mayo River. He began poor and made his fortune in farming and commerce by hard work and excellent business acumen. He fits a kind of local ideal of the successful man — one who has done well for himself, yet is good to those who work for him and does not cheat those he does business with. In speaking of him, an ambitious young man who owns a small store in Navojoa said, "When a man sees his opportunities and makes the most of them it is indeed a beautiful thing!"

A major concern of middle-class town families is the education of their children. Upper middle-class parents, like all in the local first class, send their children to private schools; most second- and all third-class parents send theirs to the public schools. And the principal reason why the rich country families move into town and join the middle class there is to make it possible for their children to attend the six-year primary schools and the high schools, because most villages have only one teacher and three grades. Middle-class parents in Navojoa are much like middle-class parents in the United States in insisting that their children go to school regularly and on time. The ambition which many have for their children presents economic difficulties in large families of modest means. If one son is more studious or more able than his brothers, the parents may decide to concentrate their efforts on him. As a friend told me, "We cannot educate all our children; there are too many. But we are going to make the struggle to educate at least one." He had high hopes that the favored son would become a doctor.

The "colonists" of Villa Juárez who have prospered during the past fifteen years and are now obviously well within the limits of the middle class are especially dominated by this concern for education. Many families in Juárez were sending children to school in Obregón about thirty miles away. A few were even occupying a second home in Obregón where mother and children lived during the week. As soon as Juárez got a new six-year primary school, it began petitioning for government aid to build a high school. When the governor told residents of this community they would have to wait another year until more funds were available, parents formed a "high school patrons' committee," rented a building, and began buying furniture for their new school. A local doctor volunteered to give classes in civics and two housewives prepared to teach sewing and cooking. All this activity by the townspeople was designed to convince the governor of their determination and to attract more attention to their demands, a frequent procedure in soliciting government aid. It was also an election year, a time when many middle-class townspeople try to make education a political issue.

The Country People

The country people have not been so much caught up in the game of emulative conspicuous ownership as the townspeople. Many would clearly like to consume more goods but their expectations have not kept up with their wants, partly because of lack of opportunities and partly because they imagine themselves inferior. Though it is true that the graft system works to the disadvantage of the poor, the peasantry are not held down by a rigorous class system here as in other parts of Latin America. The peasant's failure to improve results partly from his lack of education and the experience necessary to compete with the town Yori, but not to any deliberate, class-conscious curtailment of his opportunities.

The country people can be roughly divided into three groups on the basis of their wants and expectations. First are the conservative Indian families, usually at the bottom of the social and economic scale, who seek status through taking part in Indian ceremonial life and who will be the subject of the following chapter. At the other extreme are the Indians and Yoris referred to by some as *riquitos* (little rich). These wealthier country families enjoy a considerably higher standard of living than most of their neighbors and are among the more open and outgoing members of the peasantry. Between these two extremes are an increasing number of discontented persons, among whom can be found some symptoms of anomie. Many of these are nominally Mayo Indians, but they have lost interest in the Indian ceremonies. They avoid or denounce ceremonies and the prestige satisfaction which taking part in such ceremonies might bring. Yet they do not feel adequate to enter the Yori world, where both business and consumption are conducted largely on credit and depend so much on friends and influence.

The country families I am classifying as riquitos do not work as hired laborers, but maintain themselves independently through farming and business ventures which often require employing others. Lists of such families collected at various points along the Mayo River show that Yori riquitos consistently outnumber Indian riquitos two or three to one. Together, Indian and Yori riquitos make up five to ten per cent of the ranchería population. As we have seen, the vast majority of the country people, even most of the small landowners and ejidatarios, earn their living largely as day laborers.

Within nine rancherías of the comisaría of Tesia in the municipio of Navojoa, I encountered thirty-five riquito families, ten of which were Indian. Most of these people were either ejidatarios or private owners of small amounts of land, and most had a few head of cattle. Ten Yori families and one Indian family rented land in addition to their own. Although a fifth of both the Indian and the Yori families in this group still lived in adobe houses with dirt floors and earth roofs, most had adobe and brick houses with brick roofs, cement floors, or both, and five had brick houses. The average value of this group's housing was at least eight times the average for most rural communities along the Mayo. The group also had at least six times as many radios, sewing machines, gas stoves, sets of living-room furniture, and trucks as were found among the villagers of Las Bocas, La Florida, Buaysiacobe, Biacusi, and Vicam in house-to-house censuses. (Families in these latter villages with stoves, living-room furniture, or trucks would fall in the riquito category too.)

A fourth of the Yori and half the Indian heads of families in this Tesia riquito group had acquired their land by inheritance and had not increased their wealth. Eight of the Yoris and two of the Indians had been helped financially by relatives or through marriage. Five of the Yoris and three of the Indians had bettered their economic status by operating small stores. Like the townspeople, few work their way up without some financial help. Peasants, however, have fewer avenues to credit and are also less likely to seek it. More often they fall prey to the moneylenders who finance them *al tiempo*.

To explain the fact that Yori peasants are usually more successful than Indian peasants it is said locally that Yoris are *más entrón*, a label also frequently applied to Indians who improve their economic condition. To be más entrón is to be more aggressive, more inclined to make influential friends by maneuvering oneself into higher social circles. A man who is más entrón is not afraid to ask for credit, for example, or to form friendships with people who can make loans or otherwise help him. The Indian is said to be *muy encojido* — very timid, the opposite of entrón, because of his strong feeling of insecurity and inferiority in the presence of Yoris. This attitude may be maintained in part by the old custom of frightening children with the threat that they will be given to "el Yori" if they don't behave, but probably most important is simply the fact that Indian children sense their parents' uneasiness around Yoris at an early age and soon adopt the same attitude.

Mayo riquitos are more open in their manner and less timid than the average Mayo. Of the ten in the previously mentioned sample only one is retiring and shy, and he has improved his economic status the least of any in the group. The rest mix very smoothly with both Yoris and Indians. One of them, who owes his present prosperity to winning a lottery, has changed quite markedly from a shy, retiring young man to a quietly self-confident one who enters easily into conversations and often takes the social initiative.

As might be expected, Mayos who achieve some measure of success often become considerably more self-confident. Much of the Indians' drinking seems to be the behavior of the desperate, and the riquitos appear to drink much less than average. The case of Antonio Bacosegua illustrates the kind of metamorphosis which can take place in a Mayo when he gains some success and public recognition. According to his neighbors, this young man was often drunk before he saw and spoke with "God" near Ahome and became the founder of a small messianic movement. When I first met him he kept his head down and shifted nervously from one foot to another as he talked broken Spanish. Eighteen months later his Spanish had improved and he spoke with confidence, meeting strangers and entering social gatherings with new self-assurance. At first, many of his fellow villagers dismissed his story of talking with God as a fabrication, but when it became obvious that the change in his character was permanent, they viewed him with new respect. "He has not drunk since he saw God," they now explained. "What he says must be true, for no man could change as much as he has without God's help."

A good deal of the Indian's uneasiness around the Yori may result from the tradition of past injustice, but today there is no definite class barrier to hold the Indian in his place. Whatever hatred the "whites" may have felt for the Indian in years past as a result of the insurrections has been diluted by the great influx of people from other parts of Mexico. The Indian's lowly position on the social scale is real enough, but it is reinforced by his image of himself. The Mayo feels and acts inferior and is unable to make the most of the opportunities around him largely because of his lack of education. He feels defenseless and ill prepared to meet and compete with the Yori. The self-image of the Mayo, and of many Yori peasants as well, widens the gulf between their wants and expectations. When I have asked members of those groups if they would not like to have radios, refrigerators, modern furniture, cement floors, and tile roofs, they replied, "Of course we would. Who would not? But we are poor and how can poor people obtain such things?"

The behavior of some Mayos when drunk reveals the wide gap between their felt needs and expectations. They sometimes speak Spanish fluently and discuss longings they seldom mention when sober. Although not a typical Mayo, Manuel of Mesquital exemplifies this common tendency by his extreme behavior. Manuel is a farmer, but he also works in Navojoa as a brick-laying contractor and a foreman on construction crews. He is said to be a good worker and intelligent. When he gets drunk in his village he makes extravagant claims, saying he is not an

Indian at all, but the most Yori person in the whole village. He reviles his fellow Mayos as dirty pigs and fools for spending time and money on their religious fiestas. He claims to be richer than anyone in Mesquital and says he will build himself a two-story concrete house and a public plaza for all of the village to enjoy. Manuel is a greatly frustrated man to whom his neighbors refer with a mixture of tolerance and annoyance as "an Indian who wants to be Yori."

Another Indian who wants to be Yori is Félix of Cibacobe, who "acts like a patrón," according to his neighbors. He dresses in white and makes his sons do all the farm work. At social gatherings he mixes with Yoris and avoids his fellow Mayos. He boasts of making high profits on his crops and talks a great deal about his Yori friends. Joaquín of Tesia also likes to associate with Yoris and calls his fellow Mayos "lazy vagrants" when they are not present. He, too, claims to be wealthy and when his son was put in jail for shooting over the sheriff's head "to frighten him," Joaquín bragged that it did not matter, for he could afford the fifteen thousand pesos for bail. When he goes into town, however, he is uncomfortable around Yoris he does not know, and he sits listening quietly instead of talking enthusiastically as he does back in Tesia.

The tendency of the Indian and the poor Yori to feel inadequate in town is reinforced by the limitations in the rural environment to which he clings. When he has land, his holdings are relatively small, and if they are in irrigated areas they are expensive to farm. The water and other taxes he must pay even for only a few hectares represents a cash outlay greater than most country people can afford. If he does not have draft animals and must rent a tractor to plow, his expenses are even greater. He is forced to rent, sharecrop, or work his lands al tiempo, for he cannot hope to get enough cash. His only other recourse is to seek credit from the government lending agencies, and we have already seen why many shun this avenue.

Along the margins of the irrigation districts — near Tesia for example — there are small landowners and ejidatarios who are able to pasture cattle and draft animals in the adjoining thorn forests. Such peasants are the ones most likely to finance their own farming operations, for they can sell cattle when necessary to raise the cash to meet their planting costs. But surprisingly few take advantage of this opportunity to maintain financial independence. Ejido pasture land is frequently overrun with the livestock of more aggressive Yori neighbors while most of the Indian ejidatarios keep few or no animals at all. At Vicam Pueblo on the Yaqui reservation only two men supported themselves by keeping cattle. All the other heads of families cut firewood for a living. Yet the reserve was full of cattle owned by Yoris paying pasture taxes to the tribal authorities.

A study of farming at the ranchería Mesquital de Tesia showed that although peasants are thoroughly accustomed to planting such cash crops as sesame seed and cotton, they prefer to grow staple foods which they can both sell and eat. In this community, many of the heads of families had both irrigated and non-irrigated fields, the latter in low spots bordering the river (called "humid" lands) close to the water table. On the irrigated lands — when they did not rent these fields — they planted cash crops financed by moneylenders. But on the "humid" lands they planted corn and melons and usually financed these crops themselves, because moneylenders are seldom interested in financing outside the irrigation districts. Without water taxes, the owners merely had to buy seed and get draft animals if they did not own them. If they borrowed neighbors' animals they repaid the loan with their own labor.

The peasant is still largely oriented toward a subsistence or mixed cash and subsistence pattern of farming which has been radically altered by the development of irrigation. Cash cropping and complex credit arrangements have been made increasingly necessary by changing conditions. The peasant has a hard time adjusting to them, for his holdings are usually too small to make cash cropping very remunerative when credit arrangements are not completely to his advantage. His circumstances provide him with very meager opportunities at best, and his self-image usually adds to his difficulty.

In the Yaqui River irrigation district at Quechehueca, where ejidatarios received sixty-seven acres of irrigated land apiece (twice the average for ejidos in the Yaqui irrigation district), both Indian and Yori peasants have experienced a remarkable rise in living standards. This example shows that both groups enter readily into the pattern of emulative buying when they have the opportunity. The ejido of Quechehueca, discussed in the last chapter, is particularly interesting not only because of its generous supply of land but because it has a higher proportion of Indian members than most ejidos in the Yaqui irrigation district.

As we saw earlier (pp. 223–224) the original Quechehueca ejido was one large collective that has since separated into two individual ejidos and a small collective.[4] A comparative census was made of Aguila, one of the individual ejidos, and the collective. The two groups live mingled within the same community of Quechehueca. Aguila operates with the Ejido Bank as a modified collective in which each member irrigates, cultivates, and harvests his own plot; all preparation and planting of the land is done collectively on contract, financed by the Bank.

Aguila has forty-six members in as many households and Quechehueca forty distributed among thirty-seven households. A fourth of the Aguila households are Indian, as are half of the Quechehueca families. The predominance of Indian households in the collective is interestingly paralleled in other ejidos that have divided in the course of disagreement over collective principles. Bacobampo, on the Mayo, for example, also splintered into three ejidos. As at Quechehueca, the first group to break off from the collective had the smallest proportion of Indians, and the last group to remain collective had the highest proportion. This does not mean that the Indian is attracted to collectivism: he seems as much opposed to it as anyone. But most Mayos find it more difficult to direct their own affairs than to be directed. As we have seen, where the Indians are members of independent ejidos, they are likely to rent to Yoris and then work for the Yoris on their own plots. When they sharecrop their parcels with Yoris, who provide capital and management while the Indians provide the work, the Indians perform much the same function. Likewise, in collectives it is the Ejido Bank officials and the Yori members who make most of the managerial decisions. The true collective, then, seems to coincide in practice with the general tendency in the area for land management to pass from Indian to Yori hands regardless of the land reforms.

Aguila and Quechehueca families, formerly the peons of a nearby hacienda, now enjoy living standards comparable to or better than those of most riquitos.[5] Only fourteen per cent still have the primitive kind of housing so common among the peasantry. Most now have houses with such improvements as concrete floors, modern roofing, and brick instead of adobe construction. At least a fourth had housing worth between ten and forty thousand pesos, well within the range of the Navojoa middle class. Half had cars or trucks and the percentages with such consumer goods as gas stoves, radios, sewing machines and spring beds are slightly higher than among riquitos — between fifty and eighty per cent for each item. Over a fourth had living-room furniture and several had even purchased expensive radio-phonograph consoles.

Some differences in the consumption habits of Aguila and Quechehueca members reflect differences in the organizations of the two ejidos as well as the greater number of Indian families in the latter group. The Quechehueca collective is administered in a paternalistic fashion by Arana (pp. 224–225), who helps members finance the purchases of stoves, radios, and even automobiles or trucks. In comparing themselves to Aguileños, members of the collective claim they have "gone up more evenly," meaning that all have benefited from the paternalistic financing policies of Arana, which enable all to buy at least a few expensive consumer goods. Aguileños have had to make their own purchasing arrangements and as a result both the poorest and the wealthiest families in the two groups are to be found in the Aguila ejido. Moreover, even though the preparation and planting of Aguila lands are mechanized and done collectively, the size of harvests varies considerably on individual plots owing to differences in the diligence and skill with which they are cultivated and irrigated. Two Aguileños had purchased private land in addition to their ejido plots, something no member of the collective had done. Most of the primitive housing owned by members of the two groups belonged to members of the collective and most of the housing over ten thousand pesos in value belonged to Aguileños. Again this reflects a difference in the individual initiative of members, for Arana had not as yet been able to finance housing improvements for his members, whereas most Aguila members had been able to finance some improvement on their own.

Aguileños are acutely conscious of the differences in the consumption patterns of the two groups and admit that the members of the collective enjoy a more uniform standard of living as a result of the cooperative store and the benevolent management of Arana. But they are careful to point out that none of the collective members has done as well as the five most prosperous Aguileños. They claim their more individualistic system provides greater opportunities; as they see it, members of the collective are held back as well as helped by Arana's paternalism. They believe they have a chance for greater individual achievement without any infringements on their freedom of action and decision.

In comparing the Indian and Yori components of the two groups, we find the same pattern of change as elsewhere. In both ejidos, the most successful families are Yoris, whereas most of the families with the lowest living standards are Indian, as are the most unproductive members. Two Indian families in the collective name substitutes to work in their place. Usually this is done only by widows or elderly members unable to labor in the fields, for member families with substitute laborers receive only a fourth of the wages and a half share of the harvest while the rest goes to the substitute. Both the Indian families alluded to have able-bodied men who could do the work, yet they prefer to receive only a fraction of what they could earn by working. Although they spend on religious fiestas when they are able, their living expenses are at a minimum; they are not interested in the emulative buying of goods.

But even though the Indians depend on others for direction and as a group lag behind the Yoris in expanding their wants and expectations, these two ejidos at Quechehueca show that the majority of Indians overcome such tendencies when the opportunities are great enough. Most of the Aguila families listed as Indian would obviously prefer to have their Indian background forgotten. None of these would sponsor an Indian fiesta today, although nearly all of their parents were fiesta sponsors. All speak Spanish fluently, and some claim that they have forgotten the Indian tongue or that they never learned it well. The young children in all these households are monolingual Spanish-speakers.

Only four of the eighteen Indian families belonging to the ejido of Quechehueca still occasionally sponsor or contribute to Indian fiestas. In only two of the eighteen families do the children speak Indian as well as Spanish. The dominating tendency of Indian ejidatarios in the town of Quechehueca is to become Yori and to submerge their Indian characteristics and background. They are acquiring a townsman's desire to educate their children and are sending them to Obregón to high school after they finish the primary grades in Quechehueca. Some even hope to send their children to Mexico City or Guadalajara to become doctors or engineers.

Throughout the Mayo area town merchants have made increasing efforts to involve the peasantry in the emulative consumption boom by sending salesmen on bicycles around the country to sell everything from living-room furniture to hand lotion, all to be paid for on the installment plan. Considering the peasant's limited means, the sale of small items has been remarkably successful. As a result of the agricultural development of the area and the greater purchasing power of the country people, local merchants consider them a much better risk than formerly, particularly those peasants who are ejidatarios working on credit with the Ejido Bank. Merchants claim that the country people, especially the Indians, are very reliable. "They will even go without eating in order to make their payments," one Navojoa merchant assured me with much amusement. After buying an article, the Indian often lives in fear of losing it by defaulting on payments, for stories are prevalent among the peasantry of buyers who lost radios or bicycles by missing payments. For this reason many avoid buying things on installment, but the practice is gradually increasing in the country as the peasants gain self-confidence.

Some people tend to work hard for a certain definite objective such as a bicycle or a radio, and once they have it to reduce work effort sharply. The case of Eusevio of Las Bocas is typical. Newly married, Eusevio sold two cows to build a house. With the two hundred pesos left over he made a down payment on a bicycle he had long wanted. To make his monthly payments of a hundred pesos he worked away from home, first in the irrigation district as a field hand and later at shrimp-fishing near Agiabampo. For the first five months after he made his last payment on the bicycle, he did not leave his village and worked no more than absolutely necessary. Because his brother owns one of the stores in Las Bocas he was still living on credit and "resting" when I last saw him. He expected to make enough money at shrimp-fishing and cotton-picking in the future to pay his brother back.

Buying on time hastens the peasant's adoption of the conspicuous ownership pattern because it lowers the initial amount he must save to make the purchase, then compels him to put away additional savings for fear of losing what he has already paid. Were it not for this added incentive to save after the fact of the purchase, he would probably seldom manage to accumulate the funds for a down payment, and would spend his money on immediate pleasures, as was usual a few years ago. Installment buying is therefore affecting the peasant as it has the townspeople, but much more slowly.

The difference between town and country people in the degree to which they take part in competitive ownership is most dramatically illustrated by families with grown unmarried children. We have seen that these are often the most industrious families in the town middle class, with sons and daughters working to supplement the main income in order to remodel the family's house, buy new furniture, or buy a secondhand car. At the same point in its life cycle when the children are old enough to work for wages, the Indian family may also pool its earning potential to save money. But when an Indian family does this, it is to meet the costs of sponsoring ceremonies. A family head who vowed to help sponsor the fiesta of a certain saint often delays fulfillment until his children are old enough to help him earn the money to meet expenses. At such a time even his unmarried daughters will hire out for cotton-picking to add their earnings to the family effort. Around Tesia, where some families still make baskets, whole families work industriously all the year when saving to sponsor a fiesta. This is one of the few times when a peasant household works and saves for a definite goal, for it is one of the few times when it has sufficient incentive.

Most peasant families with several grown sons, although relatively well clothed and well fed, enjoy the greatest amount of leisure. Two families with several young wage-earners but few dependents were asked to keep a record of earnings and expenses for a month. The money earned — between twenty and twenty-five pesos a day — was sufficient to supply the bare essentials of food and clothing, although the earning potential of the families was between sixty and seventy-five pesos. There was no plan or arrangement among the members to alternate work days, but each worked as he felt inclined, and someone always looked for work when there was no more cash for food. Family heads with several daughters and no sons — a higher dependency ratio — work much more steadily. But many peasant families, particularly those who do not spend money for ceremonies, have too little expectation of advancement to enter the race to consume goods. They do not even use their leisure to improve their housing, though the materials for adobe construction are available to all. It is among those peasants who are neither ceremonial consumers nor emulative consumers that one is most likely to find the symptoms of anomie [6] and despair that were so obvious in Manuel of Mesquital.

Anomie and the Folk-Urban Continuum

It does not seem to me that the growth of town life in Sonora has wrought the social disorganization which Robert Redfield found twenty-five years ago in Yucatán.[7] Nor does the Sonoran situation resemble the conditions of Colombian city life described in Chapter V. Of course, Bogotá is a much larger city than Obregón or Navojoa. Even Mérida, Yucatán, was about twice as large in 1932 as Navojoa in 1958. But I believe differences exist here which are not attributable simply to the varying size of communities. The friction which so markedly characterizes Bogotá social life, and the greater amount of suspicion and accusation connected with witchcraft which Redfield encountered in the city of Mérida, as compared to the outlying villages, do not characterize urban development in Sonora. The difference, I believe, is because of the rate of change and growth: opportunities are expanding so fast in Sonora that there is not a great gap between the growth of expectations and the growth of felt needs.

I do not mean to say that the course of development and change in Sonora is always smooth and without conflict. For example, members of the poor classes may be persuaded by labor union organizers to squat on private lands in a movement for further redistribution of latifundios. In one such action during my stay, soldiers drove off the squatters with tear gas. The way local candidates of the dominant Revolutionary Party are elected by stuffing the ballot boxes and intimidation at the polls — where voting is anything but a secret — also stirs up resentment which occasionally rises to mob violence. But compared to the political struggles of a few years ago, such incidents are tame. The fact that PAN candidates in the last local election campaign were allowed to denounce the incumbents shows that despite bossism there is a great deal of freedom both in spirit and in fact.

But these are political events that do not really pertain to the kind of personal animosities or the sense of despair which might be associated with social disorganization and anomie. What little anomie there is seems to exist more among country people than among the townspeople. Manuel of Mesquital, the Indian who wanted to be Yori, was an extreme manifestation of the tendency toward discontent among some Indians whose expectations have not kept pace with the growth of their felt needs. The greater amount of drunkenness among country people, especially Indians, also seems to me to show a certain measure of despair. Drunken fights at dances and other social gatherings are a country phenomenon, but considering the great number of these fights, the amount and seriousness of the fighting does not seem to me to be so great as in other parts of Latin America where I have lived. What fighting does occur here is definitely more vindictive and serious among the poor Yori peasants than among the Indians. It is my impression, too, that impoverished Yori peasants are much more sensitive about their social and economic position than are their Indian counterparts.

Through their attitudes and behavior the country people in many ways demonstrate a greater degree of despondency, pessimism, and uncertainty about life than do the city people. Much of the townsman's spirit of optimism and progress is related, I believe, to his greater sense of control over his own affairs and his consequently more satisfying sense of expectation. Associated with the country peoples' weaker sense of predictability about their surroundings is their tendency toward anomie or "despair" [8] and despondency.

The country people have a greater sense of social detachment from official leadership than the townspeople. They often complain of the indifference of officials and community leaders toward them and put part of the blame for this indifference on their own poverty and lowly station. They believe that if they were rich and expensively dressed officials would pay more attention to them. There is much truth in this, of course; the attitude is probably characteristic of lower classes everywhere. But the significant thing is that townspeople are less concerned about officials' indifference and have less reason to be. The townsman has much more self-confidence in his personal relations with officials and community leaders, and through the mordida gains a greater sense of control over his dealings with the government.

Townspeople often make long-range plans to improve their economic and social position, whereas the peasants rarely have any long-range goals. They may save for a fiesta or for some immediate purchase, such as a bicycle, but they seldom plan farther ahead than that. Middle-aged peasants often confided to me that they thought they might have been able to accomplish much more in life if they had had more education. They obviously had unsatisfied longings and wants, but few expectations; many were heavy drinkers. The greater expectations of the townspeople, when converted into actions based on long-range planning, show a greater sense of control over an environment that for them is more predictable and more orderly.

The different attitudes of country people and town people toward having children also reveal much about their sense of control over the future. Townspeople have much higher aspirations for their children and a much lower expectation that they will die in childhood. Their plans and ambitions for their children, in combination with their greater sense of control over disease, is even leading to a desire for control of birth itself. The country people accept "what God wants" and hope for many births from which some offspring may survive to help them work and to provide for them when they are old. Again, the peasant's hopes are framed more in uncertainties than in any sense of predictable expectation.

The peasantry much more often than the townspeople express the belief that their lot is getting worse instead of better. They may complain, for example, that the irrigation developments have been to their disadvantage or that machines are reducing their opportunities to work or that living costs have risen so much that they can no longer eat as well as before. Some of this is true, but actually labor shortages are more acute than ever, and wages have kept up fairly well with prices. Townspeople evince a greater spirit of progress and more often complain that improvements are not being made fast enough to suit them.

The country people lament that they cannot count on their relatives, friends, and compadres (godparents) for help as they used to do, especially for church fiestas. But the same complaint is also made about help in daily living. Townspeople seem more independent and self-reliant and less concerned over the loss of reciprocal aid.

Although felt needs outdistance expectations most among the peasantry, the discrepancy is not great enough to create serious lack of integration or deep despair. In fact, developments have come so fast in this area that expectations have not always kept up with opportunities.

Whatever the degree of difference in anomie, social disorganization, and secularization between town and country, the tendencies here seem to reverse those found by Redfield in Yucatán. Peasants feel more insecure than townspeople. Town families are preoccupied with status, but they have higher expectations and take more definite steps to realize them. Redfield found an increase in the use of witchcraft in towns and cities as compared to the villages of Yucatán and believed that this tendency showed greater personal insecurity and social disorganization in urban life. In Sonora no one is much concerned with bewitchment. The cases that do crop up are usually among the Indians, but witchcraft is not a prominent preoccupation of the peasantry. In towns and cities it is very uncommon.

Life in the villages seems every bit as individualistic as in the city. There is not a great deal of visiting, and though reciprocal aid in farm work is sometimes practiced among brothers or among married sons working with their father, it is by no means general. In the cities one often finds similar working arrangements when members of a family together operate a business — a laundry, a chain of auto-supply stores, or a chain of pop-bottling concessions. Expanding chain businesses as a family enterprise is sometimes considered advantageous because of the difficulty of getting honest managers. The family seems less stable in the country and in the lower class than in the middle and upper classes. The strength of parental authority apparently depends more on whether the father owns his own land or business than on any difference between town and country.

Ceremonial cults in the villages in this area have been considerably secularized, particularly among the Mayos. The carnival accompanying church fiestas has become more important than the religious observances for most people, to judge from the behavior of those attending, and where merchants help to maintain the fiestas it is for the business they bring to the community. Some Yori peasants and third-class men are agnostics, if not outright atheists. Many are simply unconcerned and are actually more churchless than godless. In general, middle-class townsmen are the most faithful in their church attendance.

This apparent reversal of the Yucatán data does not contradict Redfield's findings; on the contrary, it complements them. The two areas are altogether different and so are the times. The Sonoran villages of 1958 are very different from the primitive Yucatán villages of 1931. They have been enmeshed in a money economy for a long time, and it has been many generations since they lost their primitive culture and social organization. Moreover, since the Sonoran cities are currently enjoying great prosperity as a result of recent economic developments, it would be equally inappropriate to equate them with Mérida in the depth of the depression. The Sonoran boom economy is permeated with optimism, and despite the differences between town and country neither part of the population has suffered severe social disorganization. Furthermore, in 1931 the lower class of Mérida apparently dominated the ethos of the city, for Redfield depends entirely upon them to characterize the urban situation. It seemed to me, on the other hand, that the rising middle class dominated the ethos and life of Navojoa, Obregón, and Huatabampo, and it is primarily that middle class I refer to in characterizing the Sonoran cities of 1958.

Redfield related the greater disorganization and individualization of life in Mérida to its greater heterogeneity. In the villages he found life much more homogeneous, and the various aspects of life much more closely interrelated. Agriculture, religion, and medicine, for example — all closely connected in the life of the villagers — were separated in city life. In the villages everyone did much the same things and there were fewer choices. Life in the city was more unstable and full of more insecurities and uncertainties. Medicine was Redfield's favorite example of a way in which the behavior in the city was more "variable, inconsistent, and unstable." Villagers tended to "follow the same line of thought and action," whereas in the city the treatments of diseases were various and inconsistent.[9]

In Sonora the villages behave the most variably and inconsistently in treating disease, as was illustrated by Mesquital in Chapter III (pp. 49–53). Though the same choices are available and employed in both the cities and the villages, the villagers more often cover a wider range of alternatives as they go from cheaper to more expensive treatments during the progress of an ailment. In the cities, however, even the lower classes today rely heavily on the modern doctor and much less than the country people on home remedies and folk curers. The changes in the villages are more additive than in the cities, where replacement is more characteristic. Despite the same range of choices there is a smaller selection of alternatives in the city. This selection is a result of increasing affluence and a cognitive choice of alternatives which gives the people using them a greater sense of control or predictability.

In a primitive closed community which is relatively homogeneous, a sense of control may virtually derive from the absence of alternatives. The sense of control there depends on social consensus. But in a completely open and heterogeneous community where there are both a multitude of alternatives and a social and economic freedom of choice, changes may take place through progressive replacements as a result of cognitive discrimination. The sense of control in the open, changing situation will also be social to the extent that choice is influenced by emulation; but the predominating difference in the open situation is the greater importance of frequency interpretation and cognition in the operation of choice. The sense of control in the open situation becomes much more directly connected with cognition than to social consensus. However, in the situation represented by the Sonoran villages (and probably by the city of Mérida in 1931), which is neither closed nor completely open, the alternatives may increase faster than the freedom to choose. For example, many Sonoran villagers would undoubtedly seek immediate medical attention were it more convenient and economically possible. Situations of additive change, where the presentation of alternatives involves new felt needs for which there are inadequate expectations, seem most likely to lead to disorganization and even anomie. For here the presentation of alternatives may reduce rather than increase people's sense of control.

XII

Religious Ceremonies and the Indians

After the Spanish conquest, older habits of conspicuous giving combined, in many parts of Latin America, with Roman Catholic ritual to form a ceremonial pattern including the sponsorship of annual calendrical fiestas for Catholic saints. Those who sponsor the fiesta often do so at great sacrifice of time and wealth, but in the process they gain public esteem. The Mayo and Yaqui Indians of Sonora still sponsor fiestas, but in both groups the practice of conspicuous giving of food is declining. Participation is declining much more rapidly, however, among the Mayos than among the Yaquis, and the reasons for that difference will concern us here.

Since the ceremonial fiesta system of the Indians requires considerable time and expense on the part of the families who support it, it conflicts with new desires for goods. Thus it persists among the more conservative groups which most clearly reject Yori values. In Sonora, taking part in these ceremonies is one of the most distinctive characteristics of "Indianness," and is the most important determinant of the social unity the Indians still have. And the disintegration of this complex is a major part of the Mexicanization of the Indian.

Yaquis are practically unanimous in supporting their ceremonial life. They refer proudly to "our religion" and assure the visitor that they

269

will never abandon their faith or their ceremonies. Most Mayos, by contrast, believe their religion is on the wane. "People no longer have faith in the saints" is frequently heard. Compared to Yaqui fiestas, those of the Mayos are much more secularized and support for the religious aspects is weaker. The difference is interesting in view of the fact that the ceremonial practices of these two neighboring groups were apparently very similar originally. The Yaquis and Mayos spoke the same aboriginal language, had very similar aboriginal cultures, and encountered the Jesuits at approximately the same time, with similar results.

Today, Mayos complain of the high cost of the fiestas and give this as a major reason for their disappearance: "They are no longer worth it" (*Ya no se costean*), they often say. Some blame the Protestant sects or "Aleluyas" (Hallelujahs), as they are called, for teaching that the fiestas are a waste of money and effort for nothing but wooden idols. The Yaquis also complain of the heavy burden of the expense of their religion, but they feel obligated to bear it. Before comparing Mayo and Yaqui participation in fiestas, it is necessary to describe some general characteristics of their fiesta organizations.

The Indian Fiesta Structure

We are concerned here with the major, public, calendrical fiestas rather than the non-calendrical, household affairs. The calendrical fiestas are held to honor a particular image, usually in connection with a native church at one of the old mission centers established by the Jesuits during the seventeenth century along the Yaqui, Mayo, and Fuerte Rivers. Though nominally Roman Catholic, the Indian maintains a religion which is almost independent of the official Roman Catholic Church, except for baptism and marriage, which are performed by an ordained priest. The native priest or *maestro* is capable of officiating at all other services of importance to the Indian.

In old mission towns the Indians have independently maintained their adobe churches for many years, and on fiesta days they and their Yori neighbors congregate there from all the surrounding rancherías. On the Mayo River most of these ceremonial towns are still important enough to be the heads of comisarías, and one of them, Etchojoa, is head of a municipio. Although people often go to fiestas in other ceremonial districts, the functionaries of a fiesta are usually from the district of the ceremonial town where it is being held. Easter fiestas, which are held simultaneously at all the ceremonial towns, are attended chiefly from within the town's own traditional ceremonial district.

The functionaries of the calendrical church ceremonies may be divided into two groups — the performers and the *fiesteros*. The former include ceremonial dancers (*matachinis* and *pascolas*), their musicians, ceremonial clowns (*fariseos* or "Jews"), native priests, and women church singers.[1] The fiesteros are the men and women responsible for organizing the fiesta, at which they must also provide and prepare the food for the performers. Not all fiestas have a special group of fiesteros, but for those which do it is this aspect of the fiesta structure which seems most sensitive to change.

Matachinis usually dance inside Indian churches, which are devoid of benches or chairs. The pascolas, the deer dancer, and the musicians perform under a special dance *ramada* a short distance away. This ramada is an open building consisting of an earth or brush roof supported by posts imbedded in the ground, built to protect the performers from the sun. Not far from the dance ramada, the fiesteros build their cooking hearths, each preparing his share of the fiesta stew in a large earthen pot.

Pascolas, deer dancers, their musicians, and the native priests are all skilled specialists, and among both Mayos and Yaquis they serve in these capacities for life. In arranging for a fiesta, the head fiesteros decide which performers they want and delegate one of the messenger fiesteros to get in touch with these men and request their services. Among the Yaquis and the Fuerte River Mayos all of these skilled performers serve as a matter of "devotion"; on the Mayo River they receive payment in addition to the traditional feast, thus greatly raising the fixed costs of Mayo River fiestas.

Other performers, including matachinis, women church singers, and the ceremonial clowns serve in fulfillment of religious vows. Almost always, these promises to serve as matachinis, "Jews," and so on, are made during an illness, when someone — usually a parent — promises the invalid to some ceremonial service in return for his recovery. Among the Yaquis these vows commit the performer to a lifetime of service, and each group of promissory performers becomes a permanent society. Among the Mayos the period of service for promissory performers is usually only three years, although skilled matachini dance leaders sometimes serve for life.

In addition to the ceremonial performers, many others take part in fiestas, for many people make vows during illness to perform various religious services. Some may promise simply to attend; to bring candles, fireworks, or alms; or to pray in the church before the saint in whose honor the fiesta is being held. Others promise to put on robes (*hábitos*), which are donned in a brief ceremony conducted by a native priest before the altar. At Mayo fiestas there is also a great deal of secular participation in the form of carnival activities: sideshows, food stands, beer dispensaries, and a public dance in the evening with music blatting from a public address system.

The number of fiesteros is variable. Among the Yaqui it is customary to have eight of each sex. Traditionally there have been twelve of each sex at the ceremonial towns along the lower Mayo River and nine of each sex at those along its upper course. As will be seen, the numbers fall far short of the ideal in many cases. Apparently twelve was the traditional number along the Fuerte River.

Since fiesteros serve either by invitation or as the result of a vow, I shall refer to them as invitational and promissory, respectively. Yaqui fiesteros are predominantly invitational. Some time after they have taken office, the incumbent fiesteros go in search of their replacements for the following year. Usually they go at night to take the candidates by surprise. It is a joke among the Yaquis that people who fear being chosen hide in the thorn forest during this period and have their meals brought to them by a member of the family. Even the devout Yaquis consider the job of fiestero *muy pesado* (very heavy).

Among the Mayos of the Fuerte River, fiesteros are predominantly promissory. The same is true along the lower course of the Mayo River at Etchoropo, Júperi, and Etchojoa. From there eastward, the percentage of invited fiesteros increases. They are outnumbered about two to one at San Pedro, but at San Ignacio and El Recodo the invited far outnumber the promissory. East of there promissory fiesteros are rare.[2]

Very often promissory fiesteros fulfill vows made many years before on condition that a child recover from an illness or that he grow to adulthood. An interview with thirteen fiesteros at Júperi disclosed that all were promissory and that in eight cases the vow had been made many years previously for a child. In four of the eight cases fulfillment of the vow was conditional on the child's attaining adulthood. There is usually no need for incumbent fiesteros to look for promissory replacements, for they volunteer when ready to accept the office.

Anywhere from a few days to a few months after a fiesta has been held — custom varies from one place to the next — the fiesteros who have agreed to serve as sponsors the following year look for their "godchildren," as they call their replacements. Godchildren of fiesteros are selected, then, a year before they become fiesteros and two years before they actually sponsor the fiesta. Where fiesteros serve voluntarily as a result of vows and there are plenty of candidates, the recruitment of godchildren is no problem. At Batacosa there are usually enough candidates to serve the popular San Bartolo for recruitment to be completed during the fiesta. As soon as replacements are found, Mayo fiesteros sponsor a small fiesta known as the *puti*, which serves as a public announcement that the godchildren have been found and as a public commitment by the godchildren to accept the obligations of the ceremonial office. Ideally, Mayo fiesteros give two more fiestas for their godchildren some time before the major fiesta. These are called the *bajítua* and the *jísuma*, the second a little bigger and more expensive than the first. Vicam Yaqui fiesteros give only one fiesta for their godchildren, the *jísuma*.

On the day before the date of the major fiesta, fiesteros kill the cattle to be eaten and deliver half of the meat to their godchildren. This meat is received ceremonially on mats before the godchildren's houses, and skyrockets are sent up to announce its delivery. The godchildren then cut up the meat and distribute it among their friends, neighbors, and relatives. Those who receive this gift of meat are then obliged to return the gift twelvefold the following year when the godchild is serving as a fiestero.

Throughout the fiesta the fiesteros must feed their godchildren as well as the performers. The godchildren may distribute part of the food to friends and relatives. But whatever these guests receive — cigarettes, coffee, skyrockets, bread, or meat — they must, theoretically, return the same thing twelvefold the following year when the godchildren are fiesteros. In this way the fiestero's economic burden is shared by his friends and relatives. The godchildren sit at a table under the dance ramada where they are periodically treated to coffee and cigarettes and where they can watch the performances of the pascolas and deer dancer. When the fiesta ends, the fiesteros turn over the remaining food to their

273

godchildren, who make a final redistribution, obligating the recipients to return the gift twelvefold the following year.

Although the fiesteros are responsible for organizing the fiesta and meeting the costs of feeding, and in some cases paying, the performers, much of the expense and consumption of food is really extrinsic to what might be termed the fixed costs of the fiesta — the expense of feeding and catering to the performers, the number of which is fairly constant for each fiesta. At the fiesta for San Juan at Tesia the total number of performers, including the musicians, dancers, and native priests, varies between fifteen and twenty men. At the fiesta for the Holy Trinity in Júperi in recent years the number has varied between fifty and seventy persons. At Tesia, therefore, the fixed costs are about nine hundred pesos (seventy-two dollars), and at Júperi over two thousand (one hundred and sixty dollars). Total costs are far more than this, however. At the San Juan fiesta at Tesia and the Holy Trinity fiesta at Júperi during 1958, total costs were at least seven times the fixed costs. Most of the expense of the fiestas goes into the distribution of food via the godchildren.

This distribution of food is a social expense which draws attention and respect to the giver. The fiestero who provides an abundance of food and who helps fellow fiesteros who cannot afford to butcher a bull for the occasion is admired for his generosity. And the poor fiestero who does the best he can with very meager resources is also admired for his attempt to live up to his obligation. The Mayos claim that formerly much attention was given to the gifts received by fiesteros from those to whom they had distributed food and fiesta goods the year before as fiestero recruits. Today, however, almost no one complies with the obligation to reciprocate twelvefold, and very few reciprocate at all. The Yaquis, in contrast, still take this obligation seriously and during the fiesta those who received token gifts the year before bring their return gifts of meat, flour, and other foods and place them on the mat before the wooden cross facing the dance ramada. On their arrival there is considerable fanfare as the fiesteros file out of the ramada to receive them and the onlookers crowd around to see who has arrived and the gifts they have brought. But even among the Yaquis the amount of public attention paid to this conspicuous giving ceremony has declined greatly in recent years.

As the interest in conspicuous giving declines, the distribution and redistribution of food through fiesteros and their godchildren becomes increasingly burdensome until in many cases the fiestas disappear. When fiestas do not disappear, costs are reduced to feeding and paying the performers, and most of the social costs are curtailed. Through such economies the fiestas sometimes outlast the office of fiestero.

The Mayos

Among the Mayos it has become more and more common to openly ridicule the sponsoring of calendrical fiestas. Mesquital de Tesia, a conservative ranchería that has long been a principal source of fiesteros for ceremonies at Tesia, contains the typical differences of opinion that have grown up among Mayo Indian families about fiesta sponsorship. Of the thirty-six Indian households in the community, twenty-three had at least one member who had at some time served as fiestero. Heads of the other thirteen households claimed that their parents had been fiesta sponsors but that they themselves had never served and would refuse if asked. Heads of two of the first twenty-three households also claimed they would refuse if asked again. Twenty-one families, therefore, were still potential fiesteros as against a total of fifteen families definitely opposed. Members of the first group said they believed it would be a sin to refuse to serve when asked, and all said fiesteros entered heaven more easily because they had served. The heads of these twenty-one "conservative" households claimed to have a high opinion of fiesteros and believed they should be treated deferentially. According to them, a man who had done his duty well in sponsoring fiestas in the past should be addressed respectfully as Don and should be invited to eat whenever he came to visit.

Members of the opposing fifteen households denied that fiesteros get into heaven more easily. Three men felt that all a fiestero gets for his trouble is more poverty and debts. Another commented that many people with only one or two cows will butcher one for a fiesta, thus giving away something which should be used for the benefit of their own families. All said that although fiesteros were well thought of among those who still favored fiestas, from their point of view they were just ordinary sinners like everyone else. As one man expressed it, "Fiesteros are not superior; they are stupid. They obligate themselves to a great expense and let their families go hungry." None of these families believed it was a sin to refuse to serve, but six said it would be a sin not to do so if a promise to a saint had been made. "It is foolish to make the promise," one man added.

In less conservative villages, the proportion of fiesteros is much smaller than in Mesquital. Out of the thirty-three households sampled in Buaysiacobe, only five contained fiesteros and these claimed they would never again serve, even if invited: "Fiestas are expensive and produce nothing." In none of the other eighteen Indian households in the sample were there persons who had ever served as fiesteros, and heads of fourteen claimed they would not take part under any circumstances. Two were not sure what they would do, and two said they would feel compelled to serve if invited.

Formerly, the danger of refusing an invitation to serve as fiestero was greatly emphasized. The incumbent fiesteros would say to a potential recruit, "Jesus Christ left this custom with us. We have done our part and now it is your turn. You do not accept for your own pleasure but for Him who made this world and gave us this custom. He ordered us to do this, and we are in this world to obey His orders. Are you going to obey? If you do not, God will punish you."

According to old people, the fear of supernatural sanctions was sufficiently strong at one time to decide the issue, but today it obviously does not carry the same weight. Some fiesteros themselves told me that they did not believe God would punish a man for refusing to do ceremonial service, saying that they knew many who had refused to serve without any mishap's befalling them.

A supernatural sanction depends for its support on strong social sanctions. Formerly the man who hesitated to give ceremonial service was so exceptional that the fear of social disapproval was enough to assure his cooperation. Conformity to tradition reinforced the supernatural beliefs and provided few exceptions to test them. But as refusal has become more common, social disapproval is no longer feared, and the supernatural sanction has lost the social foundation on which it depended. With increasing defections, a frequency interpretation becomes possible which further undermines the basis for belief.

Along the entire length of the Mayo River one repeatedly encounters men who claim they would not serve as fiesteros and do not fear supernatural punishment because they no longer "believe in the saints." This loss of faith they credit to the burning of the saints by Juan Pacheco in 1934. Pacheco is famous along the Mayo for the desecrations he carried out on the order of the state governor while serving as the local chief of rural police. He closed all the churches in the Mayo River district and removed and burned the images. Now an old man, he is healthy and prosperous. If the saints were really powerful, the argument goes, they would have punished Pacheco by now.

At first I overestimated the influence of this historical incident and thought of it as a major cause of the recent rapid disintegration of the ceremonial system. Undoubtedly it did provide a startling demonstration for many, but I later learned a less common version of the story. Not long after the burning of the images, one of Pacheco's small sons was accidentally killed by an older brother while the two were playing with a loaded gun, and many people interpreted this as punishment from God and the saints. Those who choose to proclaim their agnosticism overlook this sequel. In short, Pacheco came to symbolize successful destruction of idolatry only for those ready to be convinced.

Among the Mayos, adherence to the ceremonial pattern is related to a considerable extent to illiteracy and inability to speak Spanish. At Mesquital de Tesia, one or both heads of some two thirds of the Indian families opposed to sponsoring church fiestas were literate, whereas one or both heads were literate in only fifteen per cent of the families favoring religious fiestas. Similarly, one or both spouses spoke only the Indian tongue in two thirds of the pro-fiesta families, whereas in all but one of the opposing families both spouses were bilingual. Spanish was the household language, among a fifth of the pro-fiesta Indian families and half of the opposing ones. As Mayos gain greater facility in Spanish, their attitudes grow more and more like their Yori neighbors'. The rural schools have helped greatly to effect this change by reducing the number of monolingual Cáhita speakers.

Another important reason for the decline in support for ceremonies along the Mayo River is the change in consumption goals. This change is reflected in the attitudes of Mesquital families opposed to fiestas: the most common complaint heard against the fiestas, and the chief excuse used when a person refuses to serve as a sponsor, is their high cost. Itemizing the expenses of fiesteros at ceremonial towns along the Mayo River, I found that the total costs for the year ranged between two and three thousand pesos (one hundred and sixty to two hundred and forty dollars) at Navojoa, San Pedro, Etchojoa, and Júperi; between one and two thousand pesos (eighty to one hundred and twenty dollars) at Tesia,

Batacosa, Masiaca, El Recodo, San Ignacio, Sebampo, and Etchoropo; and less than one thousand at Camoa, Bacavachi, Tepahue, and Macoyahue. The customary daily wage in the area at this time was twelve pesos (ninety-six cents). For most fiesteros, then, the costs for the year totaled the equivalent of between eighty and two hundred and fifty working days. The burden would be comparable to that of a man in our society with an annual income of six thousand dollars making a donation to his church of between fifteen hundred and forty-five hundred dollars. No wonder all the members of the fiestero's family must pitch in to help him meet the costs. Some fiesteros go into debt, borrowing from friends and employers, but this is difficult because no one is eager to lend money for a fiesta.

It is commonly said that fiesteros come from the poorest families. Of a hundred Mayo fiesteros about whom data were gathered in 1958, ninety-three were either day laborers (fifty) or small landowners and ejidatarios (forty-three) who had to hire out as day laborers for part of the year to supplement their income. Only seven were farmers, ranchers, or ejidatarios who never worked as day laborers, and of these, four would qualify as Indian riquitos, roughly the same proportion as in the general Indian population. Though this does not bear out the common opinion that all Indians who do well financially lose interest in fiestas, it does show that the fiestas are maintained primarily by the poorer, rather than the richer Indian families.

Several fiesteros told me seriously that they were poor because all they had ever saved they had spent on fiestas. These men had been fiesteros four or five times, and no doubt this form of consumption has continually depleted their small resources. On the other hand, the wants and expectations of the wealthiest Indians seem to approximate those of the Yori and are directed more toward conspicuous ownership than toward conspicuous giving. Furthermore, they attempt to disassociate themselves from things characteristically Indian.

A very crucial breakdown in the fiestero system is the failure of those who receive gifts to reciprocate with their twelvefold donations the following year. Interviews with many fiesteros suggested that among the Mayos such returns are negligible and often non-existent. The most that any one fiestero got back from those to whom he had distributed food the year before consisted of goods worth fifty pesos, about two per cent of the man's total fiesta costs. While the Yaqui fiestero talks enthusiastically of gifts received and how they lightened his financial burden, the Mayo, in contrast, grumbles about the lack of assistance. He complains that people no longer help out, that they do not return the food given them, and that they are losing their faith. Today among the Mayo the burden of responsibility falls almost entirely upon the household of the individual fiestero.

Mayos blame inflation for the decay of the fiestas, recalling how much cheaper the necessary supplies were ten, twenty, and thirty years ago. Actually, the rise of prices has probably not been very important, because the wage scale has also risen. According to my data on prices and wages, collected in the area during 1948 and 1958, wages during the past decade have increased slightly more than food costs. The bull, for example — the most expensive single item for the fiestero — cost between twenty-five and thirty-seven days of work in 1948, when the daily wage was three to four pesos and a small animal cost about a hundred pesos. Today, with the daily wages ranging from twelve to fifteen pesos and small bulls costing between two hundred and fifty and three hundred and fifty pesos, this same item costs the fiestero between seventeen and twenty-nine days of work. One day's wages will now buy twelve kilos of corn and five kilos of beans, as compared to eight kilos and four kilos respectively in 1948.

Getting reliable figures for prices and wages for earlier periods was difficult because no merchants kept records for more than a few years. I collected estimates, however, from both merchants and peasants, for earlier periods; and despite the belief of most of them that times are harder now, their own figures showed that wages have apparently kept up with prices. Moreover, with the expansion of production in the area, opportunities to earn have greatly increased, and labor shortages are sometimes acute, especially at cotton-harvest time.

Even though fiestas really cost no more today than previously, in terms of work days necessary to pay for them, the great majority of Indians believe them more expensive now and give the high cost as a major reason for refusing to sponsor them. This price-consciousness has a number of causes. There are more things to buy now, and although the peasantry are still far behind the townspeople in the consumption of goods, their wants are increasing. In certain areas, too, the peasant has become more dependent upon money than formerly. Cash cropping in combination with subsistence farming has long been practiced, but today in the irrigated parts, where the high planting costs force the peasant to work on credit, he must grow what those who finance him want him to grow. This always means planting cotton or wheat and therefore depending more on stores for his corn and beans. Within the irrigated area most peasants also have less livestock than formerly, since the thorn forest which provided pasture has been stripped away. Formerly, people say, many fiesteros butchered their own animals for fiestas; now most have to buy them.

Though it is true that changes in cropping practices and financing within the irrigation areas have increased cash- and price-consciousness there, the fiesta is declining also over a wide area outside the irrigation districts. More important than changes in cropping and finances is the fact that the man who assumes the responsibility of sponsoring a religious fiesta no longer commands the respect he did in times past. And he who rejects ceremonial participation or goes so far as to ridicule it is not ostracized. No social sanctions are set against him, and the supernatural sanctions he no longer fears.

As a consequence, fiesta costs are being reduced in many places and in others the fiestas are disappearing. The most resilient fiesta among both Mayos and Yaquis has been the Easter celebration, for despite complaints that it comes at a time of year when money and agricultural work are scarce, it continues to be observed in nearly all the ceremonial towns. A major reason for its high survival rate is the fact that it is sponsored nearly everywhere by the "Jews" or ceremonial clowns, who meet the fixed costs with money they collect on alms-gathering trips during Lent. Only at Etchojoa, San Ignacio, Tepahue, and Tesia on the Mayo River does anyone claim that the Easter fiesta was once sponsored by fiesteros. In these four places the clowns took over the sponsorship when the fiesteros failed to find replacements.[3]

Where fiesteros still sponsor the Easter ceremonies — in Macoyahui, Camoa, Bacavachi, San Pedro, and Sebampo — the expenses and the number of fiesteros are diminishing. Expenses are reduced by eliminating the preliminary fiestas and by reducing or eliminating the distribution of food through the godchildren.[4] In some cases the number of fiesteros has diminished to less than half because of the failure of recruits to fulfill their obligation.[5] It is said of such persons that they "kept the rosaries" (*quedaron con los rosarios*). When a fiestero turns the responsibility of the fiesta over to his recruit, or godchild, he gives him the wooden rosary he wears around his neck as a symbol of office. To "keep the rosary" was formerly considered a grave sin: it meant that a fiestero had not fulfilled his duty to help sponsor a fiesta and had failed to turn it over to a replacement. It is said that such rosaries are buried with the person so that when he faces God he will carry with him the evidence of his sin. At Pueblo Viejo (Old Navojoa) and El Recodo some of the fiesteros had quit and those that remained in 1959 had sponsored the fiesta for two succeeding years because they were unable to find replacements. Each year that a group cannot find recruits to serve at the next fiesta, more of the fiesteros are forced to "keep the rosaries."

The same is true of other fiestas. Expenses are being cut, fiesteros are "keeping the rosaries," and some fiestas are disappearing entirely. On the Fuerte River at least nine major fiestas have disappeared during the past fifteen years, and four have disappeared on the Mayo River in the past seven,[6] usually because the fiesteros were unable to find replacements willing to accept the expense of the office. Several other fiestas are in a very precarious position for the same reason. Along the Fuerte River the only remaining fiesta with most of its fiestero offices still filled is the fiesta of Todos Santos at Tehueco. On the Mayo the fiesta of Espíritu Santo was sponsored in 1958 by only six fiesteros when ideally there should have been twenty-four, and these six were having difficulty finding replacements. As the fiestero complement becomes smaller, the financial burden for those remaining grows larger. And as the costs of the remaining offices rise fewer people are willing to accept them. The fiesta of Rosario in Bacavachi and the fiesta for San Miguel at Masiaca are faced with similar problems. One of the most famous fiestas in southern Sonora, the fiesta for the Holy Trinity which is held simultaneously at Júperi and Etchoropo, now has only a little more than half the traditional number of fiesteros.

Service as a fiestero in these towns is predominantly promissory and replacement for each of the twenty-four offices takes place on an individual basis. But where service is invitational, a new group of recruits may refuse to accept their offices if the incumbents are unable to find replacements for all of them. For this reason, the fiesta of San Juan at Navojoa had been given two years in succession by the same group of fiesteros in 1958. At some of those places previously mentioned where fiestas have been suddenly dropped, it was because a group of fiesteros could not bear the financial strain of continuing to sponsor a fiesta for several years in succession.

In many other ways the fiesta system is showing strain. At most places it is becoming customary for at least some of the fiesteros to divide the costs of buying a bull rather than each buying one separately, and in some cases even the offices are split. Two people may accept a single office from the same fiestero, divide the expenses, and alternately wear the official rosary. In many places, too, the preliminary fiestas to feast the recruits are being simplified or eliminated entirely. Older people can remember many fiestas that disappeared twenty to fifty years ago. The process of disintegration has been going on for a long time, although it seems to many local observers to have speeded up during the past ten years.[7]

The Mayo's felt needs have begun to increase in emulation of the townspeople; but while his heart is no longer in the old patterns of conspicuous giving, his expectations are too low to engage him in the new pattern of conspicuous ownership. But despite the lag in expectations, new wants are carrying the Mayos in the direction of new consumption goals when opportunity points the way. Moreover, the faithful and the agnostic live side by side everywhere, and the latter through dissension and ridicule has weakened the sanctions of social approval and disapproval that once made the Mayos a strong social entity.

The town of Quechehueca, discussed earlier, demonstrates the change in the consumption patterns of Mayos when their expectations increase. As noted in the preceding chapter, no dedicated fiesteros were found among the Indian families in the ejido of Aguila and only two among those in the collective. Although it was true that the Indian families as a group lagged behind the Yoris in living standards and income, the majority were decidedly turning their interests toward the acquisition of goods and the raising of living standards.

The riquitos, the better-off peasants, provide another example of the change in values. The Indians of this group are those who are usually most comfortable in the presence of Yoris and who "want to be Yoris." Usually interested in improving their housing and in buying a wider range of consumption goods, these are probably the very persons who would formerly have taken the leadership in ceremonial affairs, for according to older informants, it was often the men of greater wealth who helped most at the fiestas. This shift of interest on the part of wealthier Indians does much to weaken the power of social approbation in perpetuating the fiesta system.

Natividad, who lives in a ranchería west of Masiaca and comes from a very conservative Indian family much interested in ceremonial life and fiestas, well exemplifies this shift. He married a girl with a few head of cattle which have since increased considerably. He is in an excellent position to achieve status as a fiestero and probably would have done so a generation or more ago. Instead, he has built a small store and a brick house with a cement floor. He has a battery-powered radio, new furniture, and a shiny new Ford truck. As a matter of fact, the store loses money, for Natividad had no schooling and his accounting methods are very crude. He sells on credit and when families get too far behind he has them work off the debt by clearing land for him in the Indian comunidad, thus putting himself in the position of employer. Because this is a dry-farming area near the coast where rainfall is scanty, Natividad's crops are poor and have never justified the expense of clearing land and planting. His fifty-thousand-peso truck he uses only for periodic trips to town to replenish the stock in the store, whose inventory is worth not more than five thousand pesos. Both the store and the truck are prestige items for Natividad, and both are supported by his herd of cattle, which now numbers about a hundred and fifty head. He is proud to be a *comerciante* (merchant), and enjoys driving his new truck to Navojoa, where Yoris treat him with respect, for they have an erroneous view of his business acumen. The mainstay of Natividad's operations — his cattle — are cared for entirely by his father-in-law.

With the decline of interest in the old religious pattern, Protestant sects are now beginning to make some headway among the Mayos. Numerous small churches have sprung up along the Mayo River, and their members are usually very active both in proselytizing for their own faith and in depreciating the fiesta system. They have now gained enough strength for many conservative Mayos to view them as a major threat to the ceremonial system. It is not that they fear the Aleluyas will convert all the Mayos to their faith, but they are afraid that their arguments against "wasting money on fiestas for idols" are dissuading many people from accepting religious offices. At Etchojoa — the ceremonial center near what is probably the largest concentration of Aleluyas — the incumbent fiesteros, the native priests, and the local Indian church officials blame Aleluyas for the great difficulty in getting replacements for the fiestero offices. "People no longer want to bear the expense; they say the Aleluyas are right," they told me. None of these persons expected the traditional fiesta for Espíritu Santo to last much longer.

I interviewed twenty-four families in the vicinity of Chucarit belonging to the Church of God sect. Today this is the best-organized Protestant sect among the Mayo River peasantry, with thirteen churches and four missions (groups of less than thirty members) in various towns and rancherías along the river. In four families only the wife was an Aleluya, the husbands either unwilling to join or unable to keep the pledge not to drink. All of these families were Indian and a third of them had been fiestero families before they became Aleluyas. The parents of the present heads of another third had been fiesteros. Four of the heads of families were independent small farmers; all the rest were either full-time day laborers or small farmers who supplemented their incomes as day laborers.

Two thirds of these church members had joined simply because they liked the new religion and one third because they or a member of the family had been healed by the evangelical faith. Most of them mentioned, as a special advantage of being an Aleluya, no longer being pestered by Indian friends to assume the office of fiestero. One man who had been a fiestero five times in his life said he had never known how to refuse his friends when they came to invite him. Now that he was an Aleluya, they left him alone and he no longer had to go into debt and make sacrifices in order to save for fiestas. All were very strongly opposed to fiestas as a waste of money. A third of the men proudly testified they were reformed drunkards. Informants in several of the families commented on the relation among *hermanos* (brothers), the form of address always used among evangelists. In all these cases they expressed great satisfaction at the warmth of this relationship which they thought greater than that between fiesteros or between compadres (godparents).

Evangelical meetings are attended by both Yoris and Indians with no discrimination made between the two groups. A brother is a brother first of all. For Indians anxious to be accepted by Yoris this is very gratifying. The new religion is much less expensive than the old, yet still furnishes opportunities for social diversion. Meetings are frequent and are pleasantly informal; members join in singing hymns to the accompaniment of guitar and violin, often played by former fiesta musicians. The warmth of the relations among hermanos is heightened by their belonging to a minority group. The fact that the brethren are still viewed as an oddity by the rest of the peasantry increases their cohesiveness despite differences in economic and ethnic background.

In short, Protestant evangelical sects are providing a welcome alternative for many Indian families who are no longer interested in conspicuous giving yet feel the need for a socio-religious group.

A Religious Movement

Despite declining interest and participation in the traditional fiestas, a minor messianic movement sprang up among the Mayos during 1958 and spread very rapidly, gaining considerable local interest and support. This movement was born when God appeared at the village of La Florida on the Fuerte River in Sinaloa on October 8, 1957. God, a small man with a long white beard, was dressed in white with a red cross over his heart and a rosary and water gourd around his neck; he wore the old-style sandals which few people wear today. He appeared under the mesquite tree in front of the house of Antonio Bacosegua, a Mayo Indian of about twenty. Antonio alone witnessed the apparition, and his story of the incident has been revised since it happened, by himself and by others.

When God appeared, Antonio's mother was very sick, believed near death. In the original version of the story God told Antonio that if he gave fiestas for Him, his mother would be spared. Antonio's mother lived only a few months longer so this part of the story soon lost significance. Later, God was reported to have promised the salvation of the world in return for the fiestas. By the time I left the area in May of 1959, fiestas for God had been held at five different places along the Fuerte River, at twenty-four places along the Mayo River, at four in the Yaqui River irrigation district, and were beginning to be held at three of the eight Yaqui Indian pueblos.

With the help of a native priest from the Mayo River who had once been an evangelical pastor, Antonio's story of the appearance of God was formally written down, and copies of the statement were circulated. This statement crystallized early in June of 1958, some nine months after God's appearance. According to this version, God called to Antonio three times before Antonio saw Him. God then told him to come closer because He wanted to speak to him, and Antonio moved closer with great fear. The apparition said that He was El Señor who had formed heaven and earth and that Antonio should not be afraid. God told Antonio that many strange things would be happening soon and that it was going to rain a great deal in the next few years. He said that He was displeased with the fiestas as performed today, that too many people were failing to fulfill their religious obligations. There were too many Protestants, and not enough "Christian teaching" among the Indians. Many people were fighting "at total strength" to destroy the Indian view of Catholicism (*la idea católica indígena*). Moreover, young people no longer respected their elders.

God then told Antonio to make eight fiestas for Him on eight consecutive Mondays. These eight fiestas were to be held each year for three successive years. God also described the form in which the fiestas should be held, and promised to return with further instructions at the end of the three-year period. "But if the fiestas are not held, the world will end sooner."

The story of God's appearance, as it was spread by word of mouth, took on embellishments, particularly on the Mayo River where the movement enjoyed its greatest popularity. In the stories that spread there, God had said there would be much rain during the next three years in order to fill the dams so the poor as well as the rich would get irrigation water. God was displeased with the administration of the Office of Water Resources because irrigation water was being sold illegally to the rich, leaving little for the poor. Some versions had it that He wanted to destroy the canals because no one should charge for His water. He was also displeased that the ceremonial dancers and musicians had formed the habit of charging for their services at religious fiestas, and instructed that they should not do so at the special fiestas He had ordered. Some stories said that God was angry because people were not contributing alms for fiestas as they used to, and because those who received gifts at fiestas were not returning them twelvefold the following year.

As Antonio began holding his eight fiestas, considerable local interest was aroused. Neighbors helped him construct a ramada in front of the mesquite tree where God had stood, and on the holy spot itself an altar was erected and a cross embedded in the ground. For a while, the story drew considerable attention in the town of Los Mochis. It occurred to members of the chamber of commerce there that regular Indian fiestas might be arranged on a scheduled date each month as a permanent tourist attraction. Although the idea was not carried out, some important personages from Los Mochis attended the fiestas to talk with Antonio and take pictures, thus giving an air of official sanction and creating the impression that even the rich Yoris in Los Mochis believed Antonio's story. Without this encouragement, the movement might have died quietly at an early stage.

As the news of God's appearance spread to the Mayo River, the church officials, native priests, and fiesteros at Júperi began to consider taking the Holy Trinity from Júperi to pay a visit to the new shrine at La Florida. First, however, the *kobanaro* or "president" of the church, as he is often referred to now, was sent down to talk with Antonio and see for himself if the story was true. Much impressed with Antonio, a modest and retiring boy who spoke mostly in Cáhita, the kobanaro decided that he was *muy Yoreme* — very Indian — and therefore would not have had the courage to fabricate such a story.

After taking the Holy Trinity to La Florida, where a special reception fiesta was held for it, the Júperi functionaries reciprocated by holding a "fiesta for God" in Júperi, thus beginning the spread of the fiesta. For while Júperi was holding its eight consecutive fiestas, other villages and towns also began to "receive" the fiesta, and a procedure for this developed.

In a particular village a nucleus of ceremony-oriented families would decide to hold a "fiesta for God." The house of the informal leader of this group would usually become the site of the fiesta and there members of the group and other neighbors would construct the ramada. The informal leader or "owner" of the fiesta would then go to La Florida to ask Antonio's permission to hold the affair and to get three paper flowers and a bag of earth. One of the flowers was white, one blue, and one red; each was later fastened to one of three crosses placed in a line leading out of the ramada directly in front of the altar. They marked the path along which the matachinis danced and along which the procession took place. On the altar was a church saint if the fiesta was held in a ceremonial town, or house saints brought by the village women.

Earth brought from the site where God appeared was considered to have potent curative powers: it could be applied externally by massage or in a poultice, and it could be taken internally when cooked with water and drunk as a broth. The owner of a fiesta for God distributed a pinch of earth to every person in the village who asked for it, almost always women. They wrapped the dirt in a new handkerchief and placed it in a carton the size of a shoe box, decorated with colored paper and covered with paper flowers. During each of the two or three processions during the fiesta, the women carried their decorated cartons behind the saint as it was led down the file of crosses. While the saint was resting on the altar the cartons were placed on the ground before it.

After the eighth and final fiesta of the year, the owner of the fiesta returned three new paper flowers to Antonio to notify him that the fiesta had terminated.

At some of the villages twenty-four fiesteros (twelve of each sex) were chosen from the nucleus of interested persons. But these fiesteros were not obligated for any great expense. They helped the owner of the fiesta, who was considered head fiestero, to collect donations of food and money, to keep order, and to prepare and serve the food. The entire village always helped to support the fiesta with donations, and when these were meager most of the food was served to the performers.

As these fiestas became more numerous, the number of ceremonial dancers available along the river was nearly exhausted. In some places, trainee pascolas only ten or twelve years old were pressed into service. At the first fiesta in Júperi, more ceremonial dancers and musicians were present than many local people had ever before seen together at a fiesta: eight pascolas, three deer dancers, and thirty-one musicians. At none of the fiestas for God were the performers paid, since it was recognized that God did not want it so.

A mythology so quickly developed around the appearance of God and around the person of Antonio that within a year many supernatural stories were circulating. One variety concerned the doubter heard to say that the story of God's appearance was a lie. In these accounts the doubter was usually killed the same day, accidentally and violently: a butcher in Los Mochis was run over by a truck, a hired hand fell under the tractor he was driving, and a man was drowned while bathing in an irrigation canal. Another variety had to do with God's reappearance. A little man answering to His description was seen walking along the top of the Fuerte River dam and was told to get down by some Indians from Los Capomos. When He did not, they threw rocks at Him, and He walked across the water out of sight. Again, at the last of the eight fiestas at La Florida during the second year, 1958, hands appeared over the altar, knocked over candles, and shook the mesquite tree above the sacred spot where God had first stood.

Another myth concerned the hole from which the sacred healing earth was dug. This hole, people said, remained very shallow because God kept filling it. It was also said that the earth was normally so hard that visitors found it difficult to scoop up, but when Antonio gathered it, it loosened like sand. A story grew up about me, for I visited "fiestas for God" in many different places, always carrying a gift of food or cigarettes: I had arrived in Mexico from the United States, the story went, with a tumor on one leg so large and painful that I could hardly walk. After Antonio treated it with holy earth from the spot where God had stood, the tumor healed and out of gratitude to Antonio I now visited all fiestas for God.

The most important aspect of these fiestas was the emphasis on curing by means of the distribution and use of the holy earth. Antonio himself had become a prosperous curandero by the time I left and had bought a new bicycle and radio. He no longer had to live by farming or working as a field hand. But Antonio and his family were not the only ones to profit from the fiesta for God. The owners of fiestas in many of the Mayo villages apparently kept or tried to keep some of the alms, and in nearly all the villages there were disputes about the misuse of funds. In several villages the fiesta was moved to a different house because of quarrels. In one village the people grew angry with the owner of the fiesta because she tried to sell the holy ground that Antonio had given her: the Mexican mordida has climbed well down the social ladder.

Although these fiestas for God are burdensome in the sense that they are long and time-consuming — two work days out of every week for almost two months each year of a three-year period — they do not really reverse or even slow the trend of disintegration of the church fiestas. In the first place, the very mood of the fiestas and the rationale behind them is despair at the lapse of the traditional ceremonial system. The Mayos believe that their fiesta system is disappearing, and those most concerned about it are the ones who put their words of despair into the mouth of God. Secondly, these fiestas require no conspicuous giving. Contributions come from the populace at large and only enough help is needed to pay for feeding the performers, since they are not paid. The fiestas for God resemble the most permanent form, the Easter ceremonies, in their economic structure. Both are local and community-

sponsored, financed with alms from outside as well as within the community, and both involve only minimal costs to feed the performers,
not lavish redistribution of food and goods.

The curing aspect is of principal interest to the women, who attend
in greatest numbers and bring the contributions of food. Similarly, it
is the sickness vow more than the quest for prestige through giving
which today maintains all of the traditional church fiestas. Both depend
upon the high rate of infant mortality in the country; for, as shown
earlier, many of the fiesteros and performers in the traditional fiesta
system are promised when they are children, on the condition that they
recover from an illness or grow to maturity.

L. P. Mair has said in a recent comparison of native religious movements that when such a movement takes place within a social context
where powerful external authority can suppress subversive or destructive tendencies in the activity, sickness and cures may become a major
preoccupation of the movement.[8] Such would seem to be the case here.
Despite the political flavor of some of God's resentments against Yori
exploitation, these overtones were never dominant. And in villages near
Navojoa where permission to hold these fiestas was refused by the
municipal president, the people complained among themselves but
meekly acquiesced.

This religious movement gained its support and impetus from those
among the local Indians most likely to seek status satisfaction from
taking part in ceremonies. And it is in this search for prestige that we
find an important part of the explanation for the new behaviors and
rituals that developed with the movement. In each case where elaboration was added, such as decorating the crosses with flowers or decorating cartons to contain the sacred earth, the initiation and spread of the
practices could clearly be attributed to persons who wanted public
notice. Mayos do not usually seek public esteem in a loud or obvious
fashion. Much like other Indians of the greater Southwest, they dislike
or ridicule braggarts and others who strive to call attention to themselves. But they seek social approval, and the satisfaction an Indian gets
from holding an official position in the ceremonial organization is often
quite apparent both in his bearing while officiating and in the way he
struggles to keep his position if it is threatened by dissension within
the group. The minor elaborations of ritual which grew up within this
religious movement can be understood as a result of the Indians' desire

for prestige and its satisfactions and the random tolerance of elaborations upon existing ritual.

The Yaquis

Persecute an Indian group unjustly for a long period, exploit its labor, and then finally in remorse and reconciliation give it a communally owned parcel of land. This is one of the best recipes for creating an ethnic and cultural minority and helping it to maintain its social isolation within the larger nation. This happened to the Yaquis, as well as to many other Indian groups in the New World.

The much stronger social unity of the Yaquis as compared with the Mayos is reflected in the popular Mexican stereotypes of the Yaquis as belligerent, warlike, and cruel and the Mayos as peaceful, retiring, and sometimes even "noble." [9] The Mayos were as warlike as the Yaquis when the two groups first rose up in arms against the whites in 1740. But the topography of the Mayo country did not provide them with any defensive position for prolonged guerrilla warfare comparable to the Yaquis' Bacatete Mountains. The Mayo River flows out of the sierras across seventy-five miles of open coastal plain. From the downstream villages, which even in the eighteenth century were more populous than those upstream, the nearest mountains were seventy-five to a hundred miles away. Moreover, the sierras contained rich mines and by the beginning of the nineteenth century were well populated by whites. The Mayos had little choice but pacifism and submission to Yori infiltration. Their number has grown as a consequence, but living side by side with Yoris in the same rancherías under the same municipal governments they preserve little political or social unity. They still elect church governors, but these men have become little more than church caretakers who help keep order at fiestas. They have little authority and are sometimes referred to now as church "presidents," a position compared to the presidency of local school boards.

The Yaqui River skirts the Bacatete Mountains on its way westward, thereby putting all the Yaqui villages within about fifteen miles of a defensible mountainous retreat. This gave the Yaquis a refuge of great strategic importance, and accounts in large part for their being able to fight the Mexicans until as late as 1927. Because of conflict lasting into the present century, the Yaquis have left a very recent impression on the white population as a warlike people. Among the Yaquis, the memory and oral tradition of their bloody conflicts with the whites keeps alive a distrust and hatred recently further aggravated by the irrigation developments which dammed their river and ended the annual floods with which they had irrigated.

Thus, the years of conflict with the Yoris and the greater social isolation provided by the topography resulted in a stronger political unity among the Yaquis than among the Mayos; for example, I never heard a Mayo spontaneously speak of a Mayo "tribe," but the Yaquis constantly use the word in referring to themselves. This preoccupation with their tribal identity is frequently expressed in the same context as their dislike of Yoris or Mexicans. It rests on a deep prejudice kept alive by stories of past Yori atrocities. It also gains strength today from the Yaquis' common concern for the tribal lands finally recognized and clearly delineated during the term of President Cárdenas in the thirties. The Mayo Indians have no such unifying force as that provided by the Yaqui land reserve — a common vested interest and a common bond. Although Mayos are co-members of ejidos, this kind of land tenure tends to splinter, rather than to unify, them, for the ejidos are numerous and not exclusively Indian. In the Yaqui reserve all Indian residents are members of one tribal ejido from which Yoris are excluded by law. (Yoris may live in the reserve but are not members of the comunidad.) No other single fact does more to preserve the integrity of this minority group than its tribal land tenure. In contrast, the partitive nature of land tenure among the Mayos and their co-residence with Yoris greatly increases the chances of their social fragmentation and Mexicanization.

The word "tribe" applied to the Yaqui does not have the same meaning as when it is used to refer to primitive groups in remote parts of the world. The Yaqui are a peasant people now clearly part of the Mexican nation. As a group they have learned much better than the Mayo how to manipulate the government for their own ends. They are participants in a money economy; many are literate, and a surprising number have been in the United States or other parts of Mexico. Ralph Beals, observing the Yaqui twenty-five years ago, called them "nationalistic." He noted much the same differences as exist now in the internal organization and cohesion of the two groups and in the use of the word "tribe." But twenty-five years ago the Yaquis also thought of themselves as a nation and would "naively enough, discuss treaties and the possibility of negotiating with foreign powers on an equal basis." [10] The Yaquis no longer think of themselves as an independent nation, but their pre-occupation with tribal identity is apparently as strong as ever. But, I repeat, they are peasants, not primitive tribesmen, and their unity and *esprit de corps* are those of a minority group with certain religious and traditional practices that set them apart from the nation at large and through which they themselves act to preserve their social uniqueness.

The Yaqui reserve is divided into eight districts or pueblos, each of which has a Yaqui governor. Although Vicam pueblo is now considered the capital or head town of the reserve, Yaqui officials in the other pueblos deny that the Vicam governor has any jurisdiction over them. At Vicam Station the federal government maintains a tribal headquarters run by a federally appointed representative of the tribe. The present representative is an educated Yaqui who seems sincerely interested in the welfare of his people. Yaquis have more to do with the federal government than with state and local governments, and most Yaqui dealings with the Mexican government are channeled through his office. There is a sheriff (*comisario*) in Potam, but the Yaqui and Yori authorities divide their jurisdictions on an ethnic basis. A drunken and troublesome Yaqui apprehended by Yori officials is turned over to the Yaqui authorities. Conversely, a troublesome Yori is turned over to the sheriff by the Yaqui "soldiers."

In each pueblo the most important officials are the *firmantes* or "signers," five men who must sign all official documents. The principal of these is the first governor, who has four or five assistant governors. The second firmante is the *pueblo mayor*, head of a council of elders composed of former governors. He serves as an adviser to the governor and nowadays meets official visitors in the governor's absence. The third firmante is the "captain of infantry" whose duties most closely approximate those of a Mexican *comisario* or sheriff. He is concerned with keeping order in town, especially at fiestas, and with calling the people together for official meetings and announcements. The *guardia*, which serves as both office and jail, is under his jurisdiction. Someone must always be on duty at the guardia; and because all Yaquis are theoretically members of the infantry, all are eligible to be called into service for one week. Those who have other official or ceremonial duties, however, are excused, so the obligation usually falls on those who have no other duties and who are often referred to as the *mero pueblo* — the plain people.

The fourth firmante is the *comandante*, who is chief of the cavalry and guardian of the forest — titles largely honorific, since the Yaquis have neither infantry nor cavalry and few even own horses. The comandante, however, is in charge of collecting taxes from all Yoris who exploit the natural resources within the district: woodcutters are charged a tax on each truckload of firewood taken from the reserve, and Yori ranchers who keep cattle in the reserve must pay a head tax each year and donate cattle on demand for fiestas. The comandante relegates these tax-collecting duties to his captains and sergeants.

Fifth is the secretary, who must be fluent in Spanish and literate to some degree. He often serves as interpreter for the governors. Governors are elected for one year and are occasionally re-elected. The other four firmantes are elected for life or until the people grow dissatisfied with their services.

A serious split in the Yaqui government was only recently solved by the intervention of the federal government. Since the end of the Yaqui wars, the Mexican army has kept a small occupation force on the Yaqui reserve. The general in charge of this post during the administration of President Alemán appointed his own duplicate set of governors and firmantes for each pueblo, thus attempting to gain control of the tax money normally raised by the pueblo governors. The fact that he was able to find stooges and people willing to support them seems surprising in view of the Yaquis' strong sense of tribal identity. It suggests, however, that the Mexican mordida has penetrated even Yaqui society.

Those Yaqui who recognized the authorities appointed by the military government came to be called the *Yaquis militarizados* (military-oriented Yaquis) as opposed to the *Yaquis tradicionales* (tradition-oriented Yaquis). At La Loma de Guamuchil the military-oriented Yaquis became the dominant group because the appointed governor was more popular than the governor of the traditionalists. Most of his popularity was achieved through the distribution of graft. He helped Yori friends establish cattle ranches in his jurisdiction, but kept after them constantly for donations of cattle for fiestas. Since all major fiestas except a small Easter ceremony have disappeared at Guamuchil, cattle were frequently donated to individual Yaquis for private household fiestas, a practice which made this governor popular with the majority of his constituents.

The factionalism was finally solved by a plebiscite sponsored by the federal government in January of 1958. Traditionalists won at five pueblos and militarists at three. In the next annual elections for governor, however, in 1959, traditionalists won in all the pueblos. The federal government and its tribal "representative" are both sympathetic to the traditionalist cause, and complete withdrawal of the military occupation force is now under consideration.

Combined with the extremely difficult economic plight of the Yaquis since flood irrigation of their old fields was made impossible by the Yaqui River dams, the practice of supporting fiestas with contributions taxed from Yoris living within the reserve has tended to undermine the older dependence on conspicuous giving. Itemization of the expenses of Easter fiestas at Vicam and Torim showed that all the meat and most of the other provisions are now derived from Yori contributions. Many fiestas have almost ceased to be an expense at all for the Yaquis, and the methods of soliciting the contributions sometimes amount almost to extortion. All Yoris are fair game — the woodcutters, the merchants who operate stores and other businesses in the reserve, and especially the ranchers. The land belongs to the Yaquis, and since rumors are continually being circulated that all Yoris or all Yori ranchers are going to be put off the reserve, the Yori ranchers particularly are anxious to stay in the Yaquis' good graces. They are well aware of the Indians' attitude that anyone who lives on the reserve must "cooperate"; the Yaquis explain it to them frequently.

Although nearly all Mayo fiestas are accompanied by carnival features including sideshows, Ferris wheels, and public dances, such secular activities are permitted at only one Yaqui fiesta — the Fiesta del Camino — held in June at La Loma de Bacum. The ranchers in the Bacum district supply the beef for the fiesta, and the carnival stands are also taxed to help meet expenses. Among the Mayos, carnival taxes go to the president of the municipality, and since no close accounting is made, much of the money stays in his pocket. When the mayor of the municipio of Bacum sent police to collect taxes at the Fiesta del Camino, however, the Yaquis sent them back empty-handed with the message that the mayor could make no charges at fiestas held in a federal land reserve under Yaqui jurisdiction.

With regard to church fiestas, change has taken the same general direction among the Yaquis as among the Mayo. The Easter fiestas have shown the greatest resiliency and have survived in all eight pueblos. They are all sponsored by the ceremonial clowns and the expenses met primarily, as we have seen, with provisions collected from Yoris. The Yaquis can remember no time when Easter fiestas were sponsored by fiesteros. But they do remember many fiestas no longer held and fiestas now sponsored by the governors or some ceremonial society which were formerly supported by the contributions of fiesteros. During the period when the Yaquis were badly scattered by Porfirio Díaz's campaign to wipe them out, the fiestero groups disbanded and many never were reconstituted. Church fiestas now supported by the governors and ceremonial societies include the Fiesta de la Cruz at Potam, the Guadalupe fiestas at Potam, Vicam, and La Loma de Guamuchil (Cocorit) and the large and important Fiesta del Camino at Bacum.

Only three church fiestas sponsored by fiesteros survive among the Yaquis — the fiesta of the Holy Trinity at Potam, the fiesta of Santa Cruz at Torim, and the fiesta of San Juan at Vicam. Of these only the fiesta at Potam is still a three-day affair; the other two now last only one day. The fiesta of San Juan was revived in 1958 after not having been held for about ten years. Such a long postponement is unusual, although in times of economic hardship a postponement of a year or two is not uncommon. As among the Mayos, fiesteros often reduce costs by sharing the expense of buying cattle among two or three. There are eight fiesteros of each sex divided into two groups — the "reds" and the "blues." Each group has a separate ramada and each tries to outdo the other in the quality of its fiesta while the onlookers critically compare the two.

Despite the fact that only these three fiestero groups remain, the redistribution of food is taken very seriously and considerable pride is still derived from conspicuous giving. Those who receive food at the fiesta return a sizable contribution the following year, and, as noted earlier, great attention is paid to the gifts of food brought to the fiestas. The revival of the San Juan fiesta at Vicam after ten years was the work of the head fiestero, who by 1958 had become president of one of the Yaqui credit societies working with the Ejido Bank. Out of his salary and his mordidas he was able to spend nearly five thousand pesos (four hundred dollars), the highest I recorded for any fiestero in the Mayo-Yaqui region. (The daily wage for farm laborers in the Yaqui area is only ten pesos and in the Yaqui valley irrigation zone twelve to fifteen pesos). He was exceedingly proud of having revived the fiesta after such a long interval.

Yaqui fiesteros are invitational; no one refuses to serve. Virtually everyone agrees that refusal would be punished by God, and the strength of the supernatural sanction rests on strong social sanctions. Time and again I was told that in order to live among his fellow Yaquis one must be willing to "cooperate," the same rule which they apply to outsiders — that every Yaqui should do his part to serve the religion of his people. The sanctions of public disapproval are strong, but, on the other hand, a man who does a good job as fiestero is often called upon thereafter as a consultant about later fiestas, and he becomes a kind of respected informal leader.

Some younger Yaquis believe that their people do not progress because they spend so much time and money on fiestas. But these skeptics do not avoid their religious obligations without an acceptable excuse, for they also believe that in order to live happily with the rest they must conform. Ambivalent attitudes toward religious fiestas are not uncommon. Some Yaquis are beginning to compare their living standards unfavorably with those of people outside the reserve; they realize that the time and money spent on their many household and church fiestas could be spent for other things. But the Yaquis are still a fairly self-sufficient group so far as status is concerned; they find opportunities to achieve it within their own society by traditional means. Even the Yaqui who has traveled, is literate, and chafes under the burden of ceremonial ritual and the sponsoring of fiestas apparently finds sufficient satisfaction in the companionship of other Yaquis and in holding or the hope of holding political and religious offices to justify it all.

The high rate of Yaqui ceremonial participation strengthens both social and supernatural sanctions. Persons and families who do not take part in ceremonial life seem much more uneasy and defensive about their lack of participation than do non-participants among the Mayos, where defection and lack of interest are so much more common. And Yaquis are much more credulous about divine punishment for failure to fulfill ceremonial obligations. Although agnostics are common and outspoken among the Mayos, I never met a Yaqui who denied belief in supernatural sanction.

One of the questions asked during a census of thirty households at Vicam pueblo was the ceremonial and political offices of all family members. Such offices included governors, "cavalry" officers, church officials, ceremonial dancers, "Jews," church singers, and ceremonial musicians. Only three — ten per cent — of the households had no functionaries at all, and only six — twenty per cent — had only one. The other seventy per cent had two or more functionaries apiece. Fifty-nine per cent of the seventy-four males over sixteen in this sample were functionaries and thirty-five per cent of the sixty-two women. Even children under six were functionaries in five households. In contrast, only seven (eighteen per cent) of the thirty-eight Mayo Indian households at Biacusi had functionaries and none more than one. All were men and constituted only eight per cent of the eighty-nine adult males in the sample; all were paid performers.

On the other hand, heads in thirty-two (eighty-four per cent) of the Mayo households had been fiesteros at least once in their lifetime and most of them more than once, whereas half of the heads of the Yaqui households had never been sponsors of a major fiesta. This comparison does not give a clear picture of the situation, however, for most of the Biacusi fiesteros had sponsored the annual Fiesta de la Cruz in Biacusi, which is not a traditional ceremonial center. This fiesta began about twenty years ago, and although it is patterned exactly after church fiestas, it takes place at a private dwelling. Fiesteros buy meat, but in small quantities. For the majority of Biacusi fiesteros, the annual expense is only three hundred to five hundred pesos — twenty to forty working days. This sponsorship would not require the same personal sacrifice nor the degree of financial help from friends and relatives as the sponsorship of a Yaqui church fiesta. Nevertheless the comparisons illustrate, I believe, the quality of the difference between Yaqui and Mayo participation.

Yaqui participation emphasizes ceremonial service through permanent associations. A vow to serve as a "Jew" or a matachini, for example, entails a lifetime obligation for Yaquis, not just a three-year period of service as among the Mayos. The strong *esprit de corps* stimulated by ceremonial activities, permanent membership in associations within the ceremonial organization, and the compulsions to fulfill ceremonial obligations all increase the socially unifying effect of Yaqui religion. Conspicuous giving is disappearing, but conspicuous service persists in Yaqui ceremonial life as an integrating force which does not necessarily conflict in the Mexican environment[11] with economic distress on the one hand or with a greater interest in conspicuous ownership on the other.

Implications

Prestige through conspicuous giving is on the wane among both Mayos and Yaquis. Inflation plus increasing dependence on retail stores for food makes fiestas seem more expensive than ever to the Indians and less desirable than more individualistic forms of expenditure. The weakening of economic aid to Mayo fiesta sponsors from their friends and relatives for the same reasons has also deeply undermined the sponsorship system. Because the Mayo church fiestas depend so much on sponsorship by fiesteros the disintegration of conspicuous giving is greatly endangering their survival.

The Yaquis have kept a stronger political system as a result of the long fight for their lands and their present communal ownership of the tribal reserve, which gives them a sense of unity. Their political and social ties result in stronger social sanctions than exist among the Mayos. In a way, Yaquis are almost "nativistic" in their preoccupation with tribal integrity, their hatred of the Yori, and the maintenance of their religion. Conspicuous production in the form of ceremonial service is still important among them, though probably less so than formerly. Conspicuous giving, however, has declined and has been replaced to some extent by the tribal taxation of Yori ranchers who keep cattle on the reserve. But because of the high rate of Yaqui participation in tribal ceremonial life and the attention paid to this form of social conformity, the fiestas are surviving as an avenue for conspicuous ceremonial service which does not seriously conflict with earning a living that is within the fairly narrow limits of their expectations.

The emphasis Yaquis put on conspicuous production through ceremonial service is similar to the emphasis placed on conspicuous service within the kibbutz communities of Israel. The Yaquis show similar rejection of outsiders and also are a minority group with strong *esprit de corps*. But the Yaquis are not a highly educated people with sufficient sophistication to set up ideal intellectual and quasi-rationalistic socialist communities. Their conspicuous production takes a form they know well — ceremonial service, a form with considerable random tolerance for persistence and elaboration at different levels of sophistication. As for collectives, the Yaquis appear to be as individualistic as any of their

Sonoran neighbors. They dislike working in collectives and look forward to the promised division of ejidal lands. And Yaqui leaders frequently evince the same tendencies toward graft and conspicuous consumption as their Mexican counterparts. Though messianic movements among minority groups at a certain intellectual level may occasionally result in operating communal organizations or collectives emphasizing conspicuous production, these cases are too exceptional to serve as examples for government welfare programs in free societies. By and large the so-called collective or communal kind of community organization seems most congenial to coercive control.

The Mayos' situation is similar in the cases of the Easter fiestas and the messianic fiestas-for-God movement along the Mayo River. Conspicuous ceremonial service has taken precedence over conspicuous giving and is sustained by the families at the conservative end of the social gradient and those who seek cures. The nature of the prestige motive underlying ceremonial participation has altered among both groups and so, too, has the nature of the participation itself in some cases. Obviously there is considerable random tolerance in the persistence of ceremonial behavior. Eventually, however, the increasing reliance on modern medicine will weaken the attachment between the ceremonial complex and the desire to survive, although the most damaging consequence to the fiesta system will be the substitution of other forms of sickness vows not associated with Indianness. The emulative diffusion of other forms of vows will probably be slower among the Yaquis than among the Mayos because of Yaqui tribal consciousness and their greater desire to preserve their customs. But even among the Mayos, ceremonies may continue a long while as an expression of community and regional consciousness supported in part by local merchants' interest in annual celebrations. Perhaps the pascolas and deer dancers, who are paid performers and completely regional, will last longest.

The importance of the sickness vows in keeping up ceremonial life should not be underestimated; this is the most common reason for accepting ceremonial obligations in both groups. Even the Mayos, many of whom are coming to depend on the medical doctor to treat disease, still make sickness vows. Though treatment by a physician competes with and replaces both the home remedies and the folk curers, it does not conflict directly with the solicitation of supernatural aid. Here the process of incorporation and change is more truly additive than substitutive. But even here greater dependence on modern medicine may be correlated with differences in the popularity of various forms of sickness vows in a manner which is indirectly substitutive. While townspeople, including some of the more sophisticated Indian families, would not make vows to be fiesteros or ceremonial performers at Indian fiestas, they do make other forms of service vows according to wider Mexican and Latin American custom. Such vows may require pilgrimages, walking the length of the church on one's knees, burning candles before a certain image, or giving an image a silver replica of the afflicted part of the body. The fact that a sick person is receiving medical attention does not rule out asking for divine aid.

Sickness vows to fulfill ceremonial service at Indian fiestas are not requisites for all Indians who seek supernatural assistance. The bilinguality and literacy associated with Mexicanization and the loss of interest in the church fiestas affect the form of sickness vows which Indian families make. But the number of sickness vows and the extent of self-sacrifice they entail will obviously be affected by the morbidity and death rates of children, for, as noted earlier, such vows are frequently made on behalf of children, sometimes to insure that they reach adulthood. The high death rate of country children definitely helps to support the fiesta system by intensifying the concern for survival. Since these mortality rates, as we saw in Chapter III, are related more to poverty than to folk resistance, the Indians' low standard of living indirectly helps support the fiesta system. To the extent that the fiesta system in turn holds down the standard of living, the process becomes a vicious circle. But like all vicious circles, this one is not really circular. Regional development through greater use of natural resources — the land through roads and irrigation and the people through education — is contributing to the further Mexicanization of the Indian, particularly the less ethnically integrated Mayos. The process is slow and makes the country people look retarded by comparison with the people of the faster-changing towns. But this different rate of progress in the country must be expected even under conditions of normal, "healthy" development. Hope for uniformity in even a single region, much less an entire country, would be utopian and unrealistic.

Although a gradual increase in individual felt needs has long been competing with social or conspicuous giving in this area, conspicuous ownership has been slow to take hold among the majority of the peasantry and certainly among the Indians. Many of the Mayos are neutral with regard to status mobility. They feel little expectation of moving up in the Yori status system of conspicuous ownership, and their own former status system of ceremonial service and giving is weak or dying. But the persistence of the ceremonial system owes as much as anything to the lack of status mobility through other forms of consumption and participation. Mayos with little or no expectation of improving their finances may still find some social satisfaction in the ceremonial system, especially those whose illiteracy and language handicap estranges them most from the Yori world. Where expenses are lowered and the length of service shortened, ceremonialism becomes a pleasant social diversion which requires less personal sacrifice or competition for prestige than it formerly did.

Many Mayos no longer take part in Indian ceremonial life and refuse to sponsor fiestas. Some of these are defecting to evangelistic cults; some have accepted Yori goals and become "Indians who want to be Yoris"; a few are even to be found among the "little rich." These persons and their families form a nucleus for further change. By their very defection they weaken the social and supernatural sanctions that supported the old ceremonial system, and they demonstrate to others the increasing opportunities for mobility.

Some of the more successful Mayos who might once have been active fiesteros are now tending toward conspicuous ownership. But this does not make much impression on observers if their felt needs are not strong already, and in general the low expectations of the great majority of Indians and their tendency to feel inferior combine to keep their felt needs at a very low level of intensity. Poverty and low expectations can also make a demonstration effect — in reverse — particularly when they are widespread in a population.

In the towns, where mobility is much greater and most people are improving their standard of living, the man who lags behind feels out of step and compelled to join the trend toward conspicuous ownership. The demonstration effect of his neighbors' improvements may make his own easier; if they can buy a new stove and refrigerator, so can he. But in a sense his acts are partly forced by theirs: what everyone else is doing he must do also. Partly out of envy and partly out of pressure from within his own family, he is compelled to follow suit. When a population is making a change in sufficient numbers that the demonstration effect creates a felt need to conform to it, a social conformity effect may be said to be taking place.

In most villages along the Mayo River not enough country families have improved their circumstances to provide a demonstration effect — much less a conformity effect — in favor of further change. On the contrary, there is something tolerantly protective about the equality of poverty in the villages and the villagers' ability to say, "We are all poor here." The lack of aggressiveness and self-direction complements rather than conflicts with the greater independence of work habits in the country and the ease with which the peasant switches from work to leisure at his own discretion. Hard work may be valued, but by no means is it performed with the same diligence as in the towns where the interdependence of specialists requires a greater standardization of working hours and leads to a closer comparison of effort.

Work situations which increase the Indians' association with Mexicans and increase their facility in Spanish are important avenues of change. Recent technological developments have increased this kind of association. With the greater number of paved roads, the better maintenance of gravel ones, and the increasing number of bicycles and rural buses, country people travel to town oftener than ever before. During the cotton harvest season many villages are virtually abandoned as inhabitants go off to work as pickers, sometimes as far as a hundred or two hundred miles away. Truckers hired by large farmers visit the villages regularly at this season to recruit workers and carry them to the fields.

Miscegenation is slow, but until now it has been the most effective of all the Mexicanization processes. Because of the high birth rate, miscegenation is not taking place fast enough to convert all Indians into Yoris. In the long run education will probably be more decisive than miscegenation in fully Mexicanizing the Indian.

Rural schoolteachers assigned to teaching posts along the Mayo River twenty-five to thirty-five years ago remember how children in so many of the villages at that time were monolingual Cáhita-speakers. They believe that the rural education program is responsible for the fact that Spanish is so widely spoken among the country people today, and there is no doubt that the schools have had a tremendous influence, particularly ones where an able and dedicated teacher has taught in the same community for ten to twenty years. Most children in Indian homes where Spanish is the household language are monolingual Spanish-speakers and are much more likely to be literate than children in homes where Cáhita is the household language. Indian parents who speak Spanish at home are frequently those who "want to be Yoris" and they usually see to it that their children attend school regularly. Where Cáhita is still the household language the degree of literacy among the children depends a great deal upon the bilinguality of the parents and the amount of schooling the children have had. If the parents are bilingual, the children usually are, and a Spanish-speaking child can often learn enough in a year of schooling so that he can develop reading and writing skills for himself, because of the phonetic orthography of Spanish. But parents in the more conservative households in which Cáhita is still spoken are usually very much unconcerned about their children's education and keep their children at home for reasons that seem trivial to a town resident. In the rural village schools, boys are absent at least a third of the time and girls at least a fourth.[12] Control of truancy could improve the results of the rural education program without greatly increasing the cost of education, but this would be extremely difficult since rural education is provided by the federal government and truancy control would require local interest and supervision.

Although to the outsider the country people's need for education appears greater than the townspeople's, it is the latter who worry most about educating their children and who are most active in soliciting improvements.

Economic opportunity is also important in the growth of expectations and felt needs. Most of the small farmers and ejidatarios in the Yaqui River irrigation district enjoy more prosperity than those in the Mayo irrigation district, where the average holding is much smaller and the irrigation water more undependable. If even in this relatively underpopulated land, a slight difference in population density can make such a noticeable difference in living standards and the rise of expectations, it is obvious how important population density is for economic development. It can greatly intensify all other problems.

But by whatever means people's expectations and felt needs are increased, some cultural differences among social groups will persist. In such spheres as ritual, pageantry, art, and dress, there is the greatest amount of random tolerance for conspicuous production at all levels of social development. Cultural diversity in such spheres often provides symbols of group identity. Since the quest for prestige involves invidious comparisons within limited interest groups, it tends to preserve some diversity even though it reduces the field of random tolerance for that diversity through the accumulation of knowledge and invidious emulation.

CONCLUSIONS

XIII

Implications for the Future

T HE concept of prestige or status as used to interpret culture in this book is not to be confused with the concept of the economic man. Although I view self-interest as the underlying stimulus to action, the striving activity which results, I believe, is not directed merely toward the acquisition of useful goods. Nor have I invoked any self-regulating mechanism such as a competitive market system to keep self-interest working for the greater good of all. Here I contend that man's cognitive symbolizing ability, stimulated mainly by the desire for social recognition, accounts for the dynamic quality of progressive cultural development through the growth and spread of culture capital. As positive controls over the environment increase through specialization, social interdependence and reciprocity are extended to more people, and negative controls develop to regulate the delayed rewards of impersonal reciprocity. By this process, the cognitive component of cultural causality modifies the socially approved forms of behavior through which self-interest can seek expression. Whatever one wishes to view in this growth and expansion as a moral or ethical development must also be attributed to man's intelligence, the increasing probability of his knowledge, and a self-interest which is always socially mediated and sanctioned in some degree.

Three forms taken by the prestige motive or desire for social recognition have been given heuristic importance in this work — conspicuous giving, conspicuous ownership, and conspicuous production. The first was called characteristic of the primitive closed society, where distribution and redistribution enhanced the prestige and power of the leader or "big man." Where production provided ample food supplies beyond the needs of subsistence, redistribution favored those in command, with consequent strengthening of coercive control. Even at this level, however, there was conspicuous ownership. But the small amount of specialization so limited the variety of goods that accumulation tended toward redundancy, thus increasing the likelihood of conspicuous giving. There was also some conspicuous production at this level: craftsmen and successful warriors, for example, acquired status by virtue of their skills.

Conspicuous ownership was prominent among the privileged members of primitive coercive societies, but it became most widespread with the opening of society, as commerce and specialization increased the variety of available goods and the number of felt needs. Although conspicuous giving and conspicuous ownership still exist, conspicuous production is now in the ascendancy. In our free society, the consumer has been saturated with durable goods. Differences in consumption have become so much a matter of size, luxury, and price that even prestige advertising is becoming obvious to the consumer. Certainly conspicuous consumption is still very important in our society, but it is now finding stiff competition in conspicuous production. Men with modest salaries take increasing pride in creative work or in manipulating goods and wealth which are not their own.

The ascendancy of conspicuous production in our society as an outlet for prestige motivation is contemporaneous with the ascendancy of conspicuous giving at the international level. In the primitive closed society we saw that invidious sanction operated to keep the "big man" a conspicuous giver of redundant supplies of goods, usually food. In return for his giving, this better hunter or farmer received recognition and deference from his fellows, though probably not without some continued jealousy and envy. Today, the underdeveloped dual societies similarly employ invidious sanction to solicit foreign aid. By registering disapproval of us, sometimes even by insulting our visiting statesmen, they effectively, though not always deliberately, channel more aid in their own direction. At a time when our society is engaged in what is virtually a conspicuous production struggle for survival against a coercive society, such signs of ill will are viewed as a threat to our security. We want to increase our influence and leadership and to avoid defections to the other side. The fact that there is a rough parallel between this situation and primitive giving does not mean that international aid is primitive or wrong. This simply is another demonstration that the growth of reciprocities and negative controls is additive and substitutive. There is nothing fundamentally new under the sun in the realm of human reciprocity.

In deciding to extend foreign aid when threatened by invidious sanction at the international level, our statesmen, our lawmakers, and the sympathetic public are listening to their survival motive and in part to their own vested interest in national prestige. But those who put the giving policies into effect in the foreign countries concerned are among the rising numbers of conspicuous producers. Here is a new world for modern empirebuilders — the field of international aid and education. The simultaneous occurrence of the ascendancy of conspicuous production and international giving is no accident. The same highly productive technology which has made us the envy of the world has also freed great quantities of labor from primary productive activities and is continually freeing more. Not only are we able to increase leisure and the conspicuous production activities of leisure time, but we can also increase conspicuous production in forms of service — national and international. The growth of government services is a natural corollary of automation. And government personnel are quick to seize upon new ways of expanding services and with them jobs and opportunities for conspicuous production.

Negative Control and Students of Society

Throughout this book I have emphasized the progressive role of positive controls in cultural development. This emphasis is contrary to the idea that man's technological development has outstripped his social development. Known to social scientists as cultural lag, this idea persists with remarkable tenacity at the popular as well as the professional level. Its tenacity is probably partly explainable by its usefulness to many social scientists as a justification for their own professional existence.

An obvious implication of this cultural-lag concept is that developments in social knowledge and control must take place in order to catch up with our technological knowledge and the positive control of our natural environment. I agree, of course, that society must continually adjust to its technological changes, but it does not lag far behind them waiting for students of society to find a shortcut to Utopia. The very fact that a society *has* a given technology is sufficient evidence that it is ready for it; technological development can hardly advance beyond the limits set by the social environment. Technology consists of knowledge and skills, which, in any society, depend for their existence on the degree of specialization within that society and the way in which social reciprocities are organized and sanctioned. The development of positive controls does not take place independently of change in negative controls.

For the sake of argument, a much better case might be made for a technological — rather than social — lag in the world today.[1] Emulating more developed nations, leaders in many underdeveloped countries have very advanced ideas about social welfare measures for their people. They often attempt social welfare programs that are not economically feasible because the countries are not sufficiently developed technologically to provide the per-capita production necessary to support them.

From some points of view, a cultural lag may exist among backward people who have difficulty accepting new technologies. In this sense, "lag" may be just another way of expressing "underdevelopment." But when a group is unable to accept new techniques for so-called social reasons, there is usually a vast difference between the felt needs of the innovators and those of the people to be changed. That is, the lag is really between the felt needs of the host group and those of the donors of technology. And this is the very kind of lag which least justifies our concern if we are committed to helping first those people who want our help. Where we are faced with raising expectations — that is, with helping people satisfy needs they already feel — social conditions will no longer be a major concern, for the lag will be primarily technological.

Man's positive and negative controls are interdependent, for the progressive development of knowledge and skill, as we have seen, is dependent upon the additive and substitutive development of the social reciprocities which accompany the division of labor. The lag hypothesis is sometimes posed as a Frankenstein-and-the-monster duel between mankind and his machines, in which mankind has a hard time keeping up with its monster. But the interdependence of positive and negative controls and the socially mediated motivations which give them individual meaning and social existence vitiate such neat contrasts.

There is a further implication of the cultural-lag hypothesis that seems to me to be in error: the implication that by specializing in learning about himself man can progressively develop his negative controls in a way similar to the progressive accumulation of knowledge which takes place through continual improvements in technical observations of the physical world. Although the social "scientist" mimics the natural scientist through his use of statistical quantification, his observations do not really succeed in becoming any more technical nor his knowledge more progressively cumulative. What he accomplishes by means of specialization is a more exhaustive description of his limited subject matter, and the elaboration that takes place is characteristically additive and substitutive.

The basic difference between natural and social science is probably best dramatized at the respective professional meetings. Critical discussions of papers presented at meetings of natural scientists center upon technical considerations of method or failure to include relevant data. Ideally, the critical discussions of social scientists would follow the same course, but in practice social scientists are more concerned with the vocabulary of a speaker than with his data. While physical scientists seem to reach a consensus about the weaknesses or strengths of a paper fairly rapidly and do not usually belabor the issue, social scientists evince strong ego-involvements in their vocabulary and will argue their definitional differences into the ground. Novelty in the social sciences depends more on fresh analogies and jargon than on new frequency interpretations. This is one reason why social scientists are often said to be more "intellectual" than physical scientists. They are dialecticians, and a chief method of achieving prestige is conspicuous intellectualism. There is much to be said for the point of view that students of man's behavior are closer to being artists than scientists.

One possible danger in this situation lies in social scientists' increasing intellectual self-sufficiency. Sociologists and anthropologists, for example, depend for their living largely on colleges and universities, where they exist for the purpose of training others to someday replace

them so that these in their turn can train still more. As college enroll-
ments increase, so do the number of sociologists and anthropologists
and the number of their would-be replacements. This progressively increasing membership of professional men and students has become large
enough to make up its own reading public. Part of this public, the non-
professional students, is transitory, but through the assignment of read-
ings they are made into good, paying, captive readers. By constitut-
ing and capturing their own reading public, students of society and culture have reached the point where they can even publish books in a
professional language all their own and still sell more than enough
copies to pay printing costs. Thus, conspicuous scholars now have the
added opportunity of becoming conspicuous conceptualizers and jar-
gonists.

Since the actions of social scientists are in large part a product of
the limitations of their subject matter, the differences between social
science and physical science should not be attributed to an inferiority
of social science. Not all of the differences should be minimized by emulation of the more prestigeful physical scientist. The physical scientist's province is the expansion of positive controls; the special province
of the social scientist is the analysis and discussion of negative controls.
The purists — who would treat culture impersonally without making
judgments, in the belief that such a practice is more scientific (i.e., more
like natural science) — take their subject matter out of context. Human
behavior is cognitive and motivational and includes both choices and
values. Students of society should be conscious of their values, know
when these are intruding into their discussions, and realize that their
professional role does not preclude valuation. On the contrary, valuation could well be a major part of their activity as students of society,
for it is their major link with larger society — the most effective way
to avoid the excesses of conspicuous scholarship made possible by intellectual self-sufficiency. It is not surprising that of the two sociological
works which have been most stimulating to laymen as well as professionals in the past few years, one was written by a lawyer and the other
by a magazine editor.[2]

It is true that specialists in the physical sciences also develop their
own technical vocabularies. But their specialties can be applied to the
development of positive controls without being common knowledge.
Indeed, the development of positive controls would become impossible

if this degree of specialization had to become common knowledge. But the additive and substitutive development of voluntary negative controls in a relatively free society operating under representative government depends upon thoughtful interaction and discussion among many participants in the society, not just a few specialists. In free society, no specialist — neither physical scientist nor student of culture — has any special right by virtue of his special training and knowledge to choose for other men the negative controls by which they all must live. An opportunity is provided, however, to students of man's behavior by the society that supports them to make evaluations and thereby help provoke the discussion upon which free society depends. Such is the spirit in which I now offer some opinions on subjects treated in the course of this work.

Social Welfare and Social Emulation

The Mexican case study illustrates the ideal development opportunity for a free society. Technological developments rapidly increased the productivity of the area. Private capital had been developing the region for many years previously, but had reached a limit where only government could afford further expansion. The history of the development by private sources gave a good indication that the area was ready for government aid. This was already a commercialized farming district where the people would know what to do with the land and the water. From the standpoint of the United States government, which loaned seventeen million dollars for the irrigation developments, the even larger investment by the Mexican government was a guarantee that the country itself was ready for the project and seriously committed to it.

Development projects of this kind I consider priority projects. Nowhere could that same investment have accomplished more: the felt need was in the area, not just in the minds of social planners. In giving such assistance, however, we must not be shocked by graft, but must learn to expect it as one of the costs of development in dual society.

The different rate of change between town and country in Sonora might be interpreted as an example of the traditional form of cultural lag. It represents the kind of adjustment problem likely to occur when technological developments proceed rapidly in a dual society. But it does not echo disharmony between the society and its technology. On the contrary, this present difference is most likely to be mitigated by further technological developments to increase production, because changes among the rural population have already been greatest in those parts of the area where the ratio of land to population has permitted the most per-capita production.

An important factor in the Sonora situation has been the very rapidity with which opportunities have expanded. Economic development in southern Sonora has taken place so fast in the past decade that it has even outstripped population renewal and thereby produced a generation effect. By "generation effect" I mean the persistence of established habits within an adult population, not any mystical force of tradition. People who have reached maturity and are already deeply imbued with feelings of inferiority and self-doubt and a tendency to withdraw from new situations are not likely to change overnight, even when faced with a door opening on new opportunities. The great hope of this part of the population is the younger generation, and the best means of reaching the young is through formal education to increase the ease of communication and participation in the larger society.

The subcultural differences of some groups like the Yaquis may be enhanced by such forces as intergroup hostilities or by official recognition of collective landholdings. In such cases preserving customs that emphasize the group's distinctiveness and identity can become a defense mechanism for its members. By suppressing the felt needs and aspirations of the larger society in which they feel rejected or inadequate, they can continue to satisfy their need for self-esteem by taking part in the activities of a group made up of others like themselves. Together they can play their own prestige game until enough dissenters break away. Again, the education of the young — especially in schools attended by children of the larger outgroup — will help to integrate such peoples with the larger society. Certainly this has proved true among the Mayos who live more interspersed with "whites."

In Sonora, different rates of change between town and country or Indian and "white" do not justify giving priority to adult education programs called by such names as "self-help," "fundamental education," "extension," and "community development." The fact that development is not likely to be uniform means that everywhere there are many people at the bottom of the social ladder who cannot keep up with the rest. We have the same problem today in the United States in our city slums and in the retarded parts of our southern states. Welfare programs to help retarded people to lift their expectations and their own self-image are mopping-up operations rather than direct frontal attacks on the problem of development.

The problem of social inequality is as old as man and it does not seem likely that he will ever completely outgrow it. Even among primitive peoples like the Siriono where skill at hunting leads to higher status, chieftaincy tends to be hereditary.[3] Undoubtedly a skill like hunting depends considerably on a man's own self-esteem and confidence. The social importance of self-confidence is demonstrated by Whyte's study of a street-corner or gang society.[4] Bowling was the primary social activity among these young men; a gang member's bowling ability depended greatly on his social position and vice versa: the opinions of other members had a good deal of effect on each player's performance, either by undermining or supporting his self-confidence. Verbal attacks by the group during and after play kept members of the group in their places, even with respect to bowling ability. The criticism of hunting ability that takes place among the Siriono at their drinking bouts would undoubtedly have a similar effect.[5]

In a primitive band, which is much more permanent than a street gang, it is quite understandable that a member's position on the scale of dominance and self-confidence is likely to affect his son's position. Barring some physical handicap, the son of a chief would have a distinct advantage in acquiring the confidence to occupy his father's position of leadership. Because of the self-confidence it would inspire, the very fact that a better performance would be expected of him by other members of the group would help to assure his fulfilling the expectation. Among the Kalinga, neighbors of the Ifugao, and probably among the Ifugao as well, a man of importance could encourage his small son to wound some lower-status adult (usually an old woman) to whom compensatory damages could be paid.[6] This practice was to help the child gain the courage to become a headhunter and an important man in his own right. One can readily see how such a practice would help to prepare the child to dominate in the local prestige hierarchy and how those already dominant would have an advantage in placing their children at their own level.

Similar mechanisms exist in all societies, which helps to make status hereditary. Certainly most Mayo Indians perpetuate low-status behavior and position in their children by their own withdrawal and in-

317

security. Positive controls which increase the opportunities to rise are the major hope for reducing class differences based on ethnic distinctions. But even they cannot eliminate class distinctions altogether. The most that can be expected is that they will help to make achievement more commensurate with ability. Certainly a viable ideal of rising as a result of ability has already been stimulated in this part of Sonora, and the amount of actual mobility generated so far has provided a remarkable demonstration to justify and support the ideal.

The lifting of backward areas depends primarily on technological developments to increase the per-capita production and on the formal education of the young. But the second of these two depends upon the first; extensive formal education requires large numbers of teachers whose training and support depend on the productivity of the society. To expect uniform development in any dual society is therefore unrealistic. Certainly the United States cannot undertake to educate underdeveloped populations when it is still struggling to meet its own educational requirements.

Development in Sonora has not been utopian. Exploitation, graft, and unequal development are inevitable consequences of change in dual society. The more backward part of the population becomes a target for exploitation by the more sophisticated members. If exploitation does not take the form of outright coercion, as in Soviet society, it is very likely to take place through bureaucratic graft. Coercion and graft, of course, may go together unless the graft interferes with the objectives of the ruling class, as it might by leading to conspicuous ownership in a Communist country.

But, as we have seen, graft is not all bad. As an exploitative system it can provide a great deal more mobility and opportunity through a wider distribution of the fruits of production than can more centralized systems, particularly those that depend on feudalistic forms of land use. Also, it can provide a detour around obstacles of impractical government benevolence.

Benevolent welfare programs seem very altruistic when they are operating within a highly developed free society, because the dominantly middle-class population is sophisticated enough to keep them operating for the general welfare rather than for special interests. What appears to be governmental altruism is only a workable system of reciprocities in which the ideals or felt needs of the society at large are commensurate with its own sanctioning powers. When the sanctioning powers are not commensurate — as is so likely to be the case in the dual society — welfarism may become the vehicle for graft and corruption. This can be especially detrimental to the underdeveloped country if its appetite for social welfare programs exceeds the per-capita production necessary to sustain them.

We must face the fact that development will not be uniform even under the best circumstances. A wise course in aiding development would be to search for opportunities like that in Sonora, where middle-class expansion can be greatly aided by investment in positive controls. Strengthening the middle classes wherever we can will promote the kinds of social sanctions we approve and will help to broaden the economic base and increase the desire for popular education. Invidious emulation and conspicuous ownership can be healthy attributes of development when positive controls are employed to increase mobility and culture capital. Moreover, with the growth and strengthening of the middle class, the day draws nearer when graft will be reduced by the same social sanctions, which will increase the rewards for honest administration.

At this point one might ask whether it is necessary to spark development through invidious emulation and conspicuous ownership. Why not skip this stage of crass materialism and go straight into a benevolent development in which people learn unselfishly to help themselves by helping each other? Certainly some of the extremes of conspicuous ownership can be avoided by a coercive form of government that rewards conspicuous production. But coercive methods are the ones we most wish to avoid. Expansion of the middle classes seems the most reliable way of providing the sanctions to make government benevolent for the greatest number, and invidious emulation is the major stimulus of middle-class growth.

Self-Help: Real and Unreal

In areas of the world that are densely populated and have very low per-capita incomes, the problem of improving living conditions by stimulating the growth and expansion of the middle classes is far more difficult than in Sonora, which is a frontier area by comparison. In many cases — and here Haiti with its painful lack of natural resources is an extreme example — a significant rise in living standards may have to

319

await the development of new and cheaper forms of public power and with them a workable means of reclaiming sea water for irrigation. But again the problem is basically technological. I do not see any real hope for such areas through self-help community-development programs.

I am opposed to the notion that construction projects are quixotic and extravagant compared to the inexpensive, self-help projects through which people are supposedly taught to lift themselves by their own bootstraps.[7] Nor can I take seriously the implication of *The Ugly American* that the hope of the underdeveloped areas are retired, diamond-in-the-rough, United States millionaires who invent irrigation pumps operated by bicycles.[8] The idea that we can advance underdeveloped areas by small changes promoted by ingenious, messianic technician-inventors, the like of which are seldom encountered in the flesh, and all at little cost to ourselves, is wishful fantasy. To promote the kind of middle-class expansion that will strengthen voluntary rather than coercive negative controls, we must continue making substantial loans for the development and construction of projects that will increase energy harnessed per capita. We cannot preserve free society through some modern loaves-and-fishes miracle by sending professional do-gooders abroad to prod people into cheap, bootstrap development while we sit at home hypnotized by our television sets and by the flashing chrome on the neighbors' new cars. We must all contribute to the necessary costs of development.

Nor should we begrudge the people we try to help their turn at conspicuous consumption. The coercive way is to mobilize labor to produce capital goods while restraining the growth of felt needs for consumption goods. The free way is to help people find a new sense of optimism and self-direction through the invidious emulation of middle-class growth. And it does not take lavish conspicuous ownership to get such growth; the members of rising middle classes may derive a strong sense of achievement from changes that seem rudimentary and modest to us — a cement floor, a tile roof, or indoor plumbing. But to gain a sense of achievement and self-importance from such changes, people must want to make them because some of their "better" fellow countrymen have already done so. As long as the opportunities are sufficient to provide social mobility, conspicuous ownership and inequality are essential attributes of rapid development in free society. To go out and get people to make housing or other improvements for which the "experts" feel a need is not nearly so important as to create an environment for opportunity and emulation in which people will not only want to make improvements but expect to make them for themselves, free of dependence on "collective" or government guidance. This is the way they can gain a greater sense of personal control over their own destinies.

The kind of technical assistance which seems to me least desirable is that in which the people whose living standards are to be raised are manipulated singly or collectively in promotional programs which attempt to expand felt needs. Although theoretically these programs provide the leadership necessary to show people how to meet their own felt needs, any fundamental education program which relies heavily on personnel and persuasion in attempting such changes is actually promoting the felt needs of the innovators. When real technical research produces changes that spectacularly meet felt needs, self-help promoters are not needed to introduce or to sell them.

Isolation and the generation effect may act to keep the more retarded part of a population from changing as rapidly as an outsider might hope, but so far as the local adult population is concerned, it would seem most feasible to me to concentrate efforts on the more actively changing component. Here is where the momentum of change is greatest, and if encouraged it will, I believe, eventually draw in the retarded sectors in a permanent and "healthy" fashion, with no need for bureaucratic philosophers of self-help. By "healthy" change here I mean change which follows logically from local economic and political development. The retarded component in the Mexican case study, for example, showed some tendencies toward anomie, but the people are not, in my opinion, deeply disturbed or unhappy. I doubt that promotional fundamental education programs would have much effect on them anyway, and it seems to me that such projects would tend more to increase anomie than to lift living standards — just as when I, with all good intentions, brought Juan to the United States and introduced him to many things he could want but would never have.

A favorite argument for the self-help community-development program is that the disguised unemployment of rural areas (unused labor potential between seasonal periods of peak labor load) can be inexpensively organized and put to work on capital formation projects for the benefit of the community. This employment, too, requires promotional efforts to sell the objectives of the innovators, and, as pointed out in Chapter V, the supporting sanctions may verge on coercion in successful cases. This kind of capital formation is unquestionably best adapted to coercive negative control. The Russians and the Chinese can make it work because their political ideals are backed by an enormous amount of force. When such programs are attempted on a voluntary basis, a cooperative social organization must be cajoled into existence; and even then, work will be limited to local projects because of the difficulties of transporting workers long distances from their food supply. Using force solves all these problems much more readily.

The inexpensiveness of a fundamental-education, community-development program was questioned in Chapter VIII. Though often claimed, the cheapness has never really been demonstrated. But it is not hard to understand why the argument of economy is useful to conspicuous administrators anxious to increase the number of their subordinates. The expansion of programs depending principally on the manipulation of personnel can be made to look like a virtue by comparing annual salary costs to the total costs of some construction project. But construction projects like those in Sonora pay for themselves while lifting expectations. Personnel projects may sometimes increase felt needs, but they seldom pay for themselves and always conceal enormous amounts of Parkinsonian boondoggling. Considering their accomplishments, adult manipulation programs can be incredibly expensive.

Education and Evaluation

Though rural social welfare programs do not seem to me to deserve high priority, formal education most certainly does. Where isolation or the generation effect is keeping felt needs and expectations at a minimum, the education of the young is vital. But this must be left to the host country. We cannot afford the expense or the personnel to take over primary education in all the underdeveloped rural areas of the world. Moreover, the host countries are more likely to pace education to demand, which in the long run is probably best. In Sonora, for example, the rural areas that "need" education the most are the ones that want and get the least. But since public health has sensibly followed the same line of development as education, more children die in the illiterate areas and the population expands most in the urban area, where schooling opportunities are best. Since birth control is not yet having any important effect here, the progressive part of the population is expanding at a faster rate than the retarded part — a situation that even a eugenist could hardly object to.

The education program I consider deserving of priority attention as a method of foreign aid is the training in the United States of students from the underdeveloped areas. Qualification should be by examination, and the vocational choices offered should be based on the expressed needs of the country's industries and professions as well as its bureaucracy. Since our technical aid programs usually render assistance through government, the scholarship programs they administer tend to be weighted toward training for government jobs and the fattening of already overfed bureaucracies. Not infrequently men and women specially trained in the United States for extension and social-welfare kinds of government jobs are later not hired by their governments for reasons of political or personal discrimination. On the other hand, trained engineers, doctors, mechanics, machinists, and electricians, are not dependent on the vicissitudes of political influence and bureaucratic corruption: they can make their way in industry and private enterprise.

Admittedly there will be many severe problems in selecting, training, and educating foreign students, but the potential results of an ever-expanding program in this direction are worth a head-on collision with those problems. And we must not expect all foreign students to return home salesmen for the United States. We must aim to foster independence of spirit and thought, not demand or expect worshipful adoration. With such an attitude, we may even gain some healthy critical insights into our own way of life.

Second on the list of educational priorities are all the technical experts we send abroad, but among these priority should be given to those who have the knowledge or research ability to introduce positive controls to meet felt needs so spectacularly that their innovations will be disseminated without social-welfare promotional efforts.

The adults reached by our technical-aid programs may be divided into two kinds; first, the local technicians or counterparts of the men we send abroad; and second, the public whose living standards we hope to raise. We can most effectively serve both groups through specific research and advisory projects which will result in spectacular innovations. Plant improvement is one example. Local technicians get training in genetic selection or the control of plant diseases. The people in turn are furnished with an improved product about which they can, at their level of education, readily make a favorable frequency interpretation. Such programs require real technicians — not promoters — doing jobs of real technical assistance.

As long as there are community-development and other social-welfare programs, however, students of society will certainly be useful for helping to guide them. These are precisely the kinds of program that require a great deal of human interaction for selling new felt needs and persuading people to change their ways. But projects designed to meet specific felt needs through research and guidance, which are really technical and increase positive controls spectacularly, will not need a lot of personnel whose new intercultural "roles" must be defined and whose families must be prepared for such modern international maladies as "culture shock."

In my opinion, sociologists and anthropologists might be of greatest value in helping to select areas ripe for development through projects that involve investment in positive controls rather than persuasion. In other words, I believe they could render a very great service at the strategic level by helping to guide technical assistance into areas where the projects under consideration would have the least cause to depend upon their services thereafter.

But these students of society can also be of value at the tactical level as social cost-accountants, which, as I perceive it, may be a more modest role than some to which they occasionally aspire in the field of foreign assistance. By social cost-accounting I mean simply the weighing of costs and results of different kinds of projects. Because investments in technical assistance do not yield monetary profits, the accounting is particularly difficult. In business, the profits are a handy measure of self-correction which does not exist in foreign-aid programs.

Take the case of a certain furniture manufacturing company in Bogotá, Colombia. This company had been doing very well until the chairman of the board of directors appointed as manager a young nephew extremely concerned with efficient production. So great was his preoccupation with the efficient use of new machinery and the reduction of production costs that he completely neglected sales. The company owned its own retail outlets, and as far as the new manager was concerned, furniture sent to them was sold. But while he was concerned with production costs, the young man viewed reducing them as saving for the company rather than the consumer. He therefore kept prices very high to insure an enormous profit. As great quantities of furniture began piling up at the company's retail outlets, the store managers grew desperate and complained to several of the larger and more influential stockholders. After a brief investigation, the chairman and the manager resigned and the company was reorganized.

All this shows that in business as well as in government, circumstances may permit a person to indulge some peculiar fixation, with expensive results. Failure of a business enterprise, however, to make more money than it spends is not only an indication that some corrective action must be taken, it is a threat to its very survival. In government, on the other hand, costs must often be measured against social gains which defy quantification. But because money provides a more convenient index than do social improvements, administrators often rank themselves more by the size of the budget they are entrusted with than by any attempted measurement of the concrete results of their programs.

The social accounting so necessary to technical assistance should include not only careful analysis and evaluation but also reporting. These reports should not be issued only to operations and administrative personnel within the government, but should be made available to the general public. Social accounting in a free society must include public evaluation, of which there has been far too little to date — though not for lack of public interest. The reasons are all too clear. Evaluation is, and will remain, biased and sheltered so long as it is left to the men whose jobs depend upon the continuance of the programs in question. But with more evaluation by the public, the "entrepreneur" in government will be less likely to expend his genius and energy and the public's resources on projects in which his ego is involved as a conspicuous producer, but which are not necessarily in our best interests.

Evaluation is particularly necessary in all those programs which are most promotional in their efforts to effect cultural change. When a three-million-dollar road is built out to a dam site where a dam is never constructed, the faults of the programing are only too clear.[9] But in the promotional, adult-manipulation programs, errors of judgment can be legion, yet readily concealed. Such programs are more susceptible to boondoggling than any others; no wonder they are expanding rapidly. They provide jobs for conspicuous producers with little chance of mistakes' being noticed, and at the same time give the producers a beautiful rationalization for their only half-heartedly trying to find and correct errors. One recent writer on technical assistance neatly shelves the problem of evaluating programs by asking how it is possible to make quantitative measurements of such things as community organizations of farmers, the increasing capacity of people to solve problems for themselves, or education. This is not a fair question, of course; community organizations should not be considered as ends in themselves, and problem-solving and education are general categories rather than particular programs. If the results of a program have not been measured in some way, however inexactly, measurement has not really been attempted. The same author even goes on to ask righteously how a monetary measure can be put upon educational achievement, as if the mere desire to evaluate such programs is somehow materialistic, mercenary, and degrading.

Expropriation: Government Aid and Private Enterprise

Before concluding this book I wish to anticipate and rebut one possible criticism concerning expropriations and land reforms. I have advocated investment in positive technological controls where such investment is most likely to foment the growth of the middle classes, and I have stated a preference for this form of aid over more personal, social, and promotional forms. Since the case study I made is from an area where such overhead capital developments were preceded by land reform, some will wonder whether social overhead capital investments are as likely to produce middle classes in countries where all the land is owned or monopolized by a few.

I believe they will. As is obvious from the Mexican case study, land reforms and expropriations reshuffle the social deck, but they do not bring an end to large landholdings or the consolidation through management of large tracts of farm land. By disrupting the status quo, they give peoples and economies a chance to spurt ahead under new management by a fresh elite of ambitious social climbers. Nor do they end exploitation. The case of the American-owned sugar company in Los Mochis was most instructive in this regard. There is no question that the workers were making greater gains as a rural proletariat organized into a labor union than they did after they were turned by government fiat into a "cooperative" of small landlords. Even in countries that have not yet had land reforms, I do not think that the major problem is who owns the land or how large the holdings are. The major problem is to see that the farm laborers get a higher return for their labor. It might be a very wise move on our part to insist, as a principal condition of every loan we make for purposes of social overhead capital development abroad, that technical advisers chosen by our best and most responsible United States labor unions be sent to help organize the local labor market. Even though our labor unions are not so experienced in organizing farm labor as they are in organizing labor in industry, this kind of assistance would be preferable to inspiring land reform movements, as I have heard some colleagues suggest.

In this same context I would like to point out that in the face of the rising tide of property expropriations and land reforms throughout the world, the promotion of capital investments abroad through private United States sources is often suicidal. Men like Cárdenas in Mexico and more recently Castro in Cuba are charismatic leaders who achieve considerable power not just by coercion and force of arms but by popular support from the backward component of the dual society. We cannot afford to put ourselves in the position of opposing these social changes whenever and wherever they occur.

The fact that we cannot afford to appear to be the opponents of little people everywhere places us in an awkward position, for United States private interests in underdeveloped countries are those most likely to become the targets of the agitators and charismatic leaders who must stoke the fires of public wrath with hatred; and no hatred can be more bitter or devastating than that born of envy. It is time we reassessed the supposed advantages of lifting backward areas by means of *our* private enterprise versus the alternative of lifting them with local private enterprise stimulated by strategic technological developments.

Many Americans fail to realize how feudalistic and monopolistic capitalism usually is in backward areas. It rarely approaches the ideal form we have developed in the United States by carefully balancing the power of labor and government with that of business. Capitalism is no more intrinsically benevolent than communism. It can readily spawn fascism in a dual society, and for most Americans one kind of totalitarianism is no better or worse than another except that one may be more threatening than another at any given moment in history. Our form of capitalism is benevolent because the checks and balances of social sanction built into our political system keep it that way. We have well-educated and politically active middle and worker classes.

The "benevolent" United States businessman who goes abroad to ply his trade in an underdeveloped country does not take with him the built-in sanctions of United States society. He enters a new society with all the privileges of United States citizenship but with few of the checks and balances on his authority and power that would apply in his homeland. Many American businesses abroad have taken advantage of such situations. The threat of expropriation which has grown greater throughout the underdeveloped countries is nothing more than a manifestation of the growth of indigenous sanctioning powers on feudalistic and monopolistic capitalism both foreign and domestic. Many of our foreign companies have recognized this fact and have become much more benevolent of late. Today there are many model American companies abroad such as Sears, Roebuck de Mexico, S.A., Casa Grace of Peru, and the Creole Petroleum Corporation of Venezuela. But we should not as a nation stand behind any American-owned or American-managed corporations abroad. Nor should we even think of reimbursing American citizens from American tax funds for the loss of investments abroad because of expropriation.

Any American who votes in the elections of a foreign country forfeits his citizenship if he is discovered. But an American businessman abroad usually wields much greater political power on the local scene than that of a mere ballot-caster. If both the letter and the spirit of the law are to prevail, then any American who manages business interests abroad — except as a representative of the United States government or as a private agent authorized by the United States to work on contract or as a business consultant for foreign governments and foreign owned enterprises — might well be made to forfeit his American citizenship. This does not mean that we should prevent Americans from going into business abroad. On the contrary, they should be encouraged to do so; but without exception, any American going to a foreign country to make monetary, rather than social, profits should do so as a citizen of that country and not of ours.

Free Society, Foreign Aid, and Conspicuous Production

Whatever the faults or inadequacies of our foreign-aid programs, they are necessary. We have started something we cannot stop as long as the duel between free and coercive society continues. We wanted allies, and having set the great precedent of foreign aid in our attempt to win them, we have made the smaller nations' power of invidious sanction greater than ever before. The power contest between the United States and Russia has become a source of hope for the underdeveloped nations of the world, for as long as it is at a stalemate they can use it to their own advantage in demanding a wider distribution of the higher living standards we enjoy.

And it is to our interest that the contest remain at a stalemate, for time is on the side of free society. Our greatest responsibility, above all else, is to stay strong by keeping up in the international race of scientific, technical, and military production. If we give the ruler of a coercive state the chance to beat us, he will probably take it. But the greatest danger is within ourselves: unlike the Russians, who do not play so hard at our game of conspicuous ownership, we must keep up with our nextdoor neighbor as well as with our enemy. The need to survive by keeping up with the Russians competes for our attention with the need to succeed by keeping up with the Joneses. Through force, the coercive state gains a singleness of purpose that threatens our security, and our survival depends on our awareness of this danger.

There are many indications that the threat of coercive society is helping to accelerate the importance of conspicuous production in our own society, but the big question is whether it is weakening the distractive influence of conspicuous ownership sufficiently for our safety. The present popularity of small foreign cars that change their styles rarely, and the growing impatience with the larger American models which the Joneses buy each year, may reflect a change in consumption habits accompanying the rise of conspicuous production. The entire American concept of the "practical man" is beginning to undergo a radical alteration. The problem of national security has suddenly given new importance to scientists, technicians, educators, and government administrators. Prestige is flowing less toward the biggest buyer and more toward the conspicuous producer of ideas and action in science, education, and government.

The growing importance of conspicuous production is linked to the growing influence of government as compared with business, both changes reflecting public concern with national survival. Many resent this shift of power and influence from private enterprise to government and feel that it may lead us to become identical with the very thing we fear — coercive society. Such fears, I believe, are altogether unjustified.

Free, open society is quite capable of maintaining its freedom in spite of government's growing influence. Coercion or graft — the unpleasant alternatives faced by dual society — are products of inequality in the decision-making abilities of the populace. As long as our high standards of education prevail — and they are rising — the popular sanctions which guard our freedom will continue despite the shift of power away from private enterprise toward government. Widening our government's sphere of action is not likely to result in totalitarianism or graft. Inefficiency, however, is something else again. But the popular view of efficiency is still largely a by-product of the "practical man" concept of a conspicuous ownership society. With the increasing importance of conspicious production, the meaning of efficiency will continue to broaden. Social profits in terms of broader reciprocities will take increasing precedence over monetary and individual profits, without necessarily displacing them.

Another fear related in part to the growth of government and bureaucracy is that individuality will be smothered by an "other-directed" [10] society run by "organization" men obeying a "social ethic." [11] Along with this goes a belief in the "decline of greatness." [12] Unfortunately, our history books, which deal so much with personalities, dates, and wars, convey an impression that the course of past events was shaped by a few great men. So little is known about the common men of the past that history must be told around the names and personalities of those salient figures associated with important events. At the opposite pole, a few historians equally uninformed about details of the social matrix of past events, but less interested in personalities, give a fatalistic view of history in which the great man becomes merely the pawn of evolutionary forces. Both views are extreme. Everyone in a society has some influence on the course of its history, difficult as it may often be to measure that influence. Influence is much less equally distributed, however, in coercive than in free society, with the result that the authoritarian despot comes closest to fitting the stereotype of "greatness." But today, members of free societies enjoying representative government have more opportunities for self-expression and self-fulfillment than ever before in the history of mankind. Never before have they enjoyed such opportunities with less risk of seeing them swept away by some fellow member's rise to historical "greatness." Anyone who thinks that conformity to a social ethic has reached some new height of oppressiveness in modern free society should spend a few weeks in a dual, coercive, or primitive society to fully appreciate his own opportunities for individual action.

The recent preoccupation with "other-directedness" and "organization man" is an interesting phenomenon in itself. While *individuals* have become more important, *the* individual — that curious abstract of discussion and of biographical history — has become less important. More than ever before, men have become conscious of — and concerned with — their own individual contribution to social forces. Part of this new intensity of concern is their greater awareness of society and the nature of their duty to conform. Much of the new revulsion against conformity is not so much a result of the tightness of its strictures as a result of the seriousness which free men now impart to their own importance and sphere of action.

The technological race with coercive society must be the first concern of free men today. The gradual shift in social recognition from the merchants of soap, cigarettes, and chromium-plated automobiles to scientists, educators, and trained government personnel will help us to win the struggle with coercive society. But we should continually pay attention to our cultural expressions of the prestige motivation, to make sure that we are providing sufficient incentive for those best qualified to help win the race for free society.

Knowledge and Motives

Can men influence the forms taken by prestige motivation? Can the cognitive component of cultural causality gain some ascendancy over the motivational? It would be very comforting to believe that it could. At a time when our conspicuous-ownership or acquisitive society is moving closer to aspirations of conspicuous production it is faced with new problems of evaluation. The situation is well illustrated by two contrasting points of view that have received considerable attention of late — those of John K. Galbraith and C. Northcote Parkinson.[13] Galbraith questions the so-called conventional wisdom that puts such great emphasis in our society upon producing goods for consumption. He calls for more sales taxes and an increase in government-administrated services. But Parkinson, with tongue in cheek, uses the expansion of government bureaucracy through paper work and red tape as the prime example of his law that work expands to fill the time available.

Those who recognize the merits of both points of view are impaled on the horns of a dilemma. Even though they find the excesses of conspicuous ownership obnoxious, how do they guard against the excesses of conspicuous production?

How do we curb bureaucratic inefficiency when we need simultaneously a standard of efficiency and a method of correction? When we consider that the very men who study culture and society get so involved in their own prestige game of conspicuous scholarship that they lose objectivity about it, the prospect that they might help to curb or direct the stimulus of invidious comparison is not encouraging. There is a need, however, for full-time specialists to evaluate our government and social order critically, to help society constantly to modify its standards of social efficiency. And the student of society, by thinking less as a pure scientist and more about how his studies and judgments may help the public take part in decision-making, could aim his scholastic work at a wider audience. The increasing emergence of students of society from their ivory towers of intellectual self-sufficiency to perform more of the social cost-accounting of bigger government may help to curb the excesses of both conspicuous administration and conspicuous scholarship.

NOTES AND INDEX

Notes

I. A Man from the Past

[1] J. H. Boeke, *Economics and Economic Policy of Dual Societies as Exemplified by Indonesia*, New York: Institute of Pacific Relations, 1953, pp. 3–18.

[2] Ronald M. Berndt, "A Cargo Movement in the Eastern Central Highlands of New Guinea," *Oceania*, vol. 23, nos. 1, 2, 3, 1952, pp. 40–65, 137–158, and 202–234. Raymond Firth, *Elements of Social Organization*, London: Watts and Co., 1951, pp. 112–113. Jean Guiart, "John Frum Movement in Tanna," *Oceania*, vol. 22, no. 3, 1952, pp. 165–177.

[3] Richard T. LaPiere, *A Theory of Social Control*, New York: McGraw, 1954, pp. 45–46. David C. McClelland, "Notes for a Revised Theory of Motivation" in *Studies in Motivation*, David C. McClelland (ed), New York: Appleton-Century-Crofts, Inc., 1955, pp. 226–234.

II. Motivation and Cognition

[1] William Vogt, *Road to Survival*, New York: William Sloane Associates, 1948, pp. 186–189.

[2] Henry F. Dobyns, "Experiment in Conservation: Erosion Control and Forage Production on the Papago Indian Reservations in Arizona" in *Human Problems in Technological Change*, Edward H. Spicer (ed), 1952, pp. 209–223.

[3] *Ibid.*, p. 209.

[4] Hans Reichenbach, *The Rise of Scientific Philosophy*, Berkeley: University of California Press, 1951, p. 236.

[5] W. H. Thorpe, *Learning and Instinct in Animals*, Cambridge: Harvard University Press, 1956, p. 119.

III. Cognition and Probable Knowledge

[1] Francis L. K. Hsu, *Religion, Science and Human Crises*, London: Routledge and Kegan Paul Ltd., 1952, p. 89.

[2] *Ibid.*, pp. 8, 92. Italics mine.

[3] My classification, not Hsu's.

[4] Hsu, *op. cit.*, p. 87.

[5] *Ibid.*, p. 89.

[6] *Ibid.*

[7] Francis L. K. Hsu, "A Cholera Epidemic in a Chinese Town" in *Health, Culture and Community*, Benjamin D. Paul (ed), New York: Russell Sage Foundation, 1955, pp. 135–154.

[8] John Paul Scott, *Animal Behavior*, Chicago: University of Chicago Press, 1958, p. 102.

[9] David C. McClelland, *Personality*, New York: Dryden Press, 1951, pp. 454–455.

[10] Much of the material on Quito as well as the point of view expressed here appeared the same year as Hsu's book (above) in the *Southwestern Journal of Anthropology*, vol. 8, pp. 411–428, in an article entitled "Changing Folk Beliefs and the Relativity of Empirical Knowledge." Recently Ethel Nurge ("Etiology of Illness in Guinhangdan," *American Anthropologist*, 1958, vol. 60, pp. 1158–1172) criticized my use of questionnaires for gathering information about folk medicine. I did not make it entirely clear in the article, but the questionnaires were not employed to gather general information. No one could be more suspicious of questionnaire techniques than I. My information about folk medicine had already been gathered in many weeks of careful interviewing. The questionnaires were designed to check the results of health education programs and they served that purpose. If the results of the tests did not agree with my interview material I would be very dubious of them. Since they do, I have mentioned them here for their heuristic value.

[11] Many of these folks beliefs are widespread throughout Latin America, and were probably introduced during Spanish conquest and colonization. For excellent discussions of the provenience of Latin American folk beliefs on curing and childbirth see George M. Foster, "Relationships between Spanish and Spanish-American Folk Medicine," *Journal of American Folklore*, vol. 66, 1953, pp. 201–217, and *Culture and Conquest: America's Spanish Heritage*, Viking Fund Publications in Anthropology Number Twenty-Seven, 1960, pp. 112–123.

[12] A class of 48, half boys, half girls.

[13] In no case did a particular ailment receive a one hundred per cent response in favor of any particular method of treatment. The responses arranged themselves along a gradient in which 96 per cent favored the doctor for the treatment of tuberculosis and only one student favored him for the treatment of fright sickness. All the supernatural illnesses — malevolent air, bewitchment, and evil eye — as well as skin infections, infected wounds, urinary difficulties, facial paralysis, and colic, were among those for which more than sixty per cent of the students would consult a curandero or which they would treat at home. For such ailments as tuberculosis, malaria, bronchitis, typhoid, paralysis, whooping cough, pneumonia, dysentery, and smallpox, more than sixty per cent of the children favored the modern doctor.

[14] As the cause of typhoid fever, "fetid odors" received as many scores (twenty) as microbes, owing to the belief that typhoid may be caused by breathing a foul smell, a reason for rejecting backyard latrines in some parts of Latin America.

[15] These two public schools are adjacent, the León Mera for girls and the Brazil for boys. The test class in each school contained slightly over fifty students.

[16] This was a school for boys, and the class tested had 107 students.

[17] Thirty-four of the one hundred and seven illnesses were apparently cases of "common cold." Measles, "fever," smallpox, typhoid, and whooping cough were the next most frequently mentioned ailments, ranging from four to eight cases each. Along with tuberculosis and bronchitis, fright sickness was described three times and in each case the symptoms appeared to be those of intestinal infection with other complications. Of the remaining ailments there were only one or two cases each. They consisted of common ailments with modern names plus a few folk illnesses of the mechanical variety. In the

judgment of the Ecuadorian doctor who reviewed the symptoms given by the students, their description of the ailments with modern names was fairly accurate and indicated their familiarity with the modern terms. In a third of the cases household remedies had been relied upon for treatment, whereas drugstore remedies had been used in the other two thirds. In two thirds of the cases the students claimed that a doctor had been consulted. Despite greater reliance on modern treatment at this economic level, the explanations of ailments were still folk-like in most cases. Half the students gave causes which conformed to folk explanations of the same maladies; a fourth gave explanations combining folk and modern elements; and a fourth gave creditable modern explanations. Moreover, the responses to questions about the supernatural folk diseases indicated that these children were not nearly so familiar with those ailments as were the children in the poorer districts. Only a third gave a creditable folk definition of malevolent air and only a tenth described a folk treatment. A fourth were apparently unable to explain fright sickness.

[18] The nurses' aides consisted of two groups, sixteen beginners and thirty-nine experienced aides. The number of nursing students were twenty-three first-year, fifteen second-year, and seventeen third-year; these were the only nursing students in Quito at the time. The test was administered simultaneously to all groups and the subjects told that responses were to be anonymous. The first part of the test consisted of matching illnesses from a given list with the appropriate causes, preventive measures, and treatments. Again, the choices were based on a carefully selected combination of folk and modern causes and symptoms. The subjects were not told that they could write in comments if they felt a question was illegitimate, but it was assumed that those who were sufficiently sophisticated would object to questions about folk beliefs. This assumption proved justified, but what was not anticipated was the fact that some refused to answer. It cannot be assumed that those who gave folk answers to the questions asking for them necessarily believed in them. The responses show only that the subjects were very familiar with the folk beliefs and not sufficiently sophisticated from the modern point of view to consider denying them. The second part of the test consisted of several short-answer questions.

[19] Questions on the first part of the test which called for a folk response to a cause, prevention, or treatment which was magical or supernatural in nature were those most strongly rejected. Comments denying the validity of witchcraft were written in by persons in all groups, although most of the nurses' aides simply did not answer. They were obviously puzzled by the question; but unlike the nursing students, most of them lacked sufficient sophistication to write in a denial of witchcraft as a cause of disease. Folk answers to the question were most frequent (about forty per cent) among the beginning nurses' aides and beginning nursing students. Responses to a question concerning the magical treatment of disease ("cleaning" with herbs and guinea pigs) followed a similar pattern. Folk responses were fewest on a question about preventing disease by the use of religious medals. A question relating directly to hospital as well as folk practice was that about disposing of the placenta. Folk responses to this question were most numerous among the inexperienced aides and the first- and second-year nursing students. Two thirds of the experienced aides either refused to answer the question or denied its legitimacy. Denial increased in direct proportion to the amount of education and in the case of the third-year nursing students was unanimous. The third-year students had had the benefit of an obstetrics course which the second-year group was just beginning. The answers to this question indicated the effects of both direct and indirect experience, since folk responses were weakest among the experienced nurses' aides and the third-year students. Response to the folk cause "malevolent air" was strongly folk among all but the third-year nursing students, most of whom wrote denials. The folk responses, however, were predominantly mechanical in the more educated groups and more supernatural among the less educated. Denials were much more numerous among the better-educated nursing students to a question which limited the malevolent air concept to its supernatural

rather than its mechanical sense by asking what illnesses a child might contract from proximity to a cadaver. Folk response to the psychological cause of "sadness" was strong among all groups. Denials of the existence of "desire" as a cause of disease were numerous, however, among the nursing students, particularly at the third-year level where it was denied by all but three. Prevention of illness by avoiding "cold" foods during menstruation and the period of postnatal diet drew a strong folk response from all but the third-year nursing students, most of whom denied its validity. About a fourth of the second-year nursing students and an eighth of the persons in the other groups also wrote in denials. Prevention of illness by the regular use of laxatives drew a strong folk response but this time at all levels — even among third-year nursing students where only a third objected to the advisability of such a measure. Bad body humor, the major folk concept of contagion, provoked a very strong folk response in all groups. Only a third of the senior nursing class denied the concept and only one or two persons in each of the other groups either denied it or left the question blank. However, a question on this same cause in the second part of the test revealed that the more educated groups accepted it in a sense very close to the modern concept of contagion. The question asked whether bad body humor could lead to infection in the case of a seat still warm from a previous occupant. Most of the nursing students denied that it could, whereas most of the aides accepted this folk contagion concept as true in this — its least modern — form. One question asked the subjects to state whether microbes could or could not cause the symptoms of fright sickness, malevolent air, or bewitchment and to explain why in each case. Half the nurses' aides and a fourth of the first- and second-year nursing students gave folk answers. They reasoned that microbes could not cause these ailments since they were ailments of a different order having different causes. About a third of the nursing students gave a simplistic modern answer that microbes could not cause the symptoms of these ailments since the ailments are just superstitions and do not exist. About half of the second- and third-year nursing students, a fourth of the first-year students, but only four nurses' aides reasoned that the symptoms of these so-called diseases are often caused by microbial infection and are attributed by uneducated people to supernatural causes. Although experience had sophisticated many of the nurses' aides enough for them to give a simplistic modern answer, a deeper insight into the whole problem of the conflict between folk and modern medicine seemed to be correlated with more education.

[20] For example, one question asked the subjects what they would tell a mother who came to them with a child she said was suffering from malevolent air or fright sickness. Most of the nurses' aides would either suggest a folk remedy or tell the mother that she was superstitious. Nursing students, however, in numbers increasing with education, would explain to the mother how the child's symptoms had been caused by other factors and why he should have a doctor's care.

[21] Such tests obviously give no indication of changes in actual health practices, and these were not designed to. The purpose of these experimental lectures and retests was simply to see which kind of lecture made the students most aware and appreciative of the differences between folk and modern explanations of disease and its treatment — which, in other words, led to greater "sophistication."

[22] McClelland, op. cit., p. 443.

IV. Limitation

[1] Henry F. Dobyns, "Blunders with Bolsas," *Human Organization*, vol. 10, no. 3, 1951, pp. 25–32.

[2] S. H. Frankel, *The Economic Impact on Under-Developed Societies*, Oxford: Basil Blackwell, 1953, pp. 141–153.

[3] Anacleto Apodaca, "Corn and Custom: Introduction of Hybrid Corn to Spanish American Farmers in New Mexico" in *Human Problems in Technological Change*, Edward H. Spicer (ed), New York: Russell Sage Foundation, 1952, pp. 35–39.

NOTES

[4] *Ibid.*, p. 38.

[5] McKim Marriott, "Technological Change in Overdeveloped Rural Areas," *Economic Development and Culture Change*, vol. 1, no. 4, 1952, pp. 261–272.

[6] Apodaca, *op. cit.*, p. 38.

[7] Marriott, *op. cit.*, pp. 265–266.

[8] *Ibid.*, p. 263.

[9] *Ibid.*

[10] Arthur T. Mosher, *Technical Cooperation in Latin American Agriculture*, Chicago: University of Chicago Press, 1957, pp. 77–79.

[11] John Howland Rowe, "Inca Culture at the Time of the Spanish Conquest" in *The Andean Civilizations*, vol. 2 of the Handbook of South American Indians, Smithsonian Institution, Bureau of American Ethnology Bulletin 143, Washington, D.C., 1946, pp. 183–330.

[12] Ragnar Nurkse, *Problems of Capital Formation in Underdeveloped Countries*, Oxford: Basil Blackwell, 1953, pp. 31–37.

[13] Fred Cottrell, *Energy and Society*, New York: McGraw, 1955, pp. 134–152.

[14] *Ibid.*, p. 129.

[15] Mayone J. Stycos, "Birth Control Clinics in Crowded Puerto Rico" in *Health, Culture and Community*, Benjamin D. Paul (ed), New York: Russell Sage Foundation, 1955, p. 191.

[16] Raymond Firth, *We, The Tikopia*, New York: American Book, 1936.

[17] Raymond Firth, *Primitive Polynesian Economy*, London: George Routledge and Sons, Ltd., 1939, p. 47.

[18] Firth, *We, The Tikopia*, p. 491.

[19] *Ibid.*, p. 414.

[20] *Ibid.*

[21] *Ibid.*, pp. 527–529.

[22] *Ibid.*, p. 565.

[23] Kingsley Davis and Judith Blake, "Social Structure and Fertility: An Analytic Framework," *Economic Development and Culture Change*, vol. 4, no. 3, 1956, p. 222.

[24] Ronald Freedman, Pascal K. Whelpton and Arthur A. Campbell, *Family Planning, Sterility, and Population Growth*, New York: McGraw-Hill, 1959, pp. 322, 402.

[25] *Ibid.*, pp. 176–177.

[26] Based on a sample of 2,713 white married women selected to be a representative sample of all white wives in the national population. Freedman, Whelpton, and Campbell, *op. cit.*, p. 10.

[27] Freedman, Whelpton, and Campbell, *op. cit.*, pp. 61, 176.

[28] Stycos, *op. cit.*, p. 198, and *Family and Fertility in Puerto Rico*, New York: Columbia University Press, 1955, pp. 212, 248.

[29] See Stycos, *Family and Fertility in Puerto Rico*, pp. 182–216 for an excellent study of attitudes toward birth control in an underdeveloped area.

[30] Davis and Blake, *op. cit.*, pp. 229–230.

[31] Ayanori Okasaki, *Japan's Population Problems*, Public Information and Cultural Affairs Bureau, Ministry of Foreign Affairs, Japan, 1956, pp. 4–7.

[32] Irene B. Taeuber, *The Population of Japan*, Princeton: Princeton University Press, 1958, p. 228.

[33] *Ibid.*, pp. 272–273.

[34] Stycos, *Family and Fertility in Puerto Rico*, pp. 224–228, 250–251.

V. Limitation and Society

[1] James G. Leyburn, *The Haitian People*, New Haven: Yale University Press, 1941, p. 315.

[2] Henri Frankfort, *The Birth of Civilization in the Near East*, New York: Doubleday Anchor Books, 1956, p. 104.

[3] For this information I am indebted to my friend Jiro Suzuki, professor of social anthropology at Tokio Metropolitan University.

[4] Leyburn, *op. cit.*, pp. 51–64.

[5] See note 3 above.

[6] Allan Holmberg, "The Wells That Failed" in *Human Problems in Technological Change*, Edward H. Spicer (ed), New York: Russell Sage Foundation, 1952, pp. 113–123.

[7] Oscar Lewis, "Medicine and Politics in a Mexican Village" in *Health, Culture and Community*, Benjamin Paul (ed), New York: Russell Sage Foundation, 1955, pp. 403–434.

[8] S. C. Dube, "Cultural Factors in Rural Community Development," *Journal of Asian Studies*, vol. 16, no. 1, 1956, p. 22.

[9] William C. Gibson, Hugh B. Masters, and Ernest F. Wittee, "Report on Community Development Programs in India, Iran, Egypt and Gold Coast," International Cooperation Administration, Washington, D.C., 1955, pp. 6, 21, 55.

[10] McKim Marriott, "Technological Change in Overdeveloped Rural Areas," *Economic Development and Cultural Change*, vol. 1, no. 4, 1952, p. 270.

VI. Conspicuous Giving and Closed Societies

[1] Edward Burnett Tylor, *Primitive Culture*, London: John Murray and Co., vol. 1, 1871, p. 1.

[2] S. Herbert Frankel, *The Economic Impact on Under-Developed Societies*, Oxford: Basil Blackwell, 1953, pp. 141–153.

[3] April Smith, "Birthright," *If — Worlds of Science Fiction*, August, 1955, pp. 16–54.

[4] Shirley Jackson, "The Lottery," *New Yorker*, June 26, 1948, vol. 24, no. 18. Reprinted during the 1950's in such anthologies as *50 Great Short Stories*, Milton Crane (ed), New York: Bantam Books, 1953, pp. 175–185.

[5] For those who think in terms of culture areas and diffusion, this conclusion would be unacceptable. They would argue that there must be several cases on which to base a probability estimate, and since Western civilization cut off native Mexican development, we are left only with the example of Western tradition. Therefore we can conclude nothing except that human sacrifice is disapproved in Western civilization and tends to disappear with the spread of Western culture. This argument brings us to another important question concerning the nature of culture — how culture in the all-inclusive sense is divided into particular cultures.

Since culture has been defined as human behavior acquired through life in social groups, it must by definition have a social dimension composed of individual human units. In the past, two dimensions have been widely used by students of culture to segregate the behavorial units of culture into cultures: a spatial dimension and a social dimension. In the first case human interaction groups are used to delineate subcultures. But even though the social dimension is made the basis for delineating the cultures of bands, tribes, or communities, these cultures can also be located and described spatially. Similarly, those who make space the basis for delineating cultures also take the social dimension into consideration when they group tribal or community units within their culture areas, but for them the consideration of spatial relationships predominates.

Historically, the classification of cultures by area came into being about the turn of the century as a means of facilitating the presentation of ethnographic specimens in museums. As it was realized that artifacts from the same ecological zones were much alike, greater economy in museum preparation was achieved by exhibiting together the materials deemed most representative of a given area. This method of classification has remained a purely heuristic device for laying out museum displays and teaching courses in anthropology. Recently it has become a cause of confusion among some who are studying cultural causality but have been unable to free themselves of the spatial terms of reference implicit in classification by culture area. Part of this confusion results from the fact that almost immediately after the formulation of the culture area concept, a historical implication was added. The similarities within an area were viewed as the result of diffusion, the spread of artifacts and customs from one tribe to another — usually from the most "typical" to the least "typical." For the purposes of explaining culture areas, diffusion and ecological adaptation tended to become sufficient causes.

Julian Steward provides an example of this confusion. On pages 88 to 90 of his *Theory of Culture Change* (Urbana: University of Illinois Press, 1955) he distinguishes between "uniformities" within a single culture area or co-tradition and "regularities" — "similarities which recur cross-culturally in historically separate areas or traditions." He finds it difficult to derive causal relations from uniformities within culture areas because they result from diffusion rather than the "recurrent and independent operation of similar causal processes. . . . It is only when one compares two historically independent areas that it is possible to stipulate that a particular set of phenomena are causally interrelated . . ." Later, on page 182 he says: "The use of diffusion to avoid coming to grips with problems of cause and effect not only fails to provide a consistent approach to culture history, but it gives an explanation of culture origins that really explains nothing. Diffusion becomes a mechanical and unintelligible, though universal, cause, and it is employed, as if in contrast to other kinds of causes, to account for about 90 percent of the world's culture. One may fairly ask whether each time a society accepts diffused culture, it is not an independent recurrence of cause and effect." In the first case Steward is comparing such widely separated groups as Bushmen, Australians, and Fuegians, and he can make his argument more dramatic by emphasizing their geographic separation. In the second case he wants to treat Andean and Mexican civilizations as two examples of change, and since "most American anthropologists explain similarities between the early civilizations of the New World as a case of single origin and diffusion," it becomes expedient to make *societies* rather than areas his units of comparison.

If social structure rather than area is accepted as the basis of dividing culture into cultures, diffusion becomes a means rather than a cause of culture change. There need be no hesitation about comparing subcultures within the preindustrial components of dual societies in underdeveloped areas to derive causal relationships if cultures are distinguished on the basis of social structure rather than culture area.

⁶ My views of history and science have been influenced by Karl Raymond Popper's *The Open Society and Its Enemies* (Princeton: Princeton University Press, 1950), and those on "open" and "closed" society by Popper, Robert Redfield's work in Yucatán (*The Folk Culture of Yucatán*, Chicago: University of Chicago Press, 1941), and particularly by Eric Wolf's excellent and provocative articles on corporate and open communities ("Types of Latin American Peasantry: A Preliminary Discussion," *American Anthropologist*, vol. 57, no. 3, 1955, pp. 452–471, and "Closed Corporate Peasant Communities in Mesoamerica and Central Java," *Southwestern Journal of Anthropology*, vol. 13, no. 1, 1957, pp. 1–18).

⁷ For the best summary of Eskimo culture see Chapter 5 of E. Adamson Hoebel's *The Law of Primitive Man*, Cambridge: Harvard University Press, 1954. The description of the Siriono is taken from the monograph, *Nomads of the Long Bow*, by Allan R. Holmberg, Institute of Social Anthropology, Smithsonian Institution Publication No. 10, 1950.

⁸ Edward William Nelson, *The Eskimo about Bering Strait*, Eighteenth Annual Report of the Bureau of American Ethnology, Washington, D.C., 1899, pp. 305–306.

⁹ For a summary of Haida culture see "The Haidas of British Columbia," by George P. Murdock in his *Our Primitive Contemporaries*, New York: Macmillan, 1934, pp. 221–263. See also J. R. Swanton, *Contributions to the Ethnology of the Haida*, Memoirs of the American Museum of Natural History, vol. 8, 1909 and George P. Murdock, *Rank and Potlatch among the Haida*, Yale University Publications in Anthropology, no. 13, 1936. For the Ifugao see R. F. Barton's *Ifugao Law*, University of California Publications in American Archaeology and Ethnology, vol. 15, 1919, pp. 1–186; *Ifugao Economics*, University of California Publications in American Archaeology and Ethnology, vol. 15,

1922, pp. 385–446; and *The Religion of the Ifugaos*, Memoirs of the American Anthropological Association, no. 65, 1946. E. Adamson Hoebel has synthesized Barton's data into an excellent and very readable summary in his *The Law of Primitive Man*, pp. 100–126.

[10] Murdock, 1935, *op. cit.*, p. 246.

[11] Holmberg, *op. cit.*, p. 88.

[12] George P. Murdock, "The Common Denominator of Cultures" in *Science of Man in the World Crisis*, Ralph Linton (ed), New York, 1945, p. 139.

[13] Angel Palerm, "The Agricultural Basis of Urban Civilization in Mesoamerica," in *Irrigation Civilizations: A Comparative Study*, Social Science Monographs I, Pan American Union, Washington, D.C., 1955, pp. 28–42.

[14] Sylvanus G. Morley, *The Ancient Maya*, Stanford: Stanford University Press, 1946, pp. 154–155.

[15] The most important single reference on the aboriginal Amazon is *The Tropical Forest Tribes*, vol. 3 of the Handbook of South American Indians, Smithsonian Institution Bureau of American Ethnology Bulletin 143, Washington D.C., 1948. Page references in order of appearance: 178, 412, 336, 355, 756, 186, 389, 419, 445. See also Kalvero Oberg, *Indian Tribes of Northern Mato Grosso, Brazil*, Smithsonian Institution Institute of Social Anthropology Publication No. 15, 1953, pp. 41, 76, 40, and Charles Wagley and Eduardo Galvao, *The Tenetehara Indians of Brazil*, New York: Columbia University Press, 1949, p. 46.

[16] My source for the Taino of Hispaniola is Irving Rouse's "The Arawak," in *The Circum-Caribbean Tribes*, vol. 4 of the Handbook of South American Indians, Smithsonian Institution Bureau of American Ethnology Bulletin 143, Washington, D.C., 1948, pp. 522–539.

[17] See Morley, *op. cit.*, and Ralph L. Roys, *The Indian Background of Colonial Yucatán*, Carnegie Institution of Washington Publication 548, 1943.

[18] The most scholarly and readable general work on the Inca is John H. Rowe's "Inca Culture at the Time of the Spanish Conquest," in *The Andean Civilizations*, vol. 2 of the Handbook of South American Indians, Smithsonian Institution Bureau of American Ethnology Bulletin 143, Washington, D.C., 1946, pp. 183–330. See also Sally Falk Moore's *Power and Property in Inca Peru*, New York: Columbia University Press, 1958. This work emphasizes the fact that Inca society was not a socialistic Utopia and claims that the importance of the local nobility has been underestimated by most writers on the Inca. Even if we allow that local rule within the Inca state deserves more emphasis and attention than has been given to it in the past, the Inca state still remains a remarkable achievement for a closed society and it undoubtedly embodied more centralized, coercive control than most pre-urban or incipiently urban societies. For this reason, I have continued to make heuristic use of the Inca case as an example of well-developed centricity and redistribution in a closed society.

[19] Karl Polanyi, *The Great Transformation*, New York: Farrar and Rinehart, 1944, pp. 48–49.

[20] Moore, *op. cit.*, pp. 55–58.

VII. Conspicuous Ownership and the Opening of Society

[1] William Foote Whyte, *Street Corner Society*, Chicago: University of Chicago Press, 1943. For a brief analytic summary see George C. Homans, *The Human Group*, New York: Harcourt, 1950, pp. 156–189.

[2] All the quotations from Adam Smith in this chapter are from *The Wealth of Nations*, Book I: Chapters I, II, and III; and Book V, Part III, Article II.

[3] Karl Marx, *Capital*, 1887, Chapter XIV, section 5.

[4] Translated from the French by George Simpson, New York: Macmillan Co., 1933. See Book II, Chapters I and II.

NOTES

[5] Bronislaw Malinowski, *Argonauts of the Western Pacific*, New York: Dutton, 1950 reprint. All quotations are from pp. 60 and 96–97.

[6] For a good, concise description of ancient Mesopotamian and Egyptian life, see Henri Frankfort, *The Birth of Civilization in the Near East*, New York: Doubleday Anchor Books, 1956, chapters 3 and 4.

[7] Transportation difficulties were not the only environmental handicap to cultural development in the New World. Although the beginnings of New World plant domestication may go back nine thousand years or more to within three thousand years of its beginnings in the Old World, horticulture apparently was practiced as a supplement to hunting, fishing, and collecting for some six thousand years in the New World as compared to a period of incipient agriculture of only two to three thousand years in the Old. (L. Kaplan and R. S. MacNeish, "Prehistoric Bean Remains from Caves in the Ocampo Region of Tamaulipas, Mexico," *Botanical Museum Leaflets*, Harvard University, vol. 19, no. 2, 1960, pp. 33–56. Robert J. Braidwood, *Prehistoric Men*, Chicago Natural History Museum Popular Series, Anthropology, Number 7, 1959, pp. 110–130. Gordon R. Willey, "Historical Patterns and Evolution in Native New World Cultures," *The Evolution of Man*, Sol Tax (ed), Chicago: University of Chicago Press, 1960, pp. 124–126.) Unless the archeological record for the Old World is very deficient, the period of incipient agriculture was much shorter there. If future investigations show that the rate of agricultural development was actually slower in the New World, dearth of domesticable animals could have been largely responsible. Their flocks of goats would have given early Old World farmers a reliable source of food, making possible the greater farming risks that would have helped accelerate plant domestication.

The dearth of domesticable animals for food, transport, and plowing; the lack of any great river valleys situated in an environment comparable to that of the Nile or the Tigris-Euphrates; the distribution of the mountainous terrain and lack of strategically located inland seas all contributed to a slower rate of cultural development in the New World. Occupation of the New World (by 22,000 B.C.) and the beginnings of plant domestication there occurred early enough that without some or all of the above limitations American Indians might have been the discoverers rather than the discovered.

[8] Fred Cottrell, *Energy and Society*, New York: McGraw, 1955, pp. 48–49.

[9] G. Gordon Brown and Bruce Hutt, *Anthropology in Action*, London, 1935, p. 151.

[10] Henri Pirenne, *Economic and Social History of Medieval Europe*, New York: Harcourt, Brace and Co., 1936, Chapter I, Section III.

[11] K. William Kapp and Lore L. Kapp, *History of Economic Thought*, New York: Barnes and Noble, 1949, p. 8.

[12] Henri Pirenne, *Medieval Cities*, Princeton: Princeton University Press, 1925, "The Merchant Class."

[13] Pirenne, *Economic and Social History*, Chapters IV and V, and Max Weber, *General Economic History* (translated from the 1927 German edition by Frank H. Knight), Glencoe: The Free Press, 1950, pp. 241–248.

[14] Anne M. Chapman, "Port of Trade Enclaves in Aztec and Maya Civilizations" in *Trade and Market in the Early Empires*, Glencoe: The Free Press, 1957.

[15] Charles J. Erasmus, "Culture Structure and Process: The Occurrence and Disappearance of Reciprocal Farm Labor," *Southwestern Journal of Anthropology*, 1956, vol. 12, no. 4, pp. 444–469.

[16] George C. Homans, *English Villagers of the Thirteenth Century*, Cambridge, 1941, p. 260.

VIII. Conspicuous Production in Free and Coercive Societies

[1] Philip Drucker, *The Northern and Central Nootkan Tribes*, Smithsonian Institution Bureau of American Ethnology Bulletin 144, 1951, p. 131.

[2] David Riesman has written of conspicuous production in his *Individualism Recon-*

sidered, Glencoe: The Free Press, 1954, p. 229. He uses it in reference to modern industry and in a sense equivalent to "conspicuous corporate consumption."

[3] John Kenneth Galbraith, *The Affluent Society*, Boston: Houghton, 1958.

[4] The term *coup*, French for *blow*, is used by some writers on the Plains Indians to refer specifically to the war exploit of touching an enemy in battle. But in normal English usage the word means a sudden brilliant stratagem. In this broader sense, "counting coup" has also been applied to the several categories of successful exploits and stratagems by which distinguished warriors were ranked among Plains Indian tribes.

[5] C. Northcote Parkinson, *Parkinson's Law*, Boston: Houghton, 1957.

[6] Franz Boas, *Anthropology and Modern Life*, New York: Norton, 1928, pp. 214–215, 219–220.

[7] For an excellent discussion of different kinds of cumulation in culture change see Harvey C. Moore, "Cumulation and Cultural Processes," *American Anthropologist*, vol. 56, no. 3, 1954, pp. 347–357.

[8] Feder Belov, *The History of a Soviet Collective Farm*, New York: Praeger, 1955.

[9] Thomas P. Whitney, "The Novel That Upsets the Kremlin," *New York Times Magazine*, March 4, 1957, pp. 9, 34–40.

IX. Introduction to the Area

[1] It is customary to speak of development in terms of technology and economics rather than culture. When people wish to embrace a broader topic than technology, they usually speak of economic development and culture change. Owing to the influence of cultural relativism, "cultural change" has been considered more properly dispassionate than "cultural development." Technology and economics are a part of culture, however, so I prefer the more inclusive and less awkward term.

[2] Information was provided by the offices of Recursos Hidráulicos in Obregón and Navojoa.

The United States Export-Import Bank loaned twelve million dollars, which it later increased to seventeen and a half million, "to assist in financing the construction of the Yaqui irrigation canal, associated water distribution system, a drainage system and related roads" (correspondence with Export-Import Bank of Washington, D.C., dated February 5, 1958).

The Mayo irrigation district includes some ninety thousand hectares, but the water captured by the Macúsari dam has never been sufficient for the entire district and only about sixty-five thousand hectares (a hundred and sixty thousand acres) were irrigated during the farming cycle of 1957–1958. The original estimate of the Mayo River's rate of flow was probably too optimistic, but the main reason for the discrepancy between the amount of water and the size of the district was the unequal development of the latter at the time the government stepped in. Private canals were already irrigating land far enough south of the river to be beyond the zone expropriated earlier for the ejidos. Meanwhile, considerable ejido land in the very center of the district was still uncleared. To satisfy both private farmers and ejidatarios, the irrigation authorities were forced to overextend the district.

[3] Information provided at the offices of Recursos Hidráulicos in Navojoa and Obregón.

[4] *Séptimo Censo General de Población*, 6 de junio de 1950, Secretaría de Economía, Dirección General de Estadística, Estado de Sonora, p. 23.

[5] According to the 1950 census (*ibid.*, pp. 115–117) only about a fourth of the Mayo River population spoke Cáhita. But I was told by many rural families that they were not asked during the national census whether they could speak Cáhita, so many bilingual Indian families were probably not listed as such.

[6] For example, in the comisaría of Camoa (in the municipio of Navojoa) there are eighteen rancherías (in addition to the head village of Camoa) with a total population of about twelve hundred persons, some sixty per cent of whom are Indian. Three of the

eighteen rancherías contain all-Indian families, five all "white," three more than half Indian, four better than half "white," three are about evenly divided. Only a very few families live on their farms.

[7] Eduardo Huarte, *Eclipse Total de la Constitución para la Tribu Yaqui*, 1957, pp. 31–32.

[8] See note 13 below.

[9] An estimate supplied by Gus Dingfelder, one of the pioneer founders of Obregón.

[10] See Table 1 for maternity and mortality ratios collected in house-to-house interviews in several communities. Biacusi and La Florida are two villages not listed on the map of the area (p. 187): the first is across the Mayo River from Tesia, and the second lies very close to Ahome in Sinaloa. In Table 1, "dead children" includes only those who died before the age of eighteen and were unmarried at the time of death.

[11] W. Lloyd Warner, *Social Class in America*, New York: Harper Torchbooks, 1960.

[12] August B. Hollingshead and Frederick C. Redlich, *Social Class and Mental Illness*, New York: Wiley, 1958, p. 115.

[13] The "samples" of classes in Navojoa, Huatabampo, and Etchojoa mentioned throughout this chapter were compiled to check my impressions. I had not originally intended to make a study of town classes and became interested in this late in my field trip. I grew curious to know more about the town families who had recently improved their houses either by building new or by remodeling older structures. I wondered about the class and origins of these "progressive" families and began making lists of their names and observing and valuing their housing and other property. Later I added other names to my lists and inquired about these people in conversations and in interviews with informants. My first- and second-class samples were therefore biased toward those families which have been most diligent in keeping up appearances. This is not a serious disadvantage so far as the first class is concerned, for my samples in this case were large. But the Navojoa second-class sample is probably skewed somewhat toward the upper margins of the class.

[14] Table 2 presents quantitatively the information obtained about class occupations by the methods described in note 13. Additional businesses operated by large landowners in the first class included car agencies, gas stations, granaries, a tequila factory, a hotel, and a tractor agency. In the second class they included trucking, lime manufacture, small stores, and moneylending. "Businessmen, professionals, and employees" of the first class who farmed as a secondary interest included a motion picture theater owner, several proprietors of large stores, two gas station owners, the proprietor of a lumber yard, several doctors, and several managers of large businesses. In the second class this category included truckers, mechanics, a federal policeman, a soda pop manufacturer, small store owners, bakers, government officials, proprietors of bars, building contractors, butchers, farm foremen, and moneylenders. The category "Businessmen, professionals, and employees who do not farm," included, among the first class, owners of car agencies, proprietors of large stores, gas station proprietors, the owner of a radio station, the owner of a dry cleaning plant, a building contractor, a lawyer, several doctors, managers of several large businesses or agencies, a few important government officials, dentists, a tile manufacturer, the proprietor of an automobile repair shop, and the proprietor of a bar. Within the second class this category included many small store proprietors, bar owners, truckers, butchers, taxi drivers, repair shop proprietors (bicycles, typewriters, automobiles, adding machines, welding, hat blocking and cleaning), building contractors, the proprietor of a motion picture theater, restaurant owners, ice plant proprietors, smaller government officials, store and bank clerks, policemen, schoolteachers, and farm foremen.

The third-class samples in Huatabampo and Etchojoa were picked from families everyone would agree are third class. In Navojoa the sample is from the peripheral Rosales district, which some consider third class and others consider mixed second and third. These families are interesting as illustrations of the transition from second to third in the large towns (they include all the families in five adjoining city blocks). In seven

Table 1. Maternity and Mortality Ratios in Five Communities

	Biacusi (Mayo River)	Buaysiacobe (Mayo River)	La Florida (Fuerte River)	Vicam Pueblo (Yaquis)	Combined Villages	Navojoa
Total no. of mothers	44	32	23	34	133	56
Average age of mothers	38	33	42	43	39	43
Median age of mothers	40	33	37	39	37	43
Mothers under 45	73%	84%	61%	59%	79%	52%
Total no. of live births	270	168	164	211	813	383
Average no. of live births	6.1	5.2	7.1	6.2	6.1	6.8
Total no. of living children	161	123	111	118	513	347
Average no. of living children	3.6	3.8	4.8	3.5	3.8	6.2
Total no. of dead children	109	45	53	93	300	36
Average no. of dead children	2.5	1.4	2.3	2.7	2.2	.6
Dead children	40%	26%	32%	44%	37%	9%
No. of mothers over 45	12	5	9	14	40	27
Average no. of live births among mothers over 45	9	7.2	8.8	7.8	8.3	7.5
Average no. of dead children among mothers over 45	3.5	3	3.9	4.6	3.9	1

Table 2. Percentage of Family Heads of Each Class in Three Villages in Various Occupations

Occupation	Navojoa Classes			Huatabampo Classes			Etchojoa Classes		
	1	2	2-3*	1	2	3	1	2	3
Private farmers	36	12		49	19		63	19	
Private farmers who also own other businesses	10	3		18	14				
Businessmen, professionals, and employees who also farm	8	8		10	22		16	35	
Businessmen, professionals, or employees who do not farm	46	77	70	23	27	18	20	22	10
Ejido farmers			7		18	3		23	2
Ejido farmers who are also day laborers			23			12			25
Unskilled day laborers						66			62
Number of heads of household in sample	134	119	53	61	125	32	30	63	40

* This sample came from the Rosales district, considered third class by some, mixed second and third by others.

346

cases the heads of the households were widowed or abandoned women supporting children by making or washing clothes or both. Twelve heads were common unskilled laborers, working in construction or as loaders or night watchmen. Four were ejidatarios. Among the semiskilled and skilled employees there were three truck drivers, two taxi drivers, two door-to-door salesmen, three clerks, a policeman, a minor government official, a mechanic, three carpenters, a barber, and a musician. Those who were self-employed included two potters, six small store proprietors, a maker of fireworks, and a junk man.

Non-farming employees, professionals, and "businessmen" in the Huatabampo and Etchojoa third classes included three woodcutters, an Indian priest, two tractor drivers, a taxi owner, and a blacksmith.

[15] The information in Table 3 was collected in house-to-house interviews in all of the villages except La Loma, where it came from informants who knew the village well. All or a majority of the houses in each village were visited except in Buaysiacobe, where I interviewed the head of every fourth household. Cooperation by the peasantry was excellent in most instances. Only at Vicam Pueblo was the choice of houses affected by the refusal of families to be interviewed. "Independent households" refers to those with enough land and cattle so that the active male head of the household did not work as a day laborer nor employ himself at craft work to supplement his income. The category "Family heads, self-employed," refers to those who worked independently at such crafts, industries, or services as cutting firewood, burning lime, weaving maguey fiber bags, weaving baskets, or peddling. In Las Bocas many heads of families depended upon the sale of firewood, lime, and maguey fiber products for a large part of their income and also did some farming. At Vicam the majority of households were dependent on selling firewood cut on the reservation and some heads of families also worked as day laborers, especially at cotton harvest time. In general the people of Las Bocas and Vicam did not like working as day laborers and preferred self-employment. In all the villages but La Loma, which is so close to Navojoa that many of the heads of households work there quite regularly as day laborers, most of the families listed as day laborers also owned some land.

In Buaysiacobe most of the families were ejidatarios and worked mostly on the ejido lands. They could all be listed as day laborers in a sense, however, since this was a collective and they themselves complained that they felt more like day laborers working for the Ejido Bank than like landowners. Despite the large number of acres per family this was one of the poorest communities visited. The sixteen per cent listed as day laborers had no lands at all. For all the other villages, I have listed as day laborers family heads who depend on wages for a substantial part of their income. Many of these also hold small parcels of land.

Some of the villages listed in Table 3 are not shown on the map (p. 187). Mesquital de Tesia is just west of Tesia. La Florida is very near Ahome in Sinaloa. La Loma is across the Mayo River from Navojoa. Biacusi is across the Mayo from Tesia and refers actually to Mesquital de Biacusi, which I have shortened to "Biacusi" to avoid confusion with Mesquital de Tesia.

[16] All the housing valuations in Table 4 were made by me with the help of informants. Houses worth less than 2,000 pesos are usually of cornerpost construction with adobe or mud-and-wattle walls. Those from 2,000 to 5,000 pesos are adobe and frequently have all or part of their floors in concrete. Houses in the 5,000 to 10,000 peso category usually have both concrete floors and brick roofs. Houses above 10,000 pesos in value have brick walls or use brick facing over adobe. Expensive houses are often very elaborate and are built of brick and concrete. Little use is made of wood. In the peasant dwellings wood serves mainly for roof beams and lintels and in houses worth more than 20,000 pesos wood is often replaced by reinforced concrete. Tile floors are customary in expensive houses.

[17] The data on vehicles in Table 5 for the first and second classes were collected largely from informants while I was working up lists of families in each class (see note 13). I

Table 3. Characteristics of Country People in Various Villages

	Las Bocas	Biacusi	Buaysiacobe	La Loma	La Florida	Mesquital de Tesia	Vicam Pueblo
No. of households in the community	37	43	141	35	37	48	72
No. of households in the sample	37	43	33	35	29	48	30
Average size of households	5.4	6.3	6.2	5.8	6.8	5	8
Mixed and Yori families	35%	20%	24%	54%	66%	23%	3%
No. of independent household heads	3	4		5	2	9	1
Families with land	73%	77%	84%	46%	59%	85%	10%
Average no. of acres owned by landholding families	7	12	44	7	13.5	10	
Families with cattle	54%	40%	15%	37%	24%	23%	30%
Cattle owners with 10 head or less	80%	88%	100%	69%	100%	81%	55%
Family heads self-employed	83%	28%			7%	10%	83%
Day laborers	16%	88%	16%	86%	80%	67%	30%

Table 4. Class Differences in Value of Housing, Arranged by Place of Residence

Value of Housing	Navojoa			Huatabampo			Etchojoa			Country People						Quechehueca	
	1	2	2–3*	1	2	3	1	2	3	Pozo Dulce	Buaysi-acobe	Biacusi	La Florida	Vicam Pueblo	Las Bocas	Ejido Quechehueca	Ejido Aguila
Under 2,000 pesos (less than $160)					3%			2%	100%	96%	94%	98%	93%	97%	94%	30%	4%
2,000–5,000 pesos ($160–$400)			10%		10%	100%		52%			6%	2%	7%	3%	3%	30%	42%
5,100–10,000 pesos ($410–$800)			49%		22%			25%		2%					3%	27%	28%
11,000–25,000 pesos ($880–$2,000)	1%	4%	16%	11%	37%		4%	17%		2%						13%	15%
26,000–50,000 pesos ($2,080–$4,000)	14%	65%	6%	38%	22%		50%	4%									11%
51,000–100,000 pesos ($4,100–$8,000)	44%	25%		29%	5%		42%										
110,000–200,000 pesos ($8,800–$16,000)	20%	5%		10%	1%		4%										
210,000–300,000 pesos ($16,800–$24,000)	16%	1%		4%													
Over 300,000 pesos (over $24,000)	5%			8%													
Number of families in sample	131	117	51	52	185	30	28	48	52	66	33	43	29	30	37	37	46

* This sample came from the Rosales district, considered third class by some, mixed second and third by others.

349

Table 5. Class Differences in Vehicle Ownership, Arranged by Place of Residence

No. and Kind of Vehicles	Navojoa			Huatabampo			Etchojoa			Country People						Quechehueca	
	1	2	2–3*	1	2	3	1	2	3	Pozo Dulce	Biacusi	Buaysi-acobe	La Florida	Las Bocas	Vicam Pueblo	Ejido Quechehueca	Ejido Aguila
More than 1 car	6%																
1 car and 1 pickup	24%	2%		38%	1%		3%										
1 car	43%	16%	6%	23%	3%		13%									14%	
1 pickup	20%	35%	4%	30%	45%		68%	17%		2%	2%					8%	41%
No car other than truck used for business		5%	2%		25%		3%	11%						3%			
No car other than taxi or bus used for business		5%	6%		2%	3%										22%	9%
No cars or trucks	6%	37%	82%	9%	24%	97%	13%	72%	100%	98%	98%	100%	100%	97%	100%	56%	50%
1 bicycle	?	?	51%	?	?	23%	?	?	?	8%	?	?	21%	38%	0%	5%	0%
Number of families in sample	134	117	51	57	139	30	31	47	52	66	43	33	29	37	30	37	46

* This sample came from the Rosales district, considered third class by some, mixed second and third by others.

was able to check the information directly in many cases where I knew or observed the families, and I found no significant discrepancies. Male informants were very car-conscious and not only remembered surprisingly well who had vehicles and who did not, but could remember the makes and approximate ages. The data for the villages came directly as a by-product of house-to-house interviews.

The data on Quechehueca in Tables 4 and 5 will be discussed in Chapter XI.

[18] W. Lloyd Warner, *Social Class in America*, New York: Harper Torchbooks, 1960, p. 14.

[19] See also Jean Fourastié, *The Causes of Wealth* (translated and edited by Theodore Caplow), Glencoe: Free Press, 1960, pp. 121–122.

X. The Land Reforms

[1] For an excellent recent discussion of this question see Donald F. Gordon, "What Was the Labor Theory of Value," *American Economic Review Papers and Proceedings*, 1959, pp. 462–472.

[2] See Nathan L. Whetten, *Rural Mexico*, Chicago: University of Chicago Press, 1948, pp. 75–89, and Eyler N. Simpson, *The Ejido*, Chapel Hill: University of North Carolina Press, 1937, pp. 3–42.

[3] Rafael de Piña, *Código Agrario*, Mexico, 1954, Article 51, p. 27

[4] *Ibid.*, art. 169, p. 74.

[5] *Ibid.*, art. 159, pp. 70–71.

[6] *Ibid.*, art. 171, p. 74.

[7] *Ibid.*, art. 162, p. 72.

[8] *Ibid.*, art. 200–202, pp. 88–89.

[9] Computed from data provided by the offices of Recursos Hidráulicos in Navojoa and Obregón.

[10] Mario Gill, *La Conquista del Valle del Fuerte*, Mexico: Imprenta Técnica Moderna, 1957, pp. 134–151.

[11] Melford E. Spiro, *Kibbutz: Venture in Utopia*, Cambridge: Harvard University Press, 1956, p. 11.

XI. Mobility and Emulation

[1] This rough estimate is based on the same sources of information discussed in note 13 of Chapter IX.

[2] This information was derived from the same house-to-house interviews as the information in Table 3 (note 15 of Chapter IX). These percentages are based on marriage histories of members of the households interviewed as well as their children who had married and moved elsewhere. In Biacusi 73 marriage histories were obtained in the 43 households interviewed and at Buaysiacobe 49 histories from 33 households.

[3] In the ejido to which this man belonged, land was cleared individually by each member. Some members had cleared none of their land, but this man had cleared his full allotment.

[4] Technically, Aguila and Quechehueca are two Ejido Bank credit societies forming one ejido. They are completely separate, however, in organization and administration and are often spoken of as different ejidos. For convenience of description I have observed this popular distinction.

[5] For quantitative data on houses and vehicles of Aguila and Quechehueca members see Tables 4 and 5 (note 16 of Chapter IX).

[6] Throughout the discussion which follows I use "anomie" more in the psychological sense of a "property of individuals" than in the Durkheimian sense of "normlessness in a society" (Robert K. Merton, *Social Theory and Social Structure*, Glencoe: Free Press, 1957, p. 161). Although the spelling "anomia" has been suggested for the psychological concept to distinguish it from the sociological (see Leo Srole, Dorothy L. Meier, and

Wendell Bell, note 8 below), I have retained the older spelling here. I agree with Merton (p. 162) that the psychological concept is "a counterpart of the sociological concept of anomie, and not a substitute for it."

[7] Robert Redfield, *The Folk Culture of Yucatán,* Chicago: University of Chicago Press, 1941.

[8] Dorothy L. Meier and Wendell Bell, "Anomia and the Achievement of Life Goals," *American Sociological Review,* vol. 24, no. 2, April 1959, pp. 189–202. In their conclusions the authors note: "We may expect considerable despair in the near future among members of agricultural, nonindustrial, nonurbanized populations with low living standards — the densely settled 'underdeveloped areas.' For these people increasingly accept configurations of life goals involving political freedom and economic advancement — while facing severe obstacles as they attempt to achieve these goals. This is precisely the breeding ground of anomia." The authors are probably correct to the extent that the peoples they refer to acquire goals (felt needs) which they do not feel they can reach (which exceed their expectations). In Sonora it does not seem that felt needs have as yet greatly surpassed expectations. The items on the anomie scale (Srole's) used by the authors of this article so closely paralleled some of the attitudes and behaviors overtly expressed by country people in Sonora that I have based my discussion upon them. I made no attempt to quantify Srole's items in the field since I was unaware of them at that time. My only question about the advisability of employing the scale in underdeveloped areas has to do with the extent to which the scale proposes to test a person's exaggeration of "reality." For example, in underdeveloped areas the social detachment of the poorer people from official leadership may be a very real problem, whereas in our society it may more correctly be the peculiarly exaggerated viewpoint of a few disturbed people. For Srole's own explanation of the items see Leo Srole, "Social Integration and Certain Corollaries: An Exploratory Study," *American Sociological Review,* vol. 21, no. 6, December 1956, pp. 709–716.

[9] Redfield, *op. cit.,* p. 348.

XII. Religious Ceremonies and the Indian

[1] The performers at a Mayo fiesta include three or four pascola dancers and their seven musicians, a deer dancer and his four musicians, women church singers, and a native priest. In addition there may be matachini dancers, and at Easter fiestas there are always the ceremonial clowns called "judíos" (Jews). The costumes and dance movements of the pascola and deer dancers are the most aboriginal elements of the fiesta, but the matachinis and ceremonial clowns seem to derive from both Spanish and pre-Spanish forms. Most of the pascola musicians play harps and violins of European origin, but they also dance to the music of a drummer-flutist, which is no doubt aboriginal. Certainly the deer dancer's musicians, who accompany him by singing as they play on wooden rasps, are of aboriginal derivation.

The ceremony and ritual of Mayo and Yaqui fiestas have been described by Ralph Beals and Edward Spicer and will not be detailed here. My analysis is primarily concerned with changes in the economic structure of the fiestas and the motivations of the participants. I am greatly indebted to both Beals and Spicer for their excellent earlier studies without which I would not have worked as large an area as I did: Ralph L. Beals, *The Contemporary Culture of the Cáhita Indians,* Smithsonian Institution Bureau of American Ethnology Bulletin 142, 1945, Washington, D.C., 244 pp., Edward H. Spicer, *Pascua: A Yaqui Village in Arizona,* Chicago: University of Chicago Press, 1940, 319 pp., and *Potam: A Yaqui Village in Sonora,* American Anthropological Association Memoir No. 77, 1954, 220 pp.

[2] The difference in the distribution of the invitational and promissory forms of fiestero service is due in large part to two limiting factors — the density of the Indian population and the popularity of the saint concerned. The invitational form is best adapted to

sparsely populated areas where fewer promises would be likely to mature in time for the annual replacements. The upper course of the Mayo River, along which the invitational form occurs, is the most sparsely populated, whereas along its lower course, where the promissory form is more common, the Indian population is greatest. The outstanding exception to this tendency is Batacosa, which lies north of the Mayo River in the sparsely populated foothills of the Sierra Madres. However, the image of San Bartolo, the saint in whose honor the annual fiesta at Batacosa is held, is widely renowned as a miraculous image. People as far away as Etchojoa on the lower course of the Mayo or Quechehueca in the Yaqui irrigation district make vows to serve as fiesteros for San Bartolo.

[3] Tesia in 1953, Etchojoa in 1950, San Ignacio in 1948, and Tepahue in 1934 after the burning of the saints.

[4] At Macoyahui there is a full complement of fiesteros, but by common consent expenses have been greatly reduced. Theoretically each fiestero is supposed to butcher a bull for the occasion, but now three or four male fiesteros buy one animal among them and their female counterparts buy none. At Camoa the preliminary puti, bajítua, etc., fiestas have been given up and for the Easter fiesta itself only the fixed or minimal costs are paid to feed the performers. These are computed in advance and each fiestero must pay his share or "quota," which in 1958 amounted to only one hundred and fifty pesos (about twelve dollars) apiece. This is a very small figure compared to the three thousand pesos (two hundred and forty dollars) which it cost some fiesteros at Etchojoa the same year to meet the expenses of the Espíritu Santo fiesta and the preliminary fiestas for the fiestero recruits.

By common agreement the Camoa fiesteros have eliminated the feasting of "godchildren" and the redistribution of food and goods. This rational attempt to preserve the fiesta and reduce the costs undoubtedly results partly from Yori influence, for here as well as at Tepahue (fiesta of San Juan) and Macoyahue, Yoris also serve as fiesteros. An informal arrangement has developed whereby the sponsorship of the Easter fiestas at Camoa and Macoyahue and the San Juan fiesta at Tepahue alternates annually between predominantly Yori and predominantly Indian groups of fiesteros.

The Yoris participate "because they do not want the customs to disappear," but they try to keep expenses low. Although some Yoris actually serve as fiesteros at the fiestas, others merely pay the costs and hire Indians to stand in for them at the ceremonies. In 1957, however, when Indians at Camoa were requested to accept the fiesta, they refused to do so unless they were treated as "godchildren should be treated." This amounted to a mild form of extortion, for the Indians wanted to be feasted, so a puti was held at which the Yoris received and fed the Indian recruits. Otherwise the Yoris would have been stuck with the obligation of sponsoring the fiesta for another year. Yoris along this part of the river complain that the Indians no longer want to give their fiestas, and here the Yoris are forced to cooperate in order to keep these "pleasant" traditions alive. Storekeepers in the ceremonial towns obviously stand to gain from increased business during fiestas, so Yori support of fiestas is not always free of vested interest.

[5] At Bacavachi, San Pedro, and Sebampo.

[6] The fiestas and the approximate dates of their disappearance are listed after the names of the towns. On the Fuerte River: La Florida — San Antonio, 1943; San Miguel — San Miguel, 1956, Concepción, 1956, Guadalupe, 1952; Mochicahue — Guadalupe, 1957; Sivirijoa — Virgen de los Dolores, 1955, San Juan, 1955; Tehueco — Santa Isabel, 1949, Rosario, 1949; on the Mayo River: Macúsari (Conicarit) — Virgen del Candelario, 1952; El Recodo — Guadalupe, 1953; San Pedro — Santa Cruz, 1954, Guadalupe, 1952.

[7] The strength of the fiesta system along the Mayo River during the thirties is demonstrated by the remarkable way in which it survived the desecration of the churches that was ordered by the state governor in 1934. Yaqui churches were not molested for fear of starting another Yaqui uprising, and some of the Mayo images were saved by the devout, who hid them from the rural police. Popular San Bartolo at Batacosa is one of the few images which survived "the burning." At most of the Mayo ceremonial towns,

however, new images had to be bought a few years later when the churches were re-opened. At this time, three of the traditional ceremonial communities divided into two factions. Today El Recodo and San Ignacio carry on the fiestas of the former Cohuirimpo mission, Etchojoa and Sebampo those of the Etchojoa mission, and Júperi and Etchoropo those of the Santa Cruz mission. In spite of the persecution, popular interest in the fiestas was still strong enough in the thirties so that the number of fiestas in some areas increased rather than diminished.

The radical change in popular interest since that time is well attested by what happened in Sebampo. When this community broke away from Etchojoa after "the burning," it enthusiastically formed its own fiestero group and built its own church. But today, some twenty years later, the church is in ruins and the five remaining Sebampo fiesteros have great difficulty finding replacements. The reasons the people of Sebampo give for this state of affairs are the same ones given by Mayos everywhere along both the Mayo and the Fuerte Rivers. The fiestas are too expensive, and people are losing their faith and "devotion."

[8] L. P. Mair, "Independent Religious Movements in Three Continents," *Comparative Studies in Society and History*, vol. 1, no. 2, 1957, p. 132.

[9] Ralph Beals (*op. cit.*, pp. 210–213) apparently used these popular stereotypes in contrasting Mayo and Yaqui temperament and culture patterns. He states that though the two groups speak the same language and share almost identical culture "contents," the Mayos are traditionally a pacific people who have turned inward as a way of resisting Mexican culture. They "live *among* whites," but "rarely live *with* them." The Mayo is characteristically close-mouthed (*muy cerrado*) and reserved around whites. The Yaquis, on the other hand, have always been fighters with a "warlike nationalism." He found them "frank and aggressive" and without reticence. Beals is inclined to believe these differences in the temperament of the two groups have a long history, for he says that while the Yaquis have repeatedly taken up arms against the whites since colonization, the Mayos did so only at Yaqui instigation. Moreover, the Mayos never produced any great leaders whose names stand out in history like those of the famous Yaquis — Banderas, Cajeme, Tetabiate, and Matus.

Although it is true that history does not reveal the names of many Mayo leaders, Mayos fought alongside Yaquis in the uprisings of 1740, 1825, and 1885. In fact, the first uprising in 1740 began on the Mayo River with the burning and sacking of haciendas by Indians of Tesia, Navojoa, and San Ignacio. (Roberto Acosta, *Apuntes Históricos Sonorenses*, Mexico: Imprenta Aldina, 1949, p. 86.) According to Jesuit census figures of 1760, the Yaqui at that time were a much larger tribe than the Mayos, numbering about twenty-three thousand compared to some six thousand Mayos (Acosta, *op. cit.*, pp. 100–103). If these figures are even roughly correct, it is not surprising that the Yaquis led in doing battle with the Yoris — and it seems very probable that the proportions were correct, for even today the Yaqui River is capable of supporting a much larger population than the Mayo. With its greater flow the Yaqui River formerly inundated a much larger area than the Mayo, and it was these areas that the Indians planted when the seasonal flood waters subsided.

Moreover, Mayos have fought more recently than some people realize. A famous Mayo leader on the Fuerte River was Felipe Bachomo, who led his Indian forces in the capture of Ahome in 1914. Bachomo took advantage of the unsettled time after 1910 to try to win back the Indian lands appropriated by Yoris. In December of 1934, a small force of Mayo Indians broke into the Navojoa police station and stole arms. After a brief skirmish with some twenty-five soldiers, they scattered. The burning of the saints (pp. 276–277) and certain unpopular taxes are said to have provoked the uprising. For much the same reasons, a second minor uprising took place in Etchojoa the following year, when Mayo Indians made a night raid on the municipio of Etchojoa and looted the municipal offices. The force took shelter in the thorn forest near Pozo Dulce until dispersed by attacking aircraft. Though relatively small and insignificant, these uprisings serve to suggest that Mayos probably are no less inclined to fight than Yaquis; they simply did not have quite the same opportunities in later periods to organize and defend themselves.

As for the temperaments of the two groups, the Mayos of today are still reticent and shy, but much less so than when Beals observed them in 1932. At that time, Beals had considerable difficulty in getting information from Mayos because of their "practiced" but "unconscious evasiveness." My own impressions of the Mayos in 1948 were very much the same as Beals's, and I met with the same evasiveness. But on returning in 1958 I felt that a remarkable change had taken place during the last decade: they no longer use the excuse of the Indian tongue to evade questions, and it has become much easier to get information from them, even on short acquaintance. The Yaqui character, too, as I observed it in 1958, appeared to have changed since Beals's 1932 description. Although most of the leaders and many of the older men who were soldiers in the revolution and have traveled more than average are "frank and aggressive," this is by no means true of all Yaquis. Because a visitor is always steered through the Yaqui chain of command, he meets for the most part the leaders and their spokesmen — the aggressive, self-assured members of the tribe. But making a census of households in Vicam pueblo proved more difficult than any such investigation among the Mayos. In fact, the majority of the Yaquis seem very much like Mayos of ten years ago: they tend to be more withdrawn and evasive than the Mayos of today.

[10] Beals, *op. cit.*, p. 212.

[11] See Spicer, *Pascua: A Yaqui Village in Arizona*, concerning conflict between ceremonial service and the American job pattern among Tucson Yaquis.

[12] These estimates are based on attendance records for the seventy pupils at Mesquital de Tesia over a four-month period. In other villages I was familiar with I am sure attendance was much poorer. At Vicam pueblo, for example, the teacher neglects her classes to operate a store, and attendance is very irregular. At Las Bocas, which lies far from town in what is considered an undesirable location, teachers last only a few months at a time and arrive at intervals of seven or eight years.

XIII. Implications for the Future

[1] Very recently, Elman Service has made a similar distinction between the usual meaning of cultural lag and what he calls the "upside-down effect" or "inverse cultural lag." See Marshall D. Sahlins and Elman R. Service (eds), *Evolution and Culture*, Ann Arbor: University of Michigan Press, 1960, p. 118.

[2] I refer to David Riesman and William H. Whyte. See notes 10 and 11 below.

[3] Allan R. Holmberg, *Nomads of the Long Bow*, Institute of Social Anthropology Smithsonian Institution Publication No. 10, 1950, p. 60.

[4] William Foote Whyte, *Street Corner Society*, Chicago: University of Chicago Press, 1943, pp. 14–25.

[5] Allan R. Holmberg, "Adventures in Culture Change" in *Methods and Perspective in Anthropology*, Robert F. Spencer (ed), Minneapolis: University of Minnesota Press, 1954, pp. 112–113.

[6] R. F. Barton, *The Kalingas*, Chicago: University of Chicago Press, 1949, p. 43.

[7] See, for example, United States congressman George Meader's article "Our Foreign Aid Program — A Bureaucratic Nightmare," in *Reader's Digest*, April, 1957, pp. 93–98.

[8] William J. Lederer and Eugene Burdick, *The Ugly American*, Greenwich: Fawcett Publications, 1958, pp. 181–195.

[9] "United States Aid Operations in Iran," First Report by the Committee on Govern-

ment Operations, 85th Congress, 1st Session House Report No. 10, 1957, Washington D.C.: U.S. Government Printing Office, p. 36.

[10] David Riesman with Nathan Glazer and Reuel Denney, *The Lonely Crowd*, New Haven: Yale University Press, 1950.

[11] William H. Whyte, *The Organization Man*, New York: Simon & Schuster, 1956.

[12] Arthur M. Schlesinger, "The Decline of Greatness," *Saturday Evening Post*, November 1, 1958, p. 25.

[13] John K. Galbraith, *The Affluent Society*, Boston: Houghton, 1958. C. Northcote Parkinson, *Parkinson's Law*, Boston: Houghton, 1957.

Index

INDEX

Natividad, case of, 283

Navojoa: commercial growth of, 186, 188; map, 187; population, 190; age, 192; births, 193, 346n; social classes, 195–201 *passim*, 206, 207, 239–248 *passim*, 346n; and fiestas (Old Navojoa), 277, 281; housing, 349n; automobiles, 350n

Negative control. *See* Control

Negroes: and yaws, 26, 27; American Negroes in Haiti, 80; on Cayapas River, 151–153, 156

Nelson, Edward, 114

Newspapers and graft in Sonora, 229–230

Nursing students and changing folk beliefs. *See* Tests

Objectives of this book, 9–14

Obregón: map, 187; commercial growth, 188; population, 190; age, 192

Observations: casual, 23–26 *passim*, 31, 42, 60, 75, 78; technical, 23, 25, 31, 58, 60, 75

Occupations in Mayo River area: of social classes, 199–200, 201, 345–347n; of country people, 206; of townspeople, 239–240

Open society: and specialization, 154; free and coercive, 171–177

Organismic analogy. *See* Social organism

Organization men, 330, 331

Pacheco, Juan, 276–277

Palerm, Angel, 125, 126

PAN (Partido de Acción Nacional), 225, 263

Papago, 21, 22, 57, 58–59

Parkinson, C. Northcote, 163, 165, 331

Partido Popular, 220, 224

Pascolas, 271, 273, 288, 300

Peanut. *See* Groundnut scheme

Penicillin, 26

Performers at Mayo and Yaqui fiestas, 271, 352n

Peru, 63

Pétion, Alexandre, 89, 112

Pirenne, Henri, 145

Placenta, folk beliefs concerning disposal of, 30, 41, 337n

Plants, introduction of new or improved, 23–26, 58, 60–64, 81

Pochteca traders, 147

Political organization, Yaquis', 293

Political unity, Mayos and Yaquis compared, 292

Politics in Sonora, 263

Polygyny, 120, 121

Population: density of as limitative cause, 65–68; and types of farming, 126; Yaqui

and Mayo River areas, 190–192; density of and expectations, 304; and change, 316; density of and types of fiesteros, 352–353n

Positive control. *See* Control

Potam, 187, 192, 293, 296

Potlatch, 117–121 *passim*

Poverty: limitation of, 65–68

Practical man, society's view of, 165–166, 329, 330

Prediction: and frequency interpretation, 22, 31, 32, 42, 43, 122; and knowledge, 23; and sense of control, 26; and technical assistance, 82; and positive control, 102; and science, 111; and negative control, 170; townspeople and country people, 264

Prejudice, 204

Presentation: problems of, 78

Prestige: concern for, 12, 13, 165, 237, 310; and weakness of conspicuous production in Sonora, 236–237; and fiestas for God, 290; and ceremonial participation, 290, 300, 302; and random tolerance, 305; and self-interest, 309; and subcultures, 316; hierarchy, 317; and incentive in free society, 331. *See also* Motivation; Self-interest

Preventive medicine: and water purification program, 28; and a maternity hospital, 29–31; at folk level, 41; versus treatment in affecting folk beliefs, 45, 46, 47; and middle-class sanitation in Sonora, 53; and housing program, 80; and public health center, 83–84

Probable knowledge. *See* Knowledge

Production, conspicuous. *See* Conspicuous production

Prolonged interaction, problems of, 81–85

Promissory performers, 271

Protestants: in Mayo River area, 249–250; and attitudes toward fiestas, 270; effects on Mayo fiesta system, 283–285; and fiestas for God, 286

Public health projects: yaws eradication in Ecuador, 26–27, 29; water purification in Ecuador, 27–29; health education in Ecuador, 38, 44, 48; rural hygiene in Colombia, 79–80; health center in Bogotá, 83–84; clinic in Tepoztlán, 92–93

Puerto Rico: population growth in, 71; sterilization program, 75

Quechehueca: class, 201–202; and collective ejido, 223–225; and consumption patterns, 257–260; and fiestas, 282; housing, 349n; automobiles, 350n

Quito, 29–31, 58